PADRE PIO

PADRE PIO:
THE TRUE STORY

C. BERNARD RUFFIN

Our Sunday Visitor, Inc.
Huntington, Indiana

© Our Sunday Visitor, Inc., 1982
200 Noll Plaza
Huntington, Indiana 46750
ALL RIGHTS RESERVED

Library of Congress Catalog Card No. 81-81525
International Standard Book No. 0-87973-673-9
Printed in the United States of America
Designed by Thomas Casaletto

To the memory of

my mother

Lillian Rebecca Jones Ruffin

Contents

Acknowledgments

This book could never have come into being without the gracious assistance of several people, chief among them, the Capuchin Fathers at Our Lady of Grace Friary at San Giovanni Rotondo, whom I wish to thank for their kind permission to quote from their publications and to reproduce photographs owned by them. In particular, I am grateful for the assistance of the Reverend Joseph Pius Martin and the Reverend Alessio Parente. Both of these men shared with me their personal recollections of Padre Pio and gathered for me, through interviews with people inaccessible to me and through research in their friary archives, much valubale information.

Moreover, I wish to thank profusely Giuseppe Pagnossin, of Padua, Italy, for permission to quote from his invaluable publications *Il Calvario di Padre Pio*, in two volumes, and *Padre Pio: Storia d'una vittima*, in three volumes, and for permission to reproduce photographs contained therein. These works contain primary material not currently available elsewhere. Signor Pagnossin also permitted me to use several letters by Padre Pio that have never before been published.

Certainly no one was any more helpful than the Reverend John A. Schug of the Capuchin Friary at Garrison, New York. I could almost write another book detailing everything Father John did to help me. He graciously permitted me access to his voluminous files of letters, clippings, and interviews. He took time to search out obscure information for me, served as my source for data on the Capuchin Order, and read the first draft of my manuscript, putting forward useful comments and suggestions. I am particularly grateful for his encouragement, so important during the many times of acute frustration that occurred while I was preparing this book.

I wish to thank Mrs. Vera Calandra, director of the National Centre for Padre Pio, for providing me with valuable information. Located at 11 North Whitehall Street in Norristown, Pennsylvania 19401, her office distributes *The Voice of Padre Pio*, the publication of the canonization process. Mrs. Calandra invites requests for this magazine and other literature on Padre Pio.

I am grateful to Mr. William Carrigan of Kensington, Maryland, who helped introduce Padre Pio to American troops stationed in Italy. Carrigan's recollections have been invaluable.

Sincere thanks, too, are due to Sr. Carolyn Cossack of Brooklyn; Rev. Richard L. Cosnotti of New York City; Mrs. Concetta Gambello of Brooklyn; Dr. Emilio Ghidotti of Salto, Uruguay; Dr. Monika Hellwig, professor of theology at Georgetown University, Washington, D.C.; Barbara Ward Jackson, baroness of Lodsworth, England, now gone to her heavenly home; Miss Thérèse Lanna of New York City; Mr. and Mrs. André Mandato of North Plainfield, New Jersey; and Mr. Joseph Patterson of Hillsdale, New York.

This book could never have gone forward without help in translation from Dr. Liliana Gagliardi of Washington, D.C.; Mr. Robert H. Hopcke of North Plainfield; Dr. Louise J. Hubbard of Washington, D.C.; Mr. André Mandato; and Dr. Montserrat Sola-Solé of Bethesda, Maryland.

Finally, I wish to thank the several anonymous and confidential sources who helped me immeasurably but who prefer their names not be mentioned.

Where I have cited specific passages from Scripture, I have used either the Holy Bible, Revised Standard Version, or the King James Version.

C. Bernard Ruffin

Introduction:
'The Second Saint Francis'

National Review called him "the hottest thing in mysticism in the twentieth century" and "one of the chief religious forces in Italy."[1] By the time Padre Pio Forgione of Pietrelcina died in 1968, he was receiving five thousand letters a month, and thousands of visitors each year were converging on him from all parts of the earth, making their way through Italy's remote and rocky Gargano Mountains to the little sixteenth-century friary of Our Lady of Grace, near the town of San Giovanni Rotondo, where the venerable Capuchin priest had lived for more than half a century. There they would wait for days for a chance to make their confessions to him, packing themselves like sardines into the church adjoining the friary for a chance to see Padre Pio celebrate Mass.

Hundreds of books and articles were written about him in his native Italy, and scores of stories appeared in other countries as well. *Time, Newsweek,* and the *New York Times Magazine,* as well as other reputable American periodicals, from time to time featured lengthy, serious articles about the man who was widely known as the Second Saint Francis.

Padre Pio's visitors were predominantly Italian, but the devout, the troubled, and the curious poured in to see him from England, France, Germany, Ireland, America, Canada, the Ivory Coast, India, Sri Lanka, the Philippines, Australia, and other lands both near and far. Although his callers were overwhelmingly Roman Catholic, the Prophet of the People (as he was also known) was sought out by great numbers of men and women of other Christian denominations, especially during the Second World War, when American and British troops were stationed nearby. Although, as an old-school Italian Roman Catholic, Padre Pio believed that all other Christian denominations were less desirable than that to which he gave his heart and soul, he welcomed everyone graciously and without condescension: Protestants, Orthodox, Lutherans, Episcopalians, and even non-Christians.

Although most of the pilgrims to the Holy Man of the Gargano — another epithet applied to him — were people of humble origin, Padre Pio attracted large numbers of intellectuals and figures of international importance. During the Second Vatican Council (1962-1965), so many Roman Catholic bishops consulted him that some observers wondered aloud whether the Council was being held at Rome or at San Giovanni Rotondo.

At least two popes said privately that he was a saint. On March 9, 1952, Bishop Giovanni Battista Montini, later Pope Paul VI, told Giulio Antonacci, major general of the Carabinieri, "Padre Pio is a saint." A few minutes later, Pius XII, the reigning pontiff, having overheard the remark, saw fit to concur: "We all know that Padre Pio is a saint!"[2] Years before, Pope Benedict XV (r. 1914-1922) did not hesitate to characterize Padre Pio, even in the early years of his ministry, as "a man of God."[3]

As late as 1975, Giuseppe Cardinal Siri, the well-known archbishop of Genoa, remarked of him, "We can bow down before this figure who passes through our times as a noble, suffering standard-bearer of God."[4]

Not only churchmen but notables from the world of politics and entertainment beat their way to Padre Pio's friary door. Aldo Moro, for many years head of the Italian government, made frequent trips to see the beloved old priest, as did many other Italian politicians. Beniamino Gigli, for many years a leading star of the New York Metropolitan Opera, came to sing for Padre Pio and seek his counsel. Paul Dudley White, the celebrated American cardiologist, also visited with the padre and professed himself "deeply impressed" with his work.

The grizzled friar, described in the *National Review* article cited above as having "the greatest moral prestige of any priest in Italy," was credited by several American newsmagazines with transforming the life of the region where he lived, bringing prosperity, jobs, education, and health care to a region that had been cruelly impoverished for centuries. Because of him, the ancient monastery where he quietly and unobtrusively resided became one of the great places of Catholic pilgrimage in Europe.

And now, more than a decade after the unassuming little friar was laid to rest in a crypt beneath the main church of Our Lady of Grace — an edifice erected in 1959 expressly to accommodate the throngs who stood through the night for a chance to see the padre celebrate his 5 A.M. Mass — the devotion continues. Nearly a million people each year continue to come from all over the world to visit his tomb, view the cell where he spent the last years of his life, and see the crucifix in the "choir," or chapel, overlooking the original church where, in September 1918, he received the stigmata — the visible, bleeding wounds of Christ's Passion in the hands, feet, and side — wounds which were to be the padre's greatest glory and greatest humiliation. San Giovanni Rotondo continues to grow and to thrive as many leave their homes, not only in other parts of Italy but also in other parts of the world, to go there to live "near Padre Pio" in what someone once characterized as "a Christian ashram."

Today in southern Italy many shops prominently display pictures of Padre Pio. As the traveler nears San Giovanni Rotondo, he notices that, instead of the obscenities and Communist slogans one sees farther north, the graffiti sometimes bear the legend: LONG LIVE PADRE PIO! And for all those who knew him in life, as for many who have come to know him only after his death, Padre Pio lives indeed!

"I was drawn to him like a magnet!" an elderly lady from the city of Taranto told me when I was in San Giovanni Rotondo in September 1978. From the time of her first visit to him in 1948, she and her family traveled several times a year to see him and ask his counsel. Now she and her husband and their daughters, in-laws, and grandchildren continue to make the four-hour trip from their home at least thrice a year to "visit" with the remarkable man with whom they can commune now only in spirit. On the day they had to leave, one of the daughters told me with great feeling how sad they all were to be "leaving Padre Pio" and how they could scarcely wait to return again.

I was profoundly moved by the devotion of this family, a devotion shared by thousands who come to San Giovanni Rotondo each year. Time and again I have been struck by the fact that so many of these people — rational, levelheaded people, not cranks or neurotics — seem to experience the effectual presence of Padre Pio as if he were still on earth!

My experience in visiting San Giovanni Rotondo — seeing the tomb of Padre Pio, visiting his cell, being shown where he heard confessions and where he ate in the friary refectory — was similar to that of visiting Mount Vernon or Monticello, or like my visit to the sites associated with the founder of my own denomination, Martin Luther, in East Germany. It is a great experience to see the surroundings in which those important to the development of mankind lived and moved.

Viewing his bedroom, his shoes, his medicine bottles, his armchair, I did not feel the living presence of Padre Pio at Our Lady of Grace anymore than I feel the living presence of Jefferson at Monticello. An astonishing number of people who have been to San Giovanni, however, claim to have encountered a living power and presence. They feel that Padre Pio can and will do something for them. Padre Pio, in fact, is said to have commented more than once before his death, "I shall be able to do much more for you when I am in heaven than I can now while I am on earth." Many of Padre Pio's followers doggedly believe this.

Andre Mandato, a respected and substantial custom tailor residing in North Plainfield, New Jersey, related to me with shining eyes how "Padre Pio changed my life." He recounts how, as a young man in his native Italy, he and a friend went to see Padre Pio in 1945 — out of curiosity. He left the confessional awestruck. Not only did Padre Pio know — without ever having met Mandato before — that he had been debating in his mind whether he should take the trouble of waiting to confess to him before returning home, Padre Pio also recited, correctly and in detail, all the sins of which the young man was guilty.

"He knew everything that I had done," Mandato recounted to me in August 1978. "Padre Pio asked, 'Have you done this?. . . Have you done that?' And the answer to all his questions had to be yes."

Padre Pio referred not merely to general categories of sin but to specific acts which the confessor could not have guessed at simply through a shrewd knowledge of human nature. After Mandato left the confessional, all he could do was "cry, cry, cry." His experience had a profound, lasting effect upon him. "Many times," he says, "we ask God to forgive us, but with the mind and not the heart. Padre Pio made it possible for me to ask forgiveness of God with all my heart and soul, not just with my mind and my lips. From that moment I have really *felt* what I prayed. He made my religion real!"

Monika Hellwig, professor of theology at Georgetown University, spent three years in Italy during the time of the Second Vatican Council and visited San Giovanni Rotondo. In September 1978, Dr. Hellwig told me that she had never met anyone in Italy who was sceptical of Padre Pio. Even radicals and anticlericals, she noted, regarded the venerable friar with "respect and reverence." Moreover, she can testify that the stigmatized Capuchin did indeed lead people to "deep conversions." "What struck me most," she stated, "is how much Padre Pio mediated the presence of the divine to all who came to him. People came away from him invariably inspired and assured of God's presence and care for them. In him they experienced a most immediate revelation of God's love and concern for them."

Padre Pio was almost an exact contemporary of Rudolf Bultmann (1884-1976), the German Lutheran theologian who, out of a regard for the difficulty modern men and women have in accommodating the traditional teachings of Christianity to their twentieth-century perceptions, devised a theology that "demythologized" the Gospels, stripping away such uncomfortable baggage as miracles and other accoutrements of a first-century world view in order to get at what he believed to be the essential kernel of truth underlying all the "mythological" paraphernalia. Bultmann's approach (or at least variations of it) has strongly colored much of the theological thinking of the last few decades. How different was Padre Pio — in style, and in results. Without publishing a book or delivering a single lecture in a university, he convinced thousands, even in the age of "historical criticism" of the Bible and the "Death of God" theologians, that miracles are not mythology but reality. Through his life and ministry, thousands came to accept the Bible and all the historical doctrines of Christianity as true.

Padre Pio was also a contemporary of Paul Tillich (1886-1965), Karl Barth

(1886-1968), Pierre Teilhard de Chardin (1881-1955), and Albert Schweitzer (1875-1965); but the modest friar is attested to have communicated the existential presence of Christ more directly, more immediately, and to the satisfaction of many more people than did any of his immensely learned contemporaries in their university chairs.

Bultmann wrote in *Kerygma and Myth:* "It is impossible to use electric light and the wireless and to avail ourselves of modern medical and surgical discoveries and at the same time to believe in the New Testament world of demons and spirits."[5] Yet his contemporary, Padre Pio, convinced many a learned man that angels appeared to translate letters he received in foreign languages, that he cast out devils, and that, as late as 1964, he was knocked bodily to the floor by irate demons. These strange events were, in some instances, witnessed by reliable, reflective individuals, who described the occurrences in writing shortly after they took place.

Here was a man living in the time of air travel and astronauts, of moving pictures and mass communication, of computers and communications satellites, who lived the life of a biblical prophet or apostle and is reputed by rational people to have worked miracles similar to those performed through Moses, Elijah, Peter, Paul, and John. Here was a man in whom, if hundreds of testimonies can be believed, these words of the Lord seem to have been fulfilled: "He that believeth on me, the works that I do shall he do also" (John 14:12). Hundreds of sane, well-educated, and unbiased men and women have testified of Padre Pio, that, like Moses, "The Lord spoke unto him face to face, as a man speaketh unto his friend" (Exodus 33:11).

There is testimony that Padre Pio was gifted with the "odor of sanctity," that he frequently displayed intimate knowledge of the inner lives and thoughts of those who came to him. Without leaving his friary at San Giovanni Rotondo, Padre Pio was frequently seen and addressed in different parts of the world. While he was observed by his colleagues in his room, he was simultaneously seen in such diverse places as Rome; Salto, Uruguay; and Milwaukee, Wisconsin.

The archives of Our Lady of Grace contain volumes of testimony that, through Padre Pio's prayers, more than a thousand people pronounced hopelessly ill by their doctors were delivered of such grave maladies as cancer, heart disease, diabetes, tuberculosis, congenital birth defects, and paralysis caused by spinal injuries. There is a well-documented instance of an accident victim, through the Padre's prayers, suddenly regenerating a new eye. Even more remarkable, thousands of people — ignorant and learned, fanatical and disinterested — testify that when this man of holy reputation celebrated Mass, he inexplicably communicated to them the reality of Christ on Calvary and that, during his Mass, Padre Pio's face and form underwent visible, physical changes. Padre Alessio Parente, who assisted Padre Pio for three years late in his life, told

6 / PADRE PIO: THE TRUE STORY

me that more people were deeply touched by Padre Pio through his Mass than through his miracles, bilocations, ecstasies, and prophecies.

Perhaps more important, thousands testify that through Padre Pio's ministry, they learned to walk in holiness and to resign themselves to God's will, offering their suffering and heartache as a sacrifice to the Almighty for the conversion of souls.

Yet, not everyone was equally impressed by Padre Pio. In the 1920s he was denounced to the Vatican as a fraud by several prestigious priests and theologians. Padre Agostino Gemelli, a renowned psychologist and theologian, concluded that Padre Pio's stigmata were due to hysteria. Around the same time, Pasquale Gagliardi, longtime archbishop of Manfredonia and one of the most prestigious churchmen in Italy, swore on his pectoral cross that the controversial wounds were self-inflicted and, worse, that their bearer was demon-possessed. Dr. Amico Bignami, chief of the department of pathology at the University of Rome, wrote a report in 1919 confirming the existence of the stigmata but implying that the wounds were the result of autosuggestion. Moreover, in the last years of the padre's life there was a campaign, inspired by several highly-placed churchmen, to discredit the friar as the focus of a superstitious cult. Although all those who tried to prove Padre Pio a madman or a fraud ultimately failed and, in several cases, were themselves discredited, there are some who still believe that the Capuchin was in fact a warlock in league with the devil.

Even though Padre Pio was as contemporary a figure as Winston Churchill, Charles DeGaulle, Robert Frost, C. S. Lewis, Aimee Semple McPherson, or Kathryn Kuhlman, he seems to many much further removed. The cultural and spiritual milieu in which he moved was radically different from that with which most Americans are familiar. The difference in world view between the urban American and the rural southern Italian is perhaps as staggering today as it was in the 1890s, when Padre Pio was a boy. This fact makes it difficult for many individuals to appreciate him. In addition, the fact that much of Pio's life lies in the mysterious province of the unexplained makes him even harder to understand.

Would it not be best, then, to write Padre Pio off as a curious footnote to religious history, to dismiss him as a peculiar anachronism — a "living crucifix" — to be mentioned in the same breath with the "living pincushion" of a carnival sideshow, a prodigy deserving, at most, a sketch in Ripley's *Believe It or Not*? Should not we of the latter part of the twentieth century concern ourselves with the larger issues of peace, justice, social inequality, and human rights, rather than with the career of a bizarre old man who allegedly worked miracles that few care to believe in anymore?

Despite the aspects of his ministry that many find hard to take, one fact is incontrovertible: for thousands of people from all walks of life, Padre Pio made Christianity real. Through his ministry, a great many people were led to conversion experiences that were deep and permanent. From all available information, Padre Pio's converts did not have a high rate of recidivism, or backsliding. His American contemporary, William Ashley (Billy) Sunday, when criticized for the impermanence of many of his conversions, once responded: "They tell me a revival is only temporary. So is a bath, but it does you good!" Yet, almost all who professed a change through Padre Pio's ministry persisted and, despite inevitable highs and lows in their spiritual lives, grew as practicing Christians. This in itself is of great significance. Although Padre Pio's life may seem strange to some, no one can deny that his ministry was immensely effective.

Perhaps one reason why Padre Pio seems strange to many Americans is that he represents a tradition much different from any with which they are familiar. Many have described this short, squat man with the patriarchal beard and ethereal eyes as a medieval holy man, transplanted by God into the twentieth century to teach faith to skeptics. Certainly he was in the tradition of the holy man, elder, or spiritual guide whom the Russians call the starets, the teacher-discerner-counselor-mystic sought out by the faithful for spiritual enlightenment and direction. This, however, is not solely a medieval or prerevolutionary Russian phenomenon. The phenomenon is also exemplified by figures a few generations removed from Padre Pio, such as Seraphim of Sarov (1759-1833) in Russia and Jean-Baptist-Marie Vianney (1786-1859) in France, and played a significant role in the religious culture of Southern and Eastern Europe until well into the twentieth century.

Although the starets, or holy man, has never, outside of the cults, assumed an important role in American religious life, Padre Pio's life and work can be of deep significance to the modern reader. Through an understanding of the work, faith, and teaching of the celebrated friar, his patience in all manner of suffering, and his total submission and resignation to the will of God, even the most secularized — if sensitive — can be deeply edified.

One thing is certain: Padre Pio cannot be dismissed lightly. There are basically only four conclusions that may be drawn concerning the Capuchin and his ministry.

First, one may conclude that Padre Pio was one of the greatest frauds of the twentieth century, a showman, perhaps in league with Satan, capable of humbugging the public to a degree unimagined even by P. T. Barnum. Pasquale Gagliardi, archbishop of Manfredonia, as we will see, tried his best to convince the world that this was the case.

Second, one may conclude that Padre Pio was in large measure a product of the superstitious imaginations of an uneducated people who read into the life of a simple, holy priest what they wanted to see, building around him a cult of superstitious self-delusion.

Third, one may conclude that Padre Pio was a madman, a lunatic who was somehow able to convince thousands of people that his delusions were fact.

If none of these three scenarios be true, then we must conclude that Padre Pio of Pietrelcina was one of the most significant figures in Christian history, a man of prophetic stature who, through great personal holiness and wisdom and through a ministry in many aspects inexplicable to science, tended to confirm the truth of the Gospels and the veracity of historical Christianity to an indifferent, unbelieving age; a man capable of conveying a sense of God's love and care to an extent that can scarcely be comprehended; an evangelist who never conducted a crusade and who, though he never traveled more than a mile or two from his monastery walls in fifty years, yet seemed capable of transforming lives to a degree unimagined by Billy Graham or Oral Roberts.

Despite claims that Padre Pio was a fraud, a madman, or the unwitting subject of a superstitious cult, there is an abundance of evidence indicating that Padre Pio was a sincere and immensely effective religious teacher and leader who cannot be dismissed with a patronizing smirk. Still, whatever conclusion one draws about Padre Pio, one is forced to admit that he was tremendously significant.

Padre Pio's life and work is particularly significant in light of the "charismatic renewal" that has occurred within most Christian denominations since the 1960s. Although he died before this movement gained any real ground in Italy and played no role in promoting it — indeed may not even have been aware of it — and although his ministry and theology were somewhat different from those of many of the leaders of the present-day renewal, Padre Pio was certainly, if a tenth of what has been written and testified about him is half true, a charismatic in the New Testament sense of having a staggering abundance of spiritual gifts, or charisms.

Most of the facts of Pio's life, even those that seem most unusual, are supported by solid evidence. It is true that we have many depositions from uneducated and perhaps uncritical persons so deeply immersed in the very different culture of southern Italy as to be given slight credence by modern skeptics. Many of these accounts, however, are corroborated by the testimony of individuals who cannot be lightly dismissed.

One is fortunate to have the diary of Padre Agostino of San Marco in Lamis (1880-1963), a keen-minded, university-trained professor who observed Padre Pio closely for over fifty years. We have the testimony of at least two other colleagues, Padre Raffaele of Sant'Elia a Pianisi (1890-1974) and Padre Paolino of Casacalenda (1886-1964), who also left written accounts. We have the testimony of the doctors who examined his wounds. There is the recorded testimony of Mary Adelia Pyle (1888-1968), a native of Morristown, New Jersey, who mastered several languages and served as secretary to the celebrated educator Maria Montessori before moving to San Giovanni Rotondo to function in a similar way for Padre Pio. Moreover, we have the writings of Father Dominic Meyer (1892-1966), another highly educated American, who served for many years as the friary's official English correspondent.

Most important, we have hundreds of letters Padre Pio wrote to his spiritual directors and disciples over a period of a dozen years. In them, Pio describes his mystical life, his mission, and his theology, often in great detail.

From these documents, we can draw a clear picture of the man and his work.

I

'The God-Is-Everything People'

Padre Pio was born in Pietrelcina, a country town in the Campania region of south-central Italy. Called Pretapucina by its inhabitants, the town lies about six miles northeast of the city of Benevento, which gives its name to the province where both are found, and about forty miles northeast of Naples.

In the 1880s, Pietrelcina had a handful of merchants, professionals, and municipal employees, but the vast majority of its three thousand souls belonged to the land. They were divided into two social classes: the *possedenti* (landed gentry), and the *braccianti* (laborers or peasants), who worked for them.

There were several wealthy families who had immense estates and employed huge numbers of *braccianti*. Most of the freeholders, however, lived little differently from the peasants. They slept in their homes in town and walked (or occasionally rode) each morning to plots in the countryside only a few acres in size. There, with their wives and children and perhaps two or three hired men, they eked out a living, growing wheat, grapes, figs, and sometimes tobacco, and raising a few sheep, hogs, goats, and perhaps a cow or two. Little if any produce was taken to market. What they grew, they lived on. As Padre Pio's father recounted to Miss Pyle: "At Pietrelcina we work to eat, not to make money. The wheat is grown for bread, the vines for wine, fruit to eat, and to feed the cattle. . . . The livestock serve only for family use."[1]

The father of Padre Pio, Grazio Mario Forgione, was a member of the landed gentry. When he was born, in Pietrelcina on October 22, 1860, there was no nation of Italy. He was born a subject of King Francesco II of the kingdom of the Two Sicilies, whose capital was in nearby Naples. However, on the very day of Grazio's birth, a plebiscite ousted Francesco and his Bourbon dynasty, and the following spring Pietrelcina became a part of the new, united nation of Italy.

We know little about Grazio Forgione's youth. He was one of at least two children of Michele (Michael) Forgione and his wife, Felicita (Felicity), whose maiden name was D'Andrea. Grazio's name comes from Madonna delle Grazie (Our Lady of Grace), a title under which the Mother of our Lord is venerated in southern Italy. His nickname was Razio, and, as he grew older, he was frequently called Zio Razio (Uncle Razio). Many people from outside the community thought he was being called Zi' Orazio, and a confusion resulted as to whether his real name was Grazio — as his baptismal and marriage records show — or Orazio (Horace), which it was not. Like Hiram Ulysses Grant, who never bothered to correct people who mistakenly called him Ulysses Simpson Grant, Grazio Forgione eventually became known almost universally as Orazio Forgione. In fact, Padre Pio, when signing legal documents, always gave his father's name as Orazio, and it is ORAZIO that is carved on the old gentleman's tombstone.

Grazio's father, Michele, apparently died when Grazio was a young boy. The dominant male figure in his childhood was his godfather. We first hear of this godfather when Grazio was a small boy. His mother had made him a pair of pants of such coarse material that they could stand by themselves. After suffering torment all the way to the fields, where he would spend the day minding all three of the family sheep, young Grazio, able to endure the torture no longer, took the pants off and beat them to shreds with a rock. When he returned home with the trousers in tatters, his mother, infuriated, summoned his godfather. That good man, however, told her: "Your son is right! Why, these are no kind of trousers to be put on a human being! Make him a new pair at once!" And she obeyed.[2]

On June 8, 1881, Grazio's godfather (whose name has been lost to history) appeared at the young man's home with a crowd of male relatives and friends, all dressed in their finest, cigars in their mouths, and their pockets stuffed with the sugarcoated almonds called *confetti*. Grazio was wearing a doublet trimmed with gold buttons, kneestockings adorned with white ribbons, and white shoes. Together they went to the home of Maria Giuseppa DeNunzio, Grazio's bride-to-be. Maria Giuseppa was dressed in a red satin gown, an azure-blue apron, and a red bodice covered with gold brocade. A white scarf adorned her head, and around her neck she wore a cloth imprinted with the images of thirteen male saints. In her pocket she carried a pair of miniature scissors — to ward off the "evil eye."

After Grazio's godfather gave some advice to Maria Giuseppa, or "Beppa," she kissed the hands of her parents and left with her female companions, who were resplendent in red silk dresses nearly as lovely as her own. The little company went first to the town hall for the civil ceremony, and then to the church for the Sacrament of Matrimony. During the ceremony, Beppa tucked the hem of her skirt between Grazio's knees "to keep evil things away." The nuptials over, a band accompanied the couple back to Beppa's house, where the couple were to make their home. Thus did Grazio and Giuseppa Forgione commence forty-eight years of married life.[3]

A year after their marriage, on June 25, 1882, their first child arrived and, as was customary in the case of the first son, was given the name of Grazio's father, Michele. The second child, born two years later, was named Francesco, neither for the ex-king nor for St. Francis of Assisi, but for one of Grazio's uncles. Unhappily, this child lived only twenty days. A third child, Amalia, also died in infancy, but three months after her death, there was again occasion for joy. Around 5:30 P.M. on May 25, 1887, Beppa, who had just returned from working in the fields, gave birth to the son who would grow up to be Padre Pio. He was baptized the next day in the nearby Castle Church.

Following a custom that was common in the nineteenth century, when infant mortality was high, the child was given the name of his short-lived brother, Francesco. As time went on, Grazio and Giuseppa blessed God for the birth of three daughters: Felicita, born September 15, 1889, and named for Grazio's mother, who had died two years earlier; Pellegrina (Peregrine or Pilgrim), born March 15, 1892; and Grazia (Grace), called Graziella, born December 26, 1894. All three lived to adulthood.

What sort of people were Francesco's mother and father? Since both of them lived long lives and were still active after their son became famous, there is ample material about them. Maria Giuseppa (Mary Josepha) was the daughter of Fortunato and Maria Giovanna (Mary Jane; née Gagliardi) DeNunzio. A year and a half Grazio's senior, she was born March 28, 1859. As she was of "good family," some of her relatives were initially disapproving of her match with a man barely above peasant status. Despite the fact that she was from one of the town's most prominent families, she, like her husband, had never gone to school and could neither read nor write. Nor did she know formal Tuscan Italian, only the Neapolitan dialect. One day while engaging a tutor for Francesco, she unwittingly was a cause of mirthful embarrassment. As a woman of dignity, she tried her best to speak to the man of learning in her best Italian. Referring to her son with a term of endearment, she used the wrong word, speaking of the boy as "my darling little bastard."

Beppa Forgione was a brown-skinned woman of medium height, very thin, with deep, penetrating eyes of blue or grey. A woman of immaculately clean habits, she was known for her spotless white shawl and the snowy bandanna that ever graced her head. A quick, lively person, Beppa was nevertheless known for her grace and refinement. Even though she had never been to school a day in her life, she bore herself at all times "like a great lady," so much so that she was sometimes called the Little Princess. Friendly and kind, "She was happier when she could give than when she could receive," her friends said of her. Emmanuele Brunatto, whom we will meet in a later chapter, was struck by her sense of hospitality and impressed by her great intelligence.[4]

Grazio Forgione was described by Brunatto as "a little runt of a man." No taller than his wife, fair-skinned, black-eyed, with chestnut hair that remained full and thick into his eighth decade, he was a man of exact and impeccable morals who never let an oath or a foul word escape his lips. Although staid and somewhat puritanical, he was nevertheless a warm and joyful man. Mary Adelia Pyle, his landlady for the last nine years of his life, said that he had "a contagious joy about him which communicated itself to others. . . ." He loved to play cards (presumably not for money) and was renowned as a storyteller. So great a reverence for life had this gentle man that he would step out of the way of an ant rather than squash it. "Poor little critter," he would say, "why must it die?"[5] Although of gentle disposition, Grazio, like his famous son, had to struggle against a quick temper. Hardworking almost to a fault, in later years he regretted spending so much time struggling to earn a living that he had been unable to devote as much time as he would have liked to his children. "They never really felt comfortable in my arms," he said.[6]

Grazio and Beppa were devoted to each other and to their children. No women's libber was Beppa, however, and there was no question as to who was boss in the Forgione household. Even by nineteenth-century Italian standards, she is remembered as being submissive to her husband to an extent that few other wives were. Grazio and Beppa seem to have been caring, affectionate parents who believed in sparing the rod and relying upon the power of persuasion. Padre Pio remembered scoldings but never any spankings.

The Forgiones owned three houses, such as they were, and three small farms. Their houses were all on Vico Storto Valle (Crooked Valley Lane) in the Castle District of Pietrelcina. Number 27 was a single room one had to walk up three steps to enter. It had a brick floor, a small fireplace, and four crossbarred windows. The furniture consisted of a washstand, two chests, a table, several chairs, and a large bed. The lime-painted walls were adorned with lithographs of the Virgin Mary and with two crucifixes. This address served as the parents' bedroom, and here the children were born.

Two doors down, at number 28, the family spent most of their time. This was a two-room flat consisting of a kitchen and a room that doubled as a dining room and the girls' bedroom. It was in this kitchen that Beppa, or *Mammella* (Motherdear), as the children called her, scurried about, preparing the meals and baking bread from the grain Grazio or *Tata* (Papa) harvested. It was here, in portable washtubs, that the family took their baths. The Forgiones' other dwelling was "the Tower," a rectangular room reached by a steep flight of stairs. It was first used as the boys' bedroom and later, after Michele had married, as Pio's study and apartment.

The day at Pietrelcina was punctuated by the striking of the great bell in the Castle Church. It did not ring by the hour but according to the various periods of prayer specified by local devotion. When it rang at daybreak, the family arose for morning prayers. Then Grazio saddled his ass and started for his farm plots and vineyard in the expanse of land outside the town, known as the Piana Romana. During summer and harvest time, he would stop at the Castle Church to hire several of the day laborers who congregated there to await the landholders. Beppa and the children would follow Papa, making the one-hour trek to the Piana Romana on foot.

When there was a great deal of work to be done, the family would spend the night at the Piana Romana. On one of their farms the Forgiones had a little cottage where they stored their equipment, stabled their animals, cooked and ate their meals, and slept. The cottage had a dirt floor and no plaster on the walls. There were two beds, one for the parents and one for some of the children. The rest of the brood spent the night at the large adjacent farmhouse of Pellegrino and Daria Scocca, distant cousins who had a family of children roughly the same ages as those of Grazio and Beppa.

The Forgione farms yielded grapes, wheat, Indian corn (maize), olives, figs, and plums. Grazio also raised a few sheep and hogs, and occasionally a milch cow or two. Around the farmhouse, Beppa kept a little garden, where she grew roses, wallflowers, and carnations. When water was needed, she fetched it from a nearby well in a huge jug, which she balanced on her head.

The diet of the Forgiones was largely vegetarian. Beppa cooked not only for her husband and children but for the farmhands as well. During the week, they ate primarily greens and beans and, on Sundays, pasta. Meat was reserved for special occasions, its main source being the two or three hogs that Grazio butchered each fall. From these animals came the smoked ham and sausage that was eaten on feast days and at family celebrations.

Padre Pio maintained very pleasant memories of the farm. He and his brother and sisters played with the Scocca children, one of whom, Mercurio (1887-1968), who was exactly his own age, became the best friend of his childhood. Summer evenings when the work was done, "Franci" would go with his family and the Scoccas to visit their neighbors on nearby farms. There, in the moonlight, they would eat macaroni and sing to the accompaniment of the guitar. Music was very important to the people of Pietrelcina. Every important event was accompanied by singing, and events such as weddings and funerals demanded the use of the municipal band. Grazio is said to have had a beautiful voice and to have loved to sing. Francesco, however, apparently never exhibited any gift for music.

As an old man, Padre Pio would speak with deep affection of the green fields dotted with leafy elms and cooled by fresh spring water. Franci and his brother and sisters "roamed as little kings in a kingdom without confines, whose only law was that of the 'Good Creation.' "[7]

Winters the children, when they were young, amused themselves by playing in front of the Castle Church. The monotony of a life without television was broken on long nights by storytelling. Both Grazio and his mother-in-law, Maria Giovanna DeNunzio, were excellent raconteurs.

The year was highlighted by numerous saints' days. Gherardo Leone, who wrote extensively about Padre Pio's early years, noted that few regions in Italy observed so many saints' days as Pietrelcina: "The year was a veritable succession of feasts, novenas, High Masses, processions, with the inevitable accompaniment of fireworks [and] music. . . . "[8] Among the more significant feasts was that of Our Lady Crowned, on April 30. A statue of the Virgin with a shepherd and two bulls at her feet was carried through the streets in procession, and the priests went into the fields to bless the farm animals. On April 8, the Feast of St. Michael the Archangel was celebrated in the town of Torre, some five miles away. Thither the Pietrelcinese walked; those who wished to do penance would drag themselves on their knees to the archangel's statue. The others crowded the confession stalls, ate and drank, and enjoyed the music. In Pietrelcina, the children who remained behind went into the fields and gathered poppies, broom flowers, acacia flowers, and wild roses, and scattered the petals over the archangel's statue in the Castle Church.

Then, just before Lent, there was carnival. People decked themselves out in outlandish costumes. The air was filled with shouts. Shysters in the marketplace blew trumpets to call attention to their wares. Wine merchants stentoriously praised the quality of their goods. Butchers invited people to take advantage of their never-to-be-repeated bargains. Men dressed as women or animals danced through the streets, and the roads and lanes were alive with festive throngs, singing and laughing. When the bell in the Castle Church struck midnight, however, the youth of Pietrelcina left their revelry and took up torches to escort a straw dummy symbolizing the "man of flesh" out of town in a coffin, bringing an end to carnival.

The chief feast of the year, aside from Christmas and Easter, was that of *la Madonna della Libera* (Our Lady of Deliverance) in August. During this three-day festival, the faithful offered the first fruits of their harvest to the Madonna. The wealthier people brought candles with banknotes pinned to them as their gifts to the Madonna. The poorer people, including the Forgiones, brought ox-drawn carts laden with grain.

The highlight of the festival was the procession in which a bejeweled wooden statue of *la Libera* was carried aloft through the streets, accompanied by the municipal band. As Padre Pio was later to write: "The main street was splendidly illuminated and in the evening there was an artistic fireworks display. There were games, horse-racing, walking-the-tightrope, and theatrical performances."[9] The climax of the feast was a majestic Solemn High Mass with choir and instrumental music and a sermon, usually preached by an eminent guest speaker.

If religion was at the center of the life of the townsfolk of Pietrelcina, it was especially so in the family of Grazio and Beppa Forgione. Their neighbors characterized them as "the God-is-everything people."[10] The family attended Mass every day. Evenings they gathered together to pray the Rosary. Padre Pio's sis-

ter Graziella, who later became Suor (Sister) Pia, once told an interviewer that
in her childhood home, prayer came before anything. Whatever evening chores
or diversions were planned, they could take place only after prayers. Off-color
talk was forbidden. So great a horror of blasphemous or ribald conversation did
Papa and Motherdear instill in their young that Francesco would run home
crying if any of his playmates cursed or swore.

The few times the family ate meat had to be arranged so that they did not fall
on Wednesdays, Fridays, or Saturdays. Beppa insisted on forgoing meat on
Wednesdays and Saturdays, as well as the then-obligatory Fridays, in honor of
Our Lady of Mount Carmel. When Grazio was living in retirement at San
Giovanni Rotondo and eating his meals with the household of Miss Pyle, he
caused consternation among his fellow lodgers by insisting that during Lent the
family eat on their knees in front of a crucifix.

Most of the stories that Grazio told the children were from the Bible. Although illiterate, he had memorized much of Sacred Scripture and transmitted
his knowledge to his offspring in the form of tales of Jesus and Moses and
Samson and David and the Apostles.

Sometimes Grandmother DeNunzio would also tell the children stories. Padre
Pio never forgot a simple story she told him when he was very young. Maria
Giovanna, a regal-looking dowager with white hair, an aquiline nose, and a formal, dignified bearing, would call her grandchildren to her side and tell them
stories such as this:

> Why does the willow weep? Well, let me tell you! When Adam and Eve, our
> first parents, were put out of the Garden of Eden, they wandered all over the
> earth until, overcome with grief and exhaustion, they sat down under a
> willow tree and started to weep over their misfortunes. The Guardian
> Angels . . . stayed . . . to comfort them. They were so moved by their tears
> that they began to cry, too. They cried so much that the tree was moved to
> pity and its branches began to droop. And ever since then everybody calls
> that tree with its drooping branches the 'Weeping Willow.'[11]

Granny DeNunzio also told the children true stories. Doubtless she told them
about the wonderful miracles wrought by Pietrelcina's beloved *Madonna della
Libera*, such as how she delivered the countryside from the wrath of the Byzan-
tine armies in the seventh century. It was then that the bishop of Benevento,
known as *San Barbato* (the Holy Bearded One), taught his flock to pray to Our
Lady under the title of *la Libera*. Certainly Granny told them how, in her own
youth, back in 1854, Pietrelcina was ravaged by a terrible epidemic of Asiatic
cholera. People were collapsing on the streets, and dozens of deaths were being
reported every day. It seemed only a matter of time until no one would be left.
And so the people decided to call on their beloved *Madonna della Libera*. On
December 2, 1854, the townsfolk packed the church where the 200-year-old

wooden image of *la Libera* reposed, there to pray and weep before her. Then they carried the statue in procession through the streets in hopes that death would flee before her. From that moment, no more sickness or death was reported in Pietrelcina.[12]

For the Pietrelcinese, the saints were like members of the family. The invisible world was ever close at hand. Francesco Forgione grew up in a society that emphatically believed that God regularly intervened in His creation as dramatically as he did in the days of Moses and our Lord. It was not that the Forgiones and their neighbors were inclined to shout "*Miracolo! Miracolo!*" anytime someone recovered from a stubbed toe; but they did see everything that happened, great or small, as somehow coming from God, and they saw no reason not to believe that God could and did intervene in his world in such a way as to alter or temporarily suspend the laws that he himself had set into motion. After all, evidence of God's direct intervention was all around!

One part of Pietrelcina was called the St. Nicholas District because a spring of water there was said to have been called into existence in the fourth century when St. Nicholas was passing by and called upon God to provide a place for him to water his horses. Everyone believed the story of the origin of that spring.

As evidence of the holiness of the Roman Catholic Church, Padre Pio was especially fond of citing the example of the liquefaction of the blood of San Gennaro (St. Januarius). In doing so, Pio was not referring to a vague historical event but to a phenomenon that occurs to this very day in Naples, only some forty miles from Pietrelcina. Here the blood of San Gennaro, a bishop of Benevento who was martyred under Emperor Diocletian in 305 A.D., is kept in a glass reliquary. Normally, it is a solid mass of dark, opaque substance. When exposed several times a year before the reliquary containing the martyr's severed skull, however, the solid mass is seen to liquefy, becoming bright red and sometimes bubbling and boiling. Failure of the blood to liquefy is believed to augur some disaster. To the present day, no scientific explanation has been successfully proffered for the liquefaction of the martyr's blood.

Whereas Padre Pio's contemporaries Bultmann and Tillich could not grasp how any sensible person could believe literally in miracles, few if any in the Forgiones' environment would even think to question that the supernatural was all around them. "You don't believe in miracles? Well, what about St. Nicholas's spring? It's right here. Better yet, what about St. Gennaro's blood?" Perhaps this attitude is inherent in a remark that Padre Pio, late in life, made to a young student who asked him if God really existed. The venerable padre reportedly looked at the boy incredulously and said, "You're crazy!"

When Francesco was eight, he witnessed what appears to have been a spectacular miracle in the town of Altavilla Irpina, some fifteen miles south of Pietrelcina. Padre Pio recounted the story to his friend Padre Raffaele of Sant'Elia a Pianisi. Even if one wishes to contend that some of the facts were perhaps magnified by the passage of time, it seems quite certain that something very unusual happened and that it had a profound effect on young Francesco.

The only vacations, if such they could be called, that the Forgiones took were pilgrimages to the shrines of various saints in nearby towns and cities. From time to time, they went to Benevento, to the shrine of Our Lady of Grace, and to the shrines of Our Lady at Montevirgine and at Pompeii. On August 25, 1895, with the rest of the family remaining home, Francesco and his father set out for the shrine of San Pellegrino the Martyr, a sixth-century bishop of Amiterno who had been drowned by invading barbarians. They journeyed in a wagon drawn by a donkey through the mountain passes until they came to Altavilla Irpina.

Like Pietrelcina's feast of *la Madonna della Libera*, the feast of San Pellegrino was a curious mixture of sacred and profane. Like many of the religious shrines of the area, it was, at times, the site of rather strange and excessive devotional practices. Padre Alessio Parente recalls visiting that very shrine in the 1940s, when he was a boy, and seeing a young man, either in thanksgiving or in penance, crawling on his hands and knees all around the church, from portal to altar and back again, licking the floor with his tongue! On this earlier occasion, Papa Forgione and Franci were about to see a spectacle equally tasteless.

The church was crowded, and the air was thick with a combination of incense, garlic, and wine. Suddenly, the ceremonies were interrupted by piercing shrieks as a "raging, disheveled woman" forced her way up to the altar where the statue of San Pellegrino stood. The crowd was horrified at the sight of the young child she held in her arms. The obviously retarded boy was hydrocephalic. His huge, deformed head hung listlessly, and his shrunken, rigid limbs indicated a general paralysis. The child could not speak, but every few seconds he made a horrible, raucous sound resembling the *graaak!* of a crow. The congregation was moved by pity and horror at the sight of the unfortunate child.

Madly the mother implored the saint to heal the child. Nothing happened. The pathetic little creature in her arms continued ceaselessly his obscene "*Graaak! Graaak! Graaak!*" Just then, with a bloodcurdling shriek, still holding the child, the woman threw herself onto the steps of the altar, weeping and pleading with the saint. Still nothing happened. Then the woman began savagely to curse San Pellegrino.

Papa Forgione, sickened by the grotesque spectacle, wanted to leave, but Franci refused, saying that he wanted to pray for the child.

Moments later, the woman uttered a bone-chilling cry. With a gruesome oath, she stood up and actually threw the child at the statue of San Pellegrino, shrieking: "Why don't you cure him? Well, keep him! He's yours!" The child hit the statue, bounced off, and fell to the chapel floor with a thud. As the crowd restrained the woman from further violence, to everyone's stupefaction, the child, who had never walked before, got up and ran to his mother, crying in a clear, normal voice, "Mother! Mother!"

Cries of "*Miracolo! Miracolo!*" filled the church. Men, women, boys, and girls surged forward to behold what God and San Pellegrino had wrought. Franci and his father were nearly trampled in the pandemonium. When they finally managed to extricate themselves from the crowd, Papa was so miffed that he did not speak to Franci for miles. Francesco never forgot the day's events as long as he lived.[13]

The American reader might look askance at some of these religious practices. The evangelical Protestant especially might be inclined to exclaim: "How can these people be called Christians? Devotion to Our Lady of This and Our Lady of That? You get a toothache and you pray to St. Apollonia. You get cancer of the throat and pray to St. Blaise. You get something wrong with your eye and pray to St. Lucy. This is paganism! Didn't they know that there was only one Mary? Besides, anyone who is a Christian knows that one can and should pray to God alone, directly, without any of these confounded mediators!"

Now, most people of the Forgiones' cultural milieu believed in Christ and his centrality to the Christian faith. But very important to them was the protection of his "assistants" — the saints and angels. Some believe this to be an outgrowth of medieval feudal practice in which all relations in society were hierarchical and one appealed to the king through one of his underlings. God was seen by the Pietrelcinese as capable of intervening directly in one's life, but, most commonly, it was understood that God was to be approached through the Blessed Virgin Mary, the angels, and those Christians who had exercised heroic virtue on earth and have been accorded a special place in heaven — the saints.

To Italian Catholics such as the Forgiones, to refuse to love and honor the Madonna and the saints was tantamount to affronting a member of the family. To the end of his life, Padre Pio could not comprehend how even a lukewarm Christian could fail to pray the Rosary daily. Our Lady and the saints were so close to the Pietrelcinese that it was unthinkable to them that they should not enlist their help, just as they would in harvest time enlist the help of their neighbors.

As to the matter of the multiplicity of "Ladies," neither the Forgiones nor their countrymen believed in more than one Madonna, but they attached special importance to religious devotions associated with celestial personages who had manifested themselves locally, such as *la Madonna della Libera.* "Here is our Lady who revealed herself to *us*! Our own patroness! These are the devotions she instructed *us* to use!" This understanding, although baffling and even revolting to many Christians of a more modern and more evangelical orientation, did make for a very warm, very personal religious experience. One was not alone before the awesome throne of Jehovah, King of Tremendous Majesty; one gave homage and made supplication to the glorious Trinity *in company with* the kindly array of helpers that the Lord himself sent as guides on the way to him.

One could perhaps argue that this practice becomes paganism when more attention is paid to the saints than to God himself, when one comes to believe that it is unnecessary or futile to pray directly to him at all, when one believes that the saints are in themselves capable of granting favors or overruling the will of the Almighty.

The line is fine, however. In Italy and many other Roman Catholic societies, Mary is regarded as mediatrix and co-redemptrix of the world. In 1979, a pious priestly colleague of Padre Pio stated to me: "I don't think we can reach God straightaway. Mary is the connection between men and God, the intercession point between us and our Savior." Yet his belief is strange to Christians who know that God does answer petitions addressed to him directly.

From his letters, it is clear that Padre Pio did pray directly to Christ. He seems to have conversed with him like a friend. Pio also frequently talked to Mary, St. Francis, his guardian angel, and other celestial personages, often begging them to intercede for him with Christ. He advocated devotion to Mary and counseled the faithful to approach Jesus through her in the praying of the Rosary. Yet, once, in an ecstasy, he reportedly declared, "Beautiful Mother, dear Mary, if it were not for faith, men would make you a goddess." Obviously, Padre Pio understood that there is a point at which mediated devotion can degenerate into polytheism.

Each religious tradition has its own problems and pitfalls. The temptation to pay more attention to saints and angels and other spirits than to Jesus is inherent in the spiritual culture of southern Italy, but it is one the subject of our biography always avoided.

'Il Bello Francesco'

Even while Padre Pio was still alive, many legends grew up about his childhood. He was invariably portrayed as a child of unearthly holiness. Stories were told of how he was given to contemplation and dreams, how he "liked to remain alone, listening to the distant voices, mysterious heavenly utterances, and echoes of invisible bells that sounded only for him." Instead of playing with other children, he is described as having spent his afternoons "lost in thought, hoping that heaven would speak to him."[1]

It is hard to know which stories about Padre Pio's childhood are true. All our information, without exception, comes from testimony given long after the events took place and at a time when he was widely believed to be a saint. There is no contemporary documentation, except for birth, baptism, and confirmation records. Since Grazio and Beppa, like almost all of their contemporaries, were illiterate, there are no diaries or letters to be consulted—except for one that Grazio dictated from Pennsylvania in 1902. Padre Pio wrote no autobiography and, except in the way of example, instruction, entertainment, or in response to direct questions, said little about his early years.

Our best information comes from the recollections in old age of Pio's parents. Both of them died at the home of Mary Adelia Pyle, who realized the value of committing some of their reminiscences to paper. Grazio and Giuseppa seem to have been fairly objective. Neither hesitated to recall incidents in which the young Francesco proved difficult or exasperating. Other information was collected by two of Padre Pio's colleagues, Padres Alessandro of Ripabottoni and Lino of Prata. After Padre Pio's death, they decided that they should waste no time in interviewing the remaining people who had known Pio as a boy, people still lucid who were considered trustworthy. There is, of course, always the possibility that the good padres were told what they wanted to hear, but most of their testimony, especially in light of later, better-documented events in Padre Pio's life, seems credible.

Giuseppa Forgione, devout Christian though she was, freely admitted that after the birth of each of her children, she took them to the neighborhood fortune-teller, Giuseppe Faiella, to have their horoscopes cast. When she brought Franci to this wizened little man, Faiella said, "This child will be honored by all the world. Through his hands much money will pass, but he will possess nothing."[2]

As the months went by, it became apparent to Grazio and Beppa that there was something unusual about Franci, and this something did not seem good. Padre Pio often recounted how his mother told him that he cried incessantly. One night Grazio was driven nearly wild by the baby's continuous bawling. Finally, the crying became so loud and relentless that even so pious a Christian as Grazio lost control. Leaping from his bed, he seized the squawling infant and cried, "The good Lord must have sent a little devil into my house instead of a baby!"[3] In blind and helpless rage, he shook the child. To his horror, Franci slipped out of his hands and fell to the brick floor with a thump. Beppa, jolted awake, gathered the now frantic infant into her arms and accused her husband of trying to murder "her child." Franci soon outgrew his crying spells, and this rather difficult period in his parents' lives was nearly forgotten.

When he was a grown man and his mother reminisced about the time when she wondered whether she had borne the Antichrist or some other such unpleasant thing, Pio startled her by saying that he remembered the incident. He added that whenever she would turn down the lights, "a lot of monsters would come up close to me and I would cry."[4] Jesuit Father Giorgio Cruchon, a student of Padre Pio's life and professor of pastoral psychology at the Gregorian University in Rome, has said, "These night-time monsters can only with difficulty be interpreted as devils."[5] Nonetheless, to his dying day, Padre Pio insisted: "It was the devil who was tormenting me."[6]

From the very beginning, a deep sense of piety was evident in Franci. His parents recalled that from the time he could talk, he had only to hear the church bells ring to insist that he be taken to church. His mother used to laugh about an incident that took place when she and Franci were walking along a country road past a field of turnips. "Look at those lovely turnips." Beppa remarked. "I sure would like to eat some of them!" The little boy looked up at her with grave and solemn demeanor and observed drily, "That's a sin."

A few days later, when mother and son were again walking through the countryside, Franci saw a tree full of luscious figs. Without a word, he ran up to the tree and was about to pluck some when Motherdear said: "What's this now? It was a sin to eat the turnips, but now it's not a sin to eat the figs!"[7]

Relatives and neighbors recalled that Franci was an unusually "good" child and that he was a beautiful baby. A cousin later recalled that the fair, rosy-cheeked boy with blond hair and dark brown eyes "was so beautiful he looked like an angel."[8] Neighbors referred to him as "*il bello Francesco*" (the beautiful Francis).

When he was five years old, Franci solemnly consecrated himself to Jesus. To do this was not uncommon (except perhaps for so young a child) in southern Italy at that time. Once a year, most communities hosted teams of evangelists from one of several religious Orders. Whereas their counterparts in the southern and midwestern United States would urge their hearers to "get saved," these men would exhort their audiences to consecrate themselves either to the Sacred Heart of Jesus or, more likely, to some saint, or to the Blessed Virgin Mary. Families generally kept pictures of Jesus or Mary on the wall. Beneath them they entered the date on which each member was consecrated. Sometimes entire families made this commitment at the same time.

In Francesco's case, he dedicated himself to Jesus, probably at the encouragement of his mother. Beppa considered it vital, no doubt, that all of her children make personal commitments of their lives to Jesus at the earliest possible age.

From infancy Francesco seems to have been plagued by intestinal disorders. When he was two, his mother took him to the local witch, who lived down the street. Whenever anyone became ill in Pietrelcina, there were many who believed that someone had cast the "evil eye" on the sufferer. Someone convinced Beppa that Franci was the victim of the evil eye, so she took him to her friendly neighborhood witch.

The *strega* took Franci, massaged his abdomen, made nine crosses on it, and mumbled weird incantations. As long as he lived, Padre Pio would remember that session. "She took me by the legs and held me upside down just as if I were a lamb."[9] All the while she chanted strange formulas. This odd mélange of Christianity, the occult, and sheer humbuggery did not work, and Franci continued to be subject to recurring intestinal attacks.

When he was ten, Francesco became gravely ill. He was running an extremely high fever and had been unable to retain any food for days. This time Motherdear summoned a genuine physician, Don Giacinto Guadagna, who could not diagnose the child's illness but nevertheless told her that it was terminal. In Franci's hearing, he told the horrified parents that the boy had only a few hours to live. Franci, who remained quite calm, told his mother that if he were dying, he wanted to see his beloved Piana Romana once more. Beppa at first refused but then gave in, and Michele, now a sturdy boy of fifteen, put Franci on an ass and took him to the cottage on the farm. It was harvest time, and earlier that day Beppa had prepared fried peppers for the farmhands. They were so hot that the men had eaten comparatively few of them, and a large pot of them remained on the table. Now Franci, who loved hot peppers, asked Michele for some. Fearing that they would make him worse, the brother refused.

Beppa came in. "Close the door, Motherdear," he said, "the light is bothering me." Then he asked her to go out. "I want to be alone for a little bit."

Thereupon Franci climbed out of bed and ate every single pepper before going to bed. When Michele returned, the patient asked him for something to drink. Michele gave him a bottle of milk, and Franci drank half of it. Motherdear came back in a while, and, noticing that the peppers had completely disappeared, she turned to Michele, demanding, "Have you let the dog in here?" Michele strenuously denied having done so, but his mother would not believe him. "It's obvious the dog has been in the house," she said. "All the peppers have been eaten. The pot is clean!"

Franci fell into a deep sleep. When he awoke he was perfectly well and confessed that he had been the "dog" who had cleaned out the pot of peppers.[10]

Children in Pietrelcina received three years of compulsory education in those days. Michele never liked school, but Francesco did and was a diligent and eager student. His first teacher was Cosimo Scocca. At fourteen, he was the oldest of the boys on the neighboring farm. The next year, Franci was instructed by Mandato Saginario, who was a hemp worker by day. Classes were held at night so that teachers and students alike could work in the fields by day.

By this time, Papa Forgione had assigned Franci the task of watching all four or five of the family sheep. Mercurio Scocca was assigned by his family to watch their seven or eight sheep on the adjoining farm. With their parents' consent, the boys combined their flocks so that the two of them could play together. Sometimes they were joined by children from neighboring farms.

Some of the peasant children were amused by the manners and mannerisms of "the Little Lord," as they called Francesco. Before they left town for the Piana Romana, it was customary for mothers to give the boys a chunk of bread to eat for breakfast. Most of the boys thrust their bread into a pocket and, en route to the fields, gulped it down without ceremony. But Beppa, "the Little Princess," had taught Franci differently. She wrapped his bread in a spotless, white linen napkin, and he would wait until he got to the Piana Romana to eat it. Sitting on the ground, he would spread the linen cloth on his knees, look toward heaven, then begin to eat. If a morsel of bread fell to the ground, he would pick it up, kiss it, and then eat it.

Many of the other children thought the Little Lord was peculiar in another way, too: the minute any of them cursed or swore, he would run away. The boys liked to wrestle, and one day Franci pinned Luigi Orlando, a younger playmate. When the smaller boy failed to reverse the situation, he let escape from his lips "a strong expression." Without a word, Franci jumped up and ran away.[11]

Francesco also irritated some of his playmates because he liked to sing hymns and play church. When he and Mercurio were alone, they used to sculpt figures in clay. Franci loved to fashion figures of Christ and the saints, especially St. Michael the Archangel.

Often Franci would go off by himself and sit under the shade of an elm to read and pray. He did all his homework in the fields and was the only boy in school who consistently completed all of his assignments. It was here, beneath the elm, that Francesco claimed he conversed with his guardian angel. He often said that the companionship of his angel was more satisfying than that of mortal children.

At this point the reader may again object that these are no more than the confused ramblings of a crazy old man. But Padre Pio is not the only person outside of a lunatic asylum to have claimed intimate contact with the angelic world. William Blake (1757-1827), the British poet and painter, also told of an encounter with celestial beings. His father whipped him when young William let it be known that he had seen "a tree filled with angels, bright angelic wings spangling each bough with stars." Frances (Fanny) Crosby (1820-1915), the American Methodist hymnodist, also claimed lifelong contact with an "Angel Guide," who, she claimed, dictated poems to her. It would be unfortunate automatically to label as mad or sick anyone whose perception of reality differs from the average person's.

Indeed, as a grown man, Padre Pio, when asked, would say that from early childhood he had regularly conversed with Jesus and the Madonna, and had suffered terrifying assaults by the devil. When his friend Padre Agostino Daniele of San Marco in Lamis learned in 1911 of these supernatural experiences, he was incredulous. "You mean you actually have visions of the Madonna?" he gasped. "Of course," replied Pio. "Don't you?" When Agostino vigorously denied that he had, Pio shrugged his shoulders and said, "Surely you're saying that out of humility."

One may question the extent to which Padre Pio's mystical experiences were a result of his culture and environment. It cannot be denied that the Pietrelcinese were not only extremely pious but extremely superstitious as well. The place swarmed with witches, warlocks, fortune-tellers, and conjurers. Their art seems to have consisted of a supposed manipulation of preternatural forces by various means, such as incantations and formulas. Francesco's experiences, on the other hand, seem to have been entirely spontaneous. Moreover, there is no evidence that Giuseppa or Grazio encouraged Francesco in his mystical experiences or that they or their other children experienced any supersensible phenomena.

There is some question as to how much Francesco's family and friends knew about his spiritual life. He didn't talk about his gifts — except in instances when doing so could be of some help. One such occasion was recounted by Beppa to her friend Margherita DeCianni, who, in turn, told it to Padre Lino. It seems that Francesco had accompanied his father to the Piana Romana, where Papa was attempting to dig a well. He had dug some forty feet without finding water. Francesco, then a small boy, tugged on his arm and pleaded: "Papa, please don't be angry. You won't find any water down there."

"And how would you know, lad?"

"Jesus told me."

"Jesus told you! Indeed!"

"Yes, Jesus told me that if you want to find water, you must dig over there," said Franci, indicating another section of the field.

"All right, I'll dig where you tell me. But, if we don't find any water there, I'll throw you in the hole!"

Grazio dug three feet, four feet, five, six, seven; and then a copious spring of water gushed forth! [13]

A century earlier, in far more industrialized and sceptical England, William Blake's father had whipped him when he reported a vision of angels. In Germany or America in the 1890s, a father might have considered a son who made a statement similar to that of young Forgione to be mentally ill. But in Pietrelcina, people were more open to mystical phenomena. Certainly Francesco's parents were aware that many professed supernatural experiences were illusory, the product of a diseased mind or disordered imagination. By incidents such as the locating of the spring, they were convinced that they were the parents, not of a bizarre boy-dreamer, but of a child with true mystical gifts.

For all his incipient mysticism, goodness, and sobriety, Francesco was not entirely free of mischief. His mother often had to scold him for teasing his sisters. (Padre Alessio recalls how, even as a man of hoary years, he liked to tease.) One of his favorite capers was to sneak up quietly behind his sister Felicita while she was bathing in the tub on the kitchen floor and dunk her head in the water. Felicita, a gentle, sweet-natured child whom Padre Pio would later describe as "a saint" and "the best of all the family," never complained but merely looked at him and smiled. "Hey, Franci!" she would say, "You never stop playing, do you?" [14]

One day while Franci was taking his siesta under an elm tree, Mercurio Scocca decided to bury him with corn shocks. When Franci awoke in darkness, screaming for his mother, Mercurio burst out laughing. The next day at siesta time, it was Franci who found Mercurio sound asleep on a small farm wagon. Franci pulled the vehicle to the top of a nearby hill and, with Mercurio still asleep in it, pushed it over the brink. "He wouldn't have stopped till he got to the next town had not the wagon smashed into a pear tree!" Padre Pio said later in life. [15] Happily, his playmate emerged unhurt!

Franci also had his fling — albeit brief — at smoking. One day Mercurio's father, "Uncle" Pellegrino Scocca, hailed him, saying: "Franci, you can run fast. Take this money and go to town and fetch me a Tuscan cigar and a pack of matches. Hurry now." On his way back to the Piana Romana with the cigar, Franci grew curious and decided that he wanted to know what it was like to smoke. Sitting down on the railing of a little bridge, he lit the cigar. After one puff, his stomach turned and his head began to spin. "From that moment," he said in later years, "there has existed a great barrier between me and the smoking habit."[16]

On the whole, however, Francesco Forgione was an exemplary boy. A former playmate, Antonio Bonavita, recalled years later, "The rest of us were wicked, . . . but he was always good."[17] By the time Francesco was ten or eleven, he was determined to be a monk. "I always wanted to be a friar," Padre Pio would say in later years. At times, he would say that he first felt the call to the priesthood while listening to a sermon. Grazio and Beppa first became aware of their son's desire for the priesthood in 1897, when a young Capuchin friar from the community at Morcone — some thirteen miles north of Pietrelcina — visited the Piana Romana.

He was Fra Camillo, called Fra Cami. At twenty-six, he was the *cercatore di campagna*, or quaestor, of the friary at Morcone. That is, it was his task to go through the countryside soliciting provisions. He carried a large sack for donations of wheat, grain, flour, eggs, and similar commodities, as well as a coffer for cash contributions. The merry little man was a Pied Piper for the children, to whom he handed out holy pictures, medals, chestnuts, and walnuts. His most distinctive characteristic, a gigantic black beard, covered almost his whole face. Francesco became especially attached to this earnest, spiritual yet personable man and was especially fascinated by his beard — a mark of the Capuchin Order. Soon Franci was telling his parents that he wanted to be a Capuchin "monk." They told him that they would prefer that he go to college, promising to finance his studies.

"No, no," insisted Franci. "I want to be a friar. With a beard."

"With a beard!" laughed Motherdear. "Why, you're still a little lad. You don't know what it is to have a beard or not to have one!"[18]

But Francesco insisted that he wanted to be a Capuchin. One day, during harvest, Beppa told Fra Cami of her son's desire. "Fra Cami," she said, "we've got to make this boy a monk."

"May St. Francis bless him," Cami said, tersely but warmly, "and help him to be a good Capuchin."[19]

At about this time, Grazio and Giuseppa decided to make the journey to Morcone in their farm wagon to inspect the friary and ascertain whether the Capuchins would be interested in having Francesco come there.

Franci was on pins and needles while they were gone. When they returned, the first thing he asked was "Do they want me?" His parents smiled and nodded. The ten-year-old jumped up and down with joy. "They want me! They want me!" he cried.[20]

The Capuchins had told Grazio and Beppa that Franci needed further education beyond his three years of public schooling, which had just come to an end. This meant that he would have to be sent to a private school, which posed a problem to his parents. Although the Forgiones did not feel they lacked any necessities, they had little cash. Padre Pio recalled that they seldom had more than five lire (only a few cents) on hand. They would pay the doctor in grain, for instance, or a lawyer with eggs. Further education for Francesco, however, would have to be paid for in cold cash. Before Grazio could make any hard-and-fast decision, he felt that he had to ascertain whether the boy *really* wanted to go to school and to become a monk. At one point Michele had said he wanted to go on to further education, but he soon lost interest, and the tuition money had been wasted.

So one day Papa went to Franci while he was tending his sheep. "Franci! Do you want to go to school?" he asked.

"And how, Papa!"

"So you want to go? Well, if you learn and don't do like your brother, you'll see that Papa will make you a monk."

Some days later, the same conversation was repeated. Then Grazio let the matter drop and began waiting for some initiative from the boy. Only a few days later, Francesco came to him and asked, "Papa, when are you going to send me to school?" This was all Grazio wanted. "You really want to go to school? You *really* want to go? All right," he said, "you will go to school at once!"[21]

Grazio enrolled the boy in a private school run by Don Domenico Tizzani. In order to finance Francesco's present and future studies, Grazio made a momentous decision: he would seek work in America. By the end of the nineteenth century, southern Italians were migrating in great numbers to North and South America in search of a better life. At one time, approximately thirty percent of the men of Pietrelcina were working in America.

It was probably sometime in 1897 that Grazio first left for America. He went first to South America (some sources say to Brazil, others to Argentina), where he heard that the streets were paved with gold. When he found that they were mud and his employment opportunities almost nil, he borrowed money to return to Pietrelcina, where he arrived in the late spring or early summer of 1898. After begetting his eighth and last child, a boy named Mario, who was born March 24, 1899, and lived only eleven months, Grazio sailed away again, this time to the United States, where he found work as a laborer in Pennsylvania. Many Italian immigrants were finding jobs there in construction, toiling for wages spurned by most white Americans. In many cases the "dagoes" were housed in crude huts outside the city limits and held in contempt by the established community. It was not long, however, before the intelligent and industrious Grazio, despite his lack of a formal education, was hired as the manager of a large farm in Mahoningtown, Pennsylvania, near New Castle, and was able to earn enough money to support himself and regularly send some home to Beppa for Franci's education.

For the next three years, Francesco attended Tizzani's crowded one-room school on Via Caracciolo, where he studied reading, writing, and elementary

Latin. By the time Franci was in the fifth grade, however, it was apparent to Giuseppa that Don Domenico was not a happy choice as a teacher. Apparently it had never occurred to her or to Grazio that Tizzani, a quiet, melancholy man in his fifties who had left the priesthood to marry, would not make the best instructor for a boy bent on becoming a priest. Although Padre Pio in later years always maintained that Don Domenico was a good teacher and a kind man, it soon became clear that the former priest had little appreciation for the boy's devout ways or for his aspirations. He especially looked askance at Francesco's habit of attending Mass every morning and returning to the church every evening after school for Benediction.

One day when Giuseppa arrived for an after-school conference, Don Domenico told her bluntly: "The boy is not learning. He's not learning at all. And it's no wonder. He practically lives in church! In the morning he's at Mass. Then, in the evening, he's back in church again. He's in church right now. How can he possibly learn anything spending all his time in church?" Beppa argued with him, and the heated discussion concluded with Tizzani snarling: "The boy is a jackass! Send him to mind the sheep!"[22]

Giuseppa returned to Crooked Valley Lane in tears. When Franci came home from church, she fairly exploded. Upbraiding him, she said, "Just what am I going to write your father, who has gone all the way to America so that you can get an education?" She continued in high dudgeon until Francesco, silent up to that point, answered sadly: "Motherdear, it's not that I can't learn, and it's not that my going to church is interfering with my studies, but it's because he's a bad priest." Giuseppa dictated a letter to Grazio, apprising him of the situation.

It did not take long for Grazio to see things his son's way. Immediately he wired his wife: TAKE FRANCESCO OUT OF SCHOOL AT ONCE. FIND BETTER TEACHER.[23]

Giuseppa's choice was Don Angelo Caccavo, a man of about thirty. He was not a particularly religious man (in later years Padre Pio would write him, telling him that he prayed every day for his conversion), but anything was better than an ex-priest. Caccavo was an excellent teacher who taught first in his own private school and then in Pietrelcina's expanded public school system until shortly before his death at seventy-five in 1944. Many Pietrelcinese today remember him as a strict but competent teacher.

Don Angelo brooked no nonsense. Whenever a student got a lesson wrong, he had to take it home and copy it over several times by the next morning. Unruly children were made to hold out their hands to receive the whack of a short ruler on the open palm. If that did not work, Caccavo did not hesitate to crack the recalcitrant child on the head or put him "in jail," that is, make him kneel in front of the class, facing the blackboard. But the boys and girls learned, so parents never objected to Don Angelo's methods.

Francesco himself, on at least one occasion, felt Don Angelo's wrath, albeit undeservedly. Several of the boys drafted a passionate love letter, signed Francesco's name, and delivered it to one of the girls, who handed it over to Don Angelo. He exploded and called Francesco to the front of the room. In front of the class, he began to beat the boy with his fists. The poor child tried to take cover under the enraged teacher's desk. Hearing the commotion and knowing her husband's violent temper, Signora Caccavo hurried downstairs, interposed herself between her husband and the child, and saved him from serious injury. When Don Angelo learned that the note was a forgery, he was horrified. He regretted the beating for the rest of his life. As Padre Pio later said, "All his remorse could not take away the black and blue marks that I carried about for days!"[24]

Francesco grew into a handsome teenager, fair and blond, with regular features and a winning smile. He could have had any number of girl friends, but Franci, as he was known to his schoolmates, remained faithful to his priestly calling. He steadfastly ignored the flirtations of his female classmates, lowering his eyes to the floor when he was in their presence.

By October 1901, Francesco could write to his father in Pennsylvania: "Now I am under the guidance of a new teacher. I see that I am progressing day by day, for which I am as happy as Mama." This is the first of many letters that have been preserved. The rest of the letter provides a good picture of what was going on then in the fourteen-year-old Francesco's life. Rejoicing in his father's health, he says:

> We too are well, thanks be to the Lord, and I, in a special way, send continu-
> al prayers to our gracious Virgin, in order that she may protect you from ev-
> ery evil and restore you to our love, safe and sound.

Then he speaks of an incident about which his mother had been angry. Earlier in the year he and several school friends had made a pilgrimage to Our Lady of Pompeii. As he had gone without asking permission, Beppa upbraided him upon his return. Contrite, he tells his father, who had apparently expressed similar disapproval in his latest letter, "You are right a thousand times," but, he adds, "You should think about next year when, God willing, all festivities and amusements will be over, for I shall abandon this life to embrace a better one."[25]

The rest of the letter is quite prosaic. He promises to study, remarks about the lack of rain and the poor wheat crops, says that his mother, brother, and sisters are doing well, and inquires about a relative in America. In short, it is a most ordinary letter. Nothing about it suggests the exotic dreamer or an unbalanced neurotic. It does indicate that, at fourteen, Francesco Forgione had already committed himself to the religious life, to the abandonment of "this life" for the sake of "a better one."

As Francesco neared completion of the requirements for entrance into the Capuchin Order, he very nearly got cold feet. The decision to abandon home and family for a life of ascetic rigor and continual prayer was not an easy one for the sensitive boy. Later in life, Padre Pio said that at that time he had drunk "great draughts of the world's vanity" and found it hard to renounce the world. He was referring not to money, liquor, sex, or anything else that would automatically come to the mind of the worldly reader, but simply to the legitimate joys of life; and he was saddened at the prospect of having to forego them in the harsh austerity of the friary.

At this juncture, Francesco found a friend and confidant who was to assume great importance in his early years. He was a middle-aged priest who did much to encourage him in his vocation and help him in his thinking. Don Salvatore Maria Pannullo (1849-1926) had become pastor of Francesco's parish that year (1901), with the title *Archpriest* (similar to the American title *Monsignor*). A native of Pietrelcina with an earned doctoral degree, he had been a college and seminary professor. He was lively, cultured, and very learned. He could recite the Gospels in their entirety by heart. Zi'Tore, as the townspeople called the new archpriest, was deeply impressed by the quiet, unassuming yet spiritually precocious Forgione boy, who soon came to assist him at Mass as a *piccolo chiero* (acolyte). Moreover, with Grazio in Pennsylvania, Pannullo became almost a second father to Francesco. Evenings, the two of them would go for long walks in the countryside, during which Francesco was wont to confide to the pastor, whom he called *Pati* (Little Father), his revelations concerning the invisible world.

One night when they were walking in the company of several other *piccoli chieri*, Francesco suddenly stopped and pointed to a spot in one of the fields. "Listen," he bade them, "don't you hear the chorus of angels? Don't you hear the church bells ringing at full peal?" No one heard anything, and several of the boys began to giggle. Pati, who remained silent, believed his young friend. He would live to witness, many years later, the rise of a Capuchin church and friary on the very spot to which Francesco had pointed.[26]

By the fall of 1902, as Francesco was just about ready to enter the Capuchin Order, his vocational plans were very nearly derailed. One of his fellow *piccoli chieri* convinced Dr. Pannullo that the "little saint" had been sleeping with the daughter of the local stationmaster. This was the first of several accusations of immorality that Padre Pio would endure in the course of his long and turbulent life.

For a time, Pannullo and the other local clergy were sufficiently impressed with the allegations to suspend Francesco from all his churchly duties while they made an investigation. Though the boy was not told why he was being so treated, he did not protest or even seek to learn the reason for the measures taken against him. He had been taught by his parents, no doubt, that Christians were to imitate their Lord, who was "oppressed and afflicted," yet "opened not his mouth" (Isaiah 53:7).

Later, when asked whether he ever thought of revenge after learning the full story, Francesco, then Padre Pio, told his friend Padre Agostino, "On the contrary, I prayed for them, and I am still praying for them." He had to concede, however, that "At times I did mention to God, 'My Lord, if it is necessary to give them a whipping or two to convert them, please do it, as long as their souls are saved in the end!' "[27]

It is hard to believe that Pannullo could have taken the charges seriously. He seems to have been a man whose resolution tended to wilt under pressure. Perhaps he judged that it was better to be safe than sorry. He did, after a thorough investigation, identify the young liar and force him to admit his calumny. Then he summoned Francesco and, for the first time, explained the reason for his actions, commending the boy for his docility and patience, and announcing that the way was now clear for him to enter the Capuchin novitiate at Morcone.

On New Year's Day in 1903, Francesco was meditating on his vocation, wondering how he would ever be able to bid farewell to the world and devote himself entirely to God in the cloister, when he was favored with an "intellectual vision" (that is, a vision perceived other than through the physical senses). His physical senses were, as he put it, "suddenly suspended," and he was made "to gaze with the eye of his intellect on things quite different from those seen with bodily eyes." His vivid description begs careful reading. In it he speaks of himself in the third person.

> At his side he beheld a majestic man of rare beauty, resplendent as the sun. This man took him by the hand and said, "Come with me, for you must fight a douty warrior." He then led him to a vast field where there was a great multitude. The multitude was divided into two groups. On the one side he saw men of most beautiful countenance, clad in snow-white garments. On the other . . . he saw men of hideous aspect, dressed in black raiment like so many dark shadows.

> Between these great groups of people was a great space in which that soul was placed by his guide. As he gazed intently and with wonder . . . in the midst of the space that divided the two groups, a man appeared, advancing, so tall that his very forehead seemed to touch the heavens, while his face seemed to be that of a Blackamor, so black and horrible it was.

> At this point the poor soul was so completely disconcerted that he felt that his life was suspended. This strange personage approached nearer and nearer, and the guide who was beside the soul informed him that he would have to fight with that creature. At these words the poor little soul turned pale, trembled all over and was about to fall to the ground in a faint. So great was his terror.

> The guide supported him with one arm until he recovered somewhat from

his fright. The soul then turned to his guide and begged him to spare him from the fury of that eerie personage, because he said that the man was so strong that the strength of all men combined would not be sufficient to fell him.

"Your every resistance is vain. You must fight with this man. Take heart. Enter the combat with confidence. Go forth courageously. I shall be with you. In reward for your victory over him I will give you a shining crown to adorn your brow."

The poor little soul took heart. He entered into combat with the formidable and mysterious being. The attack [of the giant] was ferocious, but with the help of his guide, who never left his side, [the soul] finally overcame his adversary, threw him to the ground, and forced him to flee.

Then his guide, faithful to his promise, took from beneath his robes a crown of rarest beauty, a beauty that words cannot describe, and placed it on his head. But then he withdrew it again, saying, "I will reserve for you a crown even more beautiful if you fight the good fight with the being whom you have just fought. He will continually renew the assault to regain his lost honor. Fight valiantly and do not doubt my aid. Keep your eyes wide open, for that mysterious personage will try to take you by surprise. Do not fear his . . . formidable might, but remember what I have promised you: that I will always be close at hand and I will always help you, so that you will always succeed in conquering him."

When that mysterious man had been vanquished, all the multitude of men of horrible countenance took to flight with shrieks, curses, and deafening cries, while from the other multitude of men came the sound of applause and praise for the splendid man, more radiant than the sun, who had assisted the poor soul so splendidly in the fierce battle. And so the vision ended.[28]

One's first impression is that Francesco must have fallen asleep over a copy of John Bunyan's *Pilgrim's Progress* at the point at which Christian fights and subdues the fearsome giant Apollyon, but it was highly unlikely that a good Roman Catholic boy would have been caught with a book by Bunyan, who almost certainly would have been considered a heretic.

On January 3, 1903, Francesco had just received the Eucharist and was engaged "in intimate conversation with the Lord" when he was favored with another purely intellectual vision. His soul was "suddenly flooded with supernatural light," by means of which he understood in an instant that his entry into religion in the service of the heavenly monarch was to be nothing other than a prolonged combat with that mysterious man of hell with whom he had found himself in the preceding vision. Then he understood — and this was sufficient to sustain him — that although the demons would be present at his battles to ridicule his failures, there was nothing to fear because the angels would also be in attendance to applaud his victories over Satan.

He also understood that the heavenly guide was none other than Jesus Christ, who would sustain him in his battles and "reward him in paradise for the victories he would win, so long as he trusted in Him alone and fought gallantly."[29]

Two days later, the evening before he was to depart from Pietrelcina for Morcone, Francesco felt a lump in his throat. At the approaching separation from his mother and brother and sisters, he felt his "very bones crushed." The psychic pain was so great that he very nearly fainted. But now he was favored with a third vision in five days. "The Lord came to comfort him," he wrote about himself, as he described how he

> beheld in all their majesty Jesus and His blessed Mother. They encouraged him and assured him of their love. Jesus, at length, placed a hand on his head. This was sufficient to render him strong in the higher part of his soul, so that he shed not a single tear at his painful parting, although at the moment he was suffering [inwardly] agonies in soul and body.[30]

On January 6, 1903, as Francesco and two other boys who aspired to the Capuchin life, Vincenzo Masone and Antonio Bonavita, boarded the train that would take them to Morcone, Beppa, in tears, blessed Francesco and told him that he belonged henceforth, not to her, but to St. Francis. An hour later the train puffed into the station at Morcone. Don Angelo, who had accompanied them, and the three teenaged boys alighted and found their way to the unpaved, rocky path that led to the friary of Sts. Philip and James. When they knocked on the door, who should be there but their old friend Fra Cami, who embraced them and called them by name. And so Francesco went in with him to a brave new world of service and suffering.

'An Example to All'

The Order of Friars Minor, Capuchin, is the most conservative of the three men's religious Orders that trace their origin to St. Francis of Assisi (1181?-1226), who in 1206 organized a community of men whose goal was "to observe the holy Gospel of Our Lord Jesus Christ by living in obedience, without property, and in chastity."[1] Although Francesco's parents continually spoke of "making a monk" out of the boy, and although throughout his life Padre Pio was called a monk, Capuchins call themselves friars, or brothers, and are not a monastic but a mendicant Order. The difference is one that most laymen would find academic.

The older, monastic Orders had always made the vow of poverty binding upon the individual monk. No limit, however, was set to the possessions a monastery might acquire. During the Middle Ages, many monasteries acquired great corporate wealth and became bywords for luxury. Partly to remedy this, the mendicant Orders, which forbade their members to own any property, *even in common*, were established. Their members were to support themselves through their own labor and the charity of the faithful. *Mendicant* comes from the Latin word meaning "to beg," and, at least in the beginning, mendicant brothers, forbidden to take any money, solicited material sustenance through begging.

A *monk*, by technical definition, usually spends his entire life in one specific religious house, whereas a *mendicant friar* may be assigned to any number of religious communities. Padre Pio, for example, who ministered all his working life in the province of Foggia and who remained at the friary of Our Lady of Grace at San Giovanni Rotondo for more than half a century, nonetheless had nearly a dozen changes of assignment before his final one.

Further, a monk traditionally practiced a ministry of prayer and contemplation and had very limited contact with the outside world. Members of most of the mendicant Orders, on the other hand, in addition to lives of contemplation and spiritual exercises, are engaged in active service to the community. The distinction, however, between a monk and a mendicant friar is appreciated by few outside the religious Orders. Padre Pio, like most of his colleagues, seldom if ever corrected laymen who called him a monk.

At any rate, the Franciscan Order, or Order of Friars Minor, for a generation or more distinguished itself in spirituality, in learning, and in service to human need. Then, as in the case of many organizations with wonderful beginnings, it went into a moral and spiritual decline similar to that which had affected the monastic Orders whose abuses it had been organized to correct. A century and a half after the death of St. Francis, the word *friar* had become synonymous in many minds with the very opposite of the ideals of poverty, chastity, and obedience espoused by the Seraphic Father. In his vivid caricature "The Friar," in the *Canterbury Tales*, Chaucer writes:

> There was a Friar, a wanton one and merry,
> A Limiter, a very festive fellow.
> In all Four Orders there was none so mellow,
> So glib with gallant phrase and well-turned speech . . . .
>
> Sweetly he heard his penitents at a shrift,
> With pleasant absolution, for a gift.
> He was an easy man in penance-giving
> Where he could hope to make a decent living . . . .
>
> He kept his tippet stuffed with pins for curls,
> And pocket-knives, to give to pretty girls.
> And certainly his voice was gay and sturdy,
> For he sang well and played the hurdy-gurdy.
> At sing-songs he was champion of the hour . . . .
>
> He knew the taverns well in every town
> And every innkeeper and barmaid too,
> Better than lepers, beggers, and that crew,
> For in so eminent a man as he
> It was not fitting with the dignity
> Of his position, dealing with a scum
> Of wretched lepers; nothing good can come
> Of dealings with slum and gutter dwellers,
> But only with the rich and victual sellers . . . . [2]

It was the laxity and corruption parodied in the *Canterbury Tales* that called, more then a century after Chaucer, for the founding of the Capuchin Order.

Born out of the turmoil of the Reformation period, the Order was founded in 1528 by Padre Matteo of Bascio. By that time, the Franciscan Order had already split into a moderate group sometimes called the Observants and a more liberal branch known as the Conventuals. The Order of Friars Minor Capuchin was organized around a fundamentalistic observance of the Rule of St. Francis. The name *Capuchin* comes from the large hood, or *capuche*, that St. Francis always wore. In order to symbolize their intention to follow the Rule of the Seraphic Father to the letter, wearing the hood was made compulsory in the strict new Order.

Moreover, since St. Francis had worn a beard, as had Christ, Capuchins were forbidden to shave their faces. The Capuchins also adhered to St. Francis's commandment not to wear shoes. Thus, wearing sandals became a Capuchin characteristic. Each friar was given one habit made of coarse material, a small tunic without a hood, a woolen shirt, and a mantle. The habit was to be girded by a plain cord, from which a rosary was suspended. No hats or birettas were to be worn, as the hood was deemed sufficient protection from the elements.

It was this Order that played an important role in the Counter-Reformation of the sixteenth century and did much to eliminate many of the abuses of the Middle Ages and early Renaissance. For years it distinguished itself for such charitable services as nursing the sick during the great epidemics that ravaged Europe in the seventeenth and eighteenth centuries.

When young Francesco Forgione entered the Order in 1903, it was just then recovering from a period of severe persecution by the Italian civil government. The middle of the nineteenth century had seen a wave of anticlerical sentiment in many countries. During the 1860s and 1870s, France and Germany had passed a number of laws weakening the power of the Roman Catholic Church and dissolving or suppressing the religious Orders.

The same thing had happened in the newly created nation of Italy in 1866. The quarrel between the Church and the Italian government was partly over the loss of the Papacy's temporal possessions, the Papal States, which surrounded Rome and had for centuries been ruled and administered by the Holy See. But it was also due to a desire on the part of the civil government to obtain additional financial resources through dissolving the religious Orders, which were, rightly or wrongly, considered scandalously rich. Most of the friaries had been confiscated by the government, and the friars were forced either to go to other lands, take refuge in private homes, or join the ranks of the secular clergy. But in the late 1880s, the Order was once again permitted to exist.

The Capuchin province of Foggia, which comprised nearly two dozen friaries in south-central Italy, had been reorganized only a few years before by the learned Padre Pio of Benevento (1842-1908), who had ministered in England and India during the time of the suppression. In 1899 he had assumed the position of minister provincial, or governor, of the province. Although he was then a man of sixty, most of the friars whose ranks Francesco came to join in 1903 were very young men. Only a small percentage of them had entered the Order before its suppression.

Pio of Benevento saw to it that the province of Foggia, according to tradition one of the most strict provinces in Italy, maintained its ascetical rigor. It was said that, before the suppression, a significant percentage of the friars had "died in the odor of sanctity."

For Francesco, as for all religious preparing for the priesthood, there was a double formation program, the "religious," which prepared him for community life, and the "ecclesiastical," which prepared him for the priesthood. In the religious program, there were three stages: (1) the novitiate, (2) the temporary or provisional vows of poverty, chastity, and obedience, and (3) the solemn vows, which made the earlier ones permanent. The ecclesiastical program of studies was usually determined by the student's previous education. The Order usually has what are known as minor seminaries, the equivalent of a high school. Since the Order in Italy was only then beginning to reorganize, such a seminary was not available in 1903; hence Francesco had been required to complete the necessary training in the secular world under Tizzani and Caccavo.

When Francesco arrived at Morcone, he was shown to a tiny cell in which there was a mattress filled with corn husks and supported by four wooden planks, a little table, a chair, a wash stand, a jug for water, and, on the wall, a wooden cross. Like his friend Vincenzo Masone (Antonio Bonavita was too young and was sent home) and other new novices, he was directed to spend several days in solitary meditation.

On January 22, sixteen days after his arrival, Francesco was "invested" as a religious. Kneeling at the foot of the altar before the master of novices, the formidable Padre Tommaso of Montesantangelo (1872-1932), his jacket was removed and these words were said: "May the Lord strip from you the old man and all his actions." As Francesco put on his Franciscan tunic, Padre Tommaso solemnly prayed: "May the Lord reclothe you in the new man who is created, according to God, in justice, holiness, and truth." As he put on the hood with its caperon, or small scapular, the novice master said: "May the Lord put the hood of salvation upon your head to defeat the wiles of the devil." As Francesco donned the belt, or cincture, the novice master prayed: "May the Lord gird you with the cordon of purity and extinguish within your loins the fire of lust so that the virtues of continence and chastity might abide in you." Then he was given a candle. "Take the light of Christ as a sign of your immortality," Tommaso enjoined, "so that, dead to the world, you might live in God. Rise from the dead, and Christ will give you light!"[3]

Francesco was also given the symbolic monk's haircut, or tonsure, which signified his transition from the status of layman to that of cleric.

He was also given a new name in religion, as was customary. The name usually was taken either from the Bible or the calendar of saints. To this name would be attached the place of origin of the given religious. For instance, Francesco Forgione was given the name of Pio, or Pius (Pious), after St. Pius V, a sixteenth-century pope (r. 1566-1572). Thereafter, until his ordination to the priesthood, he was known as Fra (Brother) Pio of Pietrelcina. After his ordination, he was Padre Pio; though he occasionally referred to himself as "Fra Pio" to indicate his status in the Capuchin Order, which is considered a fraternity. So attached was he to his religious name that he refused to permit anyone to call him Francesco. His letters, even to his parents, were invariably signed "Fra Pio," and, after his ordination, "Padre Pio."

Capuchins are permitted to use their legal and baptismal names in order to avoid the confusion resulting from having two names in the modern world of drivers' licenses, social security cards, and similar documents. During the First World War, as we shall see, Padre Pio found himself on the verge of being court-martialed for desertion because of a mix-up caused by his having a religious as well as a legal name. When he signed any legal document, he had to use two names: Padre Pio and Francesco Forgione.

Thus Fra Pio began his year of novitiate. Since the sixteenth century, in the province of Foggia, the friary at Morcone has been a place set aside for the training of novices. These young men were assigned to a priest known as the master. Master Tommaso of Montesantangelo was a hard, stern man. According to the Constitutions, he was to teach the novices to subdue their passions and acquire such virtues as humility, obedience, "angelic purity," self-denial, sacrifice, love of poverty, and the spirit of mortification. He was to teach them to understand the Capuchin Rule and also the Breviary, which contained the "hours," or parts of the Divine Office that were to be recited by the community at seven given intervals during the day.

The Constitutions specified that none of the senior members of the community except the master and the Father Guardian (local superior) of the friary was to "speak much" with the novices. Every night except on Sundays, a bell awakened the friars a half hour after midnight to prepare for Divine Office. The sleepy friars, sandal-shod, made their way through the corridors of the house, icy-cold in winter, to the "choir," or prayer chapel of the church, there to prepare for the Divine Office. In "devotion, recollection, mortification, quiet, and silence," as the Constitution specified, they strove to "remember that they are in the presence of God and employ themselves in the angelic exercise of singing the divine praises." Then they recited the first two hours, Matins and Lauds. After that they were permitted to go back to bed.

Their repose did not last long, for they had to arise again at 5 A.M. Each friar made his bed and placed a crucifix on it to make it look like a coffin. Then they went to the choir to pray the Angelus, a prayer to remind themselves of the Lord's Incarnation. This was followed by the Litany of the Saints, in which the

Virgin Mary, the archangels, Patriarchs, prophets, Apostles, and more than thirty other saints were called upon to intercede with God for deliverance from evil. Then the community meditated for a half hour, spending time in mental prayer for the Pope, the salvation of souls, the conversion of unbelievers, and the impartation of wisdom to cardinals, bishops, prelates, kings, princes, and superiors. This period was followed by a Mass known as the *Orazione*, after which the canonical hours of Prime and Terce were recited. This Mass was followed by another, the community Mass, known as the *Messa Conventuale*. At last it was time for the community to be rewarded by a breakfast of boiled bread and oil, after which the friars went back to the chapel to pray the Divine Office of Our Lady.

It was now time for the novices to confer with Padre Tommaso on the lives of the saints, especially those of the Capuchin Order, as well as to work on memorizing the Rule. There was time to study until the moment to return to the chapel to recite the canonical hours of Sext and None.

Now it was noon. The community, still in the choir-chapel, prayed the Angelus before going to dinner. Both dinner and supper were frugal meals consisting chiefly of bread and stew. Many of the older friars living today recall the terrible hunger pains they suffered during their first weeks in the community. During most meals, there was no talking. Almost every day a lesson from the Gospels was read, followed by a reading of the Rule of St. Francis, and then by a reading from some "pious book."

From November second to Holy Saturday, except for the Christmas season, the friars fasted. They were allowed one full meal (such as it was) daily, and two smaller ones — so long as these did not add up to a full meal. No meat was served apart from the main meal. In lax provinces, the friars made up for the rest of the day with one gigantic meal of several courses, but in the province of Foggia in the early 1900s, traditions were observed in all their ancient rigor. During weekdays in Lent, no meat was served at all, and on Lenten Fridays the friars were obliged to subsist on bread and water. The reason: the teachings of St. Francis, who wrote, "It is difficult to satisfy necessity without yielding to sensuality." Everything was calculated to draw the religious away from an attachment to earthly things — even necessities — and help him focus his mind on the things of the spiritual life.

After the midday meal, the community took a brief siesta. At 2:30 P.M. they recited Vespers in the choir and then spent some time doing chores, including manual labor. Even while scrubbing the latrine in the basement, the friars were to recite the Rosary aloud or sing hymns. When chores were over, the community recited the Vespers of Our Lady, after which the novices had another conference with Padre Tommaso. Then they were allowed to recreate in the garden but were strongly encouraged to speak only about the lives of the saints or the Rule of St. Francis. At 7 P.M. they said the Rosary in the choir. Then there was another half hour of meditation, more prayers, and the final canonical "hour" of the Divine Office, known as Compline. After Compline came supper, as frugal as dinner had been, during which there were readings from the Old and New Testaments. Following the meal, the novices met for a third time with Padre Tommaso for spiritual counsel. Finally, at 9 P.M., after a thirty-minute visit to the Blessed Sacrament in the church, the friars retired for the night. Before going to bed, each friar was expected to pray and examine his conscience. Novices were instructed to sleep on their backs in their habits with their arms folded over their chests, in the form of a cross, the better to repel any assaults of the devil.

It was truly a life of great austerity, but Fra Pio and his confreres embraced it willingly, even joyfully, with the conviction that it enabled them to grow in love for God. Except for cases of necessity, the friars were allowed to converse freely only about two hours a day, during the periods of recreation in the garden and immediately after meals, but even then the Evangelical Silence was in force; that is, conversation was discouraged on any but holy and edifying subjects. The Great Silence, a total ban on all but essential conversation, was strictly observed everywhere in the friary between 9 P.M. and 5 A.M. Any man who willfully broke either the Evangelical Silence or the Great Silence was required to pray five Pater Nosters and five Ave Marias while lying on the floor with his arms extended in the form of a cross.

There was great emphasis on the practice of meditation, specifically the practice of withdrawing one's attention from the material world and focusing one's mind and soul on God. Evelyn Underhill (1875-1941), a British writer on mysticism and a contemporary of Padre Pio, called it "a stilling of the surface mind, a calling in of all our scattered interest: an entire giving of ourselves to this one activity, without self-consciousness."[4] The novices were taught to concentrate their psychic energies on one aspect of Divine Reality, such as one of the names or attributes of God, a passage of Scripture, or an event in the life of Christ. In doing so, as Miss Underhill wrote, the soul of the meditator "falls gradually and insensibly into the condition of reverie; and, protected by this holy daydream from the more distracting dream of life, sinks into itself and becomes in the language of asceticism 'recollected,' or gathered together."[5] Jacob Boehme (1575-1624), the famous Lutheran mystic, draws a vivid picture of the practice of meditation:

> Cease but from thine own activity, steadfastly fixing thine Eye upon one point. . . . For this end, gather in all thy thoughts and by faith press into the Centre, laying hold upon the Word of God, which is infallible and which hath called thee. Be thou obedient to this call and be silent before the Lord, sitting alone with Him in thy inmost and most hidden cell, thy mind being centrally united in itself, and attending His will in the patience of hope. So shall thy Light break forth as morning, and after the redness thereof is

passed, the Sun himself, which thou waitest for, shall arise unto thee, and under his most healing wings thou shalt greatly rejoice: ascending and descending in his bright and health-giving beams. . . . [6]

Not all the novices or even the older friars felt light break forth upon them as a result of this activity, but it was held to be pleasing to God to meditate as best one could.

Strict obedience to superiors was considered an essential trait for anyone aspiring to the highest state of spirituality. It was part of giving up one's will, dying to one's self. The Capuchin was at all times expected to try to learn and to carry out as diligently as possible the will and desire of his superiors. "Obedience is everything for me," Padre Pio wrote later in life. "God forbid that I should knowingly go against [a superior] who has been designated as my interior and exterior judge, even in the slightest way."[7]   Padre Bernardino of Siena recalled that even as a very old man, Padre Pio would ask his superiors for permission to do the most trivial things, such as to tonsure himself, change his habit, or put on his mantle. When he became homesick for heaven, he would even ask his superiors for permission to die. What many would consider a pathetic lack of initiative and a disturbing dependency was considered a virtue among those concerned with humility, selflessness, and the surrender to the will of God. In fact, Padre Pio once, when told that someone had accused him of disobedience, said: "If my superior ordered me to jump out of the window, I would not argue. I would jump!"[8]   Fra Pio and his fellow novices got plenty of opportunities to practice the virtues of humility and obedience under the not-so-tender care of the novice master, Padre Tommaso, who seems to have been a character straight out of a Dickens novel. The Constitutions prescribed that members of the community, novices included, "take the discipline" on Mondays, Wednesdays, and Fridays. In order to break their wills, the friars went to the choir, pulled the habit from their backs and posterior portions, and struck themselves on the bare flesh with a chain. The Constitutions, moreover, specified that during this act of discipline, which seems so strange, even barbarous, today, the friars were to think of the Passion of Jesus. The discipline was commended as a defense against sexual passions, laziness, and inconstancy.

Padre Tommaso went a step further. He reportedly ordered the novices to whip themselves until their blood ran onto the floor of the choir. Moreover, without warning, without apparent provocation, he would order boys to administer the discipline at any time or place. He seemed to be very fond of doing this at mealtimes, requiring the hapless youth to go into a corner, strip, and flagellate himself until his back was a bleeding mess. The slightest infraction of the Rule was an occasion for harsh reproofs, mortifications, and heavy punishments. Sometimes Tommaso would fasten a collar of wood around the neck of a boy who displeased him, sometimes he would blindfold him, and sometimes he would make him eat off the ground.[9] In the refectory, before eating his meager repast, each novice had to kneel at Tommaso's feet and beseech him, "Father, bless me." If Tommaso answered, "I bless you," the novice could rise and take his place in the dining hall. But if the master remained silent, the hapless boy had to stay there, kneeling on the cold floor until it was Tommaso's pleasure to dispose otherwise. Sometimes novices were forced to remain on their knees for the duration of the meal. And Padre Tommaso never gave any explanations.

Pio's friend Vincenzo Masone put up with this stifling regimen for only two months before going back to Pietrelcina, where a few years later, he married Pio's sister Felicita. A novice from Naples, whose name has not been preserved, was made to kneel, hungry, all through dinner. "Back home in Naples we pay a dime to see madmen," the boy sarcastically observed. "Here we see them for free." Tommaso overheard this and ordered the boy to strip and take the discipline there and then. The boy got up, left the friary, and never returned. Pio, however, endured Tommaso's harshness and severity without complaint.

Novices, in addition to showing detachment from all material pleasures, were supposed to show detachment from family and friends. Too strong a desire on the part of a novice to see his family was taken as a sign that the boy lacked a genuine call from God to the Order. The Capuchins took quite literally our Lord's sayings: "If any man come to me and hate not his father and mother . . . and brethren and sisters . . . he cannot be my disciple" (Luke 14:26); and "No man, having put his hand to the plow, and looking back, is fit for the kingdom of God" (Luke 9:62). This practice caused Pio's parents considerable heartbreak.

Unfortunately, no one bothered to explain to Giuseppa Forgione any of the customs of the Capuchin community life or any of the rules binding on the novices when, one day, she arrived to visit her son. She was escorted into the guest room and Fra Pio came down to meet her in the company of another friar, who never opened his mouth. He sat only a few feet away, immobile, with head down and eyes lowered. She was horrified when Pio, without showing any sign of affection, sat with his hands in his sleeves and his eyes lowered. When she gave him a number of presents, he showed no enthusiasm. "Thank you," he said, coldly and quietly, "I will take them to my superior." Unable to draw her son into any kind of conversation, she demanded: "Son, what's the matter? Why have you become mute?"

Giuseppa returned in tears to Pietrelcina without either Pio or any of his superiors having offered any explanation for his behavior. In later years Padre Pio recalled: "As soon as I saw my mother, my impulse was to throw myself into her arms. But the discipline of the novitiate did not permit this."[10]

Grazio was in Pietrelcina at the time, having returned from Pennsylvania sometime early in 1903. Horrified at what Beppa told him, he hurried to Morcone, where he demanded and received an explanation from Padre Tommaso. He was somewhat mollified but still disturbed by what he thought was unduly harsh treatment of the boys.

Extreme severity of this sort is a thing of the past. Moreover, if half of the stories told about him are true, Padre Tommaso had to have been excessive even for his time and place. Most modern Capuchins, however, suggest that not everything about traditional community life was bad. After all, at least one very positive thing can be said for the old ways: they produced Padre Pio!

As a novice, Fra Pio quickly attracted the attention of confreres and superiors through his submissiveness and spiritual fervor. Even Padre Tommaso described him as "an exemplary novice . . . an example to all."[11] He astounded Padre Tommaso by begging permission to be excused from recreation (such as it was) and even from meals in order to pray. So abstemious was he that Tommaso often had to command him to eat more. When Pio was not praying, he seemed to be reading the Bible, often on his knees.

From such a description, one might be led to conclude that Fra Pio was an unpleasant fellow, gloomy, fanatical, even neurotic. But one of the most significant arguments against such an interpretation of his personality is that people loved to be with him. Despite his penances and asceticism, he was almost always cheerful. When he was permitted to talk enough to display it, he revealed a keen sense of humor. He loved to tell jokes. Nor was he averse to playing pranks.

One midnight, after the bell had awakened the community for Matins, Pio was returning from the lavatory with a towel draped over his arm when he caught sight of another novice who was a nervous fellow, frightened of almost anything. Between Pio and his fellow student, who did not see him, there a was a large, unlighted room. On a table in the room rested a pair of tall candlesticks that jingled whenever anyone walked by. Between the candlesticks was a hideous, terrifying skull, such as friaries and monasteries kept in those days to remind their residents of the transitory nature of life. Knowing that the other boy was deathly afraid of the skull, Pio hid behind the table in the dark. When the boy passed he waved the towel in a ghostly manner and groaned a "mysterious lament."

Predictably, the nervous novice took off down the corridor, screaming. Pio, then more afraid than his victim — that Padre Tommaso would step in — took off after the boy to try to assuage his fears. But the fearful student became more terrified than ever when he heard footsteps behind him. When Pio called his name, the novice, absolutely beside himself, stumbled and fell, and his pursuer, unable to stop, fell on top of him. "Quiet! Don't be afraid. It's just I!" said Pio. By then his friend was so numb with fear he "didn't even know where he was."[12] Padre Pio, who presumably was not caught, loved to tell this story.

Whenever, for reasons of health that will be described later, Fra Pio was forced to return home, everyone in the friary was downcast. Even Padre Tommaso missed him. Padre Guglielmo recalled that his absence left "a great void in our friary and in our hearts, and we lived in hope that these absences would not be long."

At the end of the yearlong novitiate, the community held a Chapter to decide which novices should be invited to make their temporary vows and which should be recommended dismissal. For nearly two weeks before the ceremony, Pio's impatience was obvious to everyone. Padre Guglielmo recalled that he "could never forget the nine days preceding [Pio's] first religious profession, spent with such piety, prayers, and tears."[13] Finally, on January 22, 1904, Fra Pio went to the altar and knelt before the minister provincial, Pio of Benevento. He folded his hands between those of the older man and declared: "I, Fra Pio of Pietrelcina, vow and promise to the Omnipotent God, to the Blessed Virgin Mary, to St. Francis, and to all the saints, and to you, Father, to observe for three years the Rule of the Friars Minor, confirmed by Pope Honorius, living in obedience, without property, and in chastity."

Pio of Benevento answered: "And I, on the part of God, if you observe these things, promise you eternal life."

Three days later, this boy, whom his superiors described as one of "impeccable deportment" and whom they found notable for "the attraction he exerts on everyone with whom he has contact," left Morcone with Padre Pio of Benevento and another young friar and traveled the twenty miles, probably by oxcart, to the seventeenth-century friary of St. Francis of Assisi, near the town of Sant'Elia a Pianisi, some twelve miles from Campobasso. Here Fra Pio commenced six years of intensive study for the priesthood and continued his growth in community life toward the profession of his solemn vows.

At that time and place, an aspirant to the priesthood in the Capuchin Order was not sent to college, seminary, or divinity school. Nor did he normally earn an academic degree. He simply took required courses that were offered at the particular friary where the Father Lector, or professor qualified to teach the course, was residing. Therefore, during his course of study, a candidate for the priesthood could expect to be transferred to several friaries within the province, there to be instructed in logic, philosophy, theology, Sacred Scripture, dogmatic and moral theology, ecclesiastical history, patrology, canon law, pastoral theology, and the Rule. After ordination, a priest was expected to study "sacred eloquence" for a year. If he wanted permission to preach, he had to take further course work, then submit to an examination for a preaching license.

At Sant'Elia a Pianisi, Fra Pio completed the equivalent of a classical high-school course. In 1905 he was sent to the friary at San Marco la Catola, situated in a remote corner of a wildly beautiful landscape some ten miles southeast of Sant'Elia, to study philosophy. In 1906 he was back at Sant'Elia for further studies in logic and philosophy. There, the following year, he pronounced his solemn, or permanent, vows, ratifying his promise of three years previous to live the rest of his life in poverty, chastity, and obedience in accordance with the Rule of the Friars Minor.

After that he was sent to the friary at Serracapriola, about twenty miles northeast of Sant'Elia, where he studied sacred theology. The following year he had to journey some seventy miles to the west coast of Italy, where he pursued further studies at the friary in the little town of Montefusco.

Fra Pio was a diligent student. In eary 1908 he excused himself from attending the wedding of his brother, Michele, to Giuseppa Cardone on the grounds that he was too busy studying. He wrote his father, home from Pennsylvania for the occasion, that he was sure that it would be better that he pass his exams than attend the nuptials.

For all his diligence, Fra Pio does not appear to have been a brilliant scholar. Padre Bernardino of San Giovanni Rotondo, who taught him at Montefusco, described him as "not distinguished for learning" and "an ordinary student." Like all the others who met him, Padre Bernardino was most impressed by Fra Pio's conduct: "Amidst the lively, noisy students, he was quiet and calm, even during recreation. He was always humble, meek, and obedient."[14]   By the time Fra Pio was beginning his studies for the priesthood, nontraditional religious thinking was making its inroads into nearly all Christian denominations. Led by priests such as Alfred Fermin Loisy (1857-1940) in France, George Tyrell (1861-1909) in England, and Romolo Murri (1870-1944) and the youthful Ernesto Buonaiuti (1881-1946) in Italy, biblical scholars of the modernist movement were seeking to reinterpret Roman Catholic dogma and doctrine in light of modern science and philosophy. Questioning the inerrancy of Scripture, they contended that biblical writers of both the Old and New Testaments were conditioned by the times in which they lived and that, therefore, religious truth was subject to a constant evolutionary process. Rather than the inner life, emphasized by many traditional religious teachers, Catholic, Orthodox, and Protestant, they tended to stress social reform. They provoked a strong reaction from leaders of the Roman Catholic Church, and in 1907 Pope Pius X (r. 1903-1914) condemned Modernism as "the synthesis of all heresies." Eventually most of the leaders of the movement in the Roman Church were forced from the priesthood or left voluntarily.

What effect the modernist movement had on Padre Pio's intellectual or spiritual growth is conjectural. Most likely it had none at all. The generally archconservative Capuchin Order appears to have remained a bastion of historical Christianity. Fra Pio's theological training centered on the Bible, the Church Fathers, and a handful of mystical theologians.

Although knowledge of Sacred Scripture was stressed somewhat less in Roman Catholic than in Protestant seminaries, it was still considered essential. The numerous letters Padre Pio wrote over the years to his spiritual directors and spiritual children make it clear that he had virtually memorized the entire Bible;

though he never quotes chapter and verse, and sometimes he gets his quotations slightly inaccurate, as if the passages were flowing "off the top of his head." His letters are often simply series of Bible quotations or paraphrases. He seems to have been as thoroughly familiar with the minor prophets as he was with the Gospels. For him the Bible was infallible, perhaps as much or more so than for his celebrated American Presbyterian contemporary, William Ashley (Billy) Sunday (1862-1935). Frequently Pio will tell a disciple, or "spiritual child," that what he is advising is not his own opinion but God's word, because it is from the Bible. If the Bible said something, that was the end of all argument. A statement from Scripture was for him "a sure and infallible argument."

Long before Vatican II, Padre Pio insisted that his disciples study Scripture. "As regards your reading matter," he wrote, "there is little [contemporary literature] that is admirable and nearly nothing that is edifying. It is absolutely necessary for you to add to such reading that of the Scriptures, so recommended by all the Fathers of the Church."[15]

For Pio and his colleagues, on almost an equal plane with Scripture was tradition. Supreme authority lay in the Church, the authentic teacher and interpreter of the Scriptures. Pio was taught that the writings of the Fathers — the Christian theologians of the first several centuries after Christ — were simply an extension of Scripture. The weight of tradition was considered on a par with Scripture inasmuch as it was considered to be absolutely harmonious with it. If the Church is the supreme interpreter of Scripture, what would happen if she, at a given time, were to decide that various passages from the Bible had become irrelevant? That possibility was considered extremely remote if not nonexistent when Pio was a young man. In Fra Pio's early years, the popes and the bishops, who proclaimed the official interpretation of Scripture, virtually to a man, held what would today be considered a fundamentalist interpretation of the Bible. Individual theologians might deny or try to explain away various passages they considered not in accord with the latest findings of modern scholarship. They might endorse the thinking of Darwin or Spencer or Marx or Engels; but, as we have seen, in the early 1900s such men found themselves in big trouble with the Church. For Padre Pio and his contemporaries, the Church, the Scriptures, and tradition were practically synonymous, and it probably never occurred to him, at least until relatively late in life, that anyone speaking in any way even vaguely representing the authority of the Church would or even could flatly deny or contradict anything in the Bible.

Besides the Scriptures and the early Church Fathers, Fra Pio studied thoroughly the teachings of the Dominican St. Thomas Aquinas (1225?-1274) and the Franciscan St. Bonaventure (1217?-1274), whose writings centered on the building of an inner spirit of prayer and devotion, and whom the recent pope, Leo XIII (r. 1878-1903), described as "the prince par excellence who leads us by the hand to God." He was most deeply influenced by the two Spanish Carmelite mystical theologians, St. Teresa of Avila (1515-1582) and St. John of the Cross (1542-1591). Their teachings about prayer, contemplation, self-detachment, and the inner life embodied the spirit of the Capuchin Order at that time.

St. Teresa speaks of the necessity of "giving ourselves wholly to [Christ] and keeping nothing for ourselves." She was also concerned about the necessity, for the committed Christian, of suffering. "When [Christ] sees a soul who loves Him greatly," she wrote, "He knows that soul can suffer much for Him."[16] She even encouraged the devout to pray for suffering and tribulations.

Similarly, St. John advocated "dying to all things." "Cleanse your soul of every desire, attachment, and pretension," he wrote, "so that you care nothing for anything." Moreover, he contended, "It is necessary that every desire or taste be renounced, unless it is purely for the honor and glory of God, and that you remain in emptiness for love of Him who neither did nor desired to do in life other than the will of His Father."[17] In order to serve God perfectly, St. John taught, a Christian must "annihilate" himself with respect to all things, both external and internal.

Likewise, St. John urged a love of suffering and an identification with the pains of Christ. "Who does not seek the cross of Christ," he wrote, "does not seek the glory of Christ"; and "Realize that it is good to suffer in any way for Him who is God."[18]

Through his reading of St. Teresa and St. John of the Cross, Fra Pio was reinforced in two principles: total commitment and the embrace of suffering. So total must a Christian's commitment be to God that he should be able cheerfully to renounce everything else in life, even innocent pleasures; identification with Christ means identification with his cross. Suffering, when joined with Christ's, is beneficial. St. Paul writes, "Now I rejoice in my sufferings for your sake, and in my flesh I complete what is lacking in Christ's afflictions for the sake of his body, that is, the Church . . ." (Colossians 1:24).

St. Paul does not mean that Christ's saving work is insufficient or that he really needs man's help, but rather that when a Christian fully gives himself up to Christ, the closer he is drawn into the Savior's love as well as into his sufferings. Fra Pio learned from St. Teresa, St. John, and other spiritual masters that to suffer willingly is to take part in the redemption of mankind as well as to be purified and drawn nearer to Christ, who shed his blood for the redemption of the world.

Suffering, therefore, Pio was taught, might even be courted by some souls. It is not that Christ is seen as helpless without the aid of his children; rather, he grants to his beloved the *privilege* of sharing his mission. For this reason, and not for any masochistic motive, is suffering seen as desirable — because it brings about the salvation of souls.

St. John of the Cross tells us to "strive always to choose, not that which is easiest, but that which is most difficult; not what is most delightful, but what is most unpleasing; not that which gives the most pleasure, but what gives no pleasure."[19] When he was in his fifties, Pio made a statement that is comprehensible only in this context. Speaking of a deceased member of the community at San Giovanni Rotondo, he remarked: "That blessed priest, when he was here in our family, almost every day, after dinner, when I was trying to get some rest, would come to talk about his troubles to me. It took a good deal of sacrifice to listen to him. Now, every day, at the same hour, as a reward for the sacrifices he forced me to make, I say a holy Rosary for his soul, even if I feel tired and exhausted."[20]

In the tradition in which Fra Pio grew to spiritual maturity, more souls were thought to be won to Christ through the suffering of devoted men and women than through preaching, conducting evangelical meetings, or writing tracts. The idea of offering oneself as a "victim of divine love" is implied in much of what St. Teresa, St. John, and others wrote, but it seems to have been only in the century preceding Padre Pio that certain devout people came to make specific acts of offering themselves as "victims."

One such person was a recently deceased French Carmelite nun, Sr. Thérèse of the Child Jesus (1873-1897). Her autobiography was published about the time that Pio first decided that he wanted to be a Capuchin. He read *The Story of a Soul* when he was a student. Thérèse, who was canonized in 1925, two years before her death, made a special offering of herself, as "a burnt sacrifice to the merciful love of Our God."

Another recent victim of divine love was Gemma Galgani (1878-1903), an Italian servant girl who, like Thérèse, succumbed to the agonies of tuberculosis at an early age. We know that Fra Pio read her letters and was very much attracted by them. Gemma, also later canonized, had a vision in which she claimed that Jesus told her: "My child, I have need of victims, and strong victims, who by their sufferings, tribulations, and difficulties, make amends for sinners and for their ingratitude." Galgani responded: "I am the victim and Jesus the sacrificing priest. Act quickly. All that Jesus wills I desire. Everything that Jesus sends me is a gift."[21] As in the case of Thérèse, Gemma's act of offering was followed by increased physical, mental, and spiritual suffering.

Although the concept of the *victim of divine love* seems to have been more common in Mediterranean countries, it was not unknown elsewhere, nor was it an idea limited to Roman Catholicism. Frances (Fanny) Crosby (1820-1915), a Methodist, wrote numerous hymns abounding in images identifying with the sufferings of Christ. She prayed to be drawn nearer to the "precious bleeding side" of Jesus and to the cross, and declared her cheerful willingness to "toil and suffer" in order to walk more closely with Christ.

John Nelson Hyde (1865-1912), a Presbyterian missionary to India, had visions of the suffering Christ and was led to offer himself up to suffer for the conversion of souls. Like many of the Roman Catholic mystics, he urged "obedience in everything, even in the least, surrendering our wills and taking the will of God." Like many Catholic mystics, including Padre Pio, as we shall shortly see, Hyde spoke of an "inward fire burning in [his] bones."[22]

Fra Pio was early drawn to offer himself as a victim of divine love, to suffer with Christ to win souls. His specific act of oblation, however, was still a few years off.

It should be pointed out that despite the talk of "appeasing" God and "making reparations" for the sins of men, neither Teresa, John of the Cross, Thérèse, Gemma, nor Pio ever labored under the mistaken impression that he or she was doing a favor for Jesus or manipulating God, as these words of Padre Pio, spoken to Christ in an ecstasy a few years later, may elucidate:

> I want to help You. . . . Can't You make me strong? . . . I have to tell You that it grieves me to see You in this way. Have they committed many offenses against You lately? . . . They have burdened You still again! . . . O Jesus, the angel was in the Garden. . . . He too is a creature. . . . I too can help You. . . . Make it possible for me to help You with that heavy, heavy cross. . . . Can't they make it any smaller?. . . Ah, Jesus, You're right. . . . I am weak. . . but, my Jesus, what *can* I do?. . . Can't You help me?. . . I am aware of the impossibility. . . but to support You if nothing else. . . . May I help You this evening?. . . You don't need me. . . . Shall I keep myself ready?. . . You are there. . . what is there to fear?

These words were taken down by Padre Agostino, whom we shall meet shortly. The lines are a bit disconnected because a dialogue was going on, of which Agostino heard only one party. It seems clear, however, that Padre Pio had seen Jesus in an attitude of suffering. Touchingly, he volunteers to help Jesus bear his "heavy, heavy cross." Jesus, however, seems to make it clear (1) that he does not need man's works, and (2) that it is humanly impossible for a man, by his own strength, to bear Christ's cross. Yet, apparently, Pio is told that *by the grace of Christ* he can be enabled to participate in the sufferings of Christ so as to be able to assist him in his work of Redemption. Though the Lord has accorded the friar the privilege of helping him bear the cross, Pio is given to understand that this is only through the condescension of divine mercy: Pio's admission to co-redemptive suffering with the Lord is a favor accorded by Christ to Pio, not a favor accorded by Pio to Christ!

As Fra Pio, in his late teens and early twenties, pursued his seminary studies, he increasingly came to identify himself with the idea of a ministry of suffering. Co-redemption would be the dominant theme of his priestly ministry.

Heavenly Secrets

From the beginning of his seminary studies, Fra Pio heard voices and experienced visions. The modern reader, even the modern Christian reader, may tend to be somewhat sceptical about alleged visions and supernatural voices, preferring to pass over this aspect of Padre Pio's life. One cannot do this and still understand Pio, since his contact with the invisible world was an essential aspect of his existence.

From St. Teresa, St. John of the Cross, and other mystical and spiritual writers, Fra Pio learned to speak of three separate types of visions: the bodily, the imaginative, and the intellectual. A bodily vision is what most people usually have in mind when they hear about a vision. If, wide awake, I walked into my living room and, with the same organs of sight that always perceive my bookcases and my worktable, saw Padre Pio, who at this moment has been dead for twelve years, I would (assuming I am not hallucinating) be having a bodily vision. An uncle, since deceased, once recounted to me how, in 1929, when his mother was "laid out" in the parlor of his home, he, then a boy of ten, crept out of bed and went downstairs. There he found the room resplendent with celestial light. Standing around the casket, looking in, were angels. He said he touched the window blinds to make sure that he was not dreaming. If he in fact had not been dreaming or hallucinating, he was experiencing a bodily vision. Surprisingly, this type of vision was distrusted by both St. Teresa and St. John, partly because of the great difficulty involved in distinguishing a true vision from a hallucination. The only time such visions were to be considered as having even the possibility of validity was when they were totally unsought!

Padre Pio had numerous bodily visions of celestial as well as infernal beings who were as vividly present to him as were his flesh-and-blood colleagues. As we will see, he claimed that he was actually beaten and bloodied by demons and that he actually kissed the hands of Christ.

The imaginative vision is hard to describe. To say that a vision is "imaginative" by no means implies that it is a figment of the visionary's imagination. In an imaginative vision, supersensible wisdom is infused into the soul. The means of this infusion is the use of images already in the subject's imagination. It is like an allegory. Evelyn Underhill described the imaginative vision in this way: "It is an accommodation of the supersensible to our human disabilities, a symbolic reconstruction of reality on levels accessible to sense. This symbolic reconstruction is seen as a profoundly significant, vivid, and dramatic dream: and since this dream conveys transcendental truth and initiates the visionary into the atmosphere of the eternal, it may well claim precedence over that prosaic and perpetual vision which we call the 'real world.' "[1] Although at the time he used the word *intellectual* to describe it, young Francesco's vision of the black giant really corresponds to what is classically known as an imaginative vision — a vision in which, as Pio recounts, the bodily senses are suspended and the subject "sees" reality symbolically. God wished to infuse in the boy some knowledge of his future work and did so by using pictures and images already in his mind.

The intellectual vision has been described as pure understanding without any impression of images on the senses. This is a "vision," St. Teresa says, which is "not seen at all." Angela of Foligno (1248-1309), an Italian mystic, describes such visions:

> At times God comes into the soul without being called; and He instills into her fire, love, and sometimes sweetness; and the soul believes this comes from God, and delights therein. But she does not yet know or see that He dwells in her; she perceives His grace, in which she delights. . . . Beyond this the soul receives the gift of seeing God. God says to her, "Behold Me!" and the soul sees Him dwelling within her. She sees Him more clearly than one man sees another. For the eyes of the soul behold a plenitude of which I cannot speak, a plenitude which is not bodily, but spiritual, of which I can say nothing.[2]

The fifteen-year-old Francesco's "purely intellectual" revelation of January 3, 1903, when he was "suddenly flooded with supernatural light," provided the meaning of the imaginative vision of two days earlier.

We will deal more in depth with Padre Pio's spiritual life in a later chapter, but it is important to know that even as a student he was having a variety of supersensible experiences. In addition to visions, he experienced voices, or "locutions," which were sometimes heard in the same manner as the voice of another person, and sometimes experienced as purely interior.

Although Pio frequently distinguishes between intellectual and bodily visions, by the time he was in his mid-twenties, he generally referred both to his visions and his voices as "locutions," by which he apparently meant supernatural communications. He identified, basically, two kinds of locutions: "manifestations and apparitions which are purely supernatural and without form" (most intellectual visions and voices) and those "under human form" (including both bodily and imaginative visions and voices). Those manifestations which are "purely supernatural," Pio says, all "concern God, His perfections, and His attributes." He draws this analogy:

> I hope an example will clarify the matter. . . . Let's stand before a mirror. What do we see? Nothing but a human image. Our intellect, if it is not deranged, will have no doubt that this image is our own.

> Now let us suppose that all men want to prove that we are deceived in wishing to believe that the image which we see in the glass is ours. Could they possibly succeed in dissuading us from our conviction or even causing the slightest doubt to rise within us? No, certainly not.

> Well, the same thing happens to me in these manifestations and divine locutions. The soul beholds these heavenly secrets, these divine perfections, and these godly attributes much better than we see our image in a glass. My efforts to doubt their reality succeed in nothing other than making my soul stronger in its conviction. I do not know whether you have ever seen a great fire come in contact with a drop of water. This small amount of water fails to quench the flames, but, on the contrary, we see that it serves to stir them up even more. This happens to me when I try, with all my strength, to doubt that these things have their origin in God.

He says that we cannot separate the image from the glass, much less physically touch it. "And yet the image exists outside of us if not apart from us." He proceeds:

> The same thing happens to me. My soul remains fundamentally convinced that these heavenly manifestations cannot come except from God, even though with my reason I attempt to question this. But just as it is impossible to separate one's image from a mirror and touch it at the same time, it is still more difficult to succeed in committing to writing these heavenly secrets, simply because of the inadequacy of human language. The soul, without deceiving itself, can affirm only what these are not.[3]

Then he speaks of the bodily, or "human," manifestations. He says that they usually are visions of our Lord in human form — at the Last Supper, in the Garden, bound to the column and being scourged, or glorious and resplendent in the Resurrection and Ascension. There are also visions of the Virgin Mary and "other exalted heavenly beings." Although these were "in human form and appearance" and he could describe them more accurately than visions without form, he prefers to remain "in perfect reticence, because we do wrong when, in expressing ourselves, we see the great distance between the thing that is perceived within our consciousness and that which we are able to express in words."

All these supernatural manifestations produced certain effects in Pio's soul.

> I come forth from them always more penetrated by a sense of my own unworthiness. In this light I realize that I am the most miserable of the creatures that have ever seen the light. I feel greatly detached from this wretched world. I feel myself to be in a land of exile . . . and I suffer immensely in seeing how few among my companions in misery aspire as I do to the Promised Land. I always feel filled ever more full of the goodness of God, and I groan that there might be at least few who love Him wholeheartedly. I suffer in seeing myself so poor, for no other reason than that of not being able to offer anything as a sign of gratitude to so excellent a Benefactor.[4]

Another result of these "locutions" was a great, continuous peace. "I feel myself strongly consumed by an exceedingly powerful desire to please God," he wrote. "The Lord who favored me with this grace causes me to look with immense revulsion upon that which does not help me draw near to God."[5]

Although Fra Pio never spoke of his extraordinary spiritual life to his contemporaries, he was bound by obedience to do so to his superiors, who decided that it was advisable for him to be assigned a "spiritual director." St. John of the Cross believed that every committed Christian should have a spiritual guide to make plain the will of God in every circumstance of life. The disciple makes a commitment of obedience to his spiritual director. Unless the director counsels an obviously sinful act, the disciple is bound to obey him exactly, as the "internal and external judge" of his soul. If the director should lead the disciple into sin, it is the guide, not the "spiritual child," who must answer before God.

A spiritual director is supposed to be both learned and holy, and Fra Pio's superiors settled on a man who was considered to be one of the holiest and most learned in the province. He was a young professor of philosophy and physics, Padre Benedetto Nardella of San Marco in Lamis (1872-1942). Fra Pio had studied under him from 1905 to 1906, and Benedetto had been very much impressed by the young man's spiritual precocity. He felt a great affinity with him because he too was a mystic and, at least to some extent, was favored by visions and locutions.

Benedetto was born in the town of San Marco in Lamis, near San Giovanni Rotondo, where Padre Pio would minister for over fifty years. He entered the Capuchin Order when he was eighteen and was ordained at twenty-six in 1898. By the time he was in his early thirties, Benedetto, an authority on mysticism, was considered one of Italy's foremost theologians. He published nine books, most of which dealt with mysticism and the inner life. A celebrated preacher, he was greatly in demand throughout southern and central Italy. When Padre Pio of Benevento died in 1908, Padre Benedetto was elected to replace him as minister provincial.

Photographs reveal Benedetto to have been a handsome man whose regular features were almost obscured by a gigantic black beard and a profusion of black hair. Of stocky build, Benedetto was stern, almost tyrannical. Pio sometimes characterized him as hardheaded. At times he was dreadfully severe with his disciple, but the younger man always revered his "Dear Daddy." (His biological father he called Papa Dear.) Daddy insisted that Pio describe in detail all his mystical experiences. He made it plain that all locutions were to be submitted "to the judgment of the one who directs you." This Pio was ordered to do even when the locutions seemed to be certain and thoroughly reliable. Padre Benedetto warned that there was always the danger that such apparent revelations came from nature, from the devil, or from "the very propensity or fondness we have for believing what we consider to be revealed." When the younger man was unsure as to whether or not he was pleasing God, Benedetto urged him to trust in his director's judgments as totally as a blind man trusts the person or dog who leads him. Padre Pio was later to write that in his various spiritual trials, he could find calm only in the counsels of Padre Benedetto.

Around the same time, Fra Pio formed a deep and lasting relationship with another teacher, Padre Agostino Daniele of San Marco in Lamis, under whom he had first studied sacred theology at Serracapriola in 1907. Agostino was born Michele Daniele in January 1880, and entered the Order after graduation from public high school. In March 1903, two months after Fra Pio entered the novitiate, he was ordained a priest. Agostino, who was also to become renowned as a preacher, studied French and Greek in state universities and eventually earned a laureate in philosophy. Barely five feet tall, this Friar Tuck figure, nearly as wide as he was high, had a booming bass voice, a long forked beard, thick brown hair, and rubicund cheeks.

Agostino, whom Pio sometimes called "my spiritual father," was more of a best friend and confidant. He was more easygoing than Benedetto and is generally remembered as a jolly, good-natured man. Pio had the habit of pouring out his soul on paper to his "Dear Professor," then instructing him to forward the letter to Padre Benedetto for spiritual counseling. So, in a sense, Benedetto and Agostino formed a team in directing Pio.

Padre Agostino was not a mystic, however, and there were certain things he could not understand as clearly as Benedetto did. In 1946 a priest named Padre Giovanni of Baggio was visiting Padre Pio. The two began to talk about spiritual direction, and Giovanni asked Pio whether it was essential to have a spiritual director. Pio told him that it is usually sufficient to have a confessor, and that if the confessor is incapable of understanding certain spiritual matters, one should simply trust in the goodness of God.

"Don't you have a spiritual director?" Giovanni asked Pio. "I had one," Pio answered, "and he was Padre Benedetto, but since they took him from me, I have been without one."

Giovanni then asked, "You have Padre Agostino for your confessor, don't you?" "Yes," Pio allowed, "but he doesn't understand me and I have to carry on confiding in God."[6]

Even so, the mutual relationship between Pio and Agostino was very deep. Their letters abound with affection. Pio sometimes called Agostino "the most beloved person in the world." Agostino, in 1912, writes, "My dear son, I love you very much, as God wishes me to, and I desire nothing other than to embrace you here below again and then to be together with you forever in heaven with our most merciful Lord."[7]

During his student years, within the Capuchin community, knowledge of the supernatural events in Fra Pio's life was limited basically to Padre Benedetto. Even Padre Agostino knew nothing about these things until 1911. Although impressed by the young man's goodness, obedience, and diligent scholarship, Agostino was, at that time, "unaware of anything extraordinary or supernatural." Yet some remarkable occurrences were happening, and some of them are well documented.

In 1918 Daria Scocca, the Forgiones' neighbor and the mother of Pio's childhood companion Mercurio, made a deposition concerning an event that had taken place a decade earlier. "Zia Daria" testified that Fra Pio, when a student at Montefusco, used to bring her bags of chestnuts, for which the region around that friary was then celebrated. Now, Signora Scocca, who had known Pio from infancy, already believed that he was a saint and saved the bags as relics, touching them and invoking the young man's aid in times of need. One day she was alone in her home, rummaging through a drawer where she kept gunpowder. It exploded, enveloping her head and upper body in flames. Signora Scocca somehow managed to extinguish the fire but not until her face and head were horribly charred. In agony, she dragged herself to her dresser, found one of the chestnut bags, and put it over her head. When she removed it a few moments later, the burns had disappeared and her face was perfectly normal.

There are several difficulties with this story. Daria Scocca stated that she was sure that the incident took place on February 27, 1908. This, however, is impossible because Fra Pio did not go to Montefusco, whence he reportedly brought the chestnuts, until November 1908. If Signora Scocca was mistaken about the date after an interval of several years, might she not also have been mistaken about the details of the accident? By the time she made the deposition, the stigmata of Padre Pio had become common knowledge and he was generally known as a miracle worker. Is it possible that she was projecting backward into time the supernatural attributes for which the friar was being acclaimed at the time of her deposition?

Let us give Daria Scocca the benefit of the doubt and assume that she was not inventing stories to call attention to herself. Let us further assume that she was mistaken about the date only. There is still a problem: there were no witnesses. Zia Daria was alone in the house at the time of the explosion. How seriously was she burned? No one actually saw her burns. Was she herself, immediately after the accident, in a position to judge how seriously she was injured? It is quite possible to believe oneself wounded far more seriously than is actually the case.

A case in point involves my own mother. Some years ago, at her office, she plugged the cord of an electric fan into an outlet. There was a short circuit, and an explosion resulted. My mother was horrified to find her hand apparently charred coal black. In pain and shock she called her secretary, who drove her to the hospital. The doctor who examined her was at first convinced that she had sustained third-degree burns. When he washed her hand, however, the black flowed away with the water and the hand was restored to its usual whiteness. It had merely been covered with soot, and the burns were not serious.

Could the same sort of thing have happened to Daria Scocca? Perhaps the burns were not serious, and in putting the bag over her head and taking it off again, she wiped what was only soot from her face. On the other hand, the event may very well have taken place exactly as she reported it (except for the date, which has to be wrong). Another incident, which took place three or four years earlier, is much more difficult to dispute. It involves the phenomenon known as bilocation, which we will explore in depth later in the book.

The year was 1905. Fra Pio was then studying at Sant'Elia a Pianisi. At seventeen, he had the presence of mind to write down his experience within three weeks of its occurrence and consign it to his superiors. The archives of the friary of Santa Maria delle Grazie at San Giovanni Rotondo still preserve the original deposition of Fra Pio, dated February 1905. He writes:

> Several days ago, I had an extraordinary experience. Around 11:00 p.m. on January 18, 1905, Fra Anastasio and I were in the choir when suddenly I found myself far away in a wealthy home where the father was dying while a child was being born. Then there appeared to me the Most Blessed Virgin Mary, who said to me: "I am entrusting this child to you. Now she is a diamond in the rough, but I want you to work with her, polish her, and make her as shining as possible, because one day I wish to adorn myself with her."
>
> I answered, "How is this possible, since I am still a mere divinity student and do not yet know whether I will one day have the fortune and joy of being a priest? And even if I become a priest, how can I take care of this child, since I am so far away?"
>
> The Madonna said, "Do not doubt. She will come to you, but first you will

meet her at St. Peter's in Rome." After that, I found myself again in the choir.[8]

Was it Pio's imagination? Did he fall asleep and dream? Worn out by fasting and penances, was he hallucinating? That very night, January 18, 1905, some 350 miles to the north, in the city of Udine, a wealthy man by the name of Giovanni Battista Rizzani was dying. His wife, Leonilde, had just become pregnant with their sixth child when he became terminally ill. Now Rizzani was a fervent Mason and would have nothing to do with the Catholic — or any other — Church. As his illness grew worse, he grew more hardened and strictly forbade his wife to summon a clergyman. Meanwhile, as the end drew near, his Masonic friends surrounded the house day and night so as to frustrate the efforts of any priest to see the dying man.

Donna Leonilde, however, was a believing Christian and prayed fervently to God that her husband might put his trust in the Lord before he died. About the same time that Fra Pio had his experience in the choir at Sant'Elia a Pianisi, Signora Rizzani was kneeling by the bedside of her now-comatose husband, praying. Suddenly she looked up and saw a young man. She did not get a good look at his face, but he was wearing a Capuchin habit. As soon as she saw him, he left the room. Signora Rizzani got up to follow him, but he seemed to vanish into thin air.

She had no time to try to figure out an explanation for the young man's disappearance, for the family dog immediately began to howl. The baying of a dog was believed to be a harbinger of imminent death, and, naturally, the noise set the Signora's nerves on edge. Unable to stand the baying, she decided to go into the yard and untie the dog. Before she could reach the doorway, the distraught woman, then in her eighth month, was seized with labor pains. She called the family business manager, who lived on the premises and was in earshot, and he successfully delivered her of a baby girl.

Within moments, the mother, still bleeding, was able to gather the child into her arms, stagger up the stairs, lay the infant on a bed, and return to the side of her husband. The business manager went outside and demanded that the Masons let the priest in. "You might have a point about stopping him from ministering to a man who insisted that no clergy be admitted to his bedside," he shouted, "but you have no right to keep him from baptizing the premature girl to whom his wife has just given birth!" At once Rizzani's Mason friends made way for the priest, who had been trying for hours to get through. He went directly to the sickroom and began to minister to Rizzani. Suddenly the dying man opened his eyes, looked at the priest, and said distinctly, "My God! My God! Forgive me!" He drifted off into a coma again and died before morning.

In order to grasp fully what took place in 1905, we have to advance in time to the year 1922. After her husband's death, Signora Rizzani moved to Rome with her children. In the summer of 1922, the youngest girl, Giovanna, who had been born the night of her father's death, was in St. Peter's Basilica with a friend. She was about to enter college and was troubled. One of her high-school teachers had instilled serious doubts in her mind about the doctrine of the Trinity. She wanted to make her confession as well as talk to a priest about her dilemma. A guard told Giovanna and her friend that all the priests assigned to hear confessions had already gone for the day. Before they could leave, however, they encountered a young Capuchin who said that he would gladly hear Giovanna's confession.

When Giovanna told the young priest about her theological dilemma, he explained the doctrine of the Holy Trinity in such a way as to dispel her doubts. Giovanna emerged from the confessional and stood, waiting with her friend for the priest to come out of his side of the booth. The only person who appeared was an irate guard. "What are you doing here?" he demanded. "We're closed! You have to leave the basilica. Come tomorrow morning and you'll be able to make your confession."

"But I already made my confession," Giovanna told him. "We're waiting for the priest to emerge from the confessional so that we can kiss his hand. He's a Capuchin Father."

Exasperated, the guard went up to the confessional and opened the priest's compartment. "You see, young ladies, there's no one here."

"But where did he go?" Giovanna exclaimed. "We've been standing here, watching, and we haven't seen him leave!" Giovanna and her friend pondered the situation and concluded that there was no way the priest could have left the confessional without their having seen him.

That fall Giovanna entered college. Sometime the following year, she was shown a picture of Padre Pio, who was by then quite famous, though she had never heard of him. Giovanna thought that he looked very much like the Capuchin priest she had encountered at St. Peter's. She wondered whether it might have been he but then dismissed the idea and thought no more about it.

The following summer (1923), Giovanna, an aunt, and several friends decided to go to San Giovanni Rotondo to see Padre Pio. It was late afternoon when, standing in a crowd of people in the sacristy of the church, Giovanna caught her first glimpse of Padra Pio. To her amazement, he came right up to her and extended his hand for her to kiss, exclaiming: "Why, Giovanna! I know you! You were born the day your father died."

Giovanna was nonplussed. How could this man have known such a thing? The next day, after hearing her confession, Padre Pio said to her: "At last you have come to me, my dear child. I've been waiting for you for so many years!"

"Father, what do you want of me?" asked the young woman. "I don't know you. This is the first time that I came to San Giovanni Rotondo. I came with my aunt. Perhaps you're mistaken and have confused me with some other girl."

"No," said Padre Pio. "I'm not mistaken. I knew you before."

"No, Father. I don't know you. I never saw you before."

"Last year," said Padre Pio, "one summer afternoon, you went with a friend to St. Peter's Basilica and you made your confession before a Capuchin priest. Do you remember?"

"Yes, Father, I do."

"Well, I was that Capuchin!"

When he spoke those words, the young student was thunderstruck. Continuing, Padre Pio said:

> Dear child, listen to me. When you were about to come into the world, the Madonna carried me away to Udine to your mansion. She had me assist at the death of your father, telling me: "See, in this very room a man is dying. He is the head of a family. He is saved through the tears and prayers of his wife and through my intercession. The wife of the dying man is about to give birth to a child. I entrust this child to you. But first you will meet her at St. Peter's." Last year I met you at St. Peter's, and now you have come here to San Giovanni Rotondo of your own accord, without my sending for you. And now let me take care of your soul, as the heavenly Lady desires.

Giovanna burst into tears. "Father, since I'm your responsibility," she sobbed, "take care of me. Tell me what I must do. Shall I become a nun?"

"By no means," responded the Padre. "You will come often to San Giovanni Rotondo. I will take charge of your soul, and you will know the will of God."

Later, when she heard Giovanna's story, Signora Rizzani came to see Padre Pio, who told her: "Madame, that little monk whom you saw walking towards the gallery of your mansion in Udine when your husband was dying was I. I can assure you that your husband is saved. The Madonna, who appeared to me in the mansion and who bade me pray for your dying husband, told me that Jesus had pardoned all his sins and that he was saved through her maternal intercession."[9]

Both Giovanna and Leonilde Rizzani were utterly convinced. One will notice that the words both women remember Padre Pio speaking to them in 1923 were almost identical with the account that Fra Pio had written a few days after the occurrence in 1905.

Giovanna Rizzani, who became the Marchioness dei Boschi diCesena, was still alive as late as 1981. She remained a devoted disciple of Padre Pio and later gave a detailed deposition before the Archepiscopal Curia of Manfredonia. The Curia noted that her account of what Padre Pio had told her about her birth and her father's death when she first talked to him at length in 1923 accorded exactly with the account Padre Pio had written in 1905 — a document which the marchioness had not yet read! It should also be stressed that no one knew anything about Pio's bilocation experience except the superiors to whom he entrusted his deposition — and they had maintained absolute silence.

Although his colleagues were unaware of any supersensible knowledge or any miracles, they were, as we have earlier observed, struck with his character. Padre Guglielmo wrote of the "purity that was revealed by the great modesty in his eyes . . . the penances he asked with insistence to perform . . . the change in his countenance that could be observed when he unexpectedly encountered an immodest picture . . . his betrayal of distress when he observed in others an action of a dubious nature — all of these proof of his love and angelic virtue."[10]

Padre Raffaele of Sant'Elia a Pianisi (1890-1974), who studied with Pio and became a close friend, recalled, "In particular, he aroused in me a sense of great admiration for his exemplary conduct." Whenever Raffaele encountered Pio, whether in the hallway, in the choir, in the sacristy, or in the garden, the latter always seemed to be in a state of recollection, or awareness of God's presence. "There was never the danger that he would say a single word that was not necessary," Padre Raffaele recalled. "Though I was still very young and no expert on virtue, I noticed something in him that distinguished him from the other students."[11]

Padre Damaso of Sant'Elia a Pianisi (1889-1970) had a similar observation. Damaso found Pio "a little different from the others. . . . He was more lovable, and he knew how to say just the right thing to [the younger] boys. He would suggest something in the way of advice in a very sweet manner, and we used to listen to him of our own accord."[12]

Thus it was chiefly for his personal qualities rather than any supernatural or charismatic gifts that Fra Pio aroused the admiration and love of his professors and fellow students. There was something else, though, about Fra Pio that drew the attention and solicitude of others — his precarious health.

'A Holy Priest, A Perfect Victim'

Despite Fra Pio's plump, rosy-cheeked appearance, he was plagued by a variety of ill-defined physical problems from the very beginning of his novitiate, and the problems he suffered before his entry into religious life intensified in the friary. Like Martin Luther, he was beset by persistent constipation. He suffered from attacks of vomiting and sometimes was unable to retain solid food for weeks on end. Once, for a space of six months, he was forced to subsist on milk. He suffered from spasms of violent coughing, was tormented by headaches, and frequently ran high temperatures. Without warning, Fra Pio would seem to be reduced almost to the point of death, only to recover just as suddenly. His superiors, through medical consultation, tried unsuccessfully to pinpoint the cause of his physical troubles.

In 1908, while Pio was studying at the Friary of St. Egidio at Montefusco, physicians made a devastating diagnosis. Noting the asthenia, or weakness, of the twenty-one-year-old patient, coupled with his severe respiratory symptoms and his fevers, which were then most severe at night, they declared that he was suffering from an active case of tuberculosis of the lungs. This feared disease took a tremendous toll among the overworked and undernourished peasantry of southern Italy at the time. The diagnosis meant that Pio, who had already been sent home for limited periods of rest and recuperation over the years, would have to remain outside of the friary indefinitely.

Pio's parents, however, were not satisfied with the diagnosis. They took him to a young doctor in Pietrelcina, Andrea Cardone (1876-1969). Cardone, who boasted of a doctorate in medicine (many practitioners in southern Italy at the time apparently could not) as well as in veterinary medicine, is still remembered as a brilliant physician who even in his nineties kept abreast of the latest medical advances. Cardone took issue with the diagnosis of pulmonary tuberculosis. Just to be sure, he convinced Grazio and Giuseppa to send their son to specialists in Naples, who confirmed that Pio was not suffering from any form of tuberculosis.

Although the doctors in Naples were not able to say exactly what the matter was with the youth, Cardone was convinced that Fra Pio's illness was a simple case of chronic bronchitis coupled with physical exhaustion and further aggravated by his ascetical life-style. He recommended a period of rest and "abundant nourishment" in Pietrelcina. After a short time, Fra Pio seemed cured and was able to return to Montefusco. His mysterious illness, however, was to plague Pio, off and on, for the next decade, and it very nearly derailed his vocation as a religious.

Until 1909 his illness did not prevent his progress toward ordination. Pio received minor orders at Benevento on December 19, 1908, and two days later was ordained to the subdiaconate. The next month, at Morcone, he was ordained to the diaconate. Then he collapsed. His stomach could retain nothing, and he was sent home. There he seemed better.

Throughout the year, Fra Pio's superiors, as soon as they learned of an improvement, summoned him back to community life and sent him to various friaries of the province — to Morcone, to Our Lady of the Mountain at Campobasso, to Montefusco again, to Gesualdo — in the vain hope that the change in air would bring about an improvement. As soon as Pio would enter a friary door, he would be seized by violent stomach cramps and vomiting and have to be sent home again. Each time he returned to Pietrelcina he would improve; but he could not remain a single day at any friary without suffering a relapse.

Padre Benedetto, who had recently been elected provincial, decided that Fra Pio should remain with his family until further notice, since it was clear that his health would not permit his residence in any friary, even for a short time. But this posed a problem: Pio still had not completed his studies and could not be ordained unless he completed his course in moral theology. Therefore, Benedetto obtained for Pio a dispensation to live at home and pursue his studies privately. His tutor was to be a secular priest, Don Giuseppe Maria Orlando, seventy-eight years old and subject to periods of "mental derangement," but very intelligent and very pious. Under this wise but eccentric old man, Fra Pio completed the studies necessary for ordination.

During this period, Fra Pio kept in constant touch with Padre Benedetto, and his letters from this period show him to have been in very low spirits, very depressed by his poor health and inability to live in a friary, and desirous only of being ordained and then dying. Even at Pietrelcina he seems to have been constantly ill. He complains in March 1910 of continuous fever, especially at night, copious sweats, a cough, and pains in his chest and back. In April he was confined to bed. In May he suffered from chest pains. In July these pains were so bad as to render him speechless at times.

"If Almighty God in His mercy desires to free me from the sufferings of this my body, as I hope He does, through shortening my exile here on earth," he wrote Benedetto, "I shall die very happy. . . ."[1] In another letter he confides: "The notion of being healed, after all the tempests that the Most High has sent me, seems to me but as a dream, even madness. On the contrary, the idea of death is very attractive to me."[2]

Fra Pio was, however, concerned lest his illness be a visitation from God on account of unconfessed sin. Writing to Benedetto, he says:

> For several days my conscience has been continuously troubled over my past life, which I spent so wickedly. But what particularly tortures my heart and afflicts me exceedingly is the thought of being certain that I have confessed all the sins of my past life, and, more than that, whether I have confessed them well. . . . Dear Father, I need your help to still the tossings of my spirit because — and you must believe me — this is a thought that is destroying me. . . . I should like to make a general confession, but I don't know whether that would be good or bad. Please help me, O Father, for the love of our dear Jesus. . . .[3]

He is troubled that these conflicts and doubts could exist in a heart "that prefers death a thousand times to committing one sin." "I would like to make a bundle of all my bad inclinations," he wrote in July, "and give them to Jesus so that He might condescend to consume them all in the fire of His divine love!"[4]

Yet, through it all, Fra Pio is resigned to the will of God. "I do not know the reason for this, but in silence I adore and kiss the hand of Him who smites me, knowing truly that it is He Himself who, on the one hand, afflicts me, and, on the other, consoles me."[5]

Meanwhile, Padre Benedetto was working to make it possible for Fra Pio to be ordained. On July 6 he was able to write that he had obtained all the necessary dispensations and that Pio would be able to be ordained a priest about the tenth or twelfth of August. It would be necessary, however, for Pio to journey to Morcone in mid-July to learn the ceremonies involved in exercising his priestly ministry. He would also have to go to Benevento for his final examinations.

And so, on July 21, Fra Pio, along with one Padre Eugenio of Pignataro Maggiore (Capuchins had to travel in pairs), journeyed from Pietrelcina to Morcone. As soon as he arrived, he was seized with cramps and started to vomit, and the next day Tommaso of Montesantangelo, Pio's old novice master, wrote to tell Padre Benedetto that he was sending the youth home. A sympathetic Benedetto wrote Pio immediately after his return to Pietrelcina, saying that he would authorize Pannullo to instruct him on the rubrics of the Mass. "Your sufferings," he adds reassuringly, "are not punishment, but rather ways of earning merit that the Lord is giving you, and the shadows that weigh on your soul are generated by the devil, who wants to harm you." Further, he exhorts Pio to remember that "the closer God draws to a soul, the more the enemy troubles him."[6]

The longed-for day was August 10, 1910. Twenty-three-year-old Fra Pio, along with Pati and Motherdear (Papa and Michele were now in Jamaica, Long Island), boarded a horse-drawn cab and bounced over country roads to the Cathedral of Benevento. There, in the chapel, he was ordained a priest by Archbishop Paolo Schinosi. After a light lunch, which presumably Pio was able to hold down, the little party returned to Pietrelcina, arriving about 5 P.M. They were met on the edge of town by the city band, which had been hired by Michele's wife. The band accompanied Padre Pio to his home while, along the way, cheering townspeople showered him with coins and with a candy known as *raffaioli*. There, at the house, Motherdear put on a great feast. Through it all, Pio sat with his head bowed, blushing with emotion. He would always recall with pleasure "that beautiful day of my ordination," when he felt as if he were in heaven.

As a souvenir of his ordination, Padre Pio had printed on a holy card these words, which serve as a key to his ministry: "A souvenir of my first Mass. Jesus, my life and my breath, today I timorously raise Thee in a mystery of love. With Thee may I be for the world the Way, the Truth, and the Life, and through Thee a holy priest, a perfect victim."[7]

Four days later, at the new parish church of Our Lady of the Angels, Padre Pio sang his first public Mass. The sermon was preached by Padre Agostino, who spoke about the triple mission of a priest: the altar, the pulpit, and the confessional. Actually, at that point, Padre Pio was authorized to perform only one of those functions: celebrating the Eucharist. He had not taken — and never would take — the requisite courses to qualify him to undergo the examination for his preaching license, and thus far Padre Benedetto, as provincial, was unwilling to concede him the faculty to hear confessions. Benedetto hesitated because of Pio's health and because he was not sure that the young man, owing to the frequent interruptions of his studies, had the proper theological preparation. Not to be able to hear confessions was a great grief to young Padre Pio.

Ordination brought no improvement in Pio's physical health, however. Over the next few months he speaks of asthma-like respiratory symptoms as well as chest pains so severe that at times he felt as if his back and chest were exploding.

In his letters to Padre Benedetto, Padre Pio frequently speaks of assaults by the devil, which basically took three forms: temptations against purity, a sense of sin and unworthiness, and a fear of unconfessed sin. During the Easter season of 1911, he writes, "Even in these holy days the enemy tries with all his might to induce me to acquiesce to his wicked designs, and in particular, this malignant spirit tries with every sort of fantasy to tempt me into thoughts of uncleanness and despair."[8] Far from being titillated, Pio was horrified. " I tremble from head to toe with fear of offending God," he wrote.

Pio's longtime comrade Mercurio Scocca suggested that his mysterious illness was due to sexual frustration. When Scocca proposed that he cure himself by marrying (another version represents cruder advice), Pio, who always had a short fuse, picked up a pitchfork, swung it at Scocca, and chased him out of the barn where they had been talking.

Padre Pio was afflicted with a sense of being hopelessly sinful and unworthy. Martin Luther called this state *anfechtung*; and John of the Cross referred to it as "the dark night of the soul." Pio said that Satan was "forever representing the picture of my life in the grimmest possible way."[9] Again he wrote: "Our common foe has continued to wage war against me and up till now has shown no sign of wanting to give up and admit defeat. He wants me to be damned at all costs and is constantly putting before my mind the grievous picture of my life, and, what is worse, he craftily sows thoughts of despair in me."[10] In June 1911 he described himself as on the point of being "reduced to ashes" by terror over his sins and his helplessness to save his soul.

Pio was also terrified, as we have seen, by the thought of being punished by God for sins unknown to him. He was forever afraid of being condemned for the sins of his "secular life." All this anguish contributed immeasurably to his physical problems. Many years later, in 1939, Padre Pio commented to Padre Agostino, "My illnesses [in youth] stemmed from this spiritual oppression."[11]

Benedetto frequently had to remind Pio that theirs was a gracious God. "The fear of the sins you have committed is illusory and a torment caused by the devil," he counseled. "Let go, once and for all, and believe that Jesus is not the cruel exactor that you paint, but, instead, the Lamb who takes away the sins of the world and intercedes with ineffable groans for our good."[12]

Most of the time, however, Benedetto did not chide Pio for entertaining what today many would characterize as a morbid sense of sin. He told the younger man that his trials, both bodily and spiritual, were the promptings of the devil, permitted by God so as to cause him to grow in holiness. A month after Pio was ordained, Benedetto wrote him:

> I see clearly that [the Lord] has chosen you to make you close to Him, even without merit on your part. Now you can be sure that He wants to take perfect possession of your heart . . . to transfix it with pain and love like His own.[13]

In other words, to be close to Christ, one must suffer like Christ. Benedetto elaborated in another letter:

> You want to know what Jesus wants of you? The answer is simple. He wants to toss you, shake you, pound you, sift you like grain until your spirit arrives at that purity and cleanness that He desires . . . .
>
> Nonetheless, do good and desire that the Lord free you from these temptations, and also pray to this end . . . . You must not fear that the Lord will leave you at the mercy of the enemy. He will permit him to molest you only

in such a way as serves His paternal designs for the sanctification of your soul. Therefore, be strong and cheerful in heart.[14]

In still another letter, Benedetto counsels:

Hearing that the storms are raging more fiercely consoles me because it is a sign that God is establishing His reign in you. The temptations are a sure sign of divine predilection, and fearing them is the most certain proof that you do not consent to them. Be of good cheer and do not be discouraged. The more the foe increases his violence, the more you must abandon yourself in the faithful Lord, who will never permit you to be overcome. As it is written, "God is faithful and will not permit you to be tempted beyond your strength . . . .

Is not Our Lord good beyond our every thought? Is He not more interested in our well-being than we are ourselves? When we think of the love that He bears us and of His zeal for our benefit, we must be tranquil and not doubt that He will always assist us with paternal care against all our enemies . . . ."[15]

"If I did not suffer, I'd think the Lord didn't love me," Fanny Crosby once said. Basically, this is what Padre Benedetto is saying. Continually, as Padre Pio pours out his soul in anguish to him, Padre Benedetto consoles him with verses from Scripture and with reminders that physical and moral sufferings are God's way of making him pure and holy, more like Himself. "I exult," wrote Benedetto, "in knowing with certainty that the fury is permitted by . . . the celestial Father to make you like His dear Son, persecuted and beaten to death on the cross! The greater the pains, the greater the love God bears you!"[16]

Then, too, Padre Pio had his consolations. He realized that the only way to overcome his temptations was to place them in the hands of Jesus. "All the ugly phantasies," he wrote, "that the devil introduces to my mind vanish when I abandon myself to the arms of Jesus. Therefore, when I am with Jesus crucified — that is, when I meditate on His afflictions — I suffer immensely, but it is a grief which does me good. I enjoy a peace and a tranquillity which are impossible to explain." [17] On another occasion Pio wrote to his spiritual director:

From time to time Jesus alleviates my sufferings when He speaks to my heart. Oh yes, my father, the good Jesus is very much with me! Oh what precious moments I have with Him! It is a joy which I can liken to nothing else. It is a happiness that the Lord gives me to enjoy almost only in suffering. In such moments, more than ever, everything in the world pains and annoys me and I desire nothing except to love and to suffer. Yes, my dear father, in the midst of all these sufferings I am happy because I feel my heart throb in unison with the heart of Jesus. Now, imagine what consolation the knowledge of possessing Jesus with certainty infuses in my heart!

It is true that the temptations to which I am subjected are very great, but I trust in divine providence so as not to fall into the snares of the tempter. And, although it is true that Jesus very often hides Himself, what is important is that I try, with your help, always to stay in Him, since I have your assurance that I am not abandoned, but toyed with by Love.[18]

God seemed to be playing a game of hide-and-seek. This oscillation between extreme exaltation and violent depression is a common experience among mystics. Both St. Catherine of Siena (1347-1380) and St. Teresa of Avila spoke of a "game of love," in which God seems, by turns, to hide and then return to the soul. At times Pio was "almost in paradise"; at other times, he felt as if Satan were about to snatch him out of the Lord's hands. Benedetto assured him that this was a normal part of spiritual growth..

As Pio grew in faith, gradually he found himself able to rise above the temptations of the devil and worry less about the possibility of being successfully tempted. To the very end of his life, however, he never felt that his salvation was entirely secure. Far from being of the "once saved, always saved" school, he felt that the possibility of being lost remained as long as life on earth lasted. Realizing, therefore, his helplessness and his inability to save himself, in moments of spiritual desolation, he learned to cast himself into the arms of Jesus. His letters to Benedetto in the summer of 1911 reveal a growing confidence in foiling the wiles of the devil. In August of that year, he wrote:

The attacks of the devil continue, as always, to afflict my soul. Yet, meanwhile I have observed for some days a certain spiritual joy that I am unable to explain . . . . I no longer have the difficulty I once felt in resigning myself to the will of God. I even repel the calumnious assaults of the tempter with such ease that I feel neither weariness nor fatigue.[19]

The next month he again wrote Benedetto:

Jesus continues to be with me, and still the facility to repel temptations and resign myself to God has not left me, . . . doing this is growing easier. Look, then, at such a token of the sweetness and goodness of Jesus that comes to such an evil wretch as I. And meanwhile, to what can I liken such amazing grace? What can I render to Him for such benefits? How many times in the past, if only you knew, I exchanged Jesus for some vile thing of this world![20]

Padre Pio's spiritual commitment went further than merely accepting suffering for his own good. During this period he made a specific act of offering himself to God as a victim for the salvation of souls. As we have seen, he was long familiar with the concept of the "victim of divine love." Recall that the souvenir prayer card he composed for his ordination expressed the desire to be "a perfect victim." A few months after this, on November 29, 1910, he wrote to Benedetto:

For some time I have felt the need to offer myself to the Lord as a victim for poor sinners and for souls in Purgatory. This desire has grown continuously in my heart, until now it has become a powerful passion. I made this offering to the Lord on other occasions, imploring Him to lay on me the punishments that are prepared for sinners and for souls in Purgatory, even multiplying them upon me a hundredfold, so long as He converts and saves sinners and quickly releases the souls in Purgatory. . . . Now, however, I wish to make this offering to the Lord with your authorization. It seems to me that this is what Jesus wants. I am sure that you will not find it difficult to grant me this permission.[21]

Benedetto's response was an unqualified and enthusiastic assent. "Make the offering!" he advised. "Extend your arms on the cross and offer yourself to the Father as a sacrifice in union with the loving Savior. Suffer, groan, and pray for the sins of the world and the miserable ones of the other world . . . ."[22]

Two years later, in a letter to Padre Agostino, Padre Pio further defined what it meant to be a victim of divine love when he wrote:

[The Lord] chose certain souls, and among them, despite my unworthiness, He also chose me, to assist in the great work of the salvation of mankind. The more these souls suffer without any consolation, to that extent are the pains of our good Jesus made lighter. This is why I want to suffer increasingly and without comfort. And this is all my joy. It is only too true that I need courage, but Jesus will deny me nothing.[23]

Some years later, again writing to Agostino, he elaborated still further about his co-redemptive mission: "With your prayers assist this Cyrenean who carries the cross of many people, so that there might be accomplished in him the words of the Apostle, 'I make good and complete what is still lacking in the Passion of Christ.' "[24] Padre Pio liked to identify with Simon of Cyrene, the man who was forced to carry the cross to the hill of Calvary after Jesus had collapsed under its weight. Like Simon, Pio did not imagine that he had chosen this mission himself. He was certain that he had been chosen by God to be a victim, to help Jesus bear the cross.

Even by the time Padre Pio asked Padre Benedetto's authorization for his self-oblation as a victim of divine love, he had received signs in his body which led him to believe that the Lord had already accepted his offering. These signs were the marks on his body suggestive of the wounds of Christ's passion.

On the afternoon of September 7, 1910, Padre Pio appeared at Pannullo's office and showed him what appeared to be puncture wounds in the middle of his hands. Pati asked him what had happened. Pio told him that he had been praying in the Piana Romana when Jesus and Mary appeared to him and gave him the wounds. Pannullo examined the young man's hands, then insisted that Pio see a doctor. The first physician he went to diagnosed the phenomenon as tuberculosis of the skin. Pio then went to Cardone, whose response to his colleague's diagnosis was "Humbug!" He observed sores about a half inch in diameter on both the backs and the palms of Pio's hands. Although the wounds apparently did not bleed, they seemed to extend all the way through the hands. Cardone was positive that they were not of tubercular origin. Apart from that, he could not explain them.

These wounds, which Pio tried to conceal, were a source of great embarrassment. Besides Pannullo and the doctors, the only person to whom he showed them was his friend Mercurio Scocca. Pio concealed them even from Motherdear, who noticed something was wrong and remarked that he was moving his hands in a strange way. But Pio successfully evaded her questions and hid the lesions from her eyes.

A few days after seeing Cardone, Pio went to Pannullo. "Pati, do me a favor," he said. "Let's pray together to ask Jesus to take away this annoyance. I do want to suffer, even to die of suffering, but all in secret."

"Dear Son," replied Pannullo, "I'll help you to pray and ask Jesus to take this annoyance away. Yet, if it is God's will, you must yield yourself to do His will in all and over all. And remember, since this is for the salvation of souls and for the good of the entire world, you must say to Jesus, 'Do with me as Thou wilt.' "[25]

The two men prayed, and the wounds went away—for a season.

From Pannullo's comment, it seems the archpriest already knew of Pio's desire to make an offering of himself to Jesus for the conversion of souls. Only after consulting the easygoing Pati in September was Pio able to bring himself, in November, to reveal his intention to the fierce and formidable Padre Benedetto. And it was another year before he could muster the courage to tell his spiritual director about the stigmata. He did so after the wounds had reappeared, a year to the day after their first occurrence. On this occasion, Padre Pio wrote:

> Yesterday something happened, something I cannot explain or understand. In the middle of the palms of my hands there appeared a small red spot the size of a small coin, accompanied by strong, sharp pain in the middle of the red spots. The pain was most intense in the middle of the left hand, so much so that I still feel it. Also I feel some pain in the soles of my feet.
>
> This phenomenon has been going on for almost a year, yet recently there has been a brief period of time in which it has not occurred. Please do not be upset that I have not mentioned it to you before. The reason is that I had to overcome a cursed embarrassment to tell you about it. If you only knew the great effort I had to make to tell you about it! I would have told you many things, but I was unable to express myself.[26]

In later years, Padre Pio downplayed what we might call the proto-stigmata. When a confrere, Padre Raffaele of Sant'Elia a Pianisi, conducted a series of interviews with Padre Pio in 1966 and 1967, Pio, by then a very old man, at first had forgotten all about the phenomenon and, referring to the stigmata, declared that stories of an earlier stigmatization were false and that "everything happened at San Giovanni Rotondo." When he racked his brain, however, he was able to recall that while passing his time in his little hut, "in profound meditation and ecstasy, more than once I noticed fiery red spots in the palms of my hands, accompanied by extremely sharp pains that lasted several days. [I noticed] puncture wounds in my side as well. But it was only at San Giovanni Rotondo that they appeared in permanent form and with an issue of blood."[27]

From the moment he received the letter describing the marks in Pio's hands, Padre Benedetto was intent on having him return to community life at all costs.

Strange Events at Venafro

Immediately after he received Padre Pio's letter describing the stigmata, Padre Benedetto wrote to minister general of the Capuchin Order, Padre Pacifico of Seggiano, telling him about the young friar's holiness and asking about the advisability of sending him once again to live in a religious community. After describing Padre Pio as "a young priest of angelic character," the provincial mentions Pio's offering of himself as a victim of divine love and his mysterious illness, linking the two phenomena together:

> He had also asked to participate in the pains of the Savior, and has been granted this in an ineffable way. Migraine headaches, resistant to any remedy, and an illness inexplicable to any doctor, however renowned in the healing art, have come to torment him along with great spiritual suffering. It was suspected that he had been stricken with tuberculosis, and doctors ordered him to breathe the air of his native town, especially when uncontrollable vomiting prevented him from holding even a spoonful of broth for days and days.[1]

After telling Padre Pacifico about the stigmata, which he judged to be "the seal of his special calling," Padre Benedetto asked for advice. Several times in recent years, he says, Padre Pio had been sent to various friaries, only to suffer relapses and have to return home. "Well aware that until now this has been the will of God," Benedetto writes, "I want to summon him at this time to return to the cloister in any way possible. I am concerned, however [if anything should go amiss], that the fault would be mine." Then Benedetto asks, "What do you say about this?"

Padre Pacifico must have encouraged Benedetto to reassign the "angelic" young priest to a friary because, in the fall of 1911, the father provincial began to urge Padre Pio very strongly to return to community life. But he did not command him to do so. Rather, he tried to persuade Pio to consent.

Pio was extremely reluctant. "You know that I want to return to the friary," he wrote Benedetto. "The greatest sacrifice that I have made to the Lord is precisely my inability to live in community." He added, though, that he could not bring himself to believe that God wanted to kill him, for he would surely die from vomiting and inanition were he to return to the cloister. Moreover, at Pietrelcina he was able to celebrate Mass, whereas, if past experience was any guide to the future, he would be physically unable to do so if he were to go to one of the friaries. "If I must suffer alone," Pio writes, "that is well. But to be a cause of pain and anxiety without any result other than my death, to that I do not know how to respond." Pio presents his cause but offers, ultimately, obedience to his superior's command:

> It seems to me that I have the right and duty of not depriving myself of life at the age of twenty-four! It seems to me that God does not want this to happen. Consider that I am more dead than alive, and then do as you believe best, for I am disposed to make any sacrifice if it is a case of obedience.[2]

Because he was still worried that God would hold him responsible if Pio died, Benedetto was still unwilling to order him to report to a friary. He tried, however, to convince him that such a course of action would be best. On September 29, he wrote:

> I tell you that your staying with your family troubles me very much, since I would not only want to see you at one of our friaries, but also at my side, so that I could watch over you, for you know that I love you like a son. I therefore believe that your living outside the friary is serving no useful purpose. . . . If your illness is the express will of God and not a natural phenomenon, it is better for you to return to the shadow of community life. Native air cannot cure a man visited by the Most High. . . . Either at home or in community, your health will always be what God wills.[3]

Still, he falls short of summoning Pio through obedience.

Pio's answer to this letter has not been preserved. Judging from Benedetto's response, he must have insisted on further medical consultations, and complained that the provincial was not really concerned with his health. Whatever Pio said, it caused Benedetto to explode. On October 4 he wrote:

> When one writes as superior and spiritual director, you ought to listen to what he tells you with reverence and inward submission and not argue with him with a kind of resentment! As your superior and director, I declare to you that your illness has no need of doctors, since it is a *special dispensation* from God, and for this reason, I am not of a mind to arrange an examination for you by another specialist.

He goes on to recount the enormous expenditures made for Padre Pio of Benevento in his last illness and for other friars who had recently suffered serious health problems. "You see, then, how unfounded your accusation is and how wrong you are in obstinately believing in your own way!" Continuing his diatribe, Benedetto rages:

> But you do not want to submit humbly to my judgments, and you do wickedly! I hope . . . this will be the last time that you refuse to submit to my declarations. Otherwise, I will not write to you anymore. Moreover, you really hurt me by saying that I do not love you . . . that I want to kill you. . . .[4]

As soon as Pio received Benedetto's letter, he wrote a contrite and profuse apology:

> With reddened eyes and trembling hand I write you this letter to beg your forgiveness on bended knee. . . . I repent of this matter as one who loves God is able to repent of his sins. Please pardon me, Father. I know I do not deserve pardon, but your goodness towards me gives me hope. Do not be upset. Didn't you know that I am full of pride? Let us pray together to the Lord that He might smite me down ere I fall again into similar excesses![5]

After receiving this letter of subservience, Padre Benedetto acceded to Padre Pio's request for another medical examination. He sent him to Naples, where the specialists who examined him declared Pio hopelessly ill (with what disease is not clear) and maintained that it would make no difference whether he spent his last days at home or in a friary. Benedetto decided, therefore, that if Pio were to die, he might as well depart this world in community life. He ordered Padre Pio to report to the friary of San Nicandro in Venafro, a town about fifty miles north of Pietrelcina famous for its pure air, which Benedetto hoped might prolong Pio's days. While awaiting his appointment with Sister Death, Padre Pio was to study sacred eloquence, the course of study that normally followed ordination. It was to be at Venafro that the supernatural aspect of Padre Pio's life would become general knowledge among his confreres.

The friary of San Nicandro was built in 1573 adjacent to the tomb and basilica of the Roman martyr by that name. The community consisted of thirteen men, nine priests and four brothers. The father guardian, or local superior, was Evangelista of San Marco in Lamis (1878-1953). The senior member of the community was the learned, ascetical Padre Francesco Maria of Gambatesa (1843-1918). Padre Agostino was vicar as well as professor of sacred eloquence. In addition to Padre Pio, the friars included Padre Anastasio of Roio (1886-1947), who had been in the choir that January night in 1905 when Pio visited the Rizzani family in bilocation, and Padre Guglielmo of San Giovanni Rotondo (1886-1970), who later wrote an account of the early years of Padre Pio's ministry.

Pio arrived October 28, and for the first few days things proceeded smoothly. In addition to contemplation and community worship, each member of the "family"' normally had a job to perform. Padre Pio, besides his studies, was to instruct the children of the town in Christian doctrine and teach them hymns. By mid-November, though, Pio was unable to hold anything in his stomach. Soon he was able to leave his bed only to celebrate Mass and had to give up his studies and teaching.

Padre Evangelista decided to take Pio once again to Naples for medical consultation. As usual, the doctors could not diagnose the illness, and the two friars left the clinic knowing no more than before.

That evening the two priests took a room in a hotel. During the night, Evangelista was awakened by loud noises that rendered him speechless with terror. When they ceased, Pio asked him whether he had heard, then told him not to worry. He gave no explanation for the noises, though he seemed to be familiar with them. Although Padre Evangelista continued to be nervous and troubled for some time, Padre Pio awoke bright and cheerful.

The digestive ailment persisted. Before they left Naples for Venafro, Pio suggested that they stop for dinner at a restaurant. "Do you want to throw up in front of all those people?" Evangelista asked. "Do you want to make a spectacle of yourself?"

Cheerily, Pio assured him that nothing would happen, but after downing two courses, he was obliged to run to the window and vomit into the flower beds outside. At Venafro the vomiting persisted. The only nourishment that Pio was able to retain was the Sacred Host, which had to be brought to him in his room. He was now too weak even to celebrate Mass.

To this point, Padre Pio had been regarded simply as an ideal religious who had the misfortune to be suffering from an undiagnosable illness. The stigmata had disappeared again, and no one at Venafro — not even Agostino — was aware that they had ever existed. The only people who were privy to this secret — Pannullo, Benedetto, Cardone, Mercurio Scocca, and the doctor who thought the wounds were a result of tuberculosis — had done a good job of keeping their mouths shut. Toward the end of November 1911, however, the supernatural side of Padre Pio's life burst into the open.

One day Padre Agostino, advised that Pio was doing very poorly, rushed into his room, where he found the young man raving about a huge black cat that he said was about to pounce on him. Agostino was certain that Pio, unable to eat for days, was weakened to the point of hallucination. Fearing that his protégé was about to die, Agostino rushed into the chapel to pray for Pio. During his prayers, his mind wandered. He started thinking that he would probably be asked to preach at Padre Pio's funeral, and he began to fret about what he would say.

When he finished praying and returned to Pio's room, he was amazed to find his young friend lucid and cheerful. "You went to the choir to pray," he said, "and that was fine, but you also thought about my funeral eulogy. . . . There's time, Professor, there's plenty of time!"[6]

Later Pio asked Agostino to remember him in prayer while he celebrated Mass. Agostino said that he would. He remembered his promise while going downstairs to the church, but during the part of the Mass specified for recommending various persons and intentions to God, Agostino forgot all about Pio. Returning to the sick man's room, the professor, embarrassed when asked if he had remembered the request for prayer, lied and said, "Surely, I remembered."

"Well," said Pio, "at least Jesus accepted the intention that you made while you were going down the steps."[7] Agostino was nonplussed.

The professor was not the only other resident of San Nicandro Friary who observed anything unusual. One day young Padre Guglielmo and the sixty-seven-year-old doorkeeper, Fra Cherubino of Morcone, were keeping Padre Pio company. The vestments used by the priests were regularly laundered in town. Fra Cherubino looked at his watch, got up, and told his colleagues to excuse him, since the lady with the vestments was expected any moment and he had to meet her at the door.

"You don't have to go to the door now," Padre Pio told the old man. "Save your energy. Wait here. She's going to be one hour late." An hour later, Pio told Cherubino to go to the door. The old brother, doing as he was bidden, opened the door to the expected lady, who had not even had time to knock![8]

Padre Agostino began to observe Pio closely and became convinced that the priest was neither insane nor delirious. He began to spend a great amount of time in Pio's room. Sometimes, rather crassly, he invited his students in to watch, for he and Padre Evangelista agreed that some of Pio's experiences were true cases of ecstasy, and they thought the students had the opportunity of a lifetime to view such phenomena firsthand.

St. John of the Cross defines *ecstasy* as "the going out of a soul from itself and being caught up in God."[9] This "immersion" in God is how Agostino and Evangelista perceived some of the trances into which Pio was falling. On other occasions they were convinced that he was having visions inspired by the devil.

Padre Agostino observed that Padre Pio went into ecstasy two or three times a day. On seven occasions, the professor sat with pen in hand and transcribed everything that Pio said. Other ecstasies were, for various reasons, left unrecorded. These celestial encounters, in which Pio seemed to converse with Jesus, Mary, and his guardian angel, were usually either preceded or followed by diabolical vexations. The heavenly colloquies, Agostino observed, were usually longer than the infernal visitations, usually lasting between a half hour and forty-five minutes. The satanic visions usually lasted less than fifteen minutes.

In all, Padre Agostino observed ten "diabolical apparitions." The first was the vision of the black cat. On another occasion, Pio had a vision of naked women who "danced lasciviously" in his room. Another time, the devil, invisibly, spat in his face. On yet another occasion, Pio complained of hideous noises that no one else could hear.

Evangelista and Agostino were horrified one day to see Padre Pio writhing as if he were being struck repeatedly. Alarmed, they fell to their knees and began to pray and to sprinkle him and the rest of the room with holy water. After fifteen minutes, Pio came to himself and said that he had been flogged by horrible men who looked like professional torturers. Other times, he said that demons appeared to him in the form of various friends, colleagues, and superiors, even in the forms of the reigning pontiff and of Jesus, Mary, St. Francis, and his guardian angel. He recognized the diabolic ruse through a certain feeling of disgust and through his insistence that the mysterious visitors praise Jesus. When they refused, he knew that they were of the devil.

At this time, Agostino was hearing Pio's confession each day, but one morning he did not have the time and told the sick priest that he should go ahead and take the Eucharist. In the evening, Agostino would return to hear his confession. Returning to Pio's room that evening, Agostino was surprised when his friend looked at him with fear and distrust.

"Are you my professor?" he asked.

"Of course I am!" answered Agostino. "Why do you ask such a peculiar thing?"

Looking intently into his eyes, Pio demanded, "Say, 'Praise Jesus!' "

"Praise Jesus a thousand times! Now, tell me what has happened."

Pio went on to relate how, shortly after Agostino had left him in the morning, there was a knock on his door and — there was the professor, back again. Agostino — or what appeared to be Agostino — said that he was now ready to hear Pio's confession. Pio, however, felt an unaccountable disgust for him. Moreover, although "Agostino" looked true-to-life, he had a wound on his forehead that had not been there a few minutes before. "What happened to your forehead?" Pio asked.

"Oh," replied "Agostino," I fell while I was going downstairs. Now, Son, here I am to hear your confession."

At this point, Pio demanded, "Say, *Praise Jesus!*"

"No," shouted the demon who had taken the professor's ample form, and he vanished into thin air.[10] By their refusal to praise Jesus, Pio recognized his visitors' infernal origin. It will be noticed that all these apparitions were very much of the bodily type; even though no one else could see them, Pio unquestionably perceived them through his organs of sight.

When he went into ecstasy, Padre Pio was heard to talk, quite coherently, with various unseen celestial visitors. Agostino wrote down only what Pio said, seeing and hearing nothing of those to whom he was speaking. From Pio's words, however, it is possible to capture the sense of the dialogue. During these encounters, Pio prayed for conversions, pleaded, and even argued with God for the salvation of various people. He voiced his fear and horror of the devil. He expressed a desire to bear the cross. He prayed for the stigmata to return — but invisibly. He bewailed the worldly conduct of modern priests. Pio expressed concern that his illness might lead to his expulsion from the Capuchin Order. Most of all, however, Padre Pio addressed words of exalted love to his Lord and Savior.

The first ecstasy Padre Agostino transcribed took place on November 28, 1911, between 9:45 and 11:00 A.M. When it began, Pio seemed to be talking with the Virgin Mary. Then he began to pray for various souls, addressing Jesus as he would talk to a friend: "O Jesus, I commend that soul to You. . . . You *must* convert her! You can do it! . . . Convert her, save her! . . . Don't only convert her, for then it might be possible for her to lose Your grace, but sanctify her. Yes, sanctify her. . . . Oh, didn't You shed Your blood for her too? . . . O Jesus, convert that man. . . You can do it. Yes, You can! . . . I offer all myself for him. . . ."

The desire to offer himself as a victim for the conversions of sinners, in general and in particular, is a theme that runs markedly throughout his transcribed ecstasies.

After pleading with the Lord to "stay a little longer," Pio reproached him for leaving him at the mercy of the devil the previous morning. "Ah, how he frightened me!. . . Jesus, don't let him come any more!. . . I'd rather forfeit the sweetness of Your presence than have that fiend come back again!" Then, he exclaims in rapture:

> O Jesus, another thing — I love You . . . very much. I want to be all Yours. . . . Don't You see that I am burning for You? . . . You ask love from me — love, love, love. See, I love You. . . . Come within my being every morning [through the Eucharist]. Let us tarry together, let us tarry alone — I alone with You, You alone with me . . . O Jesus, give me Your love! . . . When You come into my heart, if You see anything that is not worthy of Your love, destroy it . . . I love You! . . . I will hold You tightly, so tightly! . . . I will never let You go! . . . You are free, it is true, but I . . . I will hold you closely, so very closely . . . I will almost take your freedom away. . . . "

The ecstasy closes with Padre Pio urging his angel to "praise Jesus for me. . . . My lips are unworthy and foul, but yours are pure. . . ." The angel seems to have said something, to which Pio responds, "Are you an angel of the darkness? . . . You are an angel without sin! . . . Then praise Jesus for me. . . . Dear Guardian Angel, drive that fiend away. . . ." And then he whispered the words, "O Jesus . . . Sacred Host . . . Beauty . . . Love . . . Jesus." After a few moments he became once more aware of his physical surroundings.

The next day Pio expressed concern to Jesus that he had been observed. It was acceptable that Padre Agostino had been a witness, but Pio was particularly concerned that a physician, Nicola Lombardi, a layman, had observed his ecstasy: "To friars, that's one thing . . . but to a layman! . . . I know that he's a good man, but he's still a *layman*"!

He began to pray for conversions again. "O Jesus, You can't refuse me!" he pleads. "Remember that You shed Your blood for all men . . . and what does it matter if he is a hardened sinner?"

He prayed for the colleagues who ministered to him in his sickness. "Jesus, I commend these friars to You," he says. "They get up at night. You know that. . . . After all, who am I? . . . Help them. . . . I am not good enough even to celebrate Mass, but they exercise their ministry."[12]

Pio's conversations with his guardian angel were a good deal less reverent:

> Angel of God, my angel — aren't you my guardian? God gave you to me. . . . Are you a creature or are you a creator? . . . You're a creator? No! Then you are a creature and you have a law and you have to obey — you must stay close to me whether you want to or not. . . . You're laughing! . . . What is there to laugh about? . . . Tell me one thing — You *have* to tell me. Who was it? Who was here yesterday morning? . . . You're laughing! . . . You have to tell me! . . . Who was it! . . . Either the professor or the guardian — tell me! . . . Come on now, answer me! . . . You're laughing! An angel laughing! . . . I won't let you go until you tell me!

Then Pio turned to Jesus. "If you won't tell me," he said to the angel, "I will ask Jesus . . . and then you will listen!" It is not clear what dialogue Pio had with Jesus, but soon he begins to pump the angel again:

> Well, my boy! Tell me who it was! . . . You're not answering! . . . All right, just stand there — just like a block of wood! . . . I want to know. . . . I asked you just one thing, and after such a long time, here we still are. Jesus, You tell me![13]

Jesus apparently made the angel tell him that only Agostino, "the little professor," had been watching the ecstasy of the previous day.

Toward the end of the ecstasy, Padre Pio speaks of a mysterious thirst he experiences prior to receiving Holy Communion. (It is common for mystics to feel a real hunger and thirst for the living God.) The ecstasy closes with the enraptured friar kissing the Savior's bleeding wounds.

The next day Padre Pio expressed his desire to help Jesus bear his cross. Jesus told him that he really did not need man's works, but Pio begged for the grace to participate in his redeeming sufferings. From Pio's responses, it would seem that Jesus conceded him this privilege.

But Pio remained depressed. He was quite upset over the fact that he was able to exercise his priestly duty of celebrating Mass only in his hometown.

"Why there and not here?" he asks. "Am I a priest only at Pietrelcina?" He was distressed about Padre Benedetto's refusal to permit him to hear confessions. From Pio's responses, it appears that Jesus too was unhappy about this and actually accused the provincial of having a "hard head." Even so, Pio prayed that the punishment deserved by Benedetto might fall upon himself. Yet, far from being swollen with self-righteousness, Pio immediately accused himself of being worthy of damnation. "You want to glorify Yourself in *me*?" Pio asks in amazement. "Who am I? . . . I am a priest, true, but a useless one. I don't even say Mass anymore, or hear confessions. . . ."[14] The ecstasy comes to an end with Pio praying for Benedetto, Agostino, Pannullo, and for all priests, good and evil.

The next day, December 1, was a Friday, and Pio apparently saw Jesus, crucified, bleeding, and suffering. "Jesus, I love You," he exclaims, "but don't appear like this to me anymore . . . You tear my heart to pieces. . . ." He continues, awestruck at the horrendous display of Jesus' sufferings for sinful mankind: "It's true, then, that You bore the cross all the time of Your life . . . and therefore it's wrong when wicked men say that Your suffering was only a matter of a night and a day. . . . Your suffering was . . . continuous!"[15]

Again Padre Pio offers himself as a victim and prays for the stigmata to return: "If You give me the strength, permit that those nails . . . permit it, yes, in my hands . . . if it be Your will . . . but invisibly, because men despise Your gifts. . . ."[16]

Pio suffered distress and anguish, but there were moments of sublime rapture as well. "Tell me," he asks Jesus, "if on earth it can be so lovely, what will heaven be like? . . . There we will die of love! . . . Jesus, all the things of this world are but as a shadow. . . ."[17]

Touched when told how fervently Padre Evangelista and the rest of the community are praying for him, Pio tells Jesus: "Try to console him. Maybe he doesn't even pray for himself. . . . Give him the grace [he is seeking]. . . . You can do anything!"[18]

On Sunday, December 3, as he talked to Jesus, Pio was troubled about the sins of unworthy priests. Again he offers himself as a victim, this time precisely on their behalf:

> My Jesus, why are You so bloody this morning? . . . They did wicked things to You today? . . . Alas, even on Sunday, You must suffer the offenses of ungrateful men! . . . How many abominations took place within Your sanctuary! . . . My Jesus, pardon! Lower that sword! . . . If it must fall, may it find its place on my head alone. . . . Yes, I want to be the victim! . . . Here is the usual excuse, "You are too weak.". . . Yes, I'm weak . . . but, my Jesus, You are able to strengthen me. . . . Then punish me and not others. . . . Even send me to hell, provided that I can still love You and everyone [else] is saved. Yes, everyone!"[19]

Here Pio echoes Moses, who prayed, "Alas, this people have sinned a great sin; they have made for themselves gods of gold. But now, if thou wilt, forgive their sin — if not, blot me, I pray thee, out of thy book thou hast written" (Exodus 32:31-32). He echoes St. Paul, who wrote, "For I could wish that I myself were accursed and cut off from Christ for the sake of my brethren" (Romans 9:3).

It was in this ecstasy that the Lord apparently explained to Pio that he would have to return to Pietrelcina. In previous ecstasies, as we have seen, he expressed his alarm about his inability to remain in any friary. He had been terrified when he learned that Padre Pacifico, the minister general, was thinking of dismissing him from the Order because of his ill health and that it might be necessary for him to journey to Rome to plead his cause. "O my Jesus," Pio laments, "You want to send me to that land of exile! . . . Aren't I a priest here? . . . What do I have to do [in Pietrelcina]?" At this point, Jesus apparently tells Pio his return is part of Jesus' plan to glorify himself in the friar. "You want to glorify Yourself in me?" asks Pio. "And who am I? . . . If only men could know my sins! . . . Daddy is proud of me and goes around boasting about me. . . . Oh, if he only knew, if he only knew. . . ."

St. Francis of Assisi also appeared to him. "Seraphic Father," Pio complains, "are you expelling me from your Order? . . . Aren't I your son anymore?" Pio seems to have been assured by St. Francis that he would never be expelled from the Capuchin Order and that it was God's will for him to remain in Pietrelcina for a time.

Two of Padre Pio's ecstasies were observed by Dr. Lombardi (1863-1916). On November 28, Lombardi had found Pio lying in bed and apparently staring toward the ceiling. The young man was talking to the Lord. Lombardi lit a candle and held it in front of Pio's eyes. "He's in a cataleptic trance," Lombardi explained to Agostino. "When he comes to himself, you'll see that he remembers nothing of what has happened." Lombardi was wrong. Without being told about the doctor's visit, he complained bitterly to Jesus about it the next day, as we have seen.

Lombardi was called back on December 3. Padre Pio was again talking to unseen visitors. "Take my heart and fill it with Your love," Pio was murmuring. Lombardi measured the heartbeat with his stethoscope and also took the pulse under the wrist, marveling that the two were not synchronous. The pulse of the artery in the wrist was strong and rapid, but the actual heartbeat was exceptionally so. Lombardi called the priest's name in an attempt to bring him out of the trance. "Ah, who called me?" Pio said, apparently to his angel. "My angel," he begged, "let me stay with Jesus." And he remained in the trance.

"Let me show you something, Doctor," Padre Evangelista said a few moments later. Instructing the doctor to remain in the room, the guardian went outside. Within moments Pio awoke, alert and cheerful. Evangelista, coming back into the room explained to the physician that, while standing in the corridor, he had called to Pio *in obedience*, but in such a low voice that his command could be heard by no one in Pio's room. Even so, Pio awoke. Apparently, the sick friar was not aware through his physical senses of anything going on in the room; but his angel guardian was and let him know when anything of importance was happening. When Lombardi called him, Pio was permitted to ignore him, but when a superior called him through holy obedience, even though Pio might be talking with the Lord, he was obliged to break off his conversation and obey the command.

During late November and early December, Padre Agostino brought Holy Communion to his sick friend several times while he was in ecstasy. The visionary apparently did not realize that he had received Communion because several times during the ecstasy, he asked Jesus, "Did I receive Communion this morning?" Agostino could deduce from Pio's surprised responses that Jesus had told him that the professor had indeed brought Communion to him. Jesus, moreover, told him the exact words that Agostino had uttered when he was giving him Communion: "Pio, see Jesus" and "I command you to partake [of the Sacrament], in the name of Jesus, whom I hold in my hands!" Jesus even repeated to Pio a French expression that Agostino had used: *Petit enfant*.[20]

Padre Agostino did not record all of Padre Pio's ecstasies, especially the ones that concerned Pio's personal life. He does record that Pio prayed several times that his beloved professor might be freed from the assaults of the devil. It seems that Pio at times went into more detail then Agostino cared to record. The professor later recounted:

> One day he prayed in ecstasy for a soul whom I knew as well as myself. [*Almost certainly Agostino is referring to himself.*] This soul was troubled for more than a year by terrible temptations, which were known only to God and to his confessor. Of these, Padre Pio was able to know absolutely nothing. And then one day he prayed for this soul, that the Lord might free him from those terrifying temptations. He was in ecstasy and only through divine revelation could he know the interior of that soul. Jesus answered Padre Pio that He would help that soul, but that the soul would have to be tried and tested. From that day on this soul felt strengthened, and, thank God, the temptations . . . were not so violent as before. [21]

Padre Agostino noticed that in his ecstasies Padre Pio seemed to be told to pray for certain individuals. Agostino could not identify these people. When Pio came out of his ecstasy, he had to confess that he had never met them or heard of them. Pio would later write to Benedetto, "At times I feel moved, when I am praying, to intercede for those for whom I never intended to pray, and,what is more wonderful, at times for those whom I have never known, nor seen, nor heard, nor had recommended to me by others. And, sooner or later, the Lord always grants these prayers."[22]

What can we make of these experiences at Venafro? Dr. Lombardi, who seems to have had no ulterior motive for doing so, changed his original diagnosis of catalepsy. He later decided that these experiences, in which he noted that the young priest's face assumed an unearthly beauty, were not to be explained naturally. He judged the trances to be cases of "true ecstasy" — that is, purely religious experience.[23]

In addition to the seven occasions on which Padre Agostino wrote down on the spot everything Padre Pio said, he also, within the next few years, recorded, as he found the time, other recollections from this period in Venafro. Further, we have the report written by Dr. Lombardi in February 1912, two months after the events. Though brief, his report corroborates Padre Agostino's. We also have the recollections of Padre Guglielmo, written some fifty-eight years later.

Everything Padre Pio said in his ecstasies — at least everything written down — was coherent. Dr. Lombardi was much struck by this fact. These were not the ravings of a delirious or mentally deranged man. Not only were Padre Pio's statements coherent, they also referred to real persons and real events. Of some of these he knew nothing in his normal state!

Perhaps most important, what Padre Pio said was edifying, theologically correct, and expressive of a deep love for God and man. There was nothing self-centered or uselessly sensational about Padre Pio's ecstasies. In them he asked to grow nearer to God and, in doing so, to serve individuals better.

As to Padre Pio's physical condition at Venafro, there is also some question. As we have seen, in October, specialists at Naples were unable to give a specific diagnosis, nor were they able to do so when the young priest returned to them the following month. Dr. Giuseppe De Vincenzi (1875-1969), then a young physician from the neighborhood of Venafro and a nephew of one of the doctors who had recently examined Pio in Naples, was asked to examine the sick man sometime during the last week in November. He diagnosed him as tubercular. Nicola Lombardi, however, who examined Pio twice, noted abnormal sounds in his respiration but thought the condition had more to do with the larynx than the lungs. He observed that Pio had no evening sweat or fever. The young priest showed no signs of emaciation or malnutrition, even though he vomited almost everything he ate. After noting that this phenomenon happened in every friary to which the young man was sent, but much less in his own home, Dr. Lombardi wrote, "From these facts I excluded a specific affection of the lungs, and I judged that this was a case of a nervous disturbance."[24] According to him, Pio's illness was psychosomatic.

A psychosomatic affliction is one in which the nerves or emotions work on the physical system to make one truly physically ill. This does not mean that Padre Pio was a hypochondriac or a malingerer. His illness clearly seems to have been a result, not of self-centered anxieties or repressed conflicts, but of his oft-repeated desire to suffer with Christ for the redemption of mankind. At times, as we have seen, Padre Pio asked Jesus to permit him to take on the punishment due to other people's sins; often he asked to bear the physical miseries of others simply to give them some relief.

Evelyn Underhill observes that mystics and visionaries very often suffer from ill-health, frequently from undiagnosable illnesses. Sts. Bernard of Clairvaux, Teresa of Avila, John of the Cross, Catherine of Siena, and Catherine of Genoa are in this category. Miss Underhill felt that the usual poor health of many mystics may be caused by "the immense strain which the exalted spirit puts upon a body which is adapted to a very different form of life."[25]

Of course, if one does not believe in the possibility of a mystical life or contact with a higher reality, if one does not believe in the propriety of offering oneself as a victim of divine love or the possibility of being graced with the privilege of sharing some of Christ's sufferings, Padre Pio must, at the very least, appear to be a perversely neurotic individual. If one believes in the validity of what Padre Pio stood for, then his afflictions were psychosomatic only in the sense that they were the result of something other than physical causes. In his case, they were a result of the strain of his mystical life and his offering of himself as a victim of divine love.

In whatever way Padre Pio's superiors were inclined to interpret his illness, it was both real and distressing. Padre Evangelista, concerned because Pio had been unable to retain any food for weeks, first wrote to Padre Benedetto, begging the provincial to permit the young man to return to Pietrelcina. When he received no answer, he risked offending the provincial by exercising his legal option of writing directly to the minister general, Padre Pacifico, in Rome. Evangelista told Pacifico that he had written "several" letters to Benedetto without receiving a response. In this appeal, Evangelista wrote on December 3, 1911:

> Along with all my friars here and even all the friars of the province, I am able sincerely to attest to the fact that Padre Pio of Pietrelcina, sick now for three years, is unable to retain any food in his stomach except in his native town. For nearly two years he breathed the air of his hometown, and there he never suffered from vomiting, while each time he has gone to a friary, even for a single day, he has been seized by agonizing pains and, especially, by vomiting. He has been here a month and a half and I can sincerely attest that he has never held his food for a quarter of an hour. For sixteen or seventeen days he has been bedfast and has not been able to retain even a spoonful of water. . . .
>
> Hardly did he arrive in this friary than he began to vomit, and this has persisted to the present time. Hardly does he set foot on his native soil, however, than his stomach recovers. Could this be the will of God that this poor priest must always remain at home?

In order not to give Padre Pacifico the impression that Padre Pio was malingering because he did not like life in the friary, and so as not to put him in danger of being dismissed from the Order, Evangelista adds:

> Everyone can attest to the fact that he is the best kind of priest. Therefore he has not the slightest wish to say at home, nor do we, his brethren, wish to deprive ourselves of his treasured presence.[26]

Padre Pacifico thereupon instructed Padre Benedetto to permit Padre Pio to return home. Benedetto, in a fury, wrote to Agostino, fuming: "I do not know what to make of this concern to run to Rome for a provision that is supposed to be left to my wisdom. I am troubled because it is a sign of a lack of respect and reverence towards one's immediate superiors. . . ."[27]

Benedetto nevertheless gave his consent for Padre Pio to return to Pietrelcina and authorized Agostino to accompany him. And so, on the morning of December 7, 1911, Pio and Agostino set out for Pietrelcina. The next day Padre Pio was able to celebrate Mass in his hometown — "as if he had suffered nothing."[28]

The Double Exile

There were three stages in the development of Padre Pio's ministry: his reputation for holiness became known to his hometown; then throughout Italy; finally, throughout the world.

Padre Pio called the five depressing years between 1911 and 1916 "my double exile" because he was separated from his religious community as well as from heaven, for which he fervently longed. But it was during those years that Padre Pio first gained the reputation for sanctity.

The old Capuchin Constitutions required a friar who was forced to live at home because of sickness or some other exigency to live, if possible, apart from the rest of his family and — as much as possible — to practice all the religious exercises that he would normally perform in the friary. His mother, therefore, assigned "the Tower" to Pio for his exclusive use. Against a rock and beneath a huge elm tree on the farm in the Piana Romana, she engaged friends and relatives to construct a little hut for him to use as a retreat during the warmer months.

This was not to be a time of placid retreat. Pio's health was still bad. There were difficulties with his family. There was, at first, misunderstanding on the part of the townsfolk. There was trouble with his superiors. And then there were great spiritual trials and terrifying diabolical assaults.

In addition to his usual disorders, Pio immediately began to suffer from eye problems. During much of 1912, he had difficulty reading and writing, and saying Mass posed a great problem because there are different "propers," or specified readings, for each day's Mass — too many to memorize. Pio had to struggle through the Mass holding a lamp in front of his missal. To save Pio the trouble of having to strain his weak vision every day, his superiors granted him permission to use one of two Masses every day: the Mass of Our Lady and the

Mass of the Dead. He memorized these two rituals and did not have to worry about reading different propers each day. He was also excused from reading the Divine Office and was permitted to pray the Rosary in its place. The problems with his eyesight were to recur periodically, and this permission was renewed for the rest of his life.

We know little about Padre Pio's family situation at this time. Grazio and Michele were in Jamaica, Long Island, employed by the Erie Railroad, although they returned for a long visit starting in November 1912. Michele's wife, Giuseppa, remained in Pietrelcina with their son, Franceschino ("little Frankie"). Padre Pio seems to have been very fond of this little boy, and we know that Padre Agostino, when he accompanied his friend home from Venafro in December 1911, was immediately taken by the winsome two-year-old, whom he thereafter referred to as "*le petit François*." Whenever he wrote Pio at Pietrelcina, he sent a kiss to the little boy.

Pio's oldest and best-loved sister, Felicita, was married to his friend Vincenzo Masone, who now worked as an administrator in the town hall. In February 1912, Felicita gave birth to the first of three children, a girl called Giuseppina ("little Josie"). Of all his siblings, the pious and gentle Felicita seems to have resembled Pio the most in temperament.

The second sister, Pellegrina, is the Forgione nobody likes to talk about. Almost any query about her brings an icy silence from people in a position to know. One author described her as the most vivacious of the family, a lively and fun-loving girl. In July 1913, she married Antonino Masone (no relation to Vincenzo) and three months later gave birth to a short-lived daughter named Maria Giuseppa. A few years later, the marriage broke up and Masone went to America. Pellegrina stayed behind. A few years later, she bore a child to an unknown father. Of her subsequent career, we know only that she worked as a seamstress, at times in Benevento and at times in Naples, and later found her way to the town of Chieti on the Adriatic. There is absolutely no mention of her in any of Padre Pio's correspondence or recorded conversation.

The youngest sister, Graziella, was still living at home with her mother. She has been described as a "pale, fragile little girl." As we shall see, she later became a nun. Her relationship with her brother at this time is unclear.

Motherdear, who was now managing the family farms single-handed, attributed her son's poor health to the ascetic rigor of the Order. She vigorously opposed Pio's intention to return to community life and repeatedly urged him to leave the Capuchins and become a secular priest. "My boy," she often said, "with your poor health, how can you get along in a monastery with monks? My dear, I weep for you!"[1] Perhaps it was remarks like this that led Pio to write to Agostino, "In my sore afflictions, it seems as if I no longer have a mother on earth, although I have a most merciful one in heaven."[2]

Moreover, Pio feared that certain members of his family were not saved. In

May 1913 he wrote to Agostino, "How I suffer . . . because of certain obstinate souls, and how I would even give my life that they might come to themselves and give themselves entirely to God. What devastates me the most is that among these are souls united to me by ties of kinship!"[3]

For the most part, however, Pio's family seems to have been very supportive if not always understanding. In January 1912, he was somewhat disgusted with Benedetto for making his family pay for his medical expenses. "They give their very blood for me without the slightest regret," he commented to Agostino."[4]

During his "exile" in Pietrelcina, Padre Pio celebrated Mass nearly every day, often in rural churches that were part of the parish. He also taught school. One of his students, Celestino Orlando, recalled in his seventies how diligently Padre Pio had worked to help him — a slow student — learn mathematics. Once, as a reward for mastering a particularly hard problem, Pio invited the boy to his home to enjoy a dinner of fried fish. He remembered Pio as a strict disciplinarian who always prayed before he taught. If two boys got to fighting and swore, he would not hesitate to take off one of his sandals and swat them with it.

Pio also organized adult education classes and held school in the fields, successfully teaching farmers and laborers to read and write. Moreover, he got together a choir of fifteen boys and taught them how to sing various hymns. He led them without accompaniment, singing along with them in his robust, fervent, but unmusical baritone voice.

Pannullo, the archpriest, loved Pio like a son and appreciated his assistance. Once, as the two of them took their evening walk, he tried to convince the younger man to leave the Capuchin Order and become a secular priest in the Pietrelcina parish. "Pati," answered Pio, "I'd die before I'd abandon the habit of St. Francis!"[5]

Padre Pio was not at first welcomed at the Pannullo domicile. Pati lived with a brother and his three daughters, Antonietta, Rosina, and Grazia. The oldest, Antonietta, was married and had children who lived on the premises. She feared that Padre Pio was tubercular and would contaminate her children. Whenever the young priest came to see her uncle, she and her sisters would not talk for fear of infection! They made him sit on the same chair every time he came, and drink out of the same cup, which they set apart for his exclusive use. Antonietta made Pio suffer a terrible humiliation one evening when the archbishop of Benevento came to visit with Pannullo. The archbishop invited Pio (apparently without consulting his host) to eat and pray with them. When Antonietta learned about this, she flew into a terrible rage and berated her hapless uncle for permitting a tubercular priest to come to dinner and infect her children. Cowed, Pati told the bishop, and the embarrassed prelate told Pio to stay away.

Another niece, Rosina, was horrified that Padre Pio was using the same vestments, chalice, and paten as the other priests. She demanded that her uncle provide a separate set of vestments, a chalice, and a paten for Pio's use. Again the uncle yielded to the demands of his niece, much to Padre Pio's chagrin.

One day the sacristan, Michele Pilla, got drunk and forgot to change the chalice. In the middle of Padre Pio's Mass, Rosina Pannullo, noticing that the chalice Pio was using was not the one set aside for him, called Pilla and insisted that he change chalices there and then. In front of the entire congregation, the sacristan approached the altar, interrupted the Mass, and exchanged the chalices.

This was too much for Pio. That evening, as they took their walk, he expressed his displeasure to Pati: "I must tell you that I am smarting under two offenses. First, your niece Antonietta doesn't want me in the house, lest I give my disease to her children. And secondly, the other niece, this very morning, while I was celebrating, told the sacristan to change the chalices. Well, today the Lord gave me the grace of knowing that my disease is not contagious."

The archpriest communicated this revelation to his nieces, who accepted it without question; thereafter Padre Pio was welcome in the Pannullo household.

The people of Pietrelcina sensed that there was something different about Padre Pio. He continued to observe "the discipline" on the customary days, striking himself with a metal chain until the blood ran. When he was praying at his hut in the Piana Romana, the curious would peer in to see "the mad monk." Motherdear would make his bed, but Pio considered it too luxurious and insisted on sleeping on ths ground with a rock as his pillow. This continued until Giuseppa, disgusted, reported it to her priest-cousin, Marquess Giuseppe Orlando (not to be confused with Pio's old teacher). The Marquess called on Pio and explained to him that his conduct was a breach of the obedience he owed his mother. Thereafter Pio slept on the bed. Pious practices such as these at first led many to dismiss Padre Pio as a crank and a fanatic.

Especially misunderstood was his mystical life. During the Mass, Pio tended to take interminably long pauses as, seemingly oblivious to his external surroundings, he prayed to God and conversed with celestial beings. He paused for an unconscionably long time during the Commemoration of the Living and the Dead, at which point he interceded for various souls and often was able to perceive the spiritual state of certain individuals. During the Consecration, he seemed to identify so closely with Christ's sufferings that at times he was barely able to speak the words of the liturgy. Masses that were supposed to last about a half hour were taking more than two hours, and many townspeople who were made late for their work complained to Pannullo. After a while, only old ladies were attending his Masses.

Pati had to explain to Pio that although it was a wonderful thing that he was subject to supernal raptures during the Mass, he had to be considerate of the congregation, many of whom had other obligations.

Nor did his fellow priests understand his ecstasies. After Mass, while he was making his prayer of thanksgiving, Pio frequently went into ecstasy, just as he did at Venafro. Pati knew what was happening, but other priests did not and were horrified when they left him praying in church and returned an hour or so later to find him in a state resembling death. One day the sacristan, checking the church, found Pio in ecstasy and told Pannullo that he thought the friar was dead. "No, he's not dead," said Padre Pannullo. "Let him be. Ring the midday bell and go home." Later that afternoon Pilla returned to find Pio still displaying no signs of life. "Uncle Torey," he told Pannullo, "this time the monk is dead. He's really dead." Still, Pannullo was unconcerned. "I told you, don't worry," he said. "He'll revive." Thereupon he went to the church and commanded Pio on his vow of obedience to revive — and he did! [7]

The townspeople came to realize that their native son was not a crackpot — not so much because of any miraculous events as because of his conduct and his love and concern for others.

Fairly early in his stay at Pietrelcina, in fact, the year before he went to Venafro, Pio aroused much favorable comment and made many aware of his greatness as a priest by his ministry to his old teacher Don Domenico Tizzani. Don Domenico, recall, was a former priest who gave up his vocation to marry. In later years this troubled him greatly. Many felt that if it had not been for the fact that a daughter had been born of the union, he would have returned to the priesthood. As time went on, Tizzani grew more and more melancholy and eventually became a recluse. Nobody seemed to be able to reach him. The archbishop of Benevento called on him one day, but Tizzani refused to see him. Eventually, his friends and neighbors gave up. Pannullo and the local clergy ignored their excommunicated colleague, writing him off as a lost cause.

After his ordination, Padre Pio, however, made it a point, whenever he passed Tizzani's house, to send his greetings to his old professor whenever he saw his wife or daughter outside the house. This went on for months. Finally, one day in December, he noticed that the daughter seemed quite agitated. "Assunta, how is the professor?" he asked. She broke down and told him that her sixty-nine-year-old-father was terminally ill.

"Can I visit him?" Pio asked.

"Certainly you can!" she said and led him into the house at once. "Daddy, Padre Pio is here!" she told her father, who began to weep when he saw his old pupil. The man who had been dismissed as hopelessly impenitent by every priest in the vicinity asked to make his confession, wept bitterly over his sins, and committed himself to the mercy of Jesus Christ.

When Pio told Pannullo what had happened, the archpriest was so overcome with joy that he fell to his knees, thanking the Lord. One day later, Tizzani died.

So now, a year or so later, Padre Pio, through similar acts of love and concern, was gaining the respect and love of his fellow townsmen. When he celebrated Mass in neighboring villages, he would always stop on his way back to town and talk to the farmers in the fields. Nonetheless, he wrote to Padre Benedetto:

"Most of the time it gives me great pain to talk to anyone except those of whom God speaks to me. . . . Because of this, I am a great lover of solitude. . . . When I am passing the time of day and conversations are prolonged . . . and I cannot decently get away, I force myself to remain with the greatest of effort, since these conversations give me great pain."[8]

The Pietrelcinese found Padre Pio different from other priests. Whatever he said always seemed to be of the greatest help and encouragement. No glad-handing backslapper, Pio was friendly, cheerful, polite, and witty — but basically serious. He would mince no words if he had reason to believe a parishioner was violating any of God's commandments. But so effective was he at reaching people's hearts that the townsfolk held still for rebukes and commands they would refuse to tolerate from the other clergy.

For instance, Padre Pio was totally opposed to any labor whatsoever on the Sabbath. Grazio explained that in harvest time it was necessary to gather ripe wheat as quickly as possible lest it be scorched by hot sun or beaten down by rainstorms. Surely, Grazio reasoned, God would not fault a man for working on a Sunday to provide the necessities of life. Pio disagreed. The Scriptures say: "Remember the Sabbath day, to keep it holy. Six days shalt thou labor, and do all thy work. But the seventh day is the Sabbath of the Lord thy God: in it thou shalt not do any work. . ." (Exodus 20:8-10). Was this not God's word? Could there be any excuse for breaking it? Grazio, conceding that his son was right, forewent his Sunday labors and found that his crops were none the worse for it.

In town, near the Tower where Pio stayed during the winter months, there lived a woman named Mariandreana Montella. One Sunday, coming from Mass at the new parish church, Pio espied her sitting on her front steps, sewing a ribbon onto a dress. "'Ndrianella," he said sternly, "today is Sunday. Today no one must work." 'Ndrianella made it clear that she did not want to be bothered. Pio, in a huff, went home and reappeared a few minutes later, armed with a pair of scissors. He seized the ribbon and cut it to pieces. The matron was so furious that, according to some accounts, she chased the priest down the street, but later she admitted her perversity in laboring on the Sabbath.[9]

Pio organized Sunday games for the townspeople so that they could have recreation and not think about breaking the Sabbath. The people grew to love him and came to call him "our saint." More and more people seemed to be attracted to his Mass, which, though he was making every effort to shorten it, still lasted longer than customary. During Padre Pio's Mass, they were able to apprehend the presence of God in an uncanny way. They were plunged into the mystery of the Cross as never before. Early on, it was agreed that if anyone had a special intention, the priest to be sought out to offer a Mass was "the little friar who lives in the Castle and whom everybody considers a saint."[10]

In April of 1912 or 1913, all the trees in the area were infested with lice, and the fruit crop was threatened with ruin. One day "a simple peasant" approached Padre Pio and asked him to come with him to his field to bless the trees and curse the lice. Padre Pio consented. The peasant was amazed that within a short time all the lice had fallen to the ground. When they heard about this, farmers for miles around begged Pio to go through their fields, cursing the lice on their trees. It was claimed that the lice on all the trees died and that an excellent harvest ensued. Whatever natural explanation a scientist might proffer, the Pietrelcinese were certain that a calamity had been avoided solely through the actions of their little saint.

Rosina Pannullo, who once had made trouble for Padre Pio because of his illness, wanted to test him. One day she told him she was going to the Tower to steal something to see whether he, without inspecting the room, would know what she had taken. Pio, not amused, responded, "All right, go, but you'll find a little angel behind the door, guarding my house." Rosina was afraid and did not go. A few days later, however, Padre Pio told Pati that his niece intended to steal his breviary. Pannullo went to Rosina to ask her if this was true.

"Yes," she told him. "But I said nothing about it to anyone. In fact, I merely thought of it, so as to see whether he could read my mind."[11]

Rosina's father, Alfonso Pannullo, decided to get into the game and told Pio that he was going to his house to rob him of an unspecified belonging. Pio, understandably annoyed, told him, "Don Alfonso, don't you go into my house because I don't know what would happen!"

Don Alfonso went anyway, but hardly had he put his foot on the first step when he was unable to move a step farther. His other foot just would not budge. Fearing, no doubt, that he was having a paralytic stroke, he decided to go back. He found that his feet worked perfectly going down Pio's stairs but became paralyzed when he tried to ascend them. Going back to Padre Pio, he told him, "You friars really know how to make trouble!"

"No, Uncle Alfonso," Pio told him, "I have a good guardian there, and woe betide the man who dares to set foot there!"[12]

In September 1912, Agostino gained even more impressive evidence of the presence and activity of Pio's guardian angel. It so happened that Agostino wrote Pio a letter in Greek in order to keep its contents from various local busybodies who were eager to read Pio's mail. The only problem was that Padre Pio, who was generally poor at languages, understood no Greek. In this particular letter, Agostino wrote, "What will your angel say about this? God willing, your angel will be able to make you understand it. If not, write me."

When he received the letter, Pio went to Pati's office and showed the letter to him. The learned doctor, about to translate it for him, was startled when, as he wrote, "Padro Pio . . . explained the contents to me, word for word."

"How can you read and explain that letter, my dear Pio, when you don't even know the Greek alphabet?"

"You know, Pati," came Pio's reply, "my guardian angel has explained everything to me!''[13] And that was as much of an explanation as he was to receive.

For several years, Agostino sent almost all his letters to Pio in French, another language his friend had never studied. Even so, Pio had no trouble reading the professor's letters and even once sent him a postcard entirely in French. He said that his "little angel" had told him what to write. The angel, however, must have been a poor student because a professor of French who read the text of the postcard declared Pio's French abominable, even worse than Agostino's!

In November 1912, when the professor's letters began arriving smeared with ink, Pio suspected the handiwork of devils. At the suggestion of Pati, Pio began placing a crucifix on the smudged letters. At once "they became a little lighter, at least so that we could read them, even if with difficulty," Pannullo noted.[14]

There are numerous stories concerning encounters by Padre Pio with demons in physical form both at his summer retreat in the Piana Romana and in the Tower at Pietrelcina. Several former neighbors swore that the devil or one of his minions used to interfere with Pio's prayer and meditation at the Piana Romana by appearing in the form of a snake with an enormous head.

Accounts of demonic and poltergeist activity in the Tower are better documented. Neighbors reported terrible noises — crashes, bangs, and shouts — coming from Pio's apartment, and they complained to his parents. At first they thought that his flat must be the scene of drunken brawls. Certainly the room bore evidence of terrible physical altercations. Pia Forgione-Pennelli, Michele's daughter, years later vividly recalled her grandparents talking about the condition of the house when, in response to complaints from neighbors, Grazio (recently returned from New York) and Beppa hurried to their son's apartment. Everything was thrown about the room, and Pio was exhausted. Seeing the disorder, they asked him with whom he had been fighting. "With those foul creatures," Pio said.[15]

This incident can be corroborated by a letter Padre Pio wrote to Padre Agostino on January 18, 1913, in which he described a diabolical attack. He says that he "saw nothing at first," but heard a "diabolic noise," after which a number of demons appeared "in the most abominable form." When Pio refused to do their bidding, he reports: "They hurled themselves upon me, threw me on the floor, struck me violently, and threw pillows, books, and chairs through the air and cursed me with exceedingly filthy words. It is fortunate that the apartments beside me and below me are vacant! "[16]

It is obvious that Pio is not using a metaphor for an inward temptation or a state of mind. He saw and heard and apparently felt specific phenomena — phenomena which, despite the vacancy of the adjoining apartments, were heard by neighbors several doors away.

A few days later, on February 13, 1913, he wrote Padre Agostino: "My body is all bruised because of the many blows that our enemies have rained upon me." More than once in the past month, he adds, the demons snatched away his nightshirt and beat him while he shivered, stark naked, in the cold: "Even after they left me, I remained nude for a long time, for I was powerless to move because of the cold. Those evil creatures would have thrown themselves all over me if the sweet Jesus hadn't helped me."[17]

Signora Forgione-Pennelli also stated that long after Padre Pio had left Pietrelcina, the Tower was the site of poltergeist activity. Earthen pots spontaneously shattered, chairs were thrown about, and horrible sounds were heard. Michele reported it to his brother, who told him that the apartment was still haunted by "those foul creatures" and directed him to summon a priest to perform an exorcism on the house. This was done, and there was no more trouble.

At any rate, it is indisputable that there were phenomena associated with Padre Pio that could not readily be explained. Because of contemporary documentation, they cannot be dismissed as legends.

There is much about Padre Pio, especially concerning the supersensible aspect of his life, that will probably never be completely understood. We will arrive, however, at a fuller understanding if we study his spiritual life and attempt to comprehend what was taking place in his mind and psyche during this period of his life.

The Dark Night of the Soul

Padre Pio's interior life — his prayer, his meditation, his communication with God and the invisible world — was the most important aspect of his existence. It dominated his life of action amidst daily affairs.

During his stay at Pietrelcina, Padre Pio, in good weather, spent a large segment of his day in his hut in the Piana Romana. In adverse weather, he remained in his apartment in the Tower. Wherever he was, he spent many hours each day in prayer and meditation.

For most of us, as far as our conscious experience is concerned, prayer is a one-way conversation. We trust that God hears our petitions, accepts our praise and thanksgiving, and pardons our sins; but our senses do not perceive his response. For Padre Pio, prayer was an emphatically different kind of experience. God literally spoke to him, sometimes through a word perceived through his organs of hearing, sometimes through a vision perceived through his organs of sight, but more often, through the "vision that is not seen" and the "voice that is not heard."

During his stay at Pietrelcina, Padre Pio wrote to Padre Benedetto, "My ordinary way of praying is this: hardly do I begin to pray than at once I feel my soul begin to recollect itself in a peace and tranquillity that I cannot express in words." He elaborates: "The senses remain suspended, with the exception of my hearing, which sometimes is not suspended; yet usually this sense does not cause me trouble, and . . . even if a great deal of noise were made around me, this would not bother me in the slightest."[1]

He speaks of a "continuous thought of God." Sometimes he feels "touched by the Lord . . . in a way that is so vivid and so sweet that most of the time I am constrained to shed tears of sorrow for my infidelity and for the tender mercy of having a Father so loving and so good as to summon me thus to His presence."

He felt himself "enriched by supernatural graces." He felt an irresistible "spiritual devotion" of such a nature that he speaks of his soul being "totally lost in God." . . . Other times, he experienced "an impulse so powerful that [he found himself] languishing for God, almost ready to die." He emphasizes that "all this arises, not from my own mental efforts or preparation, but from an internal flame and from a love [poured into the soul from without] so powerful that if God did not quickly come to my aid, I would be consumed!"[2]

In another letter to Padre Benedetto the "internal flame" is described:

> Hardly do I apply myself to pray than all at once I feel as if my heart were possessed by a flame of living love . . . unlike any flame of this poor world. It . . . consumes, but gives no pain. It is so sweet and delicious that the spirit finds great pleasure in it, and remains satiated in it in such a way that it does not lose its desire. Oh, God! this is a thing of supreme wonder to me. Perhaps I will never come to understand it until I reach the heavenly country![3]

Certainly, if Padre Pio himself could not understand it entirely, it is not remarkable that few others can! It is clear, however, that he was experiencing things that human language is powerless to express.

Within this mystical state, Pio was frequently visited by invisible beings from the heavenly world. Writing to Agostino in 1912, he declares, "Heavenly beings do not cease to visit me and make me anticipate the delight of the blessed."[4] On another occasion he wrote his confidant: "At night, as my eyes close, I see a veil come down and paradise opens to me, and, rejoicing in this vision, I sleep with a happy smile and with complete calm, expecting the little companion of my infancy [the angel guardian] to come to wake me and sing praises each morning with me to the delight of our hearts."[5]

Sometimes, though, Padre Pio found himself in a "great aridity of spirit," in which it was impossible for him to become recollected and pray, no matter how strongly he desired to do so. Nor was he entirely free from a nagging fear. To Benedetto he wrote in 1913: "An atrocious thought crosses my mind, namely, that all this could be an illusion without my recognizing it."[6] But most of the time, at least during the first half of his stay at Pietrelcina, he had little trouble entering into a state of prayer profound beyond the imagining of most Christians. Of the genuine nature of this state he seldom entertained doubt. Yet it was very difficult for him to communicate effectively to others what he was experiencing. Writing to Benedetto, he says:

> What happens to my soul is like what would happen were a poor shepherd led into the drawing room of a king, where . . . precious objects were displayed that he has never seen before. The shepherd, when he leaves the palace of the king, will surely carry before the eyes of his mind all those different objects . . . but he certainly will not know . . . their number, nor will

he be able to assign proper names to them. He might desire to speak with others of all that he has seen. He might gather all his intellectual and scientific powers to make a good try, but seeing that all his powers would not succeed in making known what he intends, he prefers to keep silence.[7]

Now, granted that the mystical life is in some ways incomprehensible to most people, such experience nevertheless tends to fit a definite pattern. This was true of Padre Pio. Many mystics have traced several definite states through which they pass until they attain the highest state of spiritual exaltation that can be achieved this side of heaven. Evelyn Underhill and others have distinguished five stages through which the Christian mystic usually passes on the way to "divine union."

In the first stage, which Underhill calls "the awakening of the self," the individual becomes aware of the spiritual world and begins the quest for holiness. In a poem entitled "The Valley of Silence," written when she was ninety-three, Fanny Crosby describes the state St. Teresa knew as "the prayer of quiet":

> I walk down the Valley of Silence,
> Down the dim, voiceless valley alone,
> And I hear not the fall of a footstep
> Around me, save God's and my own;
> And the hush of my heart is as holy
> As hours when angels have flown.

She goes on in the long poem to describe how she was first awakened to seek this state:

> Long ago I was weary of voices,
> Whose music my heart could not win,
> Long ago I was weary of noises
> That fretted my soul with their din;
> Long ago I was weary of places,
> When I met but the human and sin.
>
> I walked through the world with the worldly,
> I craved what the world never gave,
> And I said, "In the world, each ideal
> That shines like a star on life's wave
> Is tossed on the shores of the Real,
> And sleeps like a dream in its grave."
>
> And still did I pine for the Perfect,
> And yet found the false with the true,
> And sought mid the human for heaven,
> But caught a mere glimpse of the blue,

And I wept where the clouds of the mortal
Veiled even that glimpse from my view.

And I toiled on, heart-tired of human,
And I moaned mid the masses of men,
Until I knelt long at an altar
And heard a voice call me — since then
I have walked down the Valley of Silence
That is far beyond mortal ken.[8]

This poem very simply sums up the unfulfilled longings and the dissatisfactions with the world of a soul that is embarking upon its quest for God.

The second stage is what Underhill speaks of as "the purification of the self." For the first time the person sees the enormity of the gulf that stands between himself and the perfection of God. Through the operation of the Holy Spirit and the soul's own cooperation, the purge begins of everything in his or her life that stands between the soul and divine goodness. The soul thus commences the process of ridding itself, in Underhill's words, of "all those elements of normal experience which are not in harmony with reality: with illusion, evil, and imperfection of every kind."[9] This is usually accomplished through the mystic's own initiative, through fasting, "the discipline," and other forms of self-inflicted mortification.

The third stage is called "the illumination," in which the mystic is overcome with deep awe and a "renewed ecstatic awareness of the absolute."[10] An excellent example of this phenomenon comes from the pen of Emmanuele Brunatto (1892-1965), who was led to Christ by Padre Pio in 1919:

A supernatural presence demonstrated its truth everywhere. The day, the night, the sun, the rain, and the wind all united me with the order of creation: a nest of young chickens moved me to tears, a blade of grass made me shout with wonder. Sometimes the colors, the shapes, and the smells of the countryside exalted me almost to delirium, and, walking through the hills, I would sing hymns of thanksgiving and joy. Without a shadow of doubt I was the richest and happiest man in the world.[11]

In the fourth stage, called by St. John of the Cross "the dark night of the soul," God purges the soul, not of its carnal attachments — which have by this time been long since surrendered — but of its very selfhood. In this extremely painful stage, all physical as well as spiritual comforts are withdrawn. The operation is usually "passive"; that is, God acts upon the soul apart from any effort or preparation of its own.

This dark night (or "passive purgation," as Padre Pio called it) usually begins with oscillations between spiritual joy and spiritual distress, which, as we have seen, many mystics, including Padre Pio, have called "the game of love." These oscillations are succeeded by a deepening darkness and spiritual desolation. Often the spiritual trials are accompanied by physical and external ones. Everything seems to go wrong in the life of the person experiencing the trial. All consciousness of God's presence is swept away and the soul is kept from unbelief only by "a blind reliance on the past."[12] The mystic is, moreover, overcome by a sense of sin and worthlessness. According to St. John of the Cross, this darkness is a result of the operation of a "light" greater than the soul can bear:

> The more clear the light, the more does it blind the eyes of the owl, and the more we try to look at the sun, the feebler grows our sight. . . . So the divine light of contemplation, when it beats on the soul not yet perfectly purified, fills it with spiritual darkness, not only because of its brilliance, but because it paralyzes the natural perfection of the soul. The pain suffered by the soul is like that endured by weak or diseased eyes when suddenly struck by a strong light. . . . For in this pure light . . . the soul perceives itself to be so unclean and miserable that it seems that God has set Himself against it. . . . So great are the weakness and imperfection of the soul that the hand of God . . . is felt to be so heavy and oppressive, though merely touching it, and that, too, most mercifully; for He touches the soul, not to chastize it, but to load it with His graces.

St. Teresa, writing about the same phenomenon, says: "The majesty of Him Who can do this is manifested in such a way that the hair stands on end, and there is produced a great fear of offending so great a God, but a fear overpowered by the deepest love, new-enkindled, for One Who, as we see, has so deep a love for so loathsome a worm that He seems not to be satisfied by literally drawing the soul to Himself, but will also have the body, mortal though it is, and befouled as is its clay by all the offenses it has committed."[14]

Ultimately, the dark night gives way to the final stage of Christian growth, the stage the Eastern Orthodox call "deification" and Roman Catholics "spiritual marriage." Jeanne-Marie Bouvier Guyon (1648-1717) describes the transition in this way: "The soul, after many a redoubled death, expires at last in the arms of Love; but . . . reduced to nought, there is . . . in her ashes a seed of immortality. . . ."

Thus self-will finally dies, and the soul learns to say with Job (13:15), "Though He slay me, yet will I trust Him." Thus does the soul learn to love God, not for physical or even spiritual delights or consolations; and thus does it come to rest entirely in God. Then the self, in the words of Underhill, is "wholly penetrated — as a sponge by the sea — by the Ocean of Life and Love to which [it] has attained."[16]

According to Jacob Boehme (1575-1624), the mystic is now illuminated by the Eternal Light and inflamed with Eternal Love. Boehme describes this state by using this arresting image:

> Behold, a bright flaming piece of iron, which of itself is dark and black, and
> the fire so penetrateth and shineth through the iron that it giveth light. Now
> the iron doth not cease to be; it is iron still, and the source . . . of the fire re-
> taineth its own propriety; it doth not take the iron into it, but it penetrateth
> . . . through the iron; and it is iron then as well as before. . . . In such a man-
> ner is the soul set in the Deity; the Deity penetrateth through the soul, and
> dwelleth in the soul, yet the soul doth not comprehend the Deity, but the
> Deity comprehendeth the soul. . . .[17]

Far from distancing the mystic from human affairs, this increasing absorption
in God is almost always accompanied by increased physical and social activity.
While the mystic experiences deep intimacy with God, he is imbued with a
greater desire — and ability — to serve humankind. The more intense the
Christian's spiritual life, the more intense his response to the needs of mankind.

Now Padre Pio's spiritual life progressed *generally* along the same lines. He
has left a beautiful description of his "awakening" in a letter that he wrote to his
disciple Maria Campanile in 1922. It is the closest he ever came to writing a spiritual autobiography:

> Poor and vile creature that I am, [the Lord] from my birth showed me signs
> of a most special predilection. He showed me not only that He would be my
> Savior, my Supreme Benefactor, but also my devoted friend, sincere and
> faithful . . . my consolation, my joy, my comfort, my whole treasure.
>
> And my heart, alas, . . . all the while poured itself out, even though innocent
> and unaware, upon created things that charmed me. . . . He always watched
> over me, and inwardly recaptured me and reproved me. He reproached me,
> sweetly and paternally, it is true, but it was still a reproach that I felt in my
> soul.
>
> A sad but most sweet voice was speaking over and over in my poor heart. It
> was the warning of a loving Father, who described to the mind of His child
> the dangers that I would encounter in the warfare of life. It was the voice of
> the kind Father, who wanted to detach the heart of His son from those inno-
> cent and childish loves. It was the voice of the loving Father that whispered
> . . . to the heart of His son to detach himself from all that is of clay . . . , that
> jealously bade him consecrate himself entirely to Him. Ardently, and with
> loving sighs, and with groans incapable of translation into words, as well as
> with words that were sweet and gentle, He called me to Himself and desired
> to make me His alone.
>
> What is more . . . , He often permitted the flesh, child of earth and of clay,
> to throw stones and aim blows of ingratitude at my true self, beloved by
> Him with such tenderness and affection — all this so that I might under-
> stand how false and mistaken that love is that innocently and childishly I
> was giving to created things.

I, that ungrateful son, then understood everything, and clearly I contemplated that horrible and terrifying picture that He, in His infinite mercy showed me, a picture that truly disillusioned me and would have caused souls who were tried the most to tremble with fear.

When I understood such hideousness and such wretchedness, at once I invoked the most Holy Names of Jesus and Mary, calling the good Father with ardent yearning to come to my aid. . . . He seemed to smile and invite me to another life. He made me understand that the sure port, the harbor of peace for me, was the ranks of the army of the Church.

"Where could I serve Thee better, O Lord," [I asked] "than in the cloister and under the banner of the Poor Man of Assisi?" Beholding my bewilderment, He gazed on me, smiling, for some time. That smile left an ineffable sweetness in my heart. Sometimes I have felt Him so close to me that I have seemed to see His shadow, and my flesh and all my being have exulted in my Savior and my God! [18]

This long passage very beautifully describes the awakening that gradually unfolded during the first fifteen years of Pio's life. If he went through a purgation of the self, it was when he was a student, or even before. By the time Padre Pio came to live at Pietrelcina as a priest, he seems to have been living at the stage of illumination though experiencing a growing sense of spiritual aridity and desolation. The game of love was gradually giving place to an ever-deepening spiritual darkness and agony. By 1915 the dark-night phase, or "passive purgation," had begun to predominate in his inner life. We will see that it reached its zenith in 1918 and persisted in some sense to the end of his life. By 1944, while Padre Pio was still suffering from his "usual trial," Padre Agostino became aware that his friend and protégé lived in "a habitual intimate union with God." Even as late as 1946, when Pio was fifty-nine, Agostino commented that Pio's trial had "abated, but not disappeared." In fact, it seemed to coexist with the friar's increasing "elevation in God."

During the years 1912-1916, as we have said, Padre Pio was experiencing the illumination and the dark night side by side. Describing his spiritual exultation, Pio wrote to Agostino on March 16, 1912, "Sometimes I seem to be on the point of dying of a surfeit of sweet joy!" And five days later he writes: "Only God knows what sweetness I experienced yesterday . . . especially after Mass. . . . If only now, when I still feel almost all of His sweetness, I could bury these consolations within my heart, I would certainly be in Paradise! How happy Jesus makes me! How sweet His Spirit is! . . . He continues to love me and draw me closer to Himself. He has forgotten my sins, and . . . remembers only His own mercy. Morning by morning He comes into my poor heart and pours out all the effusions of His goodness!" [19]

On April 18, 1912, he writes Agostino again: "Oh how delightful the conversation was that I held this morning with Paradise! . . . things impossible to translate into human language. . . . The heart of Jesus and my heart were — allow me to use this expression — fused. The joy in me was so intense and so profound that I was able to contain myself no longer, and my face was bathed in the most delightful tears."[20]

Further, on July 7, 1913, Pio describes a vision of Christ. The Lord, he wrote Agostino, "immersed my soul in such peace and contentment, that all the sweetest delights of this world, even if they were doubled, pale in comparison to even a drop of this blessedness!"[21]

Yet, these spiritual joys were interspersed with periods of spiritual desolation. Pio's sweetest consolations only increased his desire for God, a desire he knew could never be consummated in this world. Because of this, he longed for death. Writing to his beloved professor on August 9, 1912, Pio says: "My spirit runs the risk of separating itself from my body because I cannot [adequately] love Jesus on earth. Yes, my soul is wounded with love for Jesus. I am sick with love. I continuously experience the bitter pain of the fire that burns but which does not consume. . . ."[22]

Again, Pio speaks of his longing to be united with Jesus in heaven when he writes Agostino a New Year's letter on December 29, 1912, speaking of another year "about to lose itself in eternity." Movingly, he laments:

> How many souls more fortunate than I will hail the dawn of the new year but not the end! How many souls [this past year] have entered into the house of Jesus, there to remain forever! . . . Life here below is . . . a grief to me. Living the life of exile is a torment so bitter to me that I can scarcely bear it. The thought that any moment I could lose Jesus is unspeakable anguish![23]

Describing an occasion when he was in ecstasy and Pilla, the church sacristan, thought he was dead, Pio wrote to Agostino: "It seemed as if an invisible force were immersing my whole being into fire. . . . My God, what fire! What sweetness! I felt many of those transports of love, and for some time I remained as if out of this world. . . . Had this lasted a moment, nay a second, longer, my soul would have been separated from my body and I would have gone to be with Jesus!"[24]

In connection with another one of these experiences, he wrote one of his most sublime passages expressing his yearning to break the bonds of the flesh:

> After my poor little soul has sighed for the moment of departure, after it has come several times to the limit of life, after it has relished the sweetness of death and has suffered all the struggle and torment that come from nature reclaiming its rights; after my soul has left my body, even to the extent of losing sight of this world below, and after I have almost touched the portals of the heavenly Jerusalem with my hand, I reawaken in this place of exile, becoming once more a pilgrim, always capable of being lost, and a new kind

of agony seizes me that is worse than death itself and worse than any kind of martyrdom. . . .

Continuing his lament to Agostino, Pio complains:

> Alas, dear Father, how terribly hard this mortal life is! As long as it lasts, eternal life is uncertain. O cruel life, enemy of the Love that loves us infinitely more than we can possibly love or understand Him . . . why do you not come to an end?

He longed to enter at once into

> that eternal rest, where I shall live forever, lost in that immense ocean of good . . . and enjoying that by which He Himself is blessed! . . . Ah, dear Father, when will that long-awaited day come when my poor little soul will break up like a foundering ship in that immense ocean of eternal truth, where we will no longer be able to sin, where we will no longer mind being creatures endowed with free will, because there all miseries are ended and it is no longer possible to turn our eyes aside from the limitless beauty nor cease to delight in God in one perpetual ecstasy of sweetest love![25]

Not only was Padre Pio in agony at being separated from God, he was also devastated by his own sinfulness, as he perceived it. His letters to Agostino and Benedetto abound with references to his own worthlessness.

In May 1914, speaking of the "deep darkness . . . thickening on the horizon of my spirit," Pio confesses, "I know that no one is spotless in the sight of the Lord, but my impurity is without bounds before Him. In the present state in which the merciful Lord, in His infinite wisdom and justice, condescends to raise the veil and reveal my secret shortcomings to me in all their malignity and hideousness, I see myself so deformed that it seems as if my very clothing shrinks in horror of my defilement!"[26]

Not only is he horrified by his actual sins, he is filled with terror at his *potential* to sin. In September 1915 he writes to Agostino that "the thought of going astray and . . . offending God fills me with terror. It paralyzes my limbs, and both body and soul feel as if they are being squeezed in a powerful vise. My bones feel as if they were being dislocated . . . crushed and ground up."[27] All this anguish at the mere *thought* of sinning!

Pio once said that the agony his soul experienced during this dark night was so great that he could not conceive of it being much less than "the atrocious pains that the damned suffer in hell." Like Luther, who said that he could not endure this utter desolation for ten minutes and still live, Padre Pio said, "Such torture does not last long, nor could it do so, because if I remain alive at all while it lasts, it is through a signal favor from God!"[28] In various letters, he speaks of being "mad with anguish," not knowing whether he is in hell or purgatory or on earth, and of being in "an endless desert of darkness, despondency, and insensibility, a land of death, a night of abandonment, a cavern of desolation in which my poor soul finds itself far from God and alone with itself."

Padre Pio was able to describe and explain this state in a clear and objective way. To one of his disciples, Margherita Tresca (1888-1965), who was suffering the same trial at approximately the same time, Pio described her sufferings as a grace ordained by God "to exalt your soul to the perfect union of love." He goes on to say that, before attaining this union, a Christian needs to be purged of his defects as well as of his attachments — to things both natural and supernatural. This is necessary, Pio says, because every "natural inclination and mode of behavior" must be surrendered to God so as to be transformed to "work in another way more divine than human."[29]

Padre Pio goes on to explain how God purges the soul, totally emptying it of itself. All self-centeredness must be replaced by "a new way of thinking and wishing that is simply and purely supernatural and celestial." In order to arrive at this state, the Christian must be subjected to this painful trial whereby he is purged by an intense light that reveals faults hitherto unseen. He sees God not as a loving Father, but as a terrifying Judge. He feels as if God were casting him out; he feels hopelessly lost.

It is through this passive purgation that God unites the soul to himself "with a chain of love." Yet this process "produces a darkness thicker than that which enshrouded the Egyptians at the time of the Exodus." This is because the intellect is incapable of receiving the light and is indisposed by many imperfections and weaknesses. This affects the intellect, the higher powers of the soul, and the physical appetites.[30]

So this "purgative light" reveals to the soul its own "nothingness, its sins, its defects, and its wretchedness." The light "eradicates every bit of esteem and conceit and complacence, to the very roots of the soul."[31] It also prepares the will and the inner man for the joy of mystical union. Moreover, the purgative light shows the soul its absolute dependency upon God for its salvation and its inability to do anything to save itself. Through this light, Padre Pio maintained, the Christian realizes that he cannot repay God's love for him, that there is nothing within him except falseness and deformity, and that God is the only fountain of truth and grace and love, the only source of salvation.

Even though Padre Pio could explain and analyze in detail his trial, this made it no less painful, nor was his anguish less acute in those moments when he felt abandoned by God, when he saw everything as darkness and desolation. All he could do was to throw himself into the arms of Jesus. Often Pio exclaimed with Job, "Though Thou slayest me, yet will I trust Thee."

Even though at times Padre Pio felt as if he were sinking through quicksand to hell, he continued to wait for his God. Constantly he repeated, as an act of faith, "Though Thou slayest me, yet will I trust Thee." He continued diligently to search the Scriptures, deriving comfort from the fact that Jonah, Jeremiah,

David, and Paul had, like him, passed through the same deep waters of desolation.

He was also comforted by Padre Benedetto. The "internal and external judge" of his soul. "You must calm yourself by means of my assurances," he told Pio, "and hold to them as if sworn by oath." That is, Pio was to have confidence and not despair of God's mercy for no other reason than that he was so ordered through obedience! This "night," Benedetto explained, was sent by God "to extinguish human understanding so that divine understanding can take its place, and you, having been stripped of the . . . usual way of using your mental faculties, might be able to rise to that supernatural and heavenly purification." Pannullo was not as helpful. "He scolds me," Pio wrote, "and I find no consolation in his sermons to me."[32]

Because of his intense spiritual life, Padre Pio saw manifestations of supernatural power where many would not. For instance, in August 1912, for a space of several days, whenever he began to write to his superiors, he was seized with violent migraine headaches and spasms in his writing arm. Recognizing this as devilish interference, he prayed and was able to write again. Many of the unseen attacks were in the form of temptations against purity.

Many of the diabolical attacks, however, were quite physical and were accompanied by terrifying noises that could be heard by neighbors. Pio was struck by actual blows that left visible bruises. Padre Pio continued to receive visits from his guardian angel, as well as from Jesus and Mary. His angel frequently rescued him from the demonic attacks. This is the subject of a strange and beautiful letter Pio wrote to Agostino:

> I cannot describe to you how those wretched creatures were beating me! Several times I thought I was near death. Saturday it seemed as if they really wanted to finish me. . . . I turned to my angel and . . . at length he appeared and flew all around me, and, with his angelic voice, sang hymns to the Divine Majesty.
>
> There ensued one of those usual arguments. I scolded him harshly for making me wait so long while I was continually calling for him to help me. In order to punish him, I did not care to look him in the face. I wanted to withdraw and get away from him. But the poor fellow overtook me, almost weeping, and caught hold of me, trying to make me look at him. And then I glanced into his face and found him full of regret. . . .
>
> "My dear boy," [he said] "I am always near. . . . My love for you will not pass away, even with your earthly life. I know that your generous heart always palpitates with yearning for Him whom we both love. . . . You would tell Him that, separated here from Him in this world, you have more sadness than joy. . . . [But] you will have to wait a little longer. As for now, He is able to give you only the ray of a star, the perfume of a flower, the note of a

harp, the caress of a wind. . . . His providence desires that you remain in exile a little longer; yet at length He will compass your desires. . . .[33]

It is clear, then, that even in the darkest depths, Padre Pio did not lose contact
entirely with the spiritual world. Even when he cried out that God had forsaken
him, he was seemingly able to consult his angel and, at times, even Jesus concerning various questions that his disciples or his superiors put to him. We will
hear more of this later.

Christ and the angels did not appear to Padre Pio for the sake of his own
pleasure, nor did Satan usually assail him on his own account. Most of Pio's visions and ecstasies revolved around his ministry to others; the devils, more than
anything, sought to derail his mission as God's instrument to save souls. Reading
through Padre Pio's letters, one sees that most of the visions he describes concern the well-being of others.

In March 1913, Pio recounts a vision revealing the grief of Jesus at the lack of
spirituality among many so-called Christians and the lack of dedication among
clergy. In this bodily vision, Jesus appeared in human form and spoke words
perceptible to the organs of hearing. At times he was silent, at others his throat
was choked with sobs. He lamented that people "make no effort to control
themselves amidst their temptations and . . . even delight in their iniquity. The
souls in whom I most delight," Jesus complained, "lose their faith when they
are put to the test. . . .

> They ignore me, day and night, in the churches. They no longer care about
> the Sacrament of the Altar. . . . No one cares any more about the love that I
> bear them. I am continually saddened. My house, for many, has become a
> theater for amusements. . . . My ministers, . . . whom I have loved as the ap-
> ple of my eye . . . ought to have comforted my heart, which is now filled
> with bitterness. They ought to have been of help to me in the redemption of
> souls, but, instead, . . . I have to receive ingratitude and thanklessness at
> their hands. My son, I see many of them who . . . betray me with hypocrit-
> ical countenances, and [there are many] sacrilegious Communions. . . .[34]

Jesus certainly seems humanly petulant in this vision, but perhaps the Lord
was appearing to Pio in a manner that the friar could comprehend. The result of
the vision was the kindling of Pio's zeal to win souls to Christ and to renew his
offering of himself as a victim.

In other visions and revelations, as we have seen, Jesus often presented to Pio
"souls" whom the friar had never met before. Through these visions he learned
about the interior state of these souls so that he would be in a position to help
them.

There are doubtless many readers of modern and secular bent who, after reading about Padre Pio's spiritual life, would still be inclined to dismiss the Capuchin as a madman or, at least, a fellow with a very vivid imagination. But they must admit that many of these supernatural experiences, particularly the hellish assaults, were accompanied by phenomena that could be seen and heard by people nearby; that the revelations and locutions usually corresponded to some generally observable reality; that the supersensible communications almost always resulted in some act of kindness or concern; and that all the supernatural experiences centered on love for God and man. Indeed, the more Padre Pio's spiritual life intensified, the more his love and concern for other people grew.

In a letter to Agostino written in the fall of 1915, Pio prays that God will give life to "dead souls," that is, people living in sin:

> I have ever implored Thee, trembling as I beseech Thee now, that, according to Thy mercy, Thou mightest deign to withdraw the thunderbolt of Thy glance from my unhappy brethren. Thou hast said, O my sweet Lord, that "Love is as strong as death and lasts as long as hell"; therefore, look with an eye of ineffable sweetness upon these dead brethren. Chain them to Thyself with a strong bond of love. May all these truly dead souls arise, O Lord! O Jesus, Lazarus made no request at all that Thou shouldst raise him. There sufficed for him the prayers of a sinful woman. Ah, behold, my Divine Lord, another soul, also sinful and guilty beyond measure, who beseecheth Thee in behalf of a multitude of dead souls who care nothing for praying to Thee. I beseech Thee to raise them. Thou knowest, my Lord and King, the cruel martyrdom occasioned to me by these Lazaruses. Call them with a cry so powerful as to give them life, and [may they,] at Thy command, issue forth from the sepulchre of their obscene pleasures![35]

All of Padre Pio's spiritual life was directed at the raising of modern-day Lazaruses. All of it fed into his ministry for the salvation of souls. Frequently he prayed to God, echoing Moses: "Either save this people or blot me out of Thy book of life!" Once someone told him of a prophecy that a member of the Franciscan Order would lead a third of the world to Christ, implying that it referred to him. Padre Pio retorted: "What do I want with a third? More! More! I want to bring everyone to God!"[36]

Between Barracks and Friary

Although Benedetto continued to function as Pio's spiritual director and Agostino continued to give him advice and counsel, both men increasingly came to look to their former pupil for wisdom in their own difficulties. It is interesting to read through the letters the three friars sent to each other during the period 1914-1922. Pio will agonize about his spiritual state and other problems. Benedetto and Agostino, in turn, will give him counsel, chide him for not surrendering himself to the "word of obedience," and then pour out their own troubles to him, beseeching him for a word of comfort.

Agostino, in particular, was forever asking questions he expected Pio to answer on the basis of his supersensible wisdom. On May 13, 1914, for instance, Agostino asks Pio about the upcoming elections in the Capuchin province. Mentioning that he has spoken to Benedetto about him, Agostino asks, "Perhaps the Lord will reveal the content of our conversation."[1] When Pio mentions none of this in his next letter, Agostino again urges him to ask the Lord to tell him what had happened in the conference with Benedetto. Eventually Pio had to tell Agostino that he did not know.

Again, in August 1914, the professor writes on behalf of a priest-friend who wants Pio to ask the Lord to reveal something about his future. Pio had to reply that Jesus did not wish the priest to know more than he already knew through natural means. Eventually Pio had to warn Agostino that he was putting the Lord to the test.

Padre Pio did appreciate questions concerning the spiritual state of the various souls whom Benedetto and Agostino were counseling, and the two older priests were very much impressed by Pio's clear and valuable advice. Despite the fact that Pio increasingly complained that he was abandoned by God and that heaven had become for him "as bronze," he seemed able to discern the will of God for other souls. In a reply to a letter from Agostino early in 1916, for instance, Pio speaks of a soul who had been recommended to him: "Jesus wants to test her some more, and for the moment He will not grant her request. Let this blessed soul have a little patience because, in the end, He will satisfy her."[2]

During the summer of 1913, Benedetto wrote about a woman who had tragically backslid in her Christian life. He asked Pio to pray to Jesus for an answer as to how this could have happened. Pio replied:

> This is how that soul was snared in the devil's net. When she saw that she was so favored by God . . ., she began to wonder at all the good that God sent her and she clearly discerned the difference between the goods of heaven and those of earth. At this point she was proceeding well.
>
> But the Enemy, who is always alert, seeing such affection, convinced her that such great confidence and certainty could never decline. . . . Furthermore, he put into her heart a clear vision of the heavenly prize, so that it seemed impossible for her to renounce so great a felicity for things so base and vile as earthly pleasures.
>
> The devil used this immoderate confidence to make her lose that holy distrust in herself, a diffidence that must never leave the soul, no matter how privileged it is by God.
>
> Meanwhile, having lost, little by little, this distrust of herself, she was cast sorely into temptation, still persuaded that she had nothing to fear. . . . This then was the origin and cause of her final ruin. What remains for us to do? Let us pray to the Lord that He might put her back on the right path. . . .[3]

Whereas many troubled people, seeking the help of clergy in time of need, were dismayed by complicated theological language, Padre Pio was always able to answer with clarity. In his diary Padre Agostino makes frequent references to Pio's "sagacity, prudence, lucidity, and charity."

Now there are many people who think that they have the answer to every situation, and many who read the advice just quoted might be uncomfortable with it. After all, how does he know this lady's soul so well? Who is he to judge? Padre Pio often said that he gave no counsel of any substance unless he was enlightened by God. Frequently, when questioned about a certain person or situation, he had no answer. On those occasions when he did speak definitively, his counsel was almost invariably helpful.

Because of this gift, Benedetto and Agostino were eager for Pio to serve as spiritual director for others. So, by 1915, when he was twenty-eight, Pio had been assigned several pious ladies as "spiritual daughters." They included Margherita Tresca, from Barletta, and Annitta Rodote (1890-1972), from Foggia, both of whom eventually became nuns. Padre Pio also had faithful spiritual daughters in two rich spinsters, Giovina Cerase (1861-1931) and her sister Raffaelina (1868-1916). According to Padre Agostino, Pio first became acquainted with them by correspondence when doctors advised Raffaelina to submit to a mastectomy. In distress, she went to Padre Agostino, upset, not so much at having cancer or losing a breast as at the prospect of having to expose her naked body to the gaze of a male surgeon. She wanted to know whether it was really necessary. Agostino passed the buck to Pio, who wrote back to him to tell her that, yes, the surgery was necessary. Soon Pio developed a regular correspondence with Raffaelina, who has been described as a lady with an angelic smile, a member of the Franciscan Third Order (an Order of laypersons following the Rule of Saint Francis) who made vigorous use of her considerable wealth in behalf of Foggia's poor. We will hear more about her later.

Padre Pio kept up an extensive correspondence with these women, making known the will of God to them in the same way that Benedetto did for him. In fact, in counseling them, he often quoted entire segments of the most recent letters of Agostino and Benedetto. In this way, a network of spiritual direction came into being. Benedetto and Agostino directed Pio, Pio directed his spiritual daughters, and, likewise, they were expected to influence other souls.

Even though they admired Padre Pio's work as an enlightened counselor of souls, Pio's superiors were not happy about his remaining away from the cloister so long. In December 1913, Benedetto began urging Pio to return to the friary. It had been two years since he had been forced to leave Venafro and, at Pietrelcina, his health had shown little improvement. "Return to community life," Benedetto urged, "even though you are convinced that in doing so, you will grow worse. It seems to be contrary to God's will . . . for you to stay outside the community so long for reasons of health. Did you enter the Seraphic Order to live and stay well and vow to remain in it only if you did not have to be ill and die?" He asked Pio to accept an appointment as vice-master of novices at Morcone. It would involve very little work — just setting an example. "And if death comes, welcome it. It will mean that the fetters of the body will be broken all the sooner!"[4]

Pio balked, saying that he would be only an encumbrance to any community where he might be sent. Instead, Pio requested a special document, known as a brief, which would allow him to remain in the secular world.

This mystified both Benedetto and Agostino. They insisted on several occasions that Pio ask Jesus to reveal why he was not to reenter the friary. On each occasion Pio said that Jesus had told him to tell them that they were not to ask. This, of course, was not satisfactory to his superiors. Thus, in August 1914, Benedetto ordered Pio to accept appointment as vice-master of novices at Morcone. "Have fear of nothing," wrote Agostino, who was to accompany him there. "Everything will result in God's glory and your good. If you die, I am sure you will go to enjoy the beauty of our Divine Bridegroom. . . . If He asked your life, would you not content him? Then let the Lord's will be done!"[5]

Padre Pio reported to Morcone but became sick immediately and had to leave after a few days. Benedetto was enraged and would not write Pio for a time. Agostino informed Pio in September that Benedetto had declared to him: "I will obtain the brief, but I will not believe in his sanctity anymore!"[6]

The professor tried to explain the provincial's position: "Like me," Agostino writes, "he is convinced that God is at work in your spirit, but he . . . does not believe that the Lord wants you there, out of the cloister. . . . 'How could God,' [Padre Benedetto asks,] 'for the purpose of greater perfection, take a soul out of the cloister and place him forever in the secular world?' . . . [He desires] that you might have the strength to come to the cloister to die, like every true son of St. Francis."[7]

Agostino took it upon himself to plead Pio's case with the minister general of the Capuchin Order, Père Venantius of Lisle-en-Rigault. Venantius was sympathetic and agreed to obtain the brief from Rome. In March 1915, Padre Pio was granted official permission to remain in the secular world — still retaining his Capuchin habit — for as long as he remained ill. For the duration of his sickness, he was to be assigned to the parish of Pietrelcina.

Although he himself had requested the brief, Pio was still upset. "What humiliation for me, my father," he wrote Agostino, "at seeing myself practically cut off from the Seraphic Order!" Agostino wrote back, comforting him, saying that he was by no means severed from the Order: "The Minister General has seen God's will and grants you the brief, but only on a temporary basis. Therefore you belong to us and even more to the Seraphic Father."[8]

Meanwhile, even more troublesome events were taking place in Italy and throughout the world. As early as May 1914, Pio had been sought for supernatural illumination on the deteriorating international situation. In response to a question by Benedetto, Pio said that Jesus didn't want him to disclose the ultimate outcome of the world situation. He would only tell the provincial: "Let's pray with true faith to our heavenly Father for a favorable outcome because the situation is getting rather grave and, if God does not bring about a solution, the outcome will be very grim. We do not deserve divine assistance, since we have willingly banished the most lovable Jesus from our hearts. . . . However, may we at least be permitted to hope in God's infinite Providence."[9]

Less than two months later, on June 28, a Serbian terrorist assassinated the heir to the Austro-Hungarian Empire, and by early August most of the world's major nations were at war. Italy, as well as America, thus far held back. Pio saw the terrifying conflict as God's punishment for man's unbelief, and he dreaded that the wrath of God would soon break out upon his country, which, like her neighbors, had apostatized from God.

The horror of the burgeoning conflict was too much for the seventy-nine-year-old pope, Pius X. When "good Catholics" from the Austro-Hungarian Empire appeared before him and asked that he bless their armaments, he broke down. Waving them away, he reproached them, saying, "We bless peace, not war." Shortly afterward he took to his bed with heart problems, and, on August 20, offering himself as a victim for the soldiers on the battlefield, he died. Padre Pio was deeply moved by the passing of "Papa Pio," whom he loved not only because he was pope but because of his tireless efforts to purge the Church of the curse of Modernism, and because of his personal holiness and his oblation of himself to God as a victim for the cessation of the war.

On September 7, Pio wrote to Agostino, begging him to pray to "disarm the hand of divine justice, rightly inflamed against the nations who do not wish to know the law of love. Above all, let us pray to disarm God's wrath towards our country," Pio begged. "She, too, has many accounts to settle with God. May she at least learn from the misfortunes of others, especially from her sister France, how harmful it is for a nation to distance itself from God!"[10]

When Italy entered the war in the spring of 1915, Pio lamented, "Italy did not want to listen to the voice of love." Meanwhile, for a time Jesus did "hold His Father's arm in check." Pio claimed that Jesus had hoped that the disasters suffered by other nations would lead Italy to repentance. But such was not to be.

Pio wrote to Agostino in May 1915: "The horrors of the war . . . keep me in constant mortal agony. I would rather die than witness such a slaughter!"[11] A few weeks later he confessed: "The horrors of the war are driving me nearly mad. My soul is plunged into extreme desolation. I had prepared myself for this, but it still has not prevented the terror and anguish that are gripping my soul!"[12] Agostino wrote, "My God, what a slaughter! What a bloodbath! What is going to happen to the world?"[13]

Even so, Pio had hopes that the war would be a "healthgiving purge" for the world, for Italy, and for the Church. He hoped that it would turn men back to God. It was his fervent prayer that after passing through a night "shrouded in thickest darkness," the like of which the world had never experienced before, mankind would emerge into a "new day." Just as Woodrow Wilson, who would take America into the war two years later, hoped that the result of the conflagration would be a "world safe for democracy," Padre Pio prayed for a world of reawakened faith and, as a consequence, of peace, love, and justice. "Ah, may all the nations afflicted by this war understand the mystery of the pacific wrath of the Lord!" He wrote:

> If He turns their poisonous joys into bitterness, if He corrupts their pleasures, and if He scatters thorns along the paths of their riot, paths hitherto strewn with the roses of slaughter, the reason is that He loves them still. And this is the holy cruelty of the physician, who, in extreme cases of sickness, makes us take most bitter and most horrible medicines. . . . The greatest mercy of God is not to let those nations remain in peace with each other who are not in peace with God. . . .[14]

Meanwhile, the World War was having more practical and immediate conse-
quences. The clergy in Italy were not exempt from the draft, and the Capuchin
Order was being decimated. By the end of May, thirteen priests and eight semi-
narians from the province of Foggia had been drafted. "My God, what a terrible
situation!" lamented Agostino, terrified at the prospect of being drafted
himself. Pio, too, was worried about being drafted, but Agostino assured him
that, with his poor health, he would surely be rejected for military service. Pio,
however, was not so sure. The medical officer for the Benevento district (where
he would have to report) was not the least bit sympathetic to complaints of physical disability.

In November it happened. Padre Pio was drafted. He went before the
"ferocious medical captain" at Benevento, who diagnosed tuberculosis. This,
under the circumstances, was not unwelcome news to Pio. He was horrified,
however, when he was sent to Caserta for further examinations and "the stupid
colonel" there pronounced him fit. When Pio protested, the colonel simply
roared, "Go to your regiment and meet your new superiors!"

Francesco Forgione (he could not use his religious name in the army) was assigned to the 10th Company of the Italian Medical Corps in Naples. Once there,
he began to vomit everything. He became so weak that his company commander ordered further examinations. For the time being he was allowed to wear his
Capuchin habit and was ordered to lodge — at his own expense — at a hotel in
town. Not having any money, he had to wire his father, who came at once with
money and provisions. Finally, the physicians came up with a diagnosis of
chronic bronchitis and, just before Christmas, granted him a year's leave for
convalescence. "Blessed be the Lord, who doeth marvelous things!" Pio exclaimed when he was permitted to return home.

Since Pio had weathered several weeks in the army without dying, Benedetto
became adamant that the young priest return to the cloister. He was especially
insistent now that so many friars were in the military and most of the religious
houses were nearly empty. On December 20, 1915, Agostino wrote Pio to tell
him the provincial wanted him back at the friary. Although Agostino professed
that he believed in Pio's excuses for not returning, he was constrained to report:
"It is being said all over the Province that you are being deceived by the devil,
who is taking advantage of your affection for your native soil!"[15]

Benedetto wrote on Christmas Eve, declaring that it was not edifying for "everyone to know that a priest remains at home because of his health. Foggia
awaits you."[16] Still Pio balked. He accused Agostino of being like one of Job's
comforters in insisting that it would be a good thing for him to return to the
cloister. When he insisted that since Benedetto did not order him *under obedience* to go to the cloister, he did not have to go, the professor wrote:

> It is an unshakable principle in the economy of our salvation that obedience
> must prevail over all worldly reasoning. Well, authority has spoken clearly

concerning your return to the cloister. Therefore no other advice and no other person can make an exception. The authority can be mistaken, but obedience is never mistaken. God Himself has never dispensed any saint from
obedience to authority.[17]

He concluded by saying, "Authority must prevail, not only in commands but
also in counsels."

Ultimately it was Raffaelina Cerase who was the direct cause of Padre Pio's
return to the friary. When Pio was first constrained to remain at home because
of his health, Agostino consulted several devoted Christians in Foggia, including Raffaelina and her sister Giovina, and asked them to pray for his friend's
permanent return to the cloister. Raffaelina was so moved by the plight of Padre
Pio that she offered herself as a victim in exchange for his return to community
life.

Meanwhile, during the fall of 1915, she had another operation, but by January it was apparent that her cancer had returned. In late January or early February, Agostino called on her and found her condition very bad. She told the professor that she knew that she was about to die and that her one desire was to see
Padre Pio before she left this world.

Agostino explained to Raffaelina the precarious state of Padre Pio's health
and described another complication, the fact that the Pietrelcinese would likely
stage a riot if Pio were taken from them. On a recent trip to Pietrelcina,
Agostino had been threatened with physical violence. "Padre Agosti," an irate
townsman had snarled, "you want to run off with our little saint, don't you? If
you do, we'll bust you in the face!" Another time Pannullo had to intervene to
prevent the professor's being mobbed when the rumor got about that he had
come to escort Pio back to the friary. Agostino had even encountered opposition
from Pio's mother. "You've got to get it into your head that Pio belongs to us,"
he pleaded with Motherdear. "You've got to give him up!"

Southern Italians have a long tradition of regarding men and women of saintly
repute as the prized possession of their particular town or village, and they have
been known to riot if that object of veneration is threatened with removal.
When St. Francis of Assisi was in his last illness, small wars nearly broke out
among the residents of nearby towns who strove for the honor of having the celebrated holy man die in their midst.

Thus the opposition of the Pietrelcinese was a real obstacle to Padre Pio's return to the friary. Even when Agostino explained this, Raffaelina, not satisfied,
replied: "Padre, don't be afraid. Make arrangements with Padre Benedetto.
Padre Pio *will* come here. He will hear my confession, and he will assist me at
my death. Make the superiors give Padre Pio the faculties to hear confessions.
He will save many souls."[18]

Agostino reported this conversation to Benedetto and then wrote Pio, urging
him to come to Foggia, if only for a few days. "Don't you want to console this

poor soul?" he asked. "Do you want to let her leave the world with this disappointment? . . . Don't you feel any obligation to this soul who has prayed so much and, indeed, is still praying for you?"[19]

So, on February 17, 1916, Padre Pio, telling his parents, siblings, and friends that he was going to Foggia for a few days to assist a dying woman, went to the Benevento railroad station where it was arranged that he would meet Agostino. The moment he set foot in the friary of St. Anne in Foggia, Benedetto, who was there to meet him, growled: "Here's a pen and paper. Write to your Mama and tell her to send your belongings because, dead or alive, you're staying here at Foggia!"[20]

It is interesting to note a belief commonly held in the Eastern Orthodox Church, which, like the Roman Catholic Church, has a long tradition of monastic holy men. According to the Orthodox, the *starets*, a priest or monk who is given the *charism* to discern in a practical way the will of God in relation to those who consult him, must withdraw from the world for a time in order to return to minister. From the time of St. Anthony of the Desert (251?-356?), many priests and lay Brothers in the tradition on which Padre Pio in many ways became a part, spent some time in partial or total isolation. As Timothy Ware, a scholar of Orthodoxy, writes:

> A monk must first withdraw, and in silence must learn the truth about himself and God. Then, after this long and rigorous preparation in solitude, having gained the gifts of discernment which are required of an elder, he can open the door of his cell and admit the world from which he formerly fled.[21]

Padre Pio's stay at Pietrelcina was certainly not intended as a flight from the world, nor was his isolation from society in any way complete. He did devote a great many hours to solitary meditation, however, and it seems that his ministry as a starets began immediately after his return to the friary.

Padre Pio's first days in Foggia were spent with Raffaelina. Padre Agostino recounts: "The meeting of Padre Pio and Miss Raffaelina was that of two souls who had known each other before the Lord for a long time. . . . The way they looked at each other — it was angelic — more eloquent than words can tell!"[22]

By March 17, Padre Pio wrote to Padre Agostino that Raffaelina was "already in the antechamber of the Supreme King. Before long," he said, "she will be led into the nuptial banquet."[23] Raffaelina's sister, Giovina, eavesdropping, heard Pio say to Raffaelina, "My dear daughter, let's tell Jesus to take me in your place."

"No, Padre," said Raffaelina. "I want to go first to Jesus myself. Then I will tell Him to send me to take you."[24]

Pio gave Raffaelina permission to go to Jesus before him, and on March 25, Pio wrote the professor: "At 4:00 this morning we gained another intercessor at the throne of the Most High. . . . Happy soul, she fell asleep in the Lord with a smile of disdain for this world!"[25] Agostino praised the "lovely soul," the "veritable treasure house of goodness and piety" who had "immolated herself" in exchange for the permanent return of Padre Pio to the cloister.

Pio now longed passionately for death. He begged Agostino, when he came to Foggia, to give him permission to die. Pio claimed that, according to his agreement with Raffaelina, the one who died first would appear to the survivor. Sure enough, Raffaelina appeared to him in her heavenly glory, but not with the message he was eager to hear. To Agostino, who had refused him permission to die, Pio wailed: "The whole lot of you are cruel! Padre Benedetto, the Provincial, says no, you say no. And now that other spirit . . . comes to tell me that she can't do anything because Jesus doesn't want it! If I had known that, I would never have given her permission to go to heaven before me! All of you are cruel!"[26] Thereafter, he referred to his friends who refused him permission to die as "my most cordial enemies."

Padre Pio remained at St. Anne's, Foggia, for about six months. During that time, he was constantly ill and spent most of his time in bed. Although he could retain scarcely any of the food he ate, he showed no signs of starvation. What his colleagues at St. Anne's noticed most, however, were the horrible noises that came from his room early every evening.

Pio's friend Paolino of Casacalenda, who was assigned to the friary of Our Lady of Grace at San Giovanni Rotondo, some twenty-five miles distant, passed through Foggia in May on his way to a nearby town where he was to undergo a medical examination for the army (which, happily, he would fail). He spent a short time at St. Anne's. There he found the friars concerned about the terrifying din that issued from Pio's room.

Paolino was somewhat sceptical until the dinner hour. The community sat down to eat, while Pio, as usual, remained upstairs in bed. During the course of the meal, everyone heard a terrific crash, just as if, as Paolino put it, a huge drum of gasoline had been dropped from a height and had crashed to the floor. Immediately Paolino ran upstairs to find Pio pale and drenched in perspiration, as if he had gone swimming in his nightshirt. The same thing happened for several successive nights.

Word of this reached the provincial, who suddenly appeared at the friary. When Paolino accidentally walked into a conference between Benedetto and Pio, the provincial asked him to remain as a witness to what he was telling Pio. Benedetto ordered Pio to have the noises stopped.

"But, Most Reverend Father," Pio humbly responded, "Your Paternity knows very well that I am not to blame and that I have nothing at all to do with what is happening. . . . It is God's will that is permitting this!"

Incredibly, Benedetto ordered Pio to "tell the Lord that I, as superior, for the greater good of this community, want to be contented . . . in having these noises stop!"[27]

Pio obediently relayed Benedetto's command, and the noises stopped. Pio explained to Paolino that the noises were in fact of demonic origin and were associated with temptations so frightening that they made him break out in a cold sweat. Of what they consisted, he did not say. The temptations continued but were unaccompanied by phenomena distressing to others.

There at Foggia, Padre Pio, despite his poor physical condition, was immediately sought out as a spiritual director. According to contemporaries, he became the center of a movement of intense spirituality. Among those who became his disciples at this time were Padre Paolino's sister, Assunta DiTommaso (1894-1953); Lucia Fiorentino (1889-1934), a native of San Giovanni who had been miraculously cured of tuberculosis while in her teens, and a mystic in her own right; and Rachelina Russo (1875-1968), who was also from San Giovanni. These three women were the center of a prayer group that Padre Pio organized. Another member of the group was Annitta Rodote, who had been Pio's spiritual daughter for nearly two years. She was associated with a remarkable phenomenon that was observed by Padre Paolino.

On one of his trips to Foggia, Annitta came to Paolino and said, "Father, yesterday something happened that never happened before in my life!" Around 2 P.M., she explained, she was working in her kitchen when she heard "a clear and intelligible voice" calling, "Annina! Annina!" (her nickname). At first Annitta thought she was dreaming, but as the voice continued to call her, she realized that she was wide awake. After calling her name twice more, the voice bade her, "Kneel down and pray for me, for I am at present very much tormented by the devil." Annitta was terrified as well as confused. The voice spoke again: "Quickly, quickly, Annina! Do not doubt because this is Padre Pio who is asking you to pray! Kneel and let's pray the litanies of the Madonna together!" At that, Annitta fell on her knees and Padre Pio's disembodied voice began the *Kyrie Eleison* (Lord, Have Mercy). Annitta responded, and they continued to the end. After he prayed the *Oremus* (Let Us Pray) to the conclusion, he said, "Thank you. I am calm now."

Paolino knew that Annitta was sincere, but he wondered whether this could have been a diabolical trick. Inasmuch as Annitta was bidden to pray for relief from diabolical temptation, however, he dismissed the possibility of the kingdom of hell being divided against itself. Then he told Annitta: "If you receive any other signs of this nature, tell the voice that you always pray for Padre Pio, but that you do not like this method of requesting prayer because you do not want to encounter illusions. You can also say that this was counseled by your confessor."

The next day Annitta called Paolino, who was staying at St. Anne's, and told him that the same thing had happened. When she had spoken of the danger of illusion, the voice had said: "But this is no illusion! I have need of souls to join with me in prayer, especially now, when I am tempted by the devil and feel the need acutely. So don't deny me the charity of praying with me!"

Padre Paolino told Annitta that she should ask Padre Pio, if he should call her in the same manner the next day, to tell her where he was at that moment. So the next day, Paolino carefully observed Pio's movements, especially around 2 P.M., the hour when Annitta had been mysteriously called to pray the past few days. The following day, when Annitta reported that the same thing had happened, Paolino asked her whether she had remembered to ask Pio where he was at the time. She repeated Pio's answer, and, to Paolino's awe, the place she indicated was the very place where Paolino had observed Pio at that hour. Satisfied, Paolino left Annitta in full liberty to pray with Pio every time he called her invisibly. He never questioned Pio on the phenomenon.[28]

Padre Pio was not to remain at Foggia for long. The summer of 1916 was very hot, and Pio suffered greatly from the heat. He was so hot at night that he could not sleep. Padre Paolino, who had become the father guardian of Our Lady of Grace at San Giovanni Rotondo in July, invited his old friend to come and spend a few days there to taste the cooler mountain air and perhaps find some refreshment.

Suffering though he was with the heat, Pio hesitated to accept without consent of the provincial. Paolino pointed out that for a visit of a few days Pio needed only the consent of his local superior. The father guardian of St. Anne's, Padre Nazareno of Arpaise, gave his permission, and Pio went with Paolino to San Giovanni Rotondo in late July 1916.

After Pio's return, Benedetto learned about the trip and, predictably, was enraged over the fact that his permission had not been asked as a matter of etiquette. Nevertheless — although not without sarcasm — Benedetto wrote to Pio, "Even though I note your willingness to please a mere priest and not [your] superior. . ., I am nonetheless happy that you went to San Giovanni Rotondo and hope that this has brought an improvement in your health."[29] Benedetto even gave him permission to live there permanently if that would help him.

After Padre Pio begged Benedetto's pardon and accepted his forgiveness, he made preparations to leave Foggia for San Giovanni Rotondo. He arrived at his new home on September 4, 1916, and, a week later, wrote Benedetto that he gave "fervent thanks to the Most High for making me worthy of finding a most edifying religious community."[30]

The same day that Pio wrote to Benedetto, Padre Paolino wrote to Agostino: "You can imagine the benefit we experience in the presence of Padre Pio! He is likewise pleased with us, with the air, the living arrangements, the quiet, the solitude, and with everything else, and, if one excepts the interior pains with which it pleases the Lord to test him, he might be said to be truly happy. What is most important is that we are happy with him!"[31]

San Giovanni Rotondo, located high in the Gargano Mountains, is the center of an agricultural community. The name is derived from an ancient circular temple of the god Janus, which, with the coming of Christianity, had been rededicated to St. John the Baptist. It was very much a rural outpost. As Emmanuele Brunatto, who was to come there in 1919, observed: "San Giovanni was a poor town, with no intercourse with the outside world, with no industry, without even a hotel. Almost all of the inhabitants were peasant farmers who went out at dawn to the harsh lands of the high plateau."[32]

About a mile from town, atop a barren hill, was the Capuchin friary. To reach it, one had to climb a zigzagging dirt road up a mountainside highlighted by stands of olive, pine, and cypress trees and rocky grainfields. Between the town and the friary there was neither a house nor a store.

The little friary had been begun in 1540 and was completed in 1601. After a severe earthquake in 1624, it had to be rebuilt. In 1667 a little church was constructed adjacent to it. The Capuchins there had long been reputed for their holiness and austerity. The community was regarded as one of the strictest in all of Italy. Although no member of the community has ever been canonized, many of the friars in the past had been popularly regarded as saints.

In December 1866, the friary was closed down during the suppression of the religious Orders and the building converted into a nursing home. It was not until November 1909 that the friary was allowed to reopen, as four religious — Padre Bernardo of Pietrelcina, Padre Luigi of Avellino, Padre Ermenegildo of San Giovanni Rotondo, and Fra Nicola of Roccabascerana — came to live there.

The friars supported themselves through the offerings contributed at the Masses of the priests and through the quests of Fra Nicola, who went begging on foot in the summer and on muleback in winter. According to Brunatto, the contributions Fra Nicola received, supplemented by fruit and vegetables from a garden and orchard, went to make up the friars' ascetic and almost vegetarian diet.

There was a long-standing feud between the friars on the hill, who had a reputation for asceticism and spirituality, and the secular clergy in town, who were notorious for their worldliness. The feud resumed with gusto after the end of government suppression, and was destined to blaze into a conflagration within a few years' time.

When Padre Pio arrived, the community at Our Lady of Grace numbered seven. Besides him, it included Padre Paolino, the guardian. A roly-poly man who looked like one of those souvenir salt-shaker monks, he was Pio's lifelong friend. There was Padre Angelico of San Marco la Catola (1888-?), the principal of the minor seminary the Capuchins ran on the premises. Not much is known about him. He seems to have left the priesthood in the mid-1920s. Padre Luigi of Seracapriola (1876-1941) was the sole professor at the seminary. Fra Nicola of Roccabascerana (1871-1943) continued as quaestor. Fra Leone of Terre (1874-1953) was the cook. There was another lay Brother, Fra Costantino of San Marco la Catola (1878-1960). Within a few months, all would be in military service except for Pio, Paolino, and Nicola.

Pio, in fact, was called to report for another physical in Naples in December, but after an examination at Trinity Hospital showed him still suffering from chronic bronchitis, he was given another six-month leave for recuperation. Paolino was excused because of a double hernia, and Nicola was too old. Agostino, despite his great bulk, had been unable to escape the draft, and was now busy organizing a military hospital for the Red Cross in northern Italy. He frequently wrote to Pio to ask for prayers and guidance.

Padre Pio's chief duties during his early years at Our Lady of Grace were teaching in the minor seminary, or seraphic college, and serving as spiritual director to the twenty or so students. He became a great favorite of the boys, who seemed unaware of his mystical interior life. To them he was simply a kind teacher and an exceptionally warm human being.

Padre Aurelio of Sant'Elia a Pianisi, a man who, at least according to some observers, bore a striking resemblance to Abraham Lincoln, studied under Padre Pio from 1916 to 1918. He admitted in an interview in July 1971 that Padre Pio was not the world's greatest teacher: "He had a superficial way of teaching. He taught history and grammar, but he knew little of the former and none of the latter. His lectures were never more than twenty minutes long, and they were unprepared. He was not strict, not even when he administered examinations. He let the kids do pretty much what they wanted."

Aurelio nonetheless recalled that there was something special about the little man with the dreamy eyes and beautiful smile: "He cast a spell over people. There was just something about him — a charm, a spell. It was only later that people considered him a saint. We boys were attracted to him in those days because he was very human, because he could understand us. He was very good with everybody. The key to his charm was his humanity. His sanctity was his humanity."

Padre Aurelio recalled how he and his fellow students, overcome by hunger, used to raid the friary kitchen at night. Padre Pio, they later discovered, knew about it but did not report them. Whenever anyone brought him fruits and candies, Pio would share them with the boys. He would sometimes even violate friary rules to help them. "One time in my life, I was desperate," recalled Aurelio more than half a century later. "Padre Pio would come into my room and sit on my bed and talk to me until 2 A.M. This was against the rules, but he did it."

Aurelio was aware of at least one supernatural occurrence. One day he scolded one of the younger boys very harshly, even going so far as to call his faith into question. That night Aurelio awoke to see a terrifying shadowy form in his room, breathing upon him with fetid breath. Objects in the room began to crash to the floor. In terror, Fra Aurelio ran to Padre Pio's room, shouting: "I don't want to go back there! There's a devil in my room!"

Padre Pio did not seem at all alarmed. He smiled and said: "Go back to your room. This is a proof that God wanted to give you so that you'll be better. . . . You did wrong in judging your fellow student so harshly. Yes, that was a devil. And thank God you didn't see his face!"

Padre Aurelio was convinced that he had not been dreaming, that a devil had really paid him a call that night, and that Padre Pio had driven him off!

As at St. Anne's, Padre Pio was encouraged to assume the spiritual direction of laypeople who sought his advice. Within weeks of his arrival, a group of pious women were meeting and praying with him twice weekly in the guest room of the friary. The group included Rachelina Russo and Lucia Fiorentino, with whom he had already been corresponding, as well as Lucia's sister Giovanna, the three Ventrella sisters — Vittoria, Elena, and Filomena — Maria Ricciardi, Maddalena Cascavilla, Maria and Lucia Campanile, Eva and Antonietta Pompilio, and Filomena Fini. Even in the ice and snow of winter, these devout ladies trudged up the hill that led to the friary to hear Padre Pio's warm and inspired words.

Padre Pio spent his spare time reading the Bible and answering correspondence from his spiritual children in other towns. At this point, his superiors were encouraging him in this ministry of correspondence, and he spent many hours a day painstakingly composing letters of spiritual counsel and enlightenment.

Pio's responsibilities grew in early 1917, after Padre Angelico was called into the military. In his absence, the man from Pietrelcina was made principal of the college. In addition to administrative work, Pio continued to teach, dividing classroom duties with Paolino, who, with most of his community away, was forced to act as a jack of all trades.

Pio's bronchial and digestive problems persisted. He ate the midday meal in the dining room but was still subject to fits of vomiting and had to keep a little box beside his seat — just in case. Then there was the matter of the fevers. On January 27 or 28, 1917, Padre Pio took to his bed. Paolino was concerned when he saw that his face was flushed and he had trouble breathing. He seemed to lack the energy to speak or even to move his limbs. The guardian was even more horrified when he tried to take his temperature. The mercury climbed to 108 degrees (F), then broke the bulb of the thermometer. Paolino hurried to the bathroom and fetched a bath thermometer, freed it from its wooden sheath, and placed it under Pio's armpit. The temperature soared to 125.5 degrees. When Paolino fed Pio some custard, the sick man vomited it "coagulated" and "almost baked." When Paolino put his hand to Pio's forehead, however, it was not hot at all. When a physician arrived, he noted the high fever, but in the absence of other specific symptoms, he prescribed the usual remedies for a bad case of the flu. To Paolino's amazement, within days the fever vanished and Pio seemed completely recovered. On February 12, he was able to write to a spiritual daughter named Maria Gargani. He spoke of the "extreme fever which the thermometer was inadequate to measure because its heat was so great as to explode it" and added: "I am neither healed nor sick, but I think that soon I will be the first to succumb."[33] He was wrong, however, and on February 23 he was able to speak of his "miraculous" recovery in a letter to Agostino.

In May, around the time of his thirtieth birthday, Pio took the longest trip of his life when, along with Padre Benedetto, he accompanied his sister Graziella to Rome, where she entered the Bridgettines. This was a semicloistered Order founded in the fourteenth century by the Swedish mystic St. Bridget and reorganized in 1911. Graziella took the name Suor Pia Dell'Addolorata (Sister Pia of Our Lady of Sorrows). Years later, incidentally, Pio confided to a friend that he had been thoroughly disgusted by the city of Rome.

Now, Pio had a six-month leave of absence from the army. He had been told to report upon receiving instructions. He had been dismissed on the second of January and was puzzled when July came and went without his hearing anything. He was even more puzzled and alarmed when, in mid-August, he received a telegram telling him to report for duty the very next day! Arriving in Naples, he found that he had almost been arrested for desertion. The original telegram had reached San Giovanni Rotondo addressed to Forgione. Nobody knew who he was, so it was sent back. Assuming that Forgione must have taken refuge in his hometown, authorities dispatched military police to Pietrelcina to arrest the deserter. Pio's sister Felicita explained that Francesco Forgione and Padre Pio were one and the same man, that he was indeed in the Capuchin friary at San Giovanni Rotondo, and that if they wanted the telegram to get through to him, they would have to use the name by which he was known in his community.

Pio was quickly placed in a hospital in Naples for observation. Two doctors diagnosed "infiltration of the pulmonary apices," but declared him fit for non-combat duty within Italy, and so he was assigned to the 4th Platoon of the 10th Company of the Italian Medical Corps.

Pio, or rather Forgione, was miserably unhappy. He had to wear an army uniform this time, which he despised. Complaining to Benedetto, he wrote, "Just thinking about these rags makes me shudder and throws me into a deathly depression." He characterized his officers as "executioners." His lieutenant, whose name was Gargani, was "a gentleman," but his captain, named Giannatasio, was "a neurotic of the first order" and "the terror of poor soldiers." Soon his stomach was refusing all food, and by mid-October he was back in Trinity Hospital with a high fever. Benedetto could not understand why Pio was not discharged. "How can you be a soldier in bed?" he asked. By October 20, he could not eat at all, and the normally stocky Pio complained that he was reduced almost to a skeleton. On November 6 he was granted his third leave of absence, this time for a period of four months.

An army certificate from this time records the thirty-year-old Padre Pio's height as just a shade over 5'5." His weight is not given, but it must have been somewhat less than the 165 pounds that was normal when he was younger. His hair is described as "chestnut" (reddish brown), as were his eyes. In other documents, however, his hair is described as "blond" or "dark blond," and his eyes as "deep blue" or "very black." His complexion is described as "rosy," and the army dentist who examined his teeth noted that they were in good condition with none missing.

After a brief visit to his parents and sister at Pietrelcina, Padre Pio returned to San Giovanni Rotondo. Despite his debilitated condition, he was comforted by a divine visitation that seemed to signal the approach of the end of the war. Just before Christmas he wrote to Padre Benedetto: "In one of the visits that I received from Jesus in recent days, I asked Him insistently to have compassion on the poor nations so tried by the misfortune of war and to cause His justice to give way at last to His mercy. It was strange. He answered only by means of a gesture that seemed to say, 'Quiet! Quiet!' 'But when?' I asked. And He, with a serious expression, but with a half smile on His lips, glanced at me briefly and, without another word, dismissed me." He told Benedetto that he never remembered Jesus making a gesture before in a vision when he questioned Him about the war. "He always observed a profound silence."[34]

Benedetto replied that he too had experienced a similar vision. Moreover, in this experience, Christ had shown Benedetto his wounds, saying, "Now they are covered, but they are not healed."

Before the Armistice, Pio had to submit to another military medical examination. On March 6, 1918, he entered Trinity Hospital once more, expressing hope that the Lord "will quickly free me from this humiliation." On March 16 he was discharged permanently with a diagnosis of "double broncho-alveolitis."

On his way back to San Giovanni Rotondo, Padre Pio stopped to see his family at Pietrelcina. It was to be his last vacation and the last time he would see his native town.

The Spiritual Director

By 1918, Padre Pio had a circle of female disciples who regularly met and prayed with him. These were his "spiritual daughters." Many of Pio's letters to these women have been preserved. Pio had spiritual sons too, but they were, at least at first, less numerous. Southern Italian men, at least in those days, were apt to feel that religion was best left to the women. So it was harder to obtain male disciples, although in the 1940s, Padre Agostino would be astounded at the number of men who came to see Padre Pio.

There is also less literature preserved about Pio's male followers. Friary rules allowed men easier access to the friars. Padre Pio had finally been accorded the faculty to hear confessions in 1917 by Pasquale Gagliardi, the archbishop of Manfredonia. Because of the schedule at the friary, Pio usually happened to hear the confessions of men, while Paolino heard those of women. While men tended to be counseled during confession, women were generally advised during their biweekly meetings and through letters.

It is the letters that convey to posterity Padre Pio's theology of spiritual direction. From them, as well as from a few other sources, we learn what he was like as a spiritual director.

Padre Pio did not accept just anybody as his spiritual child. Just as he would not correspond with people he did not "know before the Lord," he normally did not undertake to counsel or advise people about whom the Lord had not given him some "enlightenment." He would hear their confessions, of course, but it truly grieved Padre Pio to have to try to counsel without divine illumination. In such cases, as he wrote to Margherita Tresca in 1918, he had to "proceed gropingly," guiding himself with "a little cold and pallid doctrine learned in books."[1]

In the same letter, however, he says that for "certain extraordinary persons" he had "recourse to divine light." Such persons he invited to enter into a closer relationship. "It would be stupid of me to judge you without understanding the way God is leading you," he wrote to Maria Gargani. For those whom God gave him as his spiritual children, he claimed access to this understanding through "a light that Divine Goodness does not deny to ministers called to act as His proxies on earth."[2]

Despite these high-sounding words, Padre Pio was very humble. To Annitta Rodote he wrote: "To [God] alone and not to me give praise and thanksgiving. You owe nothing to me. I am but an instrument in the hands of God, capable of serving a useful purpose only when handled by the Divine Craftsman. Left to myself, I know how to do nothing except sin and sin again."[3]

The spiritual daughters met twice a week in the *foresteria*, or guest room, of the friary, where Padre Pio would discuss with them the Bible and "the means of perfection." Maria Campanile, a member of that group who was still alive in the late 1970s, recalled Padre Pio's gift for explaining difficult parts of the Bible. "He took away our doubts and illuminated our spiritual darkness," she wrote.[4]

Padre Pio established five rules for spiritual growth: weekly confession, daily Communion, spiritual reading, meditation, and examination of conscience.

Maria Campanile's father questioned her about making her confession so frequently. She asked the padre about it, and he replied, "A room needs to be dusted once a week, even if nobody is there." Some of the ladies were afraid they were unworthy of taking Communion so frequently. "Unless you are positive that you are in mortal sin," Padre Pio told them, "you ought to take Communion every day." According to Campanile, it was largely through Padre Pio's influence that daily reception of Communion became widely practiced at San Giovanni Rotondo. Pio urged a thorough study of Scripture and suggested and lent spiritual books from the friary library.

"Meditation," Padre Pio told Maria, "is the key to progress in the knowledge of self as well as the knowledge of God, and through it we achieve the goal of the spiritual life, which is the transformation of the soul in Christ."[5] In a letter to Annitta Rodote, he even suggested a physical position for meditation: "Try to put yourself in the presence of God," he suggested, "and thus understand that He, with all the celestial court, is there within your soul. Then commence your prayer and meditation. In all this, try to close your eyes, and, if possible, hold your head upright and put your forehead in the palm of your hands. . . ."[6]

As subjects for meditation, Padre Pio suggested such themes from the Bible as Jesus' passion, death, resurrection, and ascension. To Maria Gargani he wrote: "Put yourself in the presence of God, humble yourself profoundly in the consideration of who you are and Whom you are before. Ask God for the grace to make good the mental prayer that you are about to undertake, so that you can derive the fruit that God most desires. Finally, recommend yourself to the intercession of the Most Holy Virgin, as well as to all the heavenly court, so that they may help you meditate well and keep every distraction and temptation away from you."

> After you have meditated thoroughly on the subject in all its aspects, then pass to resolutions. Make it your purpose to amend yourself with regard to that defect which most hinders your union with God and which causes many other defects and sins. Propose to exercise a particular virtue. . . .

> Then ask God for all those graces and for all those helps of which you feel the need. Recommend all men to the Lord, either in general or in particular. . . . Pray for the living, pray for the dead, pray for the unbelieving, pray for heretics, and pray for the conversion of sinners.

> And after you have done this, offer your meditation and your prayer, along with yourself and those closest to your heart. Offer them all to God, along with the merits of Jesus. . . .[7]

Padre Pio urged two periods of meditation daily, as well as two periods of self-examination: in the morning, "to prepare for the battle," and in the evening, "to purify your soul from every earthly affection that might have been able to attach itself to you during the day."[8] Each of these periods of reflection and recollection was to last at least a half hour.

Padre Pio had a disconcerting tendency to lavish a great deal of attention on his newer disciples, then dealing more serverely with them as they grew in faith. Maria Campanile remembered how, when she first came to him, Padre Pio used to give her candy. She asked him why, since he himself lived in holy poverty, he would want to distribute luxuries. "Because I don't eat them, I give them to you," he told her, almost flippantly.

Marie, who was a member of the Third Order of St. Francis, asked, "But aren't I a daughter of St. Francis?"

The padre laughed and, referring to her father's first name, answered, "No, you're the daughter of *Mister* Francis!"[9]

Trying to explain Pio's indulgence with more recent disciples, Campanile wrote, "He won souls . . . by first showing compassion and catering to their wishes so that they might not fall into sin."[10] Pio felt that people who are deeply attached to material things cannot suddenly be divorced from them without the danger of falling into despair or losing interest in spiritual commitment.

Padre Pio's theology changed remarkably little over the years. His principles of discipleship embody roughly ten points, all of them applicable to daily living.

PUT YOUR TRUST IN CHRIST AS YOUR PERSONAL SAVIOR. Padre Pio often counseled his disciples to abandon themselves to Jesus "like a child to his mother's arms." He told Rachelina Russo to say repeatedly to Christ: "Whom have I on earth besides Thee; Whom in heaven but Thee, my Jesus! Thou art the God of my heart and my inheritance whom I desire eternally!"

KNOW THAT YOU HAVE NO RIGHTEOUSNESS OF YOUR OWN. To a disciple named Erminia Gargani (1883-1962), he wrote: "Consider yourself . . . what you really are: a nothing . . . the epitome of feebleness, a fountain of perversity without limit or bounds, capable of converting good to evil, of abandoning good for evil, of ascribing goodness to yourself and justifying yourself in evil, and for the love of the same evil, despising the Supreme Good." He gave Erminia the following rules:

- Never be pleased with yourself.

- Do not complain about offenses perpetrated against you.

- Forgive everyone with Christian charity.

- Always groan as a poor wretch before your God.

- Never marvel at your weakness, but recognizing yourself for what you are, blush over your inconstancy and faithlessness to God, and confide in Him, tranquilly abandoning yourself to the arms of the heavenly Father like a babe in the arms of his mother.

- Never exult in any way in any virtues, but ascribe everything to God, and give Him all the glory and honor.

Padre Pio taught that all goodness is in God and comes from God. We have no righteousness of our own. Because of this, a soul who puts his trust in Christ has nothing to fear. To Erminia Gargani, who was terrified that she could do nothing to earn her salvation, Pio wrote.

> No pilgrim soul can worthily love his God, but when this soul does everything possible on his part and trusts in divine mercy, why would Jesus reject this spirit? Has He not commanded us to love God according to our strength? If you have given and consecrated everything to God, why fear?[11]

Therefore, the Christian does his best and leaves the rest to the God in whom he trusts and to whom he prays for the grace to live righteously.

REMEMBER THAT GOOD WORKS COME ONLY THROUGH CHRIST. Good works, Padre Pio taught, are produced only in union with Christ. He told Erminia's sister Donna Maria that all of our actions are mixed with inclinations toward pride, vanity, self-love, and the like. But if our motives are God-centered and our actions consecrated to God, they are accepted and used for His glory. To his disciples the Ventrella sisters, Padre Pio wrote that a Christian should not worry about what he does so long as it is done with a desire to please God.

RECOGNIZE THAT THE DEVIL IS A REAL INDIVIDUAL, BENT ON DESTROYING YOU, BUT DO NOT FEAR HIM. Padre Pio wrote to Annitta Rodote:

> You must not marvel if our common enemy has mustered all his strength to keep you from hearing what I am writing to you. This is his job, and it is to his profit. Despise him, therefore, and arm yourself against him with ever greater steadfastness in faith, because it is written, "Your adversary the devil, like a roaring lion, walketh about seeking someone to devour. Resist him strongly in the faith" (St. Peter 5:8). Do not let the many snares of the infernal beast terrify you. Jesus, who is always with you and who fights with you and for you will never let you be deceived or conquered.[12]

ALWAYS PRAY TO GOD AND SAY, IN EVERY CIRCUMSTANCE, 'THY WILL BE DONE.' To Annita Rodote, Padre Pio wrote:

> In all human affairs . . . learn most of all to recognize and adore God's will in everything. Frequently repeat the divine words of our dear Master, "Thy will be done on earth as it is in heaven." May this beautiful exclamation always be in your heart and on your lips in all the vicissitudes of life. Repeat it in affliction. Repeat it in temptation and in the trials to which Jesus will be pleased to subject you. Repeat it still when you find yourself immersed in the ocean of Jesus' love. This will be your anchor and your salvation.[13]

LOVE THE CROSS. Padre Pio consistently taught that suffering is a special sign of God's love. "Without love for the cross," he wrote Annita Rodote, "we cannot make much profit in the Christian life." He taught that the Christian must humble himself and patiently accept suffering. A frequent reminder to his spiritual children was: "The heavenly Father wants to make you resemble His divine Son in His anguish in the desert and on the hill of Calvary."

What is the reason for so much suffering? Padre Pio put it rather gruesomely to Maria Gargani. "Religion," he wrote, "is a hospital for spiritually sick people who want to be healed. To be healed they submit themselves to suffering, namely, to bloodletting, to the lance, to the razor, to the probe, to the scalpel, to the fire, and to all the bitterness of medicine. In order to be spiritually cured, we have to submit to all the tortures of the divine Physician."

Above all, in trouble, the Christian must not grumble. Padre Pio often referred to the children of Israel, who were barred from the Promised Land because of their grumbling. "Keep your eyes fixed yonder on Him who is your guide to the heavenly country, whither He is leading you," Pio wrote to Antonietta Vona. "Why worry whether it is wastelands or meadows through which you pass, so long as God is always with you and you arrive at the possession of a blessed eternity?"[24]

The padre often used the following example to explain the necessity of suffering: "There's a woman who is embroidering. Her son, seated on a low stool, sees her work, but in reverse. He see the knots of the embroidery, the tangled threads. . . . He says, 'Mother, what are you doing? I can't make out what you are doing!' Then the mother lowers the embroidery hoop and shows the good part of the work. Each color is in place and the various threads form a harmonious design. So, we see the reverse side of the embroidery because we are seated on the low stool.''[14]

OFFER EVERY ACTION UP TO GOD. Padre Pio urged his disciples to make short mental prayers offering everything they did, no matter how simple or trivial, to Christ. "Let's refer everything to God and live and move in Him," he wrote to Maria Gargani. Along with everything else, the Christian was to offer his sufferings to God as a sacrifice. While Padre Pio did not urge everyone to offer himself as a victim, he did teach that we should offer suffering, when it comes, to God to be used for his good purposes. To the same Donna Maria, he wrote, "Physical and spiritual ills are the most worthy offering you can make to Him Who saved you by suffering."

NEVER WORRY. Anxieties, Pio taught, are a waste of time. Through the machinations of the devil, who makes use of them, anxieties befoul our good actions because of our lack of confidence in God's goodness. As he wrote to Padre Agostino, "Our sweet Lord is deprived of giving us many graces solely because the door to our heart is not open to Him in holy confidence."

ASPIRE TO THE HEAVENLY PRIZE. "How lovable an eternity in heaven is, and how miserable the affairs of this world are!" Padre Pio exclaimed in a letter to Donna Erminia. "Continually aspire to the former and fervently despise the comforts and the affairs of this mortality."

Padre Pio's vision of heaven was disarmingly traditional. In heaven the Christian is forever happy. He is united with loved ones. He watches over his family and friends on earth. When the father of the Gargani sisters died, Pio wrote to Erminia, "Comfort yourself with the sweet thought that your Daddy is not dead. . . . He lives a life of joy that will have no end. He lives in heaven. He lives in the midst of his dearest ones." When the two-year-old child of Filomena Fini died, he wrote her, "Your baby is in paradise, and there he is watching over you, assisting you, smiling on you, and preparing a place for you."

REJOICE IN THE LORD. Despite his sufferings as a victim of divine love, Padre Pio was a cheerful man. To Raffaelina Cerase he wrote: "Drive melancholy away! Even sing a few little songs! . . . Joy, with peace, is the sister of charity. . . . Serve the Lord with hilarity!" William Carrigan, an official with the American Red Cross who knew the padre during the Second World War, told me in 1979: "He couldn't stand long faces. He would jolly up any crowd."

This is what Padre Pio taught for more than fifty years. Throughout his life, his message remained basically unchanged.

From the very earliest years of his ministry, as we have seen, Padre Pio was concerned not only with people's spiritual well-being but also with their physical health. Maria Campanile recalled that from the time she first came to him when she was twenty-three, Pio expressed great concern for her family and her career (she was a teacher). He always tried to find a solution to whatever problem, spiritual or physical, was presented to him.

In this connection, Donna Maria recorded two events she described as "miracles." Padre Pio always inquired about the health of all members of his prayer group and their families. One day Maria Campanile told him that her mother was ill with double pneumonia. When she mentioned that the doctors had applied eight leeches for the purpose of drawing blood, still a common medical practice in Italy in 1918, Padre Pio, horrified, shouted, "She must not be bled!" He insisted that Signora Campanile was not suffering from pneumonia but malaria. Maria told the doctors to remove the leeches. Her mother did recover and the doctors finally had to agree that she had had malaria, not pneumonia. Without seeing or examining Maria's mother, Padre Pio, who, as far as is known, had no medical training, was able to insist — accurately — that the woman had been misdiagnosed.

The other incident concerns Padre Pio's gift of bilocation, which we have already encountered. On February 2, 1918, one of Donna Maria's sisters suffered a fall at home. She complained of violent pains in the area of her liver and then lost consciousness. The doctors who examined her determined that her liver was damaged and that there were other grave internal injuries. There was nothing they could do for her, they said; she could not live.

Immediately Maria hurried up the hill and asked for Padre Pio, who told her that her sister would recover and not to worry. Even so, the situation looked very grim that evening when Maria returned home. The sister was in a coma, vomiting every fifteen minutes. Maria called her name, tapped her, and even pinched her. The injured woman was oblivious to everything.

A lady friend was also in the room. All of a sudden, this woman, who is not identified, turned pale. Maria asked if she felt ill. "No," she replied, "the padre is here." Donna Maria confessed that she was stupefied. Up to that point she had never even heard of the phenomenon of bilocation. She asked her friend, "What do you mean, the padre is here?"

"He is here in spirit," said the friend.

"How is he dressed?" asked Maria, who saw nothing.

"Like a monk."

"If I touch him, will I feel anything?"

"Of course not. He's spirit. See," she said, poking the air. "He has come near your sister, and he has said, 'Poor child.'"

Ten minutes later the friend told Maria, "Now he has gone away." Maria went to her sister and called her name.

"How do you feel?" she asked her.

"Much better," said the sister, regaining full consciousness.

Maria looked at her watch. It was 8 P.M. The next day, with her sister well on the road to a rapid recovery, Donna Maria went to the friary and found Padre Pio in the courtyard. She asked him point-blank, "Padre, what time did you come to my house last night?"

He looked at her and, without batting an eye, answered in a matter-of-fact way, "Around eight."[15]

From this point on in Padre Pio's life there are stories of innumerable incidents involving supernatural or, at least, inexplicable phenomena. Many of those who reported them, like Maria Campanile, were quick to attribute to these unusual events a miraculous character. One thing is indisputable as we examine Pio's life at this period: he was on the threshold of renown, not only as a thaumaturge, or wonder-worker, but also as a winner of souls.

The Stigmata

The dark night into which Padre Pio's soul had been plunged during his double exile in Pietrelcina intensified with his return to the friary. Shortly after his arrival at St. Anne's in Foggia, he wrote to Padre Benedetto about periods of "celestial inebriation," which, dissipating, left him in "a prison darker than before, where eternal horror reigns." He was, as usual, perplexed at being able to see clearly into the souls of others but not into his own, and he worried about whether or not he was acceptable to God. Over and over he expressed his terror of being damned.

Benedetto would answer his letters with advice such as this: "You must calm yourself through my assurances and hold to them as if sworn by oath." Agostino, still with the Red Cross, urged him to trust blindly in the assurances of his superiors.

During 1917 and 1918, Pio spoke increasingly about God being hidden from him by what he likened to "those mists which tend to rise certain mornings around a river. . . ." He recounted to Benedetto that, while the mists hindered his soul from "fixing its gaze" on Christ, his desire and need to gaze upon the Lord grew in proportion to the difficulty. Benedetto wrote back:

> The mists are an indication of the nearness of God. Moses found the Lord in the mist of Sinai. The Hebrew people saw Him in the form of a cloud, and as a cloud He appeared in the Temple. Christ, in the Transfiguration, was at first visible and then became invisible because He was immersed in a luminous cloud. God's hiding in a mist signifies that He is growing greater in your gaze and transfiguring Himself from the visible and intelligible into the pure divine.[1]

Although Padre Pio did not feel intellectually or emotionally relieved, he re-signed himself. "I pray Thee, O my good God," he wrote, "be Thou my life, my ship, and my port." Continuing, he prayed on paper:

> Thou hast caused me to mount the cross of Thy Son, and I try to adapt my-self to it the best I can. I am convinced that I shall never come down from it and that I will never again see the air quiet about me. I am convinced that it is necessary to speak to Thee amidst the thunder and turbulence. . . . I feel the ground upon which I walk give away beneath my feet. Who will strengthen my steps? Who, if not Thou, Thou who art the staff of my weak-ness! Have mercy upon me, O God! Have mercy upon me! Let me not feel my weakness again! Let Thy faith yet once more illumine my intellect, Thy charity warm my heart, which is broken by the pain of offending Thee in the hour of trial. My God, how atrocious this thought is which never leaves me and which pierces me! My God, my God, do not make me suffer for Thee any longer! I can stand it no more![2]

In June 1918, Pio wrote to Benedetto: "How can I tell you of the agonizing pain which is causing my soul a martyrdom? . . . I feel . . . crushed by His mighty hand. Tears are my daily bread. I toss and turn, I seek Him, but I do not find Him — except in the fury of His justice." Although he still has access to su-persensible wisdom with regard to others, Pio continues to be "in the dark" about his own soul. No longer does he experience God's presence in his own life as he had as a boy and young man. "He has blotted out everything," Pio writes, "and I, alas, am lost in thickest darkness, while I return in vain to disconnected memories of a lost love. . . . O my Great Good, where art Thou to be found? I have lost Thee! I cannot find Thee again because Thou hast accepted forthwith the total offering I made to Thee!"[3]

Deprived of the light to see his own way, Pio had to rely totally upon the counsel of Benedetto and Agostino. Agostino later wrote that he felt that God brought about Pio's trial to keep him humble. For a man, even of Padre Pio's dedication to the Lord, to know how much further advanced he is spiritually than the majority of Christians would be too great a temptation to pride. This, at least, was Padre Agostino's belief. Pio speaks of his fear that he is "about to be ground into powder" beneath the heavy hand of a God who is justly angry with him. Yet he prays, "I ask of Thee the strength to suffer, stripped of all consola-tion. Make these resolutions of mine constant, steadfast, and fruitful so that they may at least suffice to disarm Thy fury."[4]

Benedetto assured Pio that his bitter anguish was part of his participation in the passion of Christ for the sake of mankind. "The Omnipotent wants to make a holocaust of you," he told Pio.

Pio frequently renewed his offering of himself as a victim for various inten-tions. In July, Pope Benedict XV urged all Christians to pray for an end to the

World War, which was still raging; and, on July 27, despite his sufferings, Pio offered himself as a victim for the end of the war. "No sooner had I made this offering," he wrote, "than I felt myself plunged into a terrible prison and heard the crash of the gate behind me." From that moment, every minute of the day he felt as if he were in hell. He told Benedetto: "I no longer know the way. I no longer have a single ray of light, not one torch, not one single guideline, no life and no more truth to understand how I can nurture or refresh myself. Thus, I hope against hope, as you suggested to me." He is willing to be swallowed by the tempest, like Jonah, but "at the bottom of the sea I fear that I will find nothing but everlasting death."[5]

Yet in the same breath with which he describes this abandonment by God, he recounts a striking vision in which Christ appears and pierces his side. Both St. Teresa of Avila[6] and St. Thérèse of Lisieux had very similar experiences. This is what befell Padre Pio on August 5, 1918:

> I was hearing the confessions of our boys . . . when suddenly I was filled with extreme terror at the sight of a heavenly Being who presented Himself to the eye of my intellect. He held some kind of weapon in His hand, something like a long, sharp-pointed steel blade, which seemed to spew out fire. At the very instant that I saw all this, I saw that Personage hurl the weapon into my soul with all His might. It was only with difficulty that I did not cry out. I thought I was dying. I told the boy to leave because I felt ill and did not feel that I could continue. . . . This agony lasted uninterruptedly until the morning of the 7th. I cannot tell you how much I suffered during this period of anguish. Even my internal organs were torn and ruptured by that weapon. . . . From that day on I have been mortally wounded. I feel in the depths of my soul a wound that is always open and causes me continual agony.[7]

Pio's letter leaves it unclear whether a physical wound was involved, but in a deposition made in February 1967, Padre Pio stated unambiguously that a visible, physical wound in his side resulted from the experience. For a time, he was able to conceal it so successfully that not even Benedetto or Agostino had an inkling that the wound was physical as well as spiritual. He did apprise them of the vision. "Is this a new punishment visited upon me by Divine Justice?" he asked his mentors. "Judge as to what verity is contained in this, and whether I have reason to fear."

Agostino wrote back immediately: "The spiritual wound from that celestial being is the token of God's love for you. Didn't you think how the 6th was the Feast of the Transfiguration of Our Lord? Jesus wanted not only to transfigure your spirit but to pierce it with a wound that He alone can cure. . . . If it pleases Him to keep it open until He calls you to Himself, so be it." Identifying the experience as a "transverberation," or piercing of the heart, Benedetto writes:

No abandonment, no vengeful justice, no unworthiness on your part deserving of rejection and condemnation! Everything that is happening to you is the effect of love. It is a trial, a calling to co-redeem, and therefore it is a fountain of glory![8]

"Will the light and joy of the Resurrection come?" Bendetto wonders. "I hope so, if it pleases Him. Kiss the hand that has given you the transverberation and sweetly cherish this wound, which is the stamp of love."

In the meantime, Padre Paolino, the only adult with whom Pio was in constant contact in these days (Fra Nicola was frequently absent), was unaware of the details of his colleague's spiritual trial. Pio never confided in him as he did in Benedetto and Agostino. Paolino, however, was aware of the increasing frequency of unexplained phenomena associated with Padre Pio in the spring and summer of 1918. During this period he made notes concerning several unusual occurrences.

One night Padre Pio was praying alone in the choir when he heard a terrible crash in the darkened church below. Hurrying downstairs, he found that the large candles at the base of the statue of the Madonna had been knocked or had fallen to the floor and lay smashed to pieces. The statue of Our Lady was up so high that it would have been difficult even for a tall man to reach the candles without a ladder. Pio looked around and was amazed to see a Capuchin Brother there, apparently attempting to so some cleaning. Pio did not know the man and asked him what he was doing there in the dark.

"I'm cleaning," he answered.

"Cleaning in the dark?" asked Padre Pio, incredulous. "Who are you, anyway? I've never met you."

"I'm a Capuchin novice, doing my purgatory," the man replied. He explained that he had died years ago, before the suppression of the friary, and was expiating his sin of laziness. "I have need of prayer," he said.

"Well," said Pio, "this is a fine way to do reparation for your sins, by breaking up all these candles. Go now. Tomorrow I will say a Mass for you so that you can be freed and no longer have to return here!"

The phantom thanked him and disappeared. A dream? Perhaps. Yet someone had broken the candles. Padre Paolino saw them, as did a visitor, Padre Emmanuele, who commented that they could never have been knocked down without a ladder.

Another mysterious encounter took place around the same time. Padre Pio was sitting in the guest room one evening, praying with his eyes closed, when he looked up and saw an old man beside him. He had never seen the fellow before and wondered how he could have entered the locked doors of the friary.

When Pio asked him who he was, the man replied: "My name was Pietro DiMauro. My father was Nicola. They used to call me Precoco. I died in this friary on September 18, 1908, in room No. 4, when this was still a poor house.

One evening I fell asleep in bed with a lighted cigar and set fire to the mattress. I died of burns and asphyxiation. I am still in purgatory and have need of a Holy Mass to be freed. The Lord has permitted me to come to ask your assistance."

Padre Pio told the specter, "Tomorrow I will celebrate a Mass for your liberation," then accompanied DiMauro to the door, which, in fact, was closed and barred. He unlatched the door, and the mysterious visitor literally vanished into the night.

Paolino and his sister Assunta, who was visiting, noticed that Pio was perturbed about something. After repeated inquiries, Pio told them what happened. Paolino thought that Padre Pio must surely have been dreaming, but, just in case, he went to the town hall and looked up the vital statistics for the year 1908. He found that on September 18 of that year, while the friary was still being used as a nursing home for the indigent, one Pietro DiMauro had in fact died of burns and asphyxiation in room No. 4!

One night Paolino was sitting in a chair in Pio's room, talking to his friend, who was lying in bed. The guardian was tired and fell asleep in his chair. Around midnight he awoke to find Pio "half lying on the bed with his right elbow raised up on the pillow, his head propped up in the palm of his hand, his usual position for meditation. He was panting . . . strenuously. . . ." By the dim light of the oil lamp, Paolino noted that Pio's face, normally florid, was pale and his eyes seemed to be fixed on something, although Paolino could see nothing unusual in the room. At the same time, Paolino heard Pio repeating, "Yes, Jesus . . . give me this grace . . . I can't remain here on earth any longer without coming to You." Then there was a deep silence. His face brightened as he said, "Why, it's you, Mary. . . ." Silence again. Then Pio smiled and said, "It seems as if you're both mocking me!" A few more moments of silence were broken when Pio proclaimed: "Thank you!. . . Thank you, Jesus! Thank you, Mary!" Then he came to himself.

Padre Paolino became curious as to how to make certain whether Pio was truly in ecstasy. Accordingly, three or four days later when he entered Pio's room and found him in a similar state, he decided to make a test. Noiselessly, he closed the door and went to the other end of the friary to a big window that overlooked the town. There, mentally, Paolino spoke the words: *Padre Pio, I command you through holy obedience to come out of your ecstasy.* Immediately he heard Pio calling him.

"What do you want?" asked the guardian.

"What do *I* want?" demanded Pio. "On the contrary, *you* tell *me* what it is that *you* want!"

Still testing him, Paolino shrugged and said: "I? I don't want anything. I came here because you called me."

Pio then smiled, looked Paolino straight in the face and said, "Father Guardian, you know only too well!"

The fact that Padre Pio responded to a command of obedience that was given *only mentally* convinced Padre Paolino that the friar was not dreaming or hallucinating but was truly in ecstasy.

Padre Paolino also had reason to believe that Padre Pio could, on occasion, read minds. Something Pio did or said annoyed Paolino, and for three days, whenever the former approached, the guardian walked away. Finally Pio could take it no longer and went to Paolino's room. "Paolino," he pleaded, "let me know what I did so that you won't treat me like this any more. If I have done something to offend you, tell me what it is and I won't do it anymore."

Paolino, still grumpy, refused to tell him. "I'll never tell you the reason for my resentment," he said. "If the Lord in His goodness wants to reveal it to you, so much the better."

Pio insisted some more, but Paolino remained obdurate. Pio then rested his elbow on the table, and supporting his head in the palm of his hand, assumed his usual meditating position and began gazing intently into Paolino's eyes. "All at once I felt as if something were being turned upside down in the inmost part of my being," Paolino wrote. "It was not a physical sensation, but I do not know how to express myself otherwise." Simultaneously Pio happily exclaimed, "So, *this* is the cause of your resentment toward me! I didn't think you would be upset over something so trivial and so beyond my control!" Padre Pio then proceeded to reveal in minute detail the precise nature of Paolino's grievance.

According to most of those who have lived with him and left a testimony, Padre Pio did not normally have the ability to read minds or tell the future. But in those instances in which God revealed what is normally hidden, Pio knew more than what was on a person's mind at a given time. Under divine revelation, Pio frequently was able to recite details of an individual's past or personality, even when the other person was not thinking of anything in particular.

Paolino also "performed experiments" relating to the presence of Padre Pio's guardian angel. Padre Paolino asked his friend many questions about this unseen guest, but Pio was unwilling to talk freely about this subject. One night, however, when Pio was ill with one of his baffling sicknesses, Paolino decided to try an experiment.

Pio had been calling Paolino during the night to come to his assistance but had been unable to rouse his superior, who was a heavy sleeper. "Pio, you know I would gladly come to your assistance at night," Paolino told him, "but if you want me to wake up, you'd better send your guardian angel to rouse me."

Now Paolino slept in the same room with the boys in the college. That night, as usual, he quickly fell into a deep sleep. Around midnight, he was roughly shaken awake. "I immediately thought of Padre Pio," he wrote, "and intended to go to him, but unfortunately dawn found me still in bed. My fatigue was so great . . . that I couldn't bring myself to get up and go to the padre."

That next morning, Paolino said to Pio: "Why did your angel guardian come to wake me only to let me fall back asleep? That was a useless effort. If he comes tonight, he must wake me in such a way that I get up."

That night, Paolino was again convinced that someone had shaken him awake, but once more he fell asleep. The next day he told Pio to bid his angel not to leave him in peace until he got out of bed. At 1:30 A.M. the third night, according to Paolino's notes: "I felt myself being shaken in such a way that I awoke so thoroughly that I immediately leapt out of bed and went to Padre Pio with a lighted candle in my hand." Knocking on the door and entering, Paolino found Pio ill and drenched in perspiration. He begged Paolino to help him change clothing.

Various episodes noted by Padre Paolino from the spring and summer of 1918 leave no doubt that he was aware that extraordinary things were taking place in Padre Pio's life; yet he was unaware of Pio's deep inward struggle and where it was leading. Most of the phenomena that Paolino reported have only himself as witness. The culmination of Padre Pio's mystical life, however, was a phenomenon that would persist for nearly five decades and be closely observed and studied by several respected scientists: the visible stigmata.

In the late summer of 1918, with the Great War still raging, the terrible pandemic of Spanish influenza struck central Italy. It is believed that more than twenty million people perished worldwide in this epidemic, which forced an estimated billion people to their beds. In San Giovanni Rotondo, the situation was scarcely less appalling. Everyone seemed to be ill. What little commerce there was in the town ground to a standstill.

Padre Pio's spiritual daughters came to him terrified, begging him to save them from this wicked strain of the flu. "Never fear," he said to Maria Campanile. "Put yourself under the protection of the Virgin, do not sin, and the sickness will not overcome you." Although some of the ladies fell ill, none of them died.

During the course of the year, as we have seen, Pio had offered himself as a victim for the cessation of the war. He also offered himself as a victim for the college of which he was the principal. On September 17, he offered himself as a victim for ending the epidemic, but the flu continued unabated.

The two dozen or so boys now in the college were almost all ill. A doctor examined them and prescribed injections. Because he was understandably overworked, he taught Paolino and Pio how to give the injections. Since alcohol was not available, the doctor left some carbolic acid to sterilize the site of the injection. Unfortunately, the exhausted doctor didn't think to tell the friars that they were to dilute the carbolic acid before applying it to their pupils' posteriors. Thus, before giving the shots, they swabbed the acid on full strength. Because they spilled some of the solution on themselves in the process of giving the injections, Paolino was left with angry red spots on his fingers and Pio with similar marks on his hands. As for the boys, Paolino recounted. "You can imagine what happened to the part of the body we had disinfected for the injection!"

When the boys were able to sit properly again, they were mystified as to why Padre Pio, during his lectures, kept his hands covered with his shawl. Paolino also noted some peculiar behavior. While praying in the choir, he noticed red spots still in evidence on Pio's hands while those on his own fingers had already disappeared. Padre Pio reacted by covering his hands with his habit.

During the last week in September, Maria Campanile bustled into the friary and told Padre Paolino that she wanted to speak to him alone. Excitedly she asked him, "Do you know that Padre Pio has received the stigmata?" The guardian burst out laughing at the credulity of the country schoolmarm and explained that the marks she saw were the result of contact with carbolic acid.

Maria disagreed. A few days before, she said, she had gone to see Padre Pio, alarmed because one of her sisters had become ill with the flu. After Pio assured her that the sister would be all right, Maria noticed a mark on one of his hands. "Padre, did you burn yourself?" she asked. Padre Pio said nothing and hid his hands in his habit.

A day or so later, she continued, another spiritual daughter had been disturbed that Padre Pio did not offer his hand for her to kiss, as he usually did. Frustrated, she had seized it and was startled to find a red mark there. She said nothing to Padre Pio but wasted no time in telling all her friends that the good friar had the stigmata "just like Francis."

Padre Paolino was still sceptical, but Donna Maria persuaded him to try to ascertain the truth. Paolino entered Pio's room one day without knocking and found him at his desk. "Go on writing," he said. "This morning I've nothing to talk to you about." As Padre Pio wrote, Paolino was able to get a good look at his hands. The marks were definitely not those left by the carbolic acid. "Drawing closer to him," Padre Paolino reports, "I was first able to see the wound on the back and in the palm of the right hand. Then I saw the wound on the back of the left hand. I could not see the palm of the left hand because he was resting it on the table to steady his paper."[10]

Paolino left the room without saying anything and immediately wrote to Padre Benedetto, who was still minister provincial. He urged him to come at once, as Padre Pio had received the stigmata. Benedetto did not come but wrote Paolino a letter in which he instructed him to observe the strictest silence about the matter.

Benedetto did not get along with Paolino and perhaps took his report with a grain of salt. Moreover, he was aware that Padre Pio had displayed the stigmata before but that the marks had proved transitory. His attitude changed when Pio wrote him, speaking of a "Personage" who had wounded his entire being. "Everything inside of me is raining blood," he complained, "and often I am forced to watch this torrent of gore streaming forth out of my body."

"My dear boy," Benedetto wrote back, "tell me everything and tell me clearly. Don't hint at it. What exactly did this Personage do? From whence does the blood flow, and how many times a day or week? Did it happen to the hands and feet, and how? I want you to provide me with every detail through holy obedience."

Pio's answer to Benedetto's letter is the fullest extant account of the definitive stigmatization. Although elsewhere he fixes the date as September 18 (and once — clearly incorrectly — as October 20), in this letter he says the date was September 20. Pio was evidently the only member of the community in the friary at the time. Padre Paolino was out of town and Fra Nicola was on his quest. The boys from the college were in the garden and, so shortly after their injections, really in no condition to take an interest in the events that were taking place in the choir that morning when Padre Pio went there to make his thanksgiving after saying Mass.

In his letter to Padre Benedetto, he writes: "I was overtaken by a repose, similar to a deep sleep. All my internal and external senses and even the very faculties of my soul were steeped in indescribable quiet. In this state absolute silence reigned within me. . . . In a moment's time I was filled with a great peace and abandonment that blotted out every other worry or preoccupation. All this happened in a twinkling."[11]

On March 29, 1966, Padre Pio gave the following deposition to Padre Raffaele of Sant'Elia a Pianisi: "Between nine and ten in the morning, while my students were taking their recreation in the garden, I was alone in the choir, sitting on the bench in the spot reserved for the vicar. I was there making my thanksgiving after Holy Mass." At this point, as Pio had reported years earlier: "All of a sudden, a great light shone round about my eyes. In the midst of this light there appeared the wounded Christ. He said nothing to me before He disappeared."[12]

In his letter to Benedetto, Pio says that he saw the same "mysterious Being" that he beheld on the evening of August 5. While he does not specifically identify him as Christ, Pio says that the hands, feet, and side of the "Being" were dripping blood, and that his countenance terrified him.

In an interview on February 6, 1967, Padre Pio went into further detail. The crucifix in the choir, he said, transformed itself into the being: "From Him there came forth beams of light with shafts of flame that wounded me in the hands and feet. My side had already been wounded on the fifth of August of the same year."[13]

According to all accounts, when the ecstasy ended, Pio found his hands and feet perforated and bleeding. He lay on the floor, his side issuing great quantities of blood.

Pio's letter to Benedetto does not say what happened next. According to the interview granted to Marquess Don Giuseppe Orlando, Pio's priest-cousin, the padre found himself in too much pain to rise and had to drag himself the length of the corridor to his cell. Once there, he cleaned the oozing wounds and went to bed. As he told Orlando, "I looked at the wounds and wept, singing hymns of thanksgiving."

Although Pio was glad at what he considered a gift from God, he was mortified that others should see the stigmata. To Benedetto he expressed the hope that Jesus would remove its external signs:

> I will raise my voice and will not cease to implore Him until, in His mercy,
> He removes, not the wounds or the pain (this is impossible inasmuch as I
> want to be inebriated with pain), but these visible signs that are an embarrassment and an indescribable humiliation.[14]

Padre Agostino wrote some years later that the Lord did hear Padre Pio's prayer and, for a time, took away the visible wounds. He was not an eyewitness however. None of those who were recalled any such temporary disappearance. Maria Campanile recalled that the padre asked her to pray with him that the visible marks would vanish, as they had in 1910 and 1911. She noted, instead, that they became more pronounced.

The stigmata did not create an immediate sensation. During the closing months of 1918, with the Armistice that finally brought an end to the Great War, and with the continuing epidemic, few people were in a position to make these mysterious marks the primary object of their concern.

On September 27 Pio was shattered by a telegram from Pietrelcina. Almost the entire Forgione family had been stricken with influenza. Pio's middle sister, Pellegrina, who had lost a baby several years before, lost her last surviving child, fourteen-month-old Alfredo. The little "Franceschino," the only child of Pio's brother Michele (still in Long Island), was stricken and seems never to have recovered fully, dying the next year at the age of eleven. Pio's mother was gravely ill. Hardest hit, however, was the family of the oldest sister, Felicita. Her oldest child, Giuseppina, was left permanently weakened and a prey to the tuberculosis that carried her to the grave several years later at the age of eighteen. The youngest child, two-year-old Ettoruccio ("little Hector"), suffered brain damage and was left subject to grand mal epileptic seizures. On September 22 the middle child, Pellegrino, went up to his father crying: "Papa! Papa! My head hurts! My head hurts!" He collapsed and died before sundown.[15]

Felicita was ill at the time, not only with the flu, but with complications from a recent miscarriage. She kept asking for Pellegrino. Her husband insisted on telling her that Pellegrino was playing with the other children in the street. She continued to lose ground until, on September 25, she raised herself on her pillow and shouted at her husband, "You deceived me!"

"But, my dear Felicita, why are you talking like this?"

"You deceived me! You said that Pellegrino was playing outside and instead, no, he's dead."

"What's making you talk like this?" replied Masone. "What's going through your mind?"

"No, he's dead, it's true," said Felicita. "See, Pellegrino is coming with all the angels, with all the child angels about him. He's coming to fetch me, and behind him, I see the face of Padre Pio!" She never spoke again. A half hour later, she was dead. She was twenty-nine. Padre Pio was almost wild with grief at the death of the sister whom he regarded as the true saint of the family. Years later he would say of her: "She was a saint. . . . I never saw her upset. Even with all the woes that befell her, she was always smiling. From childhood on, God kept her good and simple. . . . [She] surpassed everyone else in the family in goodness and loveliness." To his stricken parents he wrote:

> What can I say to you when every word I utter is strangled in my throat by the sharpness of my grief? My dear parents, in the harshness and bitterness of grief, I can do nothing except exclaim, "Just Thou art, O Lord, and righteous are Thy judgments." God gave me my poor sister and God has taken her away. Blessed be His Holy Name for it. It is only in these exclamations and in this resignation that I find sufficient strength not to succumb under the weight of grief. To this resignation to God's will I exhort you, too. In it you will find with me some respite for your grief.[16]

Soon Pio himself was ill with the flu, but, to his immense displeasure, he recovered. Assailed by the aftermath of his illness, by his grief, and by the physical pain and embarrassment of the persisting stigmata, Pio wrote Benedetto on November 13: "Unhappy man that I am! Who will free me from the body of this death? Who will free me from this . . . furnace that burns me with inextinguishable fire?" He goes on to say that all the assurances, declarations, and counsels from him and from Agostino vanish from his mind as soon as he receives them. He feels alone and complains that his heart is "turned to stone with pain" and his body "frozen rigid from the agony that is experienced in the soul, which spills over into the body."

By January 1919, Pio is a little more cheerful and writes of spiritual consolations: "I feel as if I were drowned in an immense sea of the love of my Beloved. . . . Sweet is the bitterness of this love and sweet is the burden!"

With the war over and the epidemic subsiding, the fame of the stigmatic began to spread beyond San Giovanni Rotondo. Padre Paolino blamed this on the failure of Padre Pio's spiritual daughters to keep their promise to maintain absolute silence about the stigmata. Paolino wrote, perhaps ungallantly:

> Women . . . are not made to keep secrets. And even when they have good intentions . . . they still have to reveal that secret to an intimate friend. . . . And then it happens that from the intimate friend, the secret passes to another intimate friend until, at length, the secret becomes public knowledge.[17]

This was precisely the way word of the stigmata spread through San Giovanni in late 1918 and early 1919. Maria Campanile confessed in writing that after

Paolino had confirmed to her that Pio did indeed appear to have the stigmata, she ignored his pleas for silence and told her mother and sisters. By early 1919, news of the stigmata was beginning to filter to the outside world, and Padre Pio was on the threshold of a ministry of colossal magnitude.

Holiness or Hysteria?

Few phenomena are as baffling as the stigmata. Since the first recorded instance, that of St. Francis of Assisi in 1224, three to four hundred Christians have exhibited spontaneous wounds suggesting one or more of the injuries sustained by Jesus in the process of his crucifixion. A French physician by the name of Imbert-Gourbeyre, whose exhaustive study was published in 1894, counted 321 genuine stigmatics (or stigmatists) up to that time. Of these, all were Roman Catholic, and the overwhelming majority of them were female and Italian.[1]

The stigmata have taken a variety of forms. The best-known and best-studied cases, other than that of Padre Pio, are those of St. Francis and of Pio's contemporary, the Bavarian laywoman Theresa Neumann (1898-1962).

The wounds of St. Francis, like those of Padre Pio, were found on the hands, feet, and side. While Padre Pio's side wound was on the left, St. Francis's was on the right, corresponding to the position of the wound visible on the Holy Shroud (which, as far as we know, neither man saw). St. Francis's hand and foot wounds also differed from those borne by Padre Pio. In the case of the Seraphic Father, there was not only a wound in the flesh, but, in addition, in both hands and feet there were fleshy growths that had the appearance of nails. Thomas of Celano, an early biographer, writes:

> His hands and feet seemed to be pierced through the midst with nails, the
> heads of the nails showing in the palms of the hands and upper sides of the
> feet, and their points showing on the other side; the heads of the nails were
> round and black in the hands and feet, while the points were long, bent,
> and, as it were, turned back, being formed of the flesh itself, and protruding
> therefrom.[2]

As we shall see, one physician seized upon the difference in appearance of the hand and foot wounds of St. Francis and Padre Pio in order to argue against the authenticity of the latter-day mystic. Although the wound in the side of the Seraphic Father was on the right and not on the left, as was Pio's, it was of similar appearance. The wound in St. Francis's side appeared to have been made by a spear. It often gushed blood and soaked Francis's clothing.

Padre Pio knew of Theresa Neumann and spoke favorably of her. In 1942 the Bavarian lady sent Pio her greetings and asked him to pray for her. Like Padre Pio, she was reportedly subject to bilocations, visions, ecstasies, raptures, and other mystic phenomena. She too was gifted with discernment of spirits and frequently saw and conversed orally with her guardian angel and other spirits. Like him, she bore the stigmata on her hands, feet, and left side. Further, at certain times, Neumann's wounds marked her head and face. Her stigmata were also different from those of Padre Pio in that they underwent major changes during the course of the thirty-six years they were visible.

Louise Lateau (1850-1883), a French stigmatist, also had reddish marks on her hands and feet. Every Friday these marks would each develop a blister, from which blood would flow profusely for several hours. At the same time, blood would gush from three nearly imperceptible points in her left side, which otherwise did not show any signs of a lesion.

Thus, historically, the stigmata have taken many different forms. St. Clara of Montefalco (1268-1308), an Italian Augustinian nun, bore her stigmata internally. During an autopsy, a fleshy growth of cardiac tissue shaped exactly like a crucifix was found inside her heart. During her lifetime, she maintained that she had been stigmatized in her heart; after her death, her claim was confirmed.[3] Again, St. Rita Ferdinando of Cascia (1381-1457), another Italian Augustinian nun, had a stigma in the middle of her forehead. Unlike the wounds of Padre Pio, which are widely attested to have emitted a perfume-like aroma, St. Rita's wound produced such a stench that for fifteen years she had to be segregated from the rest of her community.

The stigmata are no guarantee of sanctity. Of the several hundred stigmatists who have been carefully observed since the thirteenth century, only sixty-one have been canonized or beatified. Some, like St. Francis and St. Catherine of Siena, were obviously well balanced; others seem to have exhibited symptoms of neurosis and hysteria. Moreover, devout Mohammedans have been known to exhibit wounds similar to those suffered in battle by the Prophet, and persons allegedly possessed by Satan have sometimes been known to manifest wounds peculiar to their unsavory condition. We have, moreover, been talking only of stigmata that are of apparent spontaneous origin. For every genuine stigmatic, whether holy or hysterical, saintly or satanic, there are at least two whose wounds are self-inflicted.

Over the years, Padre Pio's wounds were carefully examined by as many as twenty people, including at least seven physicians. They included Professor Giuseppe Bastianelli (1862-1923), personal physician to Pope Benedict XV. Unfortunately, no transcript of his written evaluation is known to exist. Dr. Luigi Romanelli, physician in chief of the City Hospital at Barletta, who examined the wounds several times between May 1919 and November 1920, did leave an extensive written report. So did Dr. Amico Bignami (1862-1929), professor of pathology at the Royal University of Rome, who examined Padre Pio during the summer of 1919. There is also a detailed report from Dr. Giorgio Festa (d. 1940), a surgeon in private practice in Rome who studied Padre Pio between 1919 and 1925. Dr. Giuseppe Sala, who served as Pio's personal physician during the latter years of the friar's life, left a report, as did Dr. Andrea Cardone, the Forgione family physician, who examined the stigmata when they first appeared in 1910 as well as after 1918. We also have written accounts by several of the friars who were in close attendance on Padre Pio when he was an old man and often needed assistance in dressing and bathing.

Bignami and Festa both produced descriptions of the priest's general bodily appearance. Bignami commented on the friar's "delicate constitution." In the past, Pio's complexion had been described as ruddy or florid. Bignami found him "pale," with a "sickly, suffering look." His physique was slight, his muscles weak, and flabby. Nevertheless, the pathologist saw fit to note that "the expression of his face is full of goodness and sincerity," and that, despite his feeble appearance, he was able to work fifteen to sixteen hours straight without a bite to eat. He also noted that when Pio did eat, he consumed very little.[4]

Festa, describing Pio as "slight" and "rather emaciated," went on to remark: "His face is pale and always lit up by a very clear gaze. . . . Sometimes his eyes were half closed, as if he were waiting to welcome an inspiration." Like Bignami, Festa noted that Pio ate very little but nevertheless seemed full of "spiritual energy."

Padre Pio's wounds were clearly visible on both the upper and lower surfaces of his hands. Cardone, Festa, and Sala agree that the wounds were circular and approximately three quarters of an inch in diameter. There is some disagreement, however, as to the depth of the lesions. Dr. Festa said that "the depth of the lesions . . . does not seem to be very great," but conceded that the wounds involved "the thickness of the subcutaneous tissue because, when Padre Pio is asked to make a fist, he is not able to close his hand completely." Romanelli stated that the wounds were "not superficial." Cardone recalled that the wounds "pierced the palms of the hands completely through, so much so that one could see light through them. . . ." Padre Alessio Parente, who attended Padre Pio in the 1960s, wrote in 1969 that he believed that the wounds on the upper surface of the hand were about a half inch deep.[5] The same friar stated to me in 1978 that one could see light through the wounds. Likewise, Father Joseph Pius Martin, also an eyewitness, informed me in September of that year:

"The wounds went all the way through the hands. If he held his hand in front of a window, you could see light."

Those who examined Padre Pio observed that the lesions on his feet were similar to those on his hands. Dr. Sala states specifically that the wounds in the feet, like those in the hands, were about three quarters of an inch in diameter.

Romanelli described the wounds on the hands and feet as being covered with reddish-brown scabs. Bignami saw them as "little rounded zones of skin," perfectly symmetrical, with black scabs. Festa noted that the wounds in the hands were circular, with a black scab covering a reddish-brown lesion. Sala also observed that the wounds were circular, and Padre Alessio recounted how they were covered, when he saw them, with large, thick crusts, or scabs. Father Joseph Pius, who never saw Pio's feet, described to me the "crusts of dried blood on either side of the hands."

Both Bignami and Sala commented on the clean, clearly defined edges of the stigmata, something apparently unusual in ordinary wounds of long duration. Festa wrote, "At the edges of the lesions, the skin is perfectly normal and does not show any sign of edema, of penetration, or of redness, even when examined with a good magnifying glass. . . ."[6] Romanelli also observed that there were no signs of redness or inflammation in the surrounding skin.

The one change that did take place over the years in Padre Pio's wounds had to do with the edematous, or dropsical, swelling of the hands and feet. Although Romanelli, Bignami, and Festa were unanimous in 1919 in their statements that there was no sign of edema in the hands or feet, by the time Sala took over Pio's care in the 1950s, his extremities were swollen. In late years, his feet were so enormously swollen that one colleague said that they looked like melons. This was evidently due to the old man's failing heart and lungs rather than to any inflammation. Sala noted that there was no trace of infection. When Romanelli examined Padre Pio, he found no bleeding, nor did the wounds seem to be bleeding when Bignami made his examination. But when Festa studied them, little drops of blood oozed from the edges. Sala spoke of the wounds "flowing" with "shining blood."

As for the wound in the left side, most witnesses attest that it was shaped like a cross. Padre Paolino, who observed it in the summer of 1919, made that observation and said that he understood that the first slash had come at the time of the "transverberation," in August 1918, and the second, along with the lesions of the hand and foot, a month and a half later. Romanelli, however, was positive that when he examined Padre Pio in June 1919, the side wound "did not have the shape of a cross at all" but was, rather, "a clean cut parallel to the ribs," just under three inches long. Both Bignami and Festa, however, state that the wound was in fact cruciform.[7] Father Joseph Pius, who saw the wound in the side in the mid-1960s, stated to me in the 1978 interview that it was in the form of a cross. All witnesses agree that it was about three inches long.

As to the depth of the side wound, there is disagreement. Romanelli said it was "not very deep." Bignami stated that the skin had not even been penetrated. Festa described the wound as a pale, pink mark, like a recent scar. Later witnesses, though, were of the opinion that the wound in the side was very deep. Padre Pellegrino of Sant'Elia a Pianisi, who, like Alessio and Joseph Pius, attended Padre Pio in old age, said that the wound appeared "very deep." Of a similar opinion was Dr. Sala. The wound in the side bled more than the other four lesions. Romanelli noted that it bled profusely during his examination. The wound was not bleeding, however, when Bignami examined it. Although it was not bleeding at the time of Festa's observations, there were signs of recent profuse bleeding.[8]

Festa was explicit in stating that the wounds in the palms and backs of the hands, in the soles and tops of the feet, and in the chest region were "the only lesions that exist on the body of Padre Pio." The rest of his skin was very fair and white, "with all the normal, perfect characteristics of skin."[9] In 1943, however, Padre Pio gave one of his spiritual daughters, Cleonice Morcaldi, a white linen undershirt to wash. She was horrified to find it splattered with blood from top to bottom, as if the friar had developed wounds suggestive of the Lord's scourging. There is no record of anyone actually observing any lesions on Pio's body except for those in his hands, feet, and side.

There remains some question as to how much blood Padre Pio lost. Some authors state that he lost a pint of blood a day. None of the physicians who examined him ventured to make an estimate. Had he shed a pint of blood a day, his survival would have been truly miraculous. Even with a much less substantial loss, however, considering Pio's apparent ill health and his abstemious diet, the fact that he could endure such a work load day in and day out for many years is itself a marvel.

All the physicians who examined the wounds noted that they were extremely sensitive and painful to the touch. Whenever the overzealous grabbed his hand and squeezed it, he cried out in pain. His pat answer to those who asked whether the stigmata hurt was, "Do you think the Lord gave them to me for decoration?" Because of the wounds in his hands, Pio was given permission to wear a fingerless glove that hid the wounded part of the hand. Because of the lesions in his feet, he was permitted to replace the customary Capuchin sandals with slipperlike shoes. Even so, he walked very slowly and found it uncomfortable to be on his feet for any length of time.

A mysterious aroma emanated from the wounds. Romanelli noticed it when he first examined Padre Pio. In fact, he remarked to a priest who was with him that he thought it unsuitable for a friar to use perfume. When he determined that Pio was not using any perfume or cologne, he consulted several scientists, inquiring as to whether blood could, under any circumstances, have a sweet odor. They told him that this was impossible.

Bignami said nothing about the perfume, but Festa, though he had no sense of smell, was aware of it. He wrote:

> I can affirm that on my first visit I took from [Padre Pio's] side a small cloth stained with blood, which I brought back with me to Rome for a microscopic examination. I personally, being entirely deprived of the sense of smell, did not notice any special emanation. But a distinguished official and other persons with me in the automobile on our return to Rome from San Giovanni, not knowing that I brought with me that piece of cloth enclosed in a case, despite the strong ventilation owing to the speed of the automobile, smelled the fragrance very distinctly and assured me that it precisely corresponded to the perfume that emanates from the person of Padre Pio. In Rome, . . . for a long time after, the same cloth conserved in a cabinet in my study filled the room with perfume—so much so that many patients who came to consult me spontaneously asked me for an explanation of its origin.[10]

If medical men were unable to arrive at an explanation of the fragrance that rose from Padre Pio's wounds, they were equally at a loss to explain the stigmata themselves. Romanelli had been summoned at the request of Padre Benedetto. Nothing is known about his personality, his career, or his religious orientation — although the fact that he was scandalized at the thought that a friar should use perfume would seem to indicate traditional pious sensibilities. When Benedetto asked Romanelli about the nature and cause of Padre Pio's wounds, the physician replied, "From all that I know and all that I can tell, these lesions cannot be classified among ordinary injuries." When Padre Benedetto asked him point-blank whether these could be a true case of stigmata, Romanelli answered: "I have never found a clinical indication that would authorize me to classify the injuries. I do not wish to speak of 'stigmata' because doing so would be outside the competence of a physician."[11]

More is known of Amico Bignami. He was sent to examine Padre Pio by the Holy See. Bignami, one of Italy's foremost pathologists, was an outspoken atheist. In vain he groped for an adequate scientific explanation for the stigmata. He offered the hypothesis that the wounds were "necrobiotic" and "auto-suggestive," deriving from a "morbid state." That is, they were psychologically self-induced and characterized by the death of the tissues in a given area. What he meant by a "morbid state" he did not specify. He also felt that the wounds were kept from healing through Pio's liberal use of iodine as a disinfectant. The wounds, he concluded, were: "a multiple neurotic necrosis of the skin, perhaps unconsciously caused by a phenomenon of suggestion, artificially maintained by the use of chemicals."[12]

Because of his hunch that the stigmata were kept open by being continually drenched in iodine, Bignami ordered that Padre Pio's wounds be bandaged and sealed for eight days. This was in keeping with the standard procedure devised by Dr. Agostino Gemelli, a renowned physician, psychologist, educator, and theologian, who made extensive studies of the stigmata, and who would shortly afterward visit Pio himself. Whenever Gemelli examined a stigmatic, he bandaged the wounds for several days. He maintained that in every single instance in his experience, the scabs came off with the removal of the bandage, and the epidermis had healed.

With the sanction of Padre Benedetto, the provincial, Bignami ordered that all iodine and carbolic acid, which Pio had been using to guard against infection and, apparently, in an attempt to heal the wounds, be removed from the friar's room. Bignami bandaged and sealed the wounds in the presence of two eyewitnesses, Padre Paolino and Padre Placido. After eight days, there was no sign of healing. When the bandages were removed, his hands bled more profusely than ever. While saying Mass, Pio needed to wipe his hands constantly with handkerchiefs to keep from spoiling the altar paraments with blood.

When he learned what had happened, Bignami did not know what to make of Padre Pio's wounds. Eventually he seems to have come around to the belief that they were true stigmata and a gift from the God in whom he heretofore had not believed. A decade later, when he was stricken with an incurable illness, he seemed pleased to learn that Padre Pio had sent him his blessing.

Giorgio Festa, who was dispatched by the minister general of the Order, was a devout and faithful Catholic. He served as house doctor at the Capuchin general headquarters at Rome. This in itself would not indicate a bias in favor of Padre Pio because, at the time, many of the leaders of the Capuchin Order were undecided about the stigmata. Festa, however, after examining Padre Pio, was firmly convinced that the wounds were a genuine instance of the stigmata.

Unlike Romanelli and Bignami, Festa had the opportunity to observe the wounds over a period of nearly a decade. In September 1925, when he operated on Padre Pio to repair a hernia, he observed the wounds again and noted that they were unchanged from six years earlier. As the surgical incision healed normally, he was able to rule out the possibility of hemophilia or other abnormalities in the body's healing mechanism. He made the same observation a few years later when he operated on a cyst on Padre Pio's neck.

Pio himself showed no interest whatsoever in attempts by physicians and scientists to explain his stigmata. He was unalterably convinced that the wounds were the gift of God, though he would have preferred to suffer the pains of the Passion without any visible markings to draw the curiosity or adulation of the world. Whenever people suggested that the stigmata were caused by too great a concentration on Christ's passion, Padre Pio told them: "Go out to the fields and look very closely at a bull. Concentrate on him with all your might. Do this and see if horns grow on your head!"[13] When asked why his wounds were in the center of his hands and not in the wrists . . . Padre Pio replied, "Oh it would be too much to have them exactly as they were in the case of Christ."

The Rumor of Sanctity

By the middle of 1919, Padre Pio's hope that the war, terrible as it was, might prove a health-giving purge for Italy, and the dawn of a spiritual reawakening, was being fulfilled in his dramatically growing ministry. In Italy as elsewhere, men and women were emerging from the general carnage disillusioned and broken. Many political philosophers of the eighteenth and nineteenth centuries believed that the world was getting better and better, that ultimately mankind would build an earthly utopia of peace and justice and brotherhood — with no help from God or religion. Now this utopian vision lay shattered. While many gave themselves over to bitterness and despair, others tried to assuage the pain of their loss through the indulgence of the senses. Still others, deeply affected by man's helplessness, turned to the supernatural in their search for meaning.

The news of Padre Pio's stigmata, coming as it did just after the end of the Great War, found especially fertile soil. Large numbers of people were looking for someone who was truly close to God, someone who had answers to life's problems. Dissatisfied with the vague, relativistic teachings of secular philosophers and the abstruse and tentative doctrines of scholarly theologians, they sought someone to speak to them clearly, to tell them how to live, how to know God. Now there was rumor of someone who bore the wounds of Christ on his mortal body. In the minds of many Italians, the stigmata were a sign that a person had been marked by God, a proof of divine intimacy. Such a person was someone to whom people might turn for a solution to their dilemma. That someone, for growing numbers, was Padre Pio Forgione of Pietrelcina.

News of the stigmata was spreading throughout Italy. Padre Paolino, despite his disgust at Maria Campanile for her feminine inability to keep a secret, quickly informed his own sister Assunta in Foggia, who appeared at San Giovanni

Rotondo in the spring of 1919 with a carful of friends. The very next day a busload of people from Foggia arrived. By the close of the day, one of the group, a man who claimed to have been blind, insisted that he had received his sight after being blessed by Padre Pio. The friars had no opportunity to check his story, but the man, whose name has not been recorded, straightaway made for Foggia, where he went about for days telling everyone he met about the miracle.

Padre Benedetto had finally agreed to examine Padre Pio's stigmata in March 1919. When he left San Giovanni, he too was convinced. "They are not spots or blemishes," he wrote to Agostino, "but real wounds, perforating the hands and feet. . . . The wound in the side is a real gash that issues either blood or bloody fluid. Friday it issued blood."[1] News of the stigmata eventually reached the general headquarters of the Capuchin Order in Rome.

Five priests just discharged from the military were assigned to San Giovanni Rotondo in the spring of 1919: Padres Placido of San Marco in Lamis, age thirty-three; Basilio of Mirabello, age thirty; Raffaele of San Giovanni Rotondo, age thirty-seven; Damaso of Sant'Elia a Pianisi, age thirty; and Anastasio of Roio, age thirty-three. Immediately they found themselves swamped with work.

The life of the friary and church of Our Lady of Grace now revolved entirely around Padre Pio's ministry. By May 1919, Padre Paolino noted that it was "raining letters." A room in the friary had to be set aside for the handling of correspondence, and Padre Raffaele was assigned the task. The other priests found much of their day occupied in hearing confessions. Because of Padre Pio, there was a growing demand for this sacrament. Most of the penitents were women. Padre Pio, stationed in the sacristy, was able to handle the male penitents all by himself; but Padres Paolino, Placido, Basilio, Damaso, and Anastasio all had to work to hear the confessions of the women.

By late spring, men were waiting up to two weeks for an opportunity to make their confessions to Pio. As there were no hotels in San Giovanni Rotondo, many slept outdoors in the fields. Padre Paolino was astounded by the great numbers of farmers who neglected their crops to spend a fortnight in an effort to see the Man of God. The crowds increased as the numerous pilgrimages to the nearby time-honored shrines of Our Lady Crowned and St. Michael the Archangel began stopping at the friary too, to see Padre Pio.

By summer the scene was one of pandemonium. Padre Paolino described the little church, which held up to two hundred people, as fairly "invaded" by people from all walks of life — not only peasants, but doctors, lawyers, and journalists. Many were sick people who trusted that they would be cured. There were also many who believed they were possessed and wanted to be freed from the devil, as well as multitudes drawn simply by curiosity. Inevitably, too, there were pickpockets, who plied their trade not only in the streets and courtyard but in the very church.[2] Even Padre Pio was not exempt from thievery. In April 1919 he complained to Padre Benedetto that someone had walked off with his breviary.

The clothing of the friars was laundered in town. Whenever Padre Pio's underwear or night clothing was sent out, it was not returned. In its place was sent an identical but new garment. The original one, the friars soon discovered, was cut up into pieces and sold. Village entrepreneurs were even daubing pieces of cloth in chicken blood and selling them as articles of clothing stained by blood from Padre Pio's stigmata. The overzealous, on some occasions, forced their way into the sacristy to cut pieces from cassocks, chasubles, and albs that they had reason to believe had been used by Padre Pio. They even went so far as to remove the straw from chairs where he had been seated! To make matters worse, fistfights were breaking out among men disputing places in line for confession.

At length, policemen had to be assigned to the friary to keep order. Whenever Padre Pio appeared in public,· they had to surround him to keep the faithful from cutting his clothing right off of his back!

Padre Pio often put in a sixteen-hour day, mostly spent in hearing confessions. He spent his evening hours trying to keep up the correspondence with his spiritual daughters and usually did not retire until 1 A.M. That left him with little more than two hours to sleep. He did not mind; he was glad for the opportunity to lead souls to Christ. He expressed his attitude in the following letter to Benedetto, who had reproached him for not writing to him more often:

> I haven't a moment free. All my time is spent in freeing my brethren from the bonds of Satan. I pray you, do not afflict me more by making an appeal to charity like the others do, because the greatest charity is in snatching souls bound to Satan and winning them for Christ. And this is just what I am doing . . . day and night. . . .[3]

Likewise, one day when Padre Paolino groused that the crowds "have completely taken away our liberty and cause us so much work that we have no time to rest," Pio retorted: "I'm surprised you would talk like that! . . . You know very well that when preachers proclaim God's Word in church, they have to work hard just to get a few people there to hear their sermon. It's worse when it comes to confessions. People stay away from the confessional except when they have to fulfill their minimum obligations. Now, instead, when the Lord, through His grace and without any effort on our part, sends us so abundant a congregation, you nonetheless complain in this way and would want to let many souls go without being reconciled to their Lord! Let us work diligently and thank the Lord who has permitted us to work for His glory and for the good of souls."[4]

Inevitably there was criticism. The secular clergy of San Giovanni took an especially jaundiced view of Padre Pio's celebrity. Great numbers of people began to forsake the city churches to worship at Our Lady of Grace and make their confessions to the friars, dismissing the archpriest, Don Giuseppe Prencipe, and his staff as hypocrites and spiritual bankrupts.

One of the earliest and most vociferous critics of Padre Pio was a priest named Don Giovanni Miscio (1886-1967), a teacher in an elementary school. Early in 1919 he began to write to the newspapers, to Archbishop Gagliardi, to the Capuchin minister general, and even to the Vatican, accusing the friars of "putting Padre Pio on display for the purpose of making money."[5] He alleged that the Capuchins were running a lucrative business, hawking materials supposedly worn or handled by the stigmatized priest.

Several civil authorities were likewise hostile. One of them was a prominent politician named Fraccacreta, who was serving as a member of Italy's parliament. A Mason, Fraccacreta was hostile to all organized religion. One Sunday, in his hometown of San Severo, a certain Canon Rubino, enthusiastic about Padre Pio, announced from the pulpit that Fraccacreta had been converted through the ministry of Padre Pio. It turned out that the convert had been a nephew by the same name. When the uncle heard about the sermon, he sought out the canon and punched him in the face. In June, Fraccacreta complained bitterly to the minister of the interior about the "farce" being perpetrated by the Capuchins, and asked that police be dispatched to break up "the dirty business."[6]

Although the civil authorities took no steps to interfere, Padre Benedetto felt that some actions had to be taken to prevent abuse. Accordingly, he ordered Fra Nicola, whom Miscio had accused of soliciting money in the name of Padre Pio instead of the Order, to cease making his quests outside the friary walls. Henceforth he was merely to sit at a desk in a corner of the church and receive any offerings that the faithful cared to make. Benedetto saw to it that Pio's escort between the sacristy and the church was increased and that police cordoned off the altar area from the crowds while the padre was saying Mass. All vestments and anything else the padre used were to be carefully locked away. Moreover, the friars were ordered to exercise a "prudent reserve" in discussing Padre Pio.

For the time being, Padre Pio was allowed to exercise his ministry in relative freedom. He celebrated High Mass at noon after hearing confessions all morning. After Mass he remained in the sacristy so that the women, who did not have the opportunity to make their confessions to him, could kiss his hand and exchange a few words with him. So that he could greet those unable to find a place either in the cramped church or tiny sacristy, Padre Pio was allowed to go to a window and bless the throngs that gathered in the courtyard at certain hours. The blessing of the crowds, however, drew immediate criticism from the city clergy, who claimed that this was proof that the Capuchins were putting the stigmatist on display.

To offset the growing criticism of those who insisted that Padre Pio was a fake, Benedetto ordered a series of examinations by Dr. Romanelli, the first of which took place in May 1918. Unfortunately, this event led to further problems when Padre Raffaele, the correspondence secretary, got hold of Romanelli's preliminary report (stating that the wounds, although not scientifically explicable, were genuine) and leaked it to the press. In doing so he drew greater crowds — and Padre Benedetto's wrath.

When he read the issue of the Naples *Mattino* in which Romanelli's report was reproduced almost word for word, the provincial flew into one of his rages and wrote to Padre Paolino that he was risking the fury of the Holy See by permitting such privileged information to be disclosed to the public. He raged that what Raffaele had done was illegal and insubordinate. "Padre Raffaele ought to be sent away at once!" he fumed. Benedetto then forbade, "under pain of mortal sin," any member of the community to disclose any detailed information on Padre Pio. To do so, he said, would be "detrimental to the decorum of our Order as well as the cause of Padre Pio."[7]

Because of these directives, many who were interested in the more extraordinary aspects of Padre Pio's ministry often felt that the Capuchins were showing an excessive and unwarranted reluctance to share information on the various "miracles" that were being reported with ever greater frequency. This, of course, led some to wonder whether the Capuchins were chary in divulging details about cures and other "miracles" because such things never, in fact, took place.

Padre Benedetto and the new guardian, Padre Lorenzo, wanted to avoid all appearance of commercialism or charlatanry. With hostile city clergy writing the Vatican that miracles were being "invented" by the "monks" to bring in cash, Padre Pio's superiors felt that it was prudent to avoid speaking about miracles and other emotionally charged matters.

Despite this reserve, there are several unexplained occurrences from this period that have been at least partially documented. One of them concerned San Giovanni Rotondo's village idiot, a gaping, grotesque-looking fellow named Francesco Santarello. He was so pathetically clubfooted that he was unable to walk. Instead, he dragged himself about on his knees, supported by a pair of miniature crutches. The unfortunate little man labored up the hill to the friary to beg bread and soup, as he had done for years. Poor Santarello was a fixture in the community. Some of the wicked children of the town loved to tease the unhappy beggar, going so far at times as to knock the crutches from under his shoulders and howl with glee as he tumbled onto the pavement.

One day Santarello was positioned, as usual, near the door of the cloister, soliciting alms. A huge crowd had gathered, waiting for Padre Pio to emerge and enter the church. As Pio passed by, Santarello cried out, "Padre Pio, give me a blessing!"

Without stopping, Pio looked at him and said, "Throw away your crutches!"

Stunned, Santarello stood like a statue. This time Padre Pio stopped and shouted, "I *said*, 'Throw away your crutches!'" Without another word, Pio entered the church to say Mass.

In front of dozens of people, Santarello threw his crutches away, and for the first time in his life, began to walk on his deformed feet to the great amazement of his fellow townsfolk, who but a few minutes before had seen him lurching about, as always, on his knees.

Santarello lived for some time after that. He never used his crutches again and was able to function quite well with the aid of a cane. Miscio and other city clergy contended that it was not truly a miracle because there was no substantial change in Santarello's physical condition. His feet remained just as badly clubbed as ever, with the toes pointed in the same direction as the heels, and there was no apparent remission of his mental retardation. Yet, for the little beggar and his acquaintances, that he could now walk rather than crawl was miracle enough.[8]

One day, also in 1919, a priest from Florence came to Our Lady of Grace with a Jewish friend. Padre Naldi explained that his friend, who had recently become totally blind, had come to ask Padre Pio to intercede with God for a cure.

It is unfortunate that none of the friars ever saw fit to record whether the man's loss of sight was the result of cataracts, an accident, a war injury, or some disease. No one even saw fit to record his name. Padre Paolino, who was an eyewitness, simply left a few notes about the incident. There was no doubt that the Jew was blind. Someone had even to help him eat, putting his plate in front of him, cutting his bread and meat, and placing the glass of wine in his hand.

Padre Pio, who had a great respect for "God's ancient people," welcomed the Jew. However, he told him: "The Lord will not grant you the grace of physical sight unless you first receive sight for your soul. After you are baptized, then the Lord will give you your sight."[9]

Several months later the Jew returned, this time without his dark glasses. He explained that he had, despite opposition from his family, become a Christian and been baptized. At first he was discouraged when his blindness persisted. But gradually, over a period of months, his sight returned, and the doctor who had previously informed him that he was hopelessly blind now conceded that his eyes were in perfect condition. Padre Paolino kept in touch with the man and reported that nearly thirty years later, his vision was still perfect.[10]

We have a letter from Padre Paolino recounting to Padre Benedetto two other occurrences that he considered miraculous. In June 1919 a young woman identified only as "the niece of the archpriest of Cagli" asked Padre Pio for the grace of healing. Her legs were so unequal in length that she could just barely touch the ground with the tip of the foot of the shorter leg. Immediately after speaking to Padre Pio, she was able to rest both feet squarely on the ground and walk normally. According to Paolino, this event took place in front of numerous witnesses.[11]

That same month a more remarkable healing took place. Maria Scotto-DiFesta, forty-nine years old, came from a town near Naples. Her right leg had been paralyzed for eighteen years. After visiting Padre Pio and soliciting his prayers, she was riding home in a car. Suddenly she felt sensation returning to her paralyzed limb. When she and her friends reached Foggia, to their amazement, she was able to get out of the car and walk normally and unaided.[12]

There were also reports of other supernatural occurrences. A potter from the nearby town of Torremaggiore recounted how he was given to swearing until one night he swore "in a horrendous way" because his kiln would not light. To his horror and amazement, Padre Pio materialized before his eyes, scolded him for his blasphemies, and then made the kiln ignite![13]

There are numerous testimonies about lives changed and redirected through Padre Pio. One such instance concerns Prince Karl Klugkist (1871-1948), an exiled Russian aristocrat who lived in Florence and made a living as a painter. He was deeply involved in oriental mysticism and the occult. After reading the Romanelli material in the Naples *Mattino*, he felt compelled to seek out this new guru from San Giovanni Rotondo. Going to the friary, he asked a member of the community whether he could speak with "the saint." Klugkist was ushered through the courtyard to a small door. He describes his visit in some detail:

> I pushed the door energetically and arrived almost on top of a Capuchin who was seated on a chair, leaning with arms crossed on the back of a second chair, while a man from the country knelt on the floor beside him and made his confession. The Capuchin raised his head slowly and looked at me. It was Padre Pio!

The room was packed with men. From behind the door at the other end of the room, Klugkist could hear the noise of a scuffle as several inpatient farmers were trying to force their way past the police guards. The painter then withdrew to a corner of the room to prepare his confession. After a few seconds, however, he found himself fascinated by the beauty of Pio's face and by his whole demeanor. He goes on:

> I was able to observe . . . from the expression on his face that he only heard the words of the penitent . . . he didn't see him with bodily eyes. His body and especially his crossed arms were strangely immobile, almost cataleptic. At the end of each confession he became quite animated and answered in a clear voice, the tone of which revealed his brotherly love for the penitent. After he had spoken, his face always changed completely. His whole attention seemed to be fixed on the heart. While there had been a radiance about his head and torso before, it now seemed to be extinguished.

Klugkist then relates a most curious phenomenon, which, as far as we know, is the only instance of Padre Pio's speaking in tongues:

> Slowly, in guttural tones, he recited a rhythmic prayer, a mystical formula, in an Oriental language unknown to me. I remember the words which recurred continually: "Adai nanda" and "nanda." This unusual and mys-

terious invocation aroused my curiosity and I regretted being unable to ask
him for an explanation.

Having uttered this strange invocation, Padre Pio "raised his eyes, his face
shone, and with a solemn gesture he gave absolution." A half dozen men passed
ahead of Klugkist. The last was a priest who asked to see Padre Pio's stigmata.

"Thomas," chided the padre, "have you to touch in order to believe?" Nevertheless, he uncovered his hands and permitted the clergyman to examine and
kiss the wounds.

When it was his turn to confess, Klugkist said to Pio, "I came here hoping to
have a chat with you."

"Impossible, my good man!" replied the padre. "I don't allow people to chat
with me because there are too many. If you have something to tell me, say it
now, during confession." And so Klugkist

> started to tell him without any sort of order, jumping from one period of my
> life to another, mixing up sins and adventures, study and research, in a fan-
> tastic, pell-mell story. Padre Pio listened to me with the greatest attention,
> but always without looking at me straight in the face. . . . As I spoke, I stud-
> ied him, feeling more and more fascinated by the sincerity of his holiness.
> There was no movement, no glance, no word which might have suggested a
> personal relationship. I seemed to perceive in him something infinitely su-
> perior to this humble and frail body. I don't know whether it was due to
> some unfortunate phrase of mine . . . that he groaned and leaned over to the
> left, on the side on which he bore the bleeding lance wound. Moreover, he
> almost unconsciously blew on his hands several times as if they were burn-
> ing. I spoke for about ten minutes and would have continued to speak until
> nightfall if conscience had not stopped me. I didn't want to abuse his good-
> ness or the patience of others.

> The holy man's reply came at once, clear and beautiful, at times vivacious
> and accompanied with expressive gestures. He uttered no reproof. He spoke
> with such certainty about my supernatural experiences that I was at once
> convinced of being in the presence of a true master. He could not have been
> a scholar in the field of occult science, but it was evident that he had studied
> at the school of personal experience and possessed the Truth which shines
> forth, unique and indivisible, over and above every symbol. . . . He . . .
> spoke to me of the danger of mirages created by Lucifer and ended by
> saying what I may summarize in the words: *You are seeking the way, but
> you have already found it.*

Finally, Pio recited his "mysterious formula."

> His mind seemed to have plunged into an abyss from which those mys-
> terious words rose up. Then . . . his whole being became radiant with in-

terior light, in which he seemed merged in some indefinable and immensely exalted presence which caused the formula of absolution to issue from the human lips of this humble Capuchin.

As he kissed Padre Pio's hand, Klugkist smelled the "strong perfume which emanated from the stigmata." Leaving his presence, he concluded, "I found myself faced with the divine Ego. In [Pio] alone I found no trace of the human ego." Other spiritual teachers, he was convinced, "were men more or less imbued with the divine, while he, on the other hand, is nothing but an instrument of the divine. He has reached the goal of Union."[14]

Paul Klugkist went on to enter the Trinitarian Order in Rome, took the name Fra Pio, and became a priest. Having himself earned the reputation of being a holy man, he died in Halifax, Canada, at the age of seventy-seven.

Another man whose life was radically changed through Padre Pio also learned of him through the Naples *Mattino*. Interestingly enough, it was through the story of what turned out to be a bogus miracle.

Earlier that spring a war veteran appeared on crutches, claiming to be suffering from the effects of a wound in his foot that refused to heal. While at San Giovanni, he suddenly announced that he had been cured. Padre Paolino insisted that the veteran, Antonio Colonello, submit to an examination by three doctors. Colonello pointed to the foot that he claimed had just been healed miraculously. The doctors told Paolino that the scar was at least six months old. The guardian then wrote to Colonello's doctor and learned that the wound had, in fact, been healed for six months or more. The veteran had apparently, for reasons best known to himself, been hoping to make himself the center of attention.[15] Before the spurious nature of this "miracle" had been discovered, an account of it appeared in the *Mattino*, which was giving Padre Pio a favorable and extensive coverage.

The article was read by a twenty-six-year-old tramp named Emmanuele Brunatto. Born in a well-to-do family on September 9, 1892, Brunatto was a complex and interesting character, highly intelligent, crafty, and clever, uncompromising, volatile, and intensely loyal. Educated by the Salesian Order, Brunatto at one time entertained thoughts of becoming a priest, but by the time he grew into adolescence, he had drifted away from the Church and found that his chief interests in life were money and sex. Wanting neither to work nor to further his education, Brunatto was leading the life of a drifter and confidence man when, in 1916, he had a vivid dream about his dead father. In the dream his father blessed him. "His face irradiated an indescribable spiritual light," Brunatto wrote later. "He said, 'Kneel.' I obeyed. He put his hands on my head, and I felt a warmth go out of the palms that was like a liquid that penetrated my body and soul."[7]

When Brunatto awoke, he thought about the dream for a while, then continued his frantic pursuit of pleasure. After he read the article in the *Mattino* about

Colonello, he was seized by a sudden impulse to visit Padre Pio. At the time, Brunatto was in Naples, living with a woman named Giulietta in "a putrid alley infested by prostitutes of the very lowest kind." He began to wonder if he must consider himself a hopelessly ruined man. No, he answered himself, for God, "who had thrown me into the gutter to convince me of my weakness and my sins, was already preparing the way of my redemption. Like a call from afar," Brunatto writes, "the thought of Padre Pio came incessantly to my mind. I wanted to go to him at once but did not have the money for the trip."

Brunatto obtained some temporary work and earned enough for the bus trip as far as San Severo. He had to walk the rest of the way — ten hours — at night.

> It was a moonlit night. I passed through an inhospitable and desolate valley without encountering a living soul. Volcanic rocks immersed in a cold white light suggested illusions of the ruins of dead cities. Here and there I encountered, like motionless phantoms, the tormented forms of old Indian fig trees. I seemed to be reliving the journey of my life, a long night's journey to an unknown dawn.

Day was breaking when he came in view of a barren mountain marked by the white rectangle of the Capuchin Friary of Our Lady of Grace. Going in, he found a friar seated in much the same way that Klugkist described. The priest was hearing the confession of a farmer, who was on his knees. A crowd of men were standing around, waiting their turn. "Is this Padre Pio?" Brunatto asked a man nearby, who replied in the affirmative.

At that moment, the priest hearing confessions turned and looked at him. "Rather" writes Brunatto, "he pierced me with his gaze, which was hard and angry."

Brunatto saw before him a man with coarse features, a harsh expression, and an unkempt beard. "Is this the saint?" he asked himself. "With that bandit's face? And why does he look at me with such hatred? How lovely, to spend all my money to make this trip and then to meet — him!" Terribly shaken, Brunatto stormed out of the friary.

> There remains to me but a vague remembrance. I know that I fled the sacristy like a madman and found myself in the open, alone, along the rude fence that enclosed the monastery garden, my hands grasping the loose-fitting stones. I sobbed and wailed like a wounded child, "My Lord and my God!" It is impossible to describe the grief and the hope that tormented me as I poured out my soul.

Returning to the friary, he found Padre Pio all alone. He was waiting for him. His countenance had undergone a remarkable change. It now seemed to be "of surpassing beauty, radiating indescribable joy. Even his beard no longer appeared unkempt. And in his eyes was love." Without a word, Padre Pio signaled Brunatto to kneel.

Memories of my past rushed from my lips like the waters of a river in flood. How many errors and infamies from my youth till today! I would never have finished confessing them had not the padre stopped me: "You confessed during the war and the Lord has pardoned your sins and put a great boulder over them, and you must not try to raise it. Tell me only that which you have to regret since that time."

Brunatto recounted that at times Padre Pio helped his memory and gave advice that was "simple, clear, and compassionate."

When he came to the absolution, he had to begin over several times, as if he were struggling against an invisible adversary who was clinging to my shoulders. The sacramental words broke and came together again . . . while from his mouth there came an intense perfume of roses and violets, which bathed my face. Finally, as if freed from a great weight, I arose.

When Brunatto asked Padre Pio to bless him,

Lightly he put his two hands, covered with half-gloves, around my neck. It was then that I felt *exactly* the same warmth emanating from the palms of his hands, the same mysterious liquid that I had felt three years earlier when I dreamt that I was receiving the blessing . . . from my father.

Back home in Naples, several days later Brunatto had an unusual experience:

All of a sudden my past life began to pass before me like the projection of a film: the dangers run, the sins committed, the griefs and the joys, the gifts and the graces, the flights and the returns, all were reconstructed chronologically in a wonderful experience of my life under the incessant protection of the Mother of God. For long hours I lingered, a simple spectator, moved to tears at the film of my past. . . . One fact, however, was clear to me: the operator of this film was Padre Pio.[8]

Shortly afterward Brunatto returned to San Giovanni Rotondo, where he settled in a little hut by the town cemetery. There he raised rabbits and chickens and spent the rest of his time in prayer and meditation. Later, he was hired as a teacher at the college and given a room in the friary. He used to pray in the choir beside Padre Pio during the Office. He sometimes used to doze off during the prayers, only to be reawakened by a gentle nudge from Padre Pio, who jokingly asked him, "Now how do you expect to go to heaven if you keep falling asleep during the prayers?" One day the guardian suggested that Brunatto become a friar. Before he had a chance to answer, Padre Pio threw his hands into the air and cried, "Never! Never! Never!"[9]

Brunatto would remain at the friary until 1925, when a change in the rules excluded laymen from staying within the enclosure. He would play a very important role in Padre Pio's life during the next decade and beyond.

Many other people had experiences similar to those of Klugkist and Brunatto. Like Klugkist, some found Pio "radiant with interior light"; others, like Brunatto, experienced the mysterious passing of their past life before their eyes after their contact with Padre Pio. Almost all who came to him felt an awareness of being face to face with a man who could simply, clearly, and compassionately tell them how they stood with God. Those who sought him out were convinced that he was communicating God's will for them individually. The greatest proof of Padre Pio's effectiveness, not to mention his sanctity, was that through his ministry lives were radically and dramatically changed: men and women were led to Christ.

But not everyone thought highly of Padre Pio. He was attracting the interest of some of the Vatican higher-ups, not all of whom were friendly or sympathetic. A visit from an eminent theologian on April 18, 1920, was to create difficulties for the stigmatized priest for years to come.

Gerardo Agostino Gemelli (1878-1959), a member of the Order of Franciscan Observants, was one of Italy's most respected thinkers: a physician, a surgeon, a theologian, and the founder of Milan's Catholic University, where he was currently rector. Most important, he was a close friend of the formidable archbishop of Milan, Achille Ratti, who would soon become Pope Pius XI.

Photographs show the scholarly Gemelli as a man of unprepossessing appearance, almost entirely bald, with a big nose and huge, jug-handle ears.

Over the years he had made an extensive study of stigmatics and concluded that they were all hysterics and neurotics — except for St. Francis of Assisi and St. Catherine of Siena, whose stigmata the Church had pronounced genuine. One gets the impression that were it not for the pronouncement of the Church, Gemelli would have dismissed them, too, as mentally unbalanced.

The question remains whether Gemelli even saw Padre Pio's stigmata. In a letter of July 19, 1952, to the British scholar Father C. C. Martindale, Gemelli claimed that he had: "I accurately examined Padre Pio and his stigmata. During the examination of the stigmata, the Provincial was present. I do not remember the exact wording of the order I had from the Holy Office because I am not in the habit of saving notes of what I do for the tribunals of the Roman Curia, and I try to forget the content of my orders."[10]

There is substantial evidence that nothing of the sort took place. Gemelli arrived at the Friary of Our Lady of Grace and told Padre Lorenzo, the guardian, that he had been sent to examine Padre Pio's stigmata by the Holy Office, the Vatican congregation set up to guard the teaching of the faith and judge on heresy. Gemelli asserted to Martindale that the provincial was present. Padre Benedetto was indeed there, but he was no longer the minister provincial, having stepped down several months before. Gemelli had, in fact, written to the new provincial, Padre Pietro of Ischitella (1879-1924), telling him of his intention to come to San Giovanni to visit Padre Pio. Padre Pietro had written back that if he intended to go as a scientist to observe Padre Pio, he had to obtain written authorization from the Capuchin superiors at Rome. Gemelli responded that he was going only for "private and spiritual reasons."

As soon as Gemelli arrived, however, he began to press for an examination. Benedetto demurred, saying: "I can't help you, because the provincial told me expressly not to subject Padre Pio to this grave mortification without the proper authorization. Besides, you declared that you were not coming with such intentions." Gemelli was adamant. He insisted on at least meeting Padre Pio. Benedetto gave in and arranged an interview in the sacristy.

There were three witnesses to the meeting of Pio and Gemelli: Benedetto, Emmanuele Brunatto, and a priest, Padre Fortunato of Serracapriola. According to Padre Benedetto, the interview lasted but a few minutes. He remembered that Gemelli rather rudely said to Pio, "I want to suggest that you cure yourself of your wounds," and that Pio "dismissed him in a state of annoyance."[11]

Brunatto, then living at the friary, had similar recollections. He estimated the length of the interview as three or four minutes. He remembered, when he and Benedetto wrote their accounts about a decade later (still about twenty years before Gemelli put his recollections of the encounter on paper), that Padre Pio had asked Gemelli if he had written authorization:

"Written, no, but. . . "

"In that case," said Padre Pio, cutting him short, "I am not authorized to show the wounds to you," and started to walk away.

Gemelli, in high dudgeon, shouted after him: "All right, Padre Pio! We will meet again!"

It seems clear that there was no examination. In fairness to Gemelli, he may have thought that oral authorization from the Holy Office would be sufficient. Gemelli did write a report to Rafael Cardinal Merry del Val, secretary of the Holy Office, about Padre Pio's stigmata, in which he claimed to have made an examination. In 1931 Michele Cardinal Lega approached Padre Luigi Festa of Avellino, a Capuchin, no relation to the physician, who thought highly of Padre Pio. Lega told Festa, "If you could only read the report submitted by Gemelli, you would surely change your mind about Padre Pio." Padre Luigi asked him what it said. Lega said that he was forbidden to go into detail. "It was terrible," Lega assured him. "Had you read it, you would have changed your judgment on Padre Pio!"[12]

Whatever report Gemelli made in 1920, it had little immediate effect, for Pope Benedict XV, that little gnomelike man with gold-rimmed spectacles perched upon a large Roman nose, stood firmly behind Padre Pio. A month before Gemelli went to San Giovanni, Benedict had sent his own physician, Professor Bastianelli, to examine the stigmata in the company of two Capuchin prelates, Anselm Edward John Kenealy, archbishop of Simla, India, and Giovanni Antonio Zucchita, archbishop of Smyrna. All three men had examined the stigmata on March 24, 1920, and had spoken at length with Padre Pio. No transcript exists of their report, but it was known that they "departed San Giovanni Rotondo enthusiastic" about Padre Pio's sanctity and the supernatural character of the stigmata.

In the following months, the Pope dispatched several other Vatican officials, all with written authorization, to visit Padre Pio and examine the stigmata. A month after Gemelli's visit, Bishop Bonaventura Ceretti (1873-1933), secretary of the Congregation for Extraordinary Ecclesiastical Affairs, examined the stigmata and was convinced. Shortly thereafter, the eminent Augusto Cardinal Sili (1846-1926) visited the stigmatic priest and was likewise convinced.

Bishop Alberto Valbonesi (1868-1935), bishop of the titular see of Memphis, Egypt, who had visited Padre Pio several months before Gemelli, also came to the support of the Capuchin. Talking to Padre Pio for just a few moments, he declared, "compensated me for years of pain." Bishop Alberto Alfredo Costa of Melfi and Rapolla, who had visited Padre Pio a few days after Valbonesi, wrote, "I am convinced of the holiness of Padre Pio, not only from the signs of the Passion imprinted on his hands, but even more by his life, which is totally consecrated to the glorification of God and the conversion of sinners." He concluded his report saying, "My impressions can be boiled down to one: to that of having talked with a saint." The bishop of Allahabad, India, Angelo Police, also visited Padre Pio with the encouragement of the Pope and wrote: "I came, I saw, and I was conquered. Not the slightest doubt remains in me: the finger of God is here."[13]

Perhaps Padre Pio's most powerful advocate at the Vatican was the powerful papal secretary of State, Pietro Cardinal Gasparri (1852-1934), who as early as 1919 had recommended himself to Padre Pio's prayers. Periodically he wrote to San Giovanni to ask for "any object belonging to Padre Pio" to venerate as a relic.

Pope Benedict seems to have been fully convinced that Padre Pio was neither a neurotic nor a charlatan but truly a man of great holiness. He told Cesare Festa, a noted attorney (who, unlike Padre Luigi, was related to the physician): "Padre Pio is truly a man of God. Take care to make him known because he is not appreciated as he deserves to be." To a Church official in Uruguay he remarked, "Truly Padre Pio is an extraordinary man, the like of whom God sends to earth from time to time for the purpose of converting men." To Archbishop Gagliardi, who was passing on to the Vatican the denunciatory letters of Miscio, Fraccacreta, and others, Benedict warned: "You must proceed cautiously concerning Padre Pio. It's bad to be too unbelieving."[14] As long as he lived, Pope Benedict XV would keep Padre Pio's enemies at bay.

The Friar and the Archbishop

Between 1919 and 1922, Padre Pio struggled to ignore the controversy that swirled about him. His life was the altar, the confessional, and the prayer chapel. He had time for little else, really, since by early 1920 he was working a nineteen-hour day. He still made time to answer the letters of his spiritual children, although his replies tended to grow more telegraphic. Understandably, he was extremely reluctant to take on additional correspondence and, as usual, refused to do so unless he received some illumination concerning the spiritual state of the people who wanted to correspond with him. Yet even if he refused to carry on a correspondence with most of those who wrote to him, he promised nevertheless to "pray very hard for them, that they might be illuminated concerning the things they desire."

Despite his long hours of dealing with human need, Padre Pio's spiritual life appeared to intensify. Like many people of highly developed spiritual or intellectual life, he seemed to need very little sleep. Besides, it was when he was trying to rest that the pain of the stigmata became unbearable. As he told a friend some years later: "One thing carries me to the next, and so the day passes. It is the nights [that are hard to bear.] If ever I allow myself to sleep, the pain of these [wounds] . . . is multiplied beyond measure."[1] If he had any free time in the evening, much of it he would devote to prayer.

Pio's spiritual life continued much the way it had been before the onset of his fame. He still had highs and lows. The lows stemmed not so much from his existential anguish as from "the failure of men to respond to heavenly favors." In October 1920, he wrote to Padre Benedetto:

> The thought of being unable to bring spiritual relief to those whom Jesus
> sends me, the thought of so many souls who foolishly want to justify their

evil in defiance of their Chief Good afflicts me, tortures me, martyrs me, overcharges my mind, and rends my heart. . . . Of late I have felt two desires growing gigantically within my spirit. . . . I want to live, so as to be of use to my brethren in exile, and, on the other hand, I wish to die to be united with my heavenly Spouse.[2]

In the same vein he wrote, again to Benedetto, on November 20, 1921:

Everything can be summed up in this: I am devoured by the love of God and the love of my neighbor. God is always fixed in my mind and stamped in my heart. I never lose sight of Him. I can admire His beauty, His smiles, His vexation, His mercy, His vengeance, or, rather, the rigors of His justice. . . .

How is it possible to see God saddened . . . and not to grieve, too? I see God on the verge of hurling His thunderbolts, and it seems that there is no remedy except to raise a hand to stop His arm. And we must wave the other hand frantically to warn our brother to cast the evil out of his life . . . , since the hand of the judge is about to discharge itself upon him!

I feel nothing except to have and to will that which God desires. And in Him I always feel at peace, at least within my soul. Externally, sometimes, I am somewhat vexed, for the sake of my brothers.[3]

Benedetto and Agostino continued to be a support to Pio, although he seldom saw either man now. Benedetto, after stepping down as minister general, was assigned for a time to the Capuchin headquarters in Rome. Agostino was now the guardian of the friary at San Marco la Catola. Padre Pio still looked to them for advice, not only in spiritual but also in temporal matters.

One thing that now troubled Pio was how to dispose of the considerable sums of money that were handed to him for the purpose of furthering his ministry. As a Capuchin, he had taken a vow to live without money, and he did not want anyone to have the slightest grounds for accusing him of "running a racket." Benedetto advised him that it was all right for him to accept offerings so long as he knew the precise purpose of the donor and carried it out. Thus, when people pressed money into his hands, Padre Pio would often hand it back, giving the donors the names and addresses of various people in need and urging them to give the funds directly to those individuals. When the donors insisted that Pio keep the money, urging him to use it as he saw fit, he would quickly distribute it to people he knew to be in need.

Although Benedetto continued to advise Pio, their roles gradually came to be reversed. More often than not, the younger man proved to be Benedetto's comforter. As Agostino had been doing for several years, Benedetto was now barraging Pio with questions about his spiritual state. The former pupil tried his best, both with and without supersensible intuition, to advise and comfort him.

Both Agostino and Benedetto were now showering Pio with requests for prayer and supernatural intuition, to many of which he found himself unable adequately to respond. The letters of the two older priests give a good illustration of the type of request that was coming before Padre Pio constantly. Agostino asked Pio whether a doctor who had died in the war was saved or damned. Pio had to answer, "I know nothing." Benedetto asked him about a friar who was listed as missing in action. Pio responded: "'Concerning Fra Luca of happy memory, I know nothing on the part of God. But my mind tells me that he must not be sought among the living. May it please God to disprove my presentiment." God was so pleased, and Padre Pio was proved wrong: Fra Luca turned up alive.

In one letter, Benedetto submitted these requests: "A doctor from Naples has a poor demented daughter and prays that the Lord relieve her. A good lady from here wants to be healed of a chronic cough. . . . Fra Gerardo is suffering from an inflamed arm and wants to be healed so that he can serve God more effectively." In another letter, Benedetto wrote: "There is a woman with a son who is fourteen years old, retarded, and incapable of functioning on his own. He is like a block of wood. She would like the Lord to illuminate his intelligence, at least so that he might be able to function minimally, or else take him to heaven." On another occasion, Benedetto forwarded a dollar from an American lady who thought she could pay Padre Pio to regain her health. On yet another, he recommended Maria Giuseppina Giosafatta Ciardi-Apicelli, the wife of San Marco la Catola's town secretary, who was terminally ill but unwilling to die because she had small children. In another letter he recommended a seminarian who had tuberculosis, as well as the archpriest of San Marco in Lamis, Don Giuseppe Maria Bozzuto, who was dying from cancer of the tongue.

We do not know the results of most of these requests. It is known that Signora Ciardi-Apicelli died less than three months after her request for healing, and that Bozzuto, too, had succumbed to his sickness. Often Padre Pio lamented that God would not answer his prayers.

Life at the friary was more hectic than ever. After Padre Pietro succeeded Padre Benedetto as provincial, he made a number of changes. Padre Paolino — who was partly blamed for leaking Romanelli's report to the press, — was transferred to the friary at Gesualdo. Next to Benedetto and Agostino, Paolino was probably Pio's closest friend at the time, and the stigmatist was overcome with "extreme bitterness" at the transfer of his confrere, writing him that their separation left "an abyss in [his] soul."

Meanwhile, the secular clergy, especially the canons, the priests on the staff of the Cathedral of Manfredonia, continued to bombard the Vatican with complaints about Padre Pio. Archpriest Don Giuseppe Prencipe (1872-1956), a man who seems to have supported whatever party had the upper hand, had, like much of his flock, taken to making his confessions to Padre Pio. He wrote in his diary that he recognized that he was "in the presence of a man graced with an extraordinary gift." In 1920 he warned Padre Pio, "I'm under great pressure from the canons to denounce you, and you're not praying for me!"

"If I didn't pray, things would be worse," Pio explained. Prencipe was mollified, and for the time being he leaned toward Padre Pio.

For the moment, any disturbances on the part of dissident and radical clergy were stifled by the terrible civil strife that was sweeping Italy and exploded with deadly violence in the heart of San Giovanni Rotondo. In the economic slump following the World War, Italy was plagued with strikes, lockouts, and labor violence. The Socialists won about a third of the seats in the 1919 parliamentary elections, and strife between that party and the increasingly powerful Fascists was growing.

In San Giovanni Rotondo, the Socialists were of the extreme left-wing variety. Although they did not actually call themselves Communists, they openly promised to bring about a "soviet regime." They found their support mostly among the large numbers of landless laborers, promising to confiscate and redistribute the great landed estates. When they made gains in the municipal elections in that autumn of 1920, the stage was set for trouble. The Fascists hotly disputed the election, and violence was in the air. Forty state troopers and eighty-two soldiers from the Italian army were called in to preserve order.

Alarmed, Padre Pio summoned the mayor of San Giovanni Rotondo, Francesco Morcaldi (1889-1976). Morcaldi, who served as mayor during much of Padre Pio's working life, has been described as a kind, quiet, gentle, and pious man but something of a political chameleon who managed to accommodate himself to whoever happened to be in power. Pio insisted that Morcaldi use his influence to keep the peace. "Go into the countryside and calm the people down," he enjoined the mayor.

Despite Morcaldi's efforts, the catastrophe occurred on October 14. Socialists tried to storm the city hall, haul down the flag of Italy, and replace it with the red flag of Marxism. They could not succeed in cracking the wall of troops surrounding the edifice. Hordes of Fascists appeared on the scene, whereupon the two factions went at each other with sticks, stones, and knives. A Socialist seized a rifle from one of the state troopers and killed him with it. In panic, some of the troopers began to open fire on the crowd. Then some of the Socialists began to retaliate by exploding a couple of homemade bombs. Within moments six people lay dead, seven more were dying, and more than eighty were injured.

In tears, Morcaldi hurried to the friary, wailing, "Padre Pio! Padre Pio! What are we going to do?" Pio laid his hand on Francesco's shoulder and said, "Reconcile, my son, reconcile." Within a few days, Pio suggested a program of pacification to the mayor. Morcaldi announced the following proposals a short time later, maintaining that they were the expression of Padre Pio's wishes:

> The inhabitants of San Giovanni were to be given a fuller voice in the municipal government.

To improve the plight of the rural laborers, a municipal Office of Labor was to be established.

Mobile units from agricultural schools were to be engaged to teach better farming methods.

A permanent Committee of Assistance was to be set up to aid the children of soldiers killed in the war.

A municipal hospital with an operating room was to be established to provide free health care for the indigent.

A system of good roads was to be built in the community and in the countryside.

Sanitation was to be improved by the construction of sidewalks and public toilets, and by the removal and replacement of numerous slum dwellings, many of which had been built of dried mud.

A telephone network was to be constructed.[4]

Though Morcaldi attempted to pursue the program of improvement that he had discussed with Padre Pio, nonetheless Pio and the Capuchins were somehow blamed for the "Massacre of San Giovanni Rotondo." Their detractors claimed that by their alleged support of the establishment, they were the cause of the bloodshed. One canon in particular, Don Domenico Palladino (1890-1977), whose sympathies lay with the Socialists, charged Padre Pio and the friars from the pulpit with being tools of the Fascists! At any rate, the Socialists, discredited by the violence, were soundly defeated in the next election.

Violence arose not only over political issues. Not too far away, court hearings were in progress in the town of Vieste over a religious riot that had taken place a year before, on May 15, 1919. The center of the unrest was the archbishop of Manfredonia, Pasquale Gagliardi. The sixty-year-old prelate had occupied his see since 1897, when he was thirty-eight. Gagliardi had taught philosophy and theology for a number of years before being appointed to his archepiscopate by Pope Leo XIII. Since most of the information that has survived about him comes from the somewhat poisoned pens of Morcaldi and Brunatto, who hated him and portrayed him almost as the incarnation of evil, it is hard to get an objective picture of the man. About the only person who recorded for posterity a single kind word about him was Padre Raffaele D'Addario of Sant'Elia a Pianisi (1890-1974); not to be confused with Padre Raffaele Gorgoglione of San Giovanni Rotondo. Raffaele D'Addario resided at Our Lady of Grace for more than three decades and was guardian there toward the end of the Gagliardi affair. When, toward the end of his life, he was approached by an interviewer for his opinion on Gagliardi, he said that he thought that the archbishop was probably a good man but that he was poisoned in his thinking by the hostile clergy at

San Giovanni Rotondo. According to Padre Raffaele, the real culprit was Don Giuseppe Prencipe.

Contemporary churchmen are extremely reluctant to talk about Gagliardi. "Why do you want to know anything about that sick man?" replied one such person in response to my inquiry. As far as is known, Padre Pio left nothing for the record concerning his attitude toward the archbishop. Pio's position was probably similar to that of his mother, who, as we shall see, remarked when Gagliardi was being excoriated in her presence, "We must not judge others because we can see only the deeds men do, but God alone knows the reasons why."

The saintly Padre Agostino, however, minced no words in his diary, charging that Gagliardi instigated "a veritable satanic war" against Padre Pio, personally soliciting "innumerable letters filled with accusations, exaggerations, and calumnies" to forward to the Vatican against Padre Pio.

Although they were far from impartial, Brunatto and Morcaldi amassed an impressive amount of solid evidence concerning the career of Gagliardi, evidence in the form of letters, papers, memoranda, and depositions, all of which occupies nearly three hundred pages in the massive two-volume set *Il Calvario di Padre Pio*, compiled and edited by Giuseppe Pagnossin in 1978. The facts are sordid but give one an idea of the type of man who was leading the Archdiocese of Manfredonia.

Among their materials is a photograph of Gagliardi. It reveals a rather sullen-looking young man with close-cropped hair, beetle brows, deep-set eyes, a huge Roman nose, and thick lips. By the period of time with which we are dealing, he was so disliked by the laity of his archdiocese that he was often hooted and hissed when he appeared in public.

Fairly early in his career as archbishop, Gagliardi had been arrested by civil authorities on a charge of rape.[5] Other records show that, even into his sixties, Gagliardi was on several occasions publicly accused of sexual molestation and unchastity.[6] Even his valet testified that Gagliardi was profligate.[7]

Although there is no solid evidence for any practice of homosexuality on Gagliardi's part, it was beyond question that he showed a preference for priests who had been convicted of this crime. Several instances were cited in a long report made to the Vatican in April 1927. There is no need to recall from the dust the names of these unfortunate men. In one instance, however, a certain priest was convicted of sodomy in both the lower and appellate courts. Gagliardi refused to remove him from his office as archpriest of Carpino until the unhappy man was actually jailed. Again, Gagliardi appointed as archpriest in the town of Vico a man who had been arrested and convicted three times for sodomy. In the same town, the archbishop appointed another priest who had an extensive police record for "continued and habitual pederasty."[8] Several witnesses testified that many of these homosexual priests sent Gagliardi expensive gifts after he gave them positions in his archdiocese.

Gagliardi liked to depict himself as a champion of the needy. He frequently remarked that the elaborate artwork found in many of the churches ought to be sold and the proceeds given to the poor. The Poor Clares at Manfredonia, however, complained that Gagliardi had taken their golden statues and other costly works of art and sold them, only to pocket the monies received.

According to Padre Agostino, Gagliardi was highly critical of the canonization of St. Joan of Arc in 1919 and revealed that he had voted against her elevation to the altar, apparently because of the number of extravagant supernatural phenomena associated with her ministry.

It is hard to know what Gagliardi's initial attitude was toward Padre Pio. His first contact was rooted in an incident that occurred long before Pio's arrival at San Giovanni. Gagliardi had decided one day to take his brother and pregnant sister-in-law on a guided tour of one of the numerous convents in Manfredonia, even though it was strictly forbidden for laypersons to enter the enclosure.

"But this is a grave infraction of the papal enclosure!" warned the mother superior.

"Well, I'll take that up with the Pope myself!" sniffed the archbishop.

"Violate the enclosure," said the superior in a menacing tone, "and your brother's child will be born either blind or dumb!"

All three Gagliardis immediately burst out laughing at this example of primitive superstition, but a few months later the sister-in-law gave birth to a daughter, and it shortly became apparent that the child was deaf.

Shortly after Padre Pio's fame began to spread, the archbishop, in the company of his longtime acquaintance, Padre Agostino, came to call on Padre Pio. Kissing the friar's hand, Gagliardi begged for Pio's prayers for the healing of his niece. That the child was not healed was apparently a factor in turning Gagliardi against Padre Pio. So too was the riot in the town of Vieste, where the archbishop held the position of perpetual administrator and maintained a splendid mansion.

Smoldering resentment against Gagliardi broke out into an angry conflagration when a beloved statue of the Virgin Mary, commonly believed to be miraculous, disappeared from its niche in the Mother Church at Vieste. Word spread around town that the archbishop had taken it to sell, and a mob stormed the church as Gagliardi was celebrating Mass in a side chapel. Even when a nervous sacristan produced the statue from a storage room and explained that it had merely been set aside for repairs, the crowd continued to howl for the archbishop's blood.

Within moments, a mob of more than six hundred — men, women, and children — cornered Gagliardi in the side chapel. They pelted him with stones, seized his missal, from which he was reading the service, and the paten, and hurled them at his head. They began to punch and kick him until several agitated priests intervened to spirit the prelate into an adjoining room and slam the door against the raging mob.

Still cursing and crying for vengeance, the people pounded on the door. When they began to smash it in, two policemen escorted Gagliardi out of the church. Getting wind of this, the mob quickly poured into the street and surrounded the quaking archbishop and his terrified protectors. They and the archbishop received severe beatings from the mob. Just in time, a small army of state troopers arrived to rescue the prelate intact. Even so, he was carried to his palace unconscious and bleeding. When he finally came to, the pain in his testicles was so great that he could not speak for days. His nose was badly smashed and he was bedridden for a month.[9]

This incident could only have intensified Gagliardi's aversion to Padre Pio. Although no one in his right mind could claim that the friar had the slightest responsibility for the riot at Vieste, for Gagliardi, Padre Pio was associated in his mind with the superstitious religiosity that very nearly led to his being forever deprived of his capacity for amorous pursuits; and much of his resentment he visited upon Padre Pio. From about that time, Gagliardi commenced his campaign against Padre Pio.

Pope Benedict, as we have seen, took a dim view of Gagliardi and eventually told him he was not interested in the anti-Pio smut that the archbishop solicited and cheerfully forwarded to him. Thus, for the duration of Benedict's pontificate, there was little that Gagliardi or other like-minded individuals could do to undermine Padre Pio's ministry.

The earliest extant photo of Padre Pio. Taken during the fall of 1911.

Our Lady of Grace Friary
as it appeared when Padre Pio first arrived in 1916

Giovanni Rizzani,
marchioness dei Boschi.
Padre Pio appeared
in bilocation at her
birth and, again, in
St. Peter's Basilica,
around the time of
this 1922 photograph.

Giuseppina Masone,
Padre Pio's beloved
niece, who died of
consumption at eighteen.
She was the daughter
of Pio's favorite sister,
Felicita.

Giuseppa and Grazio Forgione,
Padre Pio's parents, in their sixties

Suor Pia, Padre Pio's sister.
She scandalized him by leaving
her Order after fifty years.

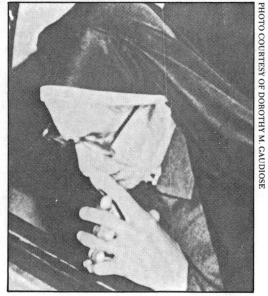

Michele Forgione, Padre
Pio's brother

Padre Pio, in his early
thirties, saying Mass

Italian army medical corpsman Francisco Forgione.
Taken in 1916, this is the only photograph
showing Padre Pio in other than religious garb.

Padre Benedetto Nardella,
Pio's spiritual director

Padre Agostino Daniele. For more than
fifty years he was Pio's confessor,
confidant, and best friend.

Padre Paolino Di Tomasso
of Casacalenda, Padre
Pio's lifelong friend
and colleague; guardian
of Our Lady of Grace
Friary at the time when
Pio received the visible
wounds—1918.

Padre Pio, in his sixties,
in a typical attitude

This photograph, taken August 19, 1919, under holy obedience,
clearly shows the stigmata in Padre Pio's hands.

Padre Pio was praying before this crucifix
in the friary chapel
when he received the visible stigmata.

Padre Pio in his
mid-thirties

Pasquale Gagliardi,
archbishop of Manfredonia
from 1897 to 1929. His
hostility toward Padre Pio
led to a decade of harassment
by the Vatican.

Padre Pio in his mid-seventies

Padre Pio
in his fifties

Padre Pio's cell as
it appeared in the 1950s

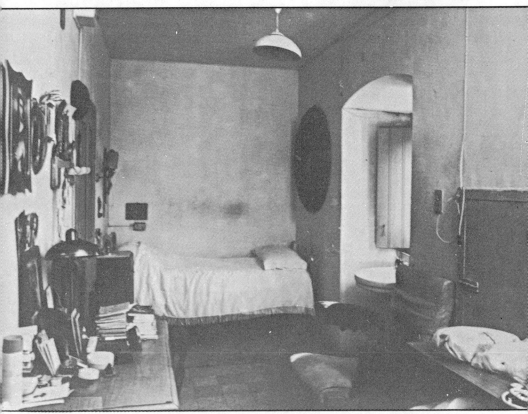

The faithful Mary Adelia
Pyle. Photograph taken
a few months before her
death at eighty.

Emmanuele Brunatto at age seventy

Dr. Guglielmo Sanguinetti,
mastermind of the *Casa
Sollievo* project, and one
of Padre Pio's close friends

Padre Pio in conversation.
Taken about 1965.

The *Casa Sollievo della Sofferenza* a year after Padre Pio's death

The Raging Tempest

The situation changed dramatically for Padre Pio when Pope Benedict died unexpectedly after a brief siege of pneumonia in January 1922, at the early (for a pope) age of sixty-seven. Elected as his successor was the archbishop of Milan, sixty-five-year-old Achille Ratti, the son of a textile worker, who took the name Pius XI. A short, stocky, round-faced, bald-pated, bespectacled man, Pope Pius had nevertheless an awe-inspiring presence. Severe, and so distant that even his closest relatives had to apply like total strangers to the master of the chamber for an audience with him and then wait for a card of invitation, he exuded an aura of majestic dignity. Even the dread Hermann Goering, second in command in Nazi Germany, quaked before him. "You know me," he wrote to a Romanian official in the 1930s. "You know that I've never in my life lacked courage; but before that little figure robed all in white I felt my heart jump as never before. For the first time in my life I believe I was afraid."[1]

Although he was far from being a theological liberal, according to Father C. C. Martindale, this no-nonsense pope was "reluctant to admit, hastily, the preternatural,"[2] and investigating a controversy involving an alleged holy friar in a remote and rocky corner of Italy was not of high priority. Italy was on the eve of a Fascist takeover by Benito Mussolini, Russia reddened under the murderous regime of Lenin, and Germany was full of unrest stemming from the brutally harsh Treaty of Versailles, an unrest that would lead, eleven years later, to the rise of Adolf Hitler. Many nations were experiencing disastrous upheavals in the wake of World War I. With so many international crises having so many grave implications for the Roman Catholic Church, Pope Pius had to relegate matters of lesser importance to others. Too busy to look into the Padre Pio case himself, the Pontiff decided to rely upon trusted aides to learn of the character and ministry of Padre Pio and to form a judgment on the growing controversy concerning him. Unfortunately, among those upon whom Pius relied were Agostino Gemelli and Pasquale Gagliardi.

Immediately after the accession of Pius, Gagliardi went to the Vatican in person and gave him an earful about the dreadful friar who, with his mercenary cronies, was tearing his archdiocese apart. Among other things, Gagliardi deplored Padre Pio's "horrible manner of hearing confessions" that left souls "in a state of agitation."[3] With an expression of downcast contrition, Gagliardi lamented to Pius, "I think I have to answer to God for having authorized Padre Pio to hear confessions."

According to Gagliardi, Padre Pio was more than a misguided, undereducated, superstitious backwoods friar; he was a demoniac. Gagliardi went so far as to appear before the bishops and archbishops of the Consistorial Congregation, which regulated all matters concerning the government of dioceses, where he denounced Padre Pio. He concluded his harangue: "Padre Pio is demon-possessed. I declare to you that he has a devil and the friars of San Giovanni Rotondo are a band of thieves. With my own eyes I saw Padre Pio perfume himself and put makeup on his face! All this I swear on my pectoral cross!"[4]

Padre Pio had at least one friend at the meeting, Bishop Alberto Valbonesi, the Vatican canon who held the titular see of Memphis. He was thoroughly disgusted with Gagliardi and wrote to Padre Pietro, Pio's provincial, detailing the archbishop's charges.

After declaring that Padre Pio was demon-possessed, Gagliardi announced to the assembled bishops that Pio habitually slept in the friary's guest room, where he was attended by young girls with whom he took liberties.

Gagliardi also charged that the friars had been paying newsmen to write sensational stories about Padre Pio and invent accounts of miracles and conversions. The Capuchins, he claimed, were living in "unspeakable luxury," even to the extent of parting and pomading their hair!

Gagliardi charged that the friars were raking in huge sums of money. Some of them, he claimed, had literally come to blows, actually drawing blood over the pocketing of the filthy lucre.

No sooner had he received Bishop Valbonesi's letter than Padre Pietro heard from an alarmed Padre Giuseppantonio Bussolari of Persiceto, the minister general of the Capuchin Order. He had learned of Gagliardi's charges and did not know what to believe. He questioned Pietro about the charges that the friars were having fistfights over the mountains of money. Indignant, Padre Pietro wrote back, telling the minister general that the goodness of the friars at San Giovanni Rotondo

> is such as not to leave me a moment's doubt as to even the possibility of a crime of any gravity. The most perfect peace has reigned among them, and

the spirit of love renders them incapable of resorting even to an offensive word, let alone the crime of which they are accused, which is as unbelievable as the motive said to cause it is false and stupid![5]

"Is it lawful," Pietro asked, "to defame with impunity people who are far removed from suspicion? I want to know . . . the name of the person who, with unspeakable cunning and malignity, has had the nerve to report, nay, invent, these deep black lies to vilify my religious! Such information would enable me to force a retraction from this crafty and malevolent liar. . . ."

Of course, Padre Giuseppantonio did not reveal the name of the "crafty and malevolent liar" (which Pietro knew anyway), who was far from finished. Throughout 1922, Gagliardi encouraged priests to forward anonymous letters of denunciation to Rome. Whereas Benedict had discouraged this practice, Pius allowed such correspondence to be handed over to the Holy Office.

One of the most shocking libels came from Don Giovanni Miscio, who had been the first to complain about Padre Pio to Gagliardi. Miscio wrote a long letter to the Holy Office alleging that Padre Pio was suffering from tuberculosis, a nervous disorder, epilepsy, and venereal disease. Some of the charges that Miscio leveled against Padre Pio were so luridly repulsive that they do not bear repeating.

Criticism of Padre Pio poured into the Holy Office, now even from Vatican circles. Bishop Carlo Perosi, a member of the Holy Office who would be created a cardinal in 1926, with unbelievable pettiness accused Padre Pio of causing his sister's divorce. His sister and her husband regularly made their confessions to Padre Pio. They got a divorce. The ex-husband continued to go to Padre Pio for confession, while the ex-wife did not. Therefore, according to the erudite bishop, Padre Pio was to blame for the divorce!

With accusations against Pio pouring in from right and left, the Holy Office, in the spring of 1922, felt it necessary to investigate. Headed by the eminent London-born Spanish prelate, Rafael Cardinal Merry del Val (1865-1930), the Holy Office sifted through the medical reports of Romanelli, Bignami, Festa, and Bastianelli, and heard testimony in Pio's behalf from the powerful secretary of state, Cardinal Gasparri, as well as from Cardinal Sili, the prefect of the Supreme Tribunal of the Holy See. Bishops Costa and Valbonesi also spoke on Padre Pio's behalf.

The chief witnesses against Padre Pio were Gagliardi, the enormously influential Gemelli, and some of the clergy from San Giovanni Rotondo whom they brought along, notably Giovanni Miscio and Domenico Palladino. As a result of the hearing, Cardinal Merry del Val decided upon certain steps, which he communicated to Padre Giuseppantonio, the Capuchin minister general.

To avoid any possibility of rumor or scandal, Padre Pio was to be restricted to activities that pertained to the "common life of religious." To discourage crowds, the hour of Padre Pio's Mass was to vary each day — and be unannounced. Perferably it would take place very early in the morning and in a private chapel. No longer was Padre Pio to bless crowds from the window, nor was he to be permitted to show the stigmata to any visitors or even speak of the marks.

Moreover, the Holy Office directed the minister general of the Capuchin Order to transfer Padre Pio from San Giovanni Rotondo to a friary outside the province of Foggia, preferably in northern Italy. In addition, Padre Pio was ordered not to answer letters from "devout people seeking counsel, graces, and other things." This effectively ended his correspondence with his spiritual children.

Perhaps the hardest of Merry del Val's dispositions concerned Padre Benedetto. For reasons never made clear, the Holy Office decided that Benedetto's spiritual direction left something to be desired, that the former provincial, "under the pretence of zeal," had actually been sowing "spiritual confusion." The Holy Office therefore decreed that Padre Pio's spiritual director should be "someone other than Padre Benedetto." Padre Pio was heartbroken over the loss of his spiritual father.

Whatever the reason for the Holy Office's action, Padres Pio and Benedetto never met again on earth. According to Padre Agostino, Padre Pio, although shattered, "submitted to the disposition with holy resignation." The same was true of Benedetto. In the twenty years of life that remained to the former provincial, not a word of complaint escaped his lips. Whenever he passed by San Giovanni Rotondo by car or by bus, he saluted Padre Pio — mentally — but never tried to see him. When Benedetto was dying, the guardian of the friary of San Severo, where he was staying, asked the old man if he would like to send for Padre Pio. "No, it is not necessary," answered Benedetto. "He is here beside me."[6]

Padre Pietro responded to the minister general, who had forwarded him the directives from Cardinal Merry del Val. Padre Pietro assured Padre Giuseppantonio that all the letters addressed to Padre Pio would be opened by the guardian or vicar of the friary, or by friars of "indisputable sobriety and prudence"; that letters seeking counsel "in matters of conscience" would be answered with the simple exhortation to submit to the judgment of a prudent confessor; and that letters asking for graces or favors would not be answered, or would be answered simply with a promise of prayer.

The greatest problem for Padre Pietro was Padre Pio's transfer. The civil authorities warned the provincial that to move the holy man would be to risk even greater bloodshed than the "Massacre of San Giovanni Rotondo." Accordingly, Pietro wrote Giuseppantonio that they would have to prepare for violent riots if an attempt to transfer him were made. Moreover, the provincial told the general that "it would be difficult to find another place in which [Padre Pio] could be better protected and in greater isolation than in San Giovanni Rotondo." Pietro cited the inaccessibility of the town in winter, the lack of inns and hotels, and the great distance of the friary from the town proper. Giuseppantonio seems to have felt that Pietro was making sense and, for the time being, did not press for Padre Pio's transfer.

The next May, the Holy Office issued a cautious declaration concerning the inquiry about Padre Pio of the previous year:

> The Supreme Holy Congregation of the Holy Office, which is charged with upholding the integrity of Faith and Tradition, held an inquiry on the phenomena attributed to Padre Pio of Pietrelcina of the Minor Capuchins of the friary of San Giovanni Rotondo . . . declares that it cannot confirm from this inquiry the supernatural character of these phenomena and exhorts the faithful to conform their practices to this declaration.[7]

That is, the faithful were not to treat Padre Pio as a saint or venerate his reputed supernatural gifts.

Merry del Val and his Holy Office hoped that this statement would thin the immense crowds that were pouring ever more copiously into San Giovanni Rotondo. It seems to have had the opposite effect, however. More people than ever came, and there were reports of conversions, healings, and prophecies.

By now the minister general, Padre Giuseppantonio, was furious, convinced that Padre Pietro was purposely dragging his feet in carrying out the instructions of the previous year. Although Merry del Val had never insisted that Padre Pio's Mass be celebrated privately, he stated in his directives that he preferred that this be the case. Moreover, it was clear that his intention was that Padre Pietro was to follow his instructions for the purpose of eliminating the crowds and the publicity. It was also clear that since lesser measures had not succeeded in accomplishing this, more stringent ones were in order. Accordingly, Padre Giuseppantonio considered Padre Pietro deliberately remiss in failing to implement the stricter alternative. Thus he now *ordered* the provincial to permit Padre Pio to celebrate Mass only in the inner chapel of the friary, with no congregation. Reluctantly, Padre Pietro relayed this order to Padre Ignazio of Ielsi, who was now the guardian of Our Lady of Grace.

Even though Padre Pio was supposed to be celebrating Mass at irregular times, the faithful seemed to have a good idea when to expect him, for, on June 25, 1923, a crowd was waiting for him to appear in church. They waited in vain. As Francesco Morcaldi noted that evening in his diary:

> Padre Pio did not come to the church. He has received the order to celebrate Holy Mass behind closed doors in the inner chapel of the friary, without anyone assisting him. The faithful, who saw his usual assistant [Brunatto] come into the church alone, his eyes filled with tears, came at once to understand the order of segregation.[8]

Led by Mayor Morcaldi, the Sangiovannese responded quickly, forming a People's Association and staging a massive demonstration the next day in which nearly five thousand people — half of the population of the metropolitan area — took part. That night the crowds turned ugly and attacked the home of the truculent Don Domenico Palladino, who had been routinely attacking Padre Pio from his pulpit. It was only the pleas of Morcaldi that kept them from burning Palladino's house to the ground — with him in it! The mayor barely dissuaded them from burning the city church, pastored by the inconstant Prencipe, who was now regarded as an enemy of Padre Pio. Morcaldi managed to lead the crowds out of town up the road to the friary.

The friars were astounded, looking out their windows at a sea of torches that stretched more than a half mile down the road. Morcaldi had commandeered the town band, which was playing as he and other city fathers marched to the friary door.

When Padre Ignazio appeared, Morcaldi demanded that he permit Padre Pio to celebrate Mass in public. "If you don't," he warned the father guardian, "I will resign as mayor and fight as an ordinary citizen in the riot that is bound to ensue!"

Presented with an ultimatum, Ignazio capitulated. Afraid, as he said, of "encountering the fanaticism of an entire citizenry who are disposed to undertake all manner of violent measures," the guardian telegraphed Padre Pietro, "Today I carried out the order not to [let Padre Pio] celebrate Mass in public. This evening, because of an impressively enormous public demonstration, it has become impossible to continue to comply. I am forced to suspend the measures again."[9]

During the next few days, members of the People's Association sent telegrams to every ecclesiastical and civil authority they could think of, expressing their support for Padre Pio and their displeasure at the attempts to restrict his ministry. They also expressed their chief concern: that the measures they were protesting were merely a prelude to Padre Pio's removal from San Giovanni Rotondo.

The Association sent a delegation to the archbishop. Gagliardi smiled an unctuous smile and told them, "I will do everything possible to prevent the removal of Padre Pio," adding, "Since, however, such measures do not come from my initiative, I will send my secretary to Rome at once to plead the cause of the People's Association to the minister general of the Capuchins." When the delegation left, however, Gagliardi turned to an aide and snapped, "The next time these blinking Sangiovennese come here, I'll call the police!"

Immediately he dashed off a haughty letter to Morcaldi, with a carbon copy to be sent to the archpriest, Don Giuseppe Prencipe. In it he said: "Let me repeat, neither I nor the local priests have ever requested the removal of Padre Pio from there. Such an allegation is unfounded. It is slanderous of you to make such an imputation!"[10] Along with the carbon copy, however, he sent Prencipe a note in which he implies that he knows Rome is planning to transfer Padre Pio. He concludes by saying that his chief reason for pushing the removal of Padre Pio is to keep people from being hurt by preventing intolerant fanatics from wreaking harm on their neighbors.

At that very moment Merry del Val and Giuseppantonio were searching for a way to transfer Padre Pio. Their reasons were somewhat different from those of Gemelli and Gagliardi. They were genuinely concerned about the huge crowds of fanatical followers who were making a travesty of the Christian faith with their vulgar shenanigans, as well as the apparent inability of the local superiors to control them. The fistfights continued. The women continued to elude Padre Pio's bodyguards so that they might snip away pieces of his clothing. Small-time entrepreneurs continued to hawk pieces of cloth stained with chicken and rabbit blood as relics of "the Man of God." One day as Padre Pio was trying to pray in the choir, he could hear the noisy crowd outside. Above the din, a leather-throated sidewalk vendor kept bellowing: "Padre Pio for two cents! Padre Pio for two cents!" He was selling crudely painted picture postcards. Pio burst out laughing, remarking to a colleague, "The Guardian might hold me in great esteem, but, instead — look at this — Padre Pio is worth two cents!"[11]

This was no laughing matter to Giuseppantonio or Merry del Val. They admitted that Padre Pio might be a holy man, but they did not want him to be the center of a carnival. They wanted to send him to a friary beyond the reach of aggressive, fanatical crowds. There seemed to be no hope of bringing even a semblance of sobriety to San Giovanni Rotondo. Therefore, they thought it might be a good thing to transfer Pio to a friary in an urban center in the more sceptical north. Padre Giuseppantonio decided on a friary in Ancona.

The People's Association, through Brunatto, was aware of everything. To prevent the transfer, three of Padre Pio's closest followers headed for Rome: Brunatto to see Padre Gemelli; Francesco Morcaldi to see Donato Cardinal Sbaretti, prefect of the Congregation of the Council (which oversaw, among other things, the discipline of the clergy); and the Marquess Don Giuseppe Orlando to see Padre Alessandro Lottini of the Holy Office.

Brunatto was particularly disgusted when he learned that Gemelli was falsely telling everyone, including the Pope, that he had examined Padre Pio's stigmata. Brunatto called on Gemelli at the friary of San Antonio in Rome. He ruffled the psychologist's feathers by reminding him that he, Brunatto, was an eyewitness to the fact that Gemelli had not examined Padre Pio. "In response," Brunatto reported, "the magnificent rector warned me of the risks to which I was exposing myself in challenging a man of his stature." Gemelli angrily dismissed his interrogator. "I'll have you destroyed!" he roared. "Thank you for your Franciscan advice," said Brunatto quietly, and left.[12]

Mayor Morcaldi told Cardinal Sbaretti: "If Padre Pio had to leave San

Giovanni Rotondo for a just reason, we would accompany him from town with music and banners. But if he must leave as one guilty of a crime, at the instigation of an immoral, belligerent, and dishonest clergy who would continue to corrupt our population after banishing a holy priest with ignominy, then, Your Eminence, I will throw away [the insignia of my office] and, in order to take Padre Pio away, you will have to trample on our dead bodies!"[13]

Despite Morcaldi's emotional appeal, the cardinal was noncommittal. The mayor was pleased, however, to know that the papal secretary of state, Cardinal Gasparri, was as supportive as ever; but since the restrictions had come through the Holy Office, of which he was not a member, the prelate was unable to be as helpful as he would have liked.

Giuseppe Orlando was partially successful in his visit to Padre Lottini, the commissioner of the Holy Office. Lottini told Orlando of Gagliardi's "detailed report" about Padre Pio, and the fact that the archbishop attributed the stigmata to "fakery and fanaticism." Further, he told Orlando, Gagliardi had publicly remarked, "Either Padre Pio goes, or I go!"

Lottini was chiefly concerned about Padre Pio's alleged disobedience. He was convinced that Pio had resisted Merry del Val's planned transfer of him the previous year. "We sent him the order," Lottini said, "calling him under obedience to be transferred. . . . Instead of obeying, [he] has, by means of the fanatical women who surround him, fostered demonstrations of such magnitude as to put not only the town but even the civil and military authorities into confusion."

The marquess told the commissioner that he would go in person to Padre Pio to verify the truth of these accusations. Lottini agreed. "Go, then," he said. "Swear here upon this missal." Orlando knelt, kissed Lottini's right hand, and swore upon the book that he would question Padre Pio and accurately report his response.

When Orlando reached the friary of Our Lady of Grace, he told Padre Pio: "They are accusing you of all kinds of things, but, most of all, they say that you are disobedient to the orders of your superiors who have imposed upon you the obedience to leave this place."

Padre Pio fell onto one knee, opened his arms, and declared: "Peppino, I swear to you on this crucifix . . . that I never received such an order. If my superiors ordered me to jump out of the window, I would not argue. I would jump."[14] The Marquess Giuseppe Orlando conveyed this singular response to Padre Lottini.

In the meantime, the townspeople were maintaining a round-the-clock guard at the friary, in case someone might try to spirit away their beloved padre. When Brunatto, returning from Rome, roundly execrated Gemelli, Gagliardi, and other less-than-helpful ecclesiastical officials, Pio rebuked him. "You did a wicked thing!" he said. "We must respect the decrees of the Church. We must be silent, and suffer!"[15] To Morcaldi, who bitterly reviled the Church, Pio said:

"Do all within the Church, act only within the Church! We must beware of putting ourselves against our Mother. . . . Sweet is the hand of the Church, even when it batters us!"[16]

Late in July 1923, Padre Giuseppantonio summoned Padre Luigi Festa of Avellino. The general announced that he had at last made a firm decision to transfer Padre Pio, probably to Ancona. Giuseppantonio wanted Luigi to go to Pio and "receive his obedience" to go wherever he might be sent.

On August 7, Padre Luigi arrived at San Giovanni. Although it was midnight, he went to Padre Pio's room and read him the order from the father general. Pio bowed his head, crossed his arms on his chest, and replied: "I'm at your disposal. Let's depart at once. When I am with my superior, I am with God."

"You mean you want to come with me at once? Now?" asked Luigi, incredulous. "Why, it's the middle of the night! Where would we go?"

"I don't know," responded Pio. "I only know that I am going with you, when and where you wish."

"All I have is the order to communicate the obedience to you," said the startled Luigi. "It will be carried out when I receive further instructions from Rome."[17]

Meanwhile, the minister general was having second thoughts about sending Padre Pio to the friary at Ancona. The minister provincial there had told him frankly, "Ancona is not a place suitable for saints." Giuseppantonio began weighing the possibility of sending Pio to Spain or even America. Before he had a chance to make a final decision, however, he received a report from Dr. Carmelo Camillieri, who had been sent to discuss with the local authorities the possibility of moving Padre Pio.

After interviewing a great number of people, Camillieri concluded that the only people who really opposed Padre Pio in the San Giovanni area were Gagliardi, the secular clergy, and the Franciscan Observants from the friary of San Matteo in San Marco in Lamis, who were very friendly with Gagliardi. After conferring with the police, Camillieri concluded that Padre Pio could be taken away only by force "with the certainty of an effusion of blood."

This was illustrated only too vividly on August 10, during Vespers. Padre Pio was about to bless the faithful from the altar with the Blessed Sacrament enclosed in a receptacle called a monstrance. He had opened the tabernacle, which contained the consecrated Communion wafers, and was about to place one of them in the monstrance when a man, identified only as Donato, a bricklayer, lunged forward and, brandishing a revolver, leveled it at Padre Pio's head. "Either dead or alive," he shouted, "you're going to stay with us in this town!"[18] The frenzied declaration of the would-be assassin gave worshippers and police the chance to wrestle him to the ground before he could squeeze the trigger, but the incident only underscored the explosive nature of the situation.

Pio, who must have been badly shaken, pleaded for mercy for his assailant.

That night he put his thoughts in writing: "Lord, what do these people want of me? . . . Tomorrow may bring I don't know what. I don't know where my superiors are going to send me. As a faithful son of holy obedience, I will obey without a murmur. . . ."[19]

Padre Pio was ready to leave San Giovanni if need be, but if he had to go, he preferred the mission field. In fact, he had recently written to his superiors for permission to work as a missionary in India. Permission was refused. Pio must have wondered why his superiors refused, since he was evidently such a thorn in their sides. At any rate, he resigned himself to whatever was to be and urged his supporters to do the same. In this spirit, in a moving letter on August 12, he wrote to Morcaldi:

> The events that have unfolded in recent days have profoundly troubled me . . . because they give reason to fear that I might be the unwilling cause of grievous events in this my beloved town.
>
> I pray to God that He might prevent such a catastrophe. . . . Yet, if, as you have told me, my transfer has been decided upon, I pray you employ the proper means to bring it about, since the will of my superiors, which is the will of God, must be carried out. . . .
>
> I will always remember this high-spirited people in my poor but earnest prayers, imploring peace and prosperity for them, and, as a token of my love for them, since I can do nothing else, I hereby make known my desire that, as long as my superiors do not oppose it, my bones [shall] rest in some tranquil corner of this soil.

Doubtless the murder attempt impressed Padre Giuseppantonio as to the truth in Dr. Camillieri's warning, for on August 17 a telegram arrived from the Holy Office stating that the transfer order was suspended until further notice.

A story is told by Countess Virginia Sili-Salviucci, who related it to Padre Pio Dellepiano before her death in 1948. The countess was a relative of the eminent Augusto Cardinal Sili. The cardinal told her that he was present at an important meeting with Pope Pius XI during the summer of 1923. The Holy Office had been debating what to do with Padre Pio. Pius himself tended to think of Padre Pio as a fanatic, willing to incite a riot rather than be transferred. During this meeting of the top officials of the Holy Office as well as other pertinent congregations, Pope Pius announced that he was ready to suspend Padre Pio *a divinis* (that is, from all priestly functions). Suddenly, while he was speaking, a Capuchin friar appeared, knelt, and kissed his feet, saying only, "Your Holiness, for the good of the Church, do not take this course of action." He then asked the Pope's blessing, kissed his feet again, rose, and left.

"Who let that confounded friar in?" the Pope demanded. The prelates ran outside the meeting room to upbraid the guards for letting the friar in. The guards, however, all strenuously denied having seen any friar either enter or leave the room. When this was reported to the Pope, he grew silent and ordered no one to speak of the incident. He ordered Cardinal Sili, however, to ascertain where Padre Pio was that day and hour. When Sili learned that Pio was in the choir of his friary, saying his Office, he was bewildered. So was the Pope when he received the report. After that, Pius said no more about suspending Padre Pio from his priestly faculties. According to the countess, Cardinal Sili felt that this was the real reason why the Holy Office stopped pressing the Capuchins to transfer Padre Pio.

Whether or not the story, related by a second party fifteen years after the event, is true, Padre Pio's troubles were far from over!

'The Light of the Gargano'

Now in his mid-thirties, Padre Pio had lost the emaciated appearance of his first years at San Giovanni Rotondo, and his compact frame began to assume a robust aspect. A newspaper reporter during this period remarked on the dissimilarity between his actual appearance and the unflattering portraits of him that were being sold all over the south of Italy. Padre Pio, the reporter wrote, was "a beautiful young man" with dark blond hair and beard, now liberally shot with gray. He wore a "meek and serene" expression, and spoke in a voice of unusual sweetness, "which implants itself in the soul as soon as it is heard, and is never forgotten."[1] Other visitors noted his pale, rosy-hued complexion, his bright, penetrating eyes, and his radiant smile.

Despite disruptions, restrictions, and controversies, Padre Pio's ministry went on. Although he retained what his followers called a holy serenity, his heart was not made of stone, and he was at times deeply grieved. In December 1922, in the midst of the Gagliardi-Gemelli affair, he wrote to one of his supporters in the Vatican, Bishop Alberto Costa: "At present I am passing through a period of continuous mortification. . . . Pray to the Lord that . . . He might free me immediately from this harsh prison and from this body of death, calling me to Himself. I definitely cannot stand this any longer!"[2]

Although the Holy Office forbade the Light of the Gargano to answer their letters, people from all over the world continued to write to Padre Pio, unburdening their hearts and asking for his prayers. The letters were not only from the humble but from the mighty as well. In March 1923, a letter arrived from none other than King Alfonso XIII of Spain (1886-1941). No doubt as a result of generations of inbreeding, his immediate family was a virtual museum of pathology. Two of his sons, Alfonso and Gonzalo, were afflicted with the curse of hemophilia. A third son, Jaime, was born a deaf-mute. Alfonso wrote to Padre Pio:

> Having learned that your prayers are heard by the Most High and that on various occasions you have obtained the complete cure of . . . persons . . . so ill that only divine intervention could save them, I take the liberty of turning to you, Father, in earnest supplication.[3]

He went on to describe his family's health problems and request prayers for a cure. None was forthcoming. Both Don Alfonso and Don Gonzalo died after automobile accidents in the mid-1930s, of massive hemorrhaging from minor cuts, and Don Jaime remained totally deaf.

There were a number of dramatic cures and other supersensible phenomena, however. One of them took place in Montevideo, Uruguay, in 1921. Vicar General Fernando Damiani, to whom Pope Benedict had praised Padre Pio as "an extraordinary man," had heeded that pontiff's advice and done all he could to make the stigmatist known in Uruguay. Among those deeply impressed by what Damiani had to say was Mother Teresa Salvadores, superior of the Miraculous Medal Atelier School of Montevideo.

In January 1921, Mother Teresa became ill with inoperable stomach cancer, further complicated by a heart condition. By November of that year she was completely bedridden, unable to eat, kept alive by injections, and made comfortable only by morphine. There was a palpable tumor, the size of a fist, in her side. Another, in her throat, was slowly suffocating her.

The mother superior was almost at her last gasp when a relative of Bishop Damiani came to see her. Bringing with her a glove that had been worn by Padre Pio, this lady touched it to Mother Teresa's throat and side. As the nun later recounted:

> I fell asleep. In my dream I saw Padre Pio; he touched my side where the pain was, breathed into my mouth, and told me so many things that are not of this world. . . . After three hours, I woke up, asked for my habit so that I could get out of the bed in which I had been lying for three months . . . and went down to the chapel. . . . At noon I went to the refectory, and I, who hadn't eaten for so long, ate more than my sisters. . . . From that day on I have had no further illness.[4]

Another inexplicable recovery from grave illness took place in Florence two years earlier. Maria Cozzi-Giuliano was diagnosed as having an epithelioma (a type of cancer) of the tongue and on August 18, 1919, was in the hospital of Santa Maria Novella awaiting surgery. For several months, Signora Giuliano had suffered intense pain and had been unable to chew. Three days before surgery was scheduled, she decided to invoke Padre Pio's intercession. The following day she was examined by the dental surgeon who was to extract her teeth prior to the operation. He was dumbfounded to find that the cancer had vanished and the tongue was entirely cured. Professor Marchetti, Signora Giuliano's surgeon, examined her, found her perfectly normal, and dismissed her![5] When she wrote her deposition in the early 1930s, she was still without any recurrence of her illness.

There were also many reports of bilocations, often in connection with healings. Early in 1925, a young mother named Paolina Preziosi fell ill with a severe case of pneumonia. She is described as a devout Catholic and a member of the Franciscan Third Order.

She apparently lived in or near San Giovanni Rotondo. There was no penicillin available in 1925, and whatever treatment was being attempted was having no effect. In alarm, her relatives went to the friary to ask Padre Pio to intercede with God for the young mother's life. "Tell her to have no fear," he said late on Good Friday night, "since she will be resurrected with Our Lord."

Later that night, Signora Preziosi was praying to God to heal her for the sake of her five little children. Suddenly she looked up and saw Padre Pio. "Have no fear, have faith and hope," he told her. "Tomorrow, when the bells ring, you will be cured."

Within moments Preziosi sank into a coma, and her relatives, holding out no further hope, spent the day making preparations for her funeral, even preparing the Franciscan habit in which tertiaries frequently requested to be buried. They were stunned when, at the stroke of midnight, as the bells announcing the Risen Christ began to peal, Signora Preziosi leapt from her bed "as if she had been pushed by a superhuman force."

From that moment on, she was perfectly well.[6]

A similar occurrence was related to Charles Mortimer Carty, an American priest, by his friend, Bishop D'Indico of Florence. On July 21, 1921, the bishop was alone in his study, quite worried about a sister in the same town who was gravely ill. Suddenly, as he told Carty, he felt the sensation of having someone at his back. Turning, he saw a man in monk's attire who then vanished into thin air. Thinking that he was losing his mind, he went to see the chaplain of the seminary, where he was studying. The chaplain dismissed the phenomenon as a hallucination brought on by anxiety and overwork.

After his talk with the chaplain, D'Indico decided to call on his sister. The sick woman, who had been in a deep coma, was now, to his happy amazement, conscious and quite lucid. She reported seeing a monk in her room at the very moment her brother was having his "hallucination." "Don't be afraid," the monk told her. "Tomorrow your fever will disappear and after a few days there will be no trace of your illness on your body."

"Are you a saint?" asked the sick woman.

"No," said the mysterious monk, "I am a creature who serves the Lord through His mercies."

"Let me kiss your habit, Father," asked the bishop's sister.

"Kiss the sign of the Passion," he said, and revealed hands exhibiting the stigmata.

After agreeing to keep the sick woman's husband and son under his protection, the monk vanished. The bishop's sister awoke from her coma, felt an immediate improvement, and, within eight days, was completely well again.[7] (This incident, by the way, took place before Merry del Val's decree that Pio was to show the stigmata to no one.)

We have seen how Padre Paolino had recounted that many people came to San Giovanni claiming to be possessed by the devil. There are many reports of expulsion of demons through Padre Pio. Father John Schug interviewed an eyewitness who testified to one such occurrence. One day a woman disrupted the Mass in the crowded church with her yelling. The woman's face was so hideously contorted and she had such an uncanny light in her eyes that many fled in terror.

"I'm the owner of this church!" the woman roared, "and I'm the only person who gives orders here." As she approached a picture of the Archangel Michael, who cast Satan from heaven, she bellowed, "You didn't win! I won!"

Padre Pio was hearing confessions in the sacristy when he heard the commotion and went into the church. When the sacristan urged him not to go out because the woman was surely possessed, Pio said: "Don't be afraid. When were we afraid of the devil?"

He walked up to the raving woman, who was crouching beside one of the confessionals "like a tigress," waiting to spring at him. "Go away from there!" Pio commanded her.

"Please don't send me away! Please don't send me away!" she pleaded.

"Go away until I finish hearing confessions," insisted Padre Pio. "Then come back here."

When Padre Pio finished hearing the confessions of men, he went into the church and found the wretched woman, now quiet. He ordered her into one of the confessionals. When she left, according to eyewitnesses, her face was "like that of an angel."[8]

Father Schug also tells the story of a young wife who had lain in a coma for over a year. She was carried into the church one evening when Padre Pio was leading the Vespers service. As he blessed the congregation with the Blessed Sacrament, the woman awoke, "snorted like a bull, and her body began to puff up." After Vespers, Padre Pio hurried the woman and her husband into the sacristy and began the formal rite of exorcism. While he prayed, the frantic woman tried to claw his habit and beard. After he finished, the woman suddenly became calm. It was quite undramatic, unlike *The Exorcist* and other popular films on the subject. The woman, quite restored to her senses, took her husband's hand, marveled at her disheveled appearance, asked for a comb, and walked out.[9] Padre Pio frequently prayed over, and brought peace to, people who were — or were thought to be — possessed.

Sometime in the early 1920s Padre Pio began to hear the confessions of women on a routine basis. The women's confessions he heard in the closed confessionals in the church, while he continued to hear those of the men in the sacristy. Padre Pio was known to be extremely abrupt with those who had come for the sake of curiosity or were not sincerely repentant. A lady from Naples told me in 1979 that, years before, an uncle of hers, incurably ill, attempted to make his confession to Padre Pio in hopes of a cure, but, to his great indignation, the monk refused to speak to him and sent him away. The sick man returned home in a rage and died embittered about a year later. The niece, however, recalls that the older man was never a firm believer and was looking to Padre Pio to manipulate the will of heaven. Moreover, he really was not interested in making his confession but simply in demanding a cure from Padre Pio.

Padre Pio reasoned that since there were scores of people coming each day to make sincere confessions and genuinely seek spiritual counsel, he simply could not afford to waste time with people who came merely to test his alleged occult powers.

Many complained about Padre Pio's "rough" manner in the confessional. When Archbishop Gagliardi complained to the Pope about Padre Pio's "horrible manner of hearing confessions," he was doubtless referring to this. Pio's superiors themselves were sometimes concerned. In November 1921, a few months before he was dismissed as Pio's spiritual director, Benedetto expressed his worry about the younger man's "fits of temper" in the confessional. Padre Pio admitted that he did at times have "bursts of temper," which he said were due in part to overwork. The sight of so many hardened and unrepentant sinners, he explained, moved him to an anger reflective of God's indignation.[10]

It is a fact that a great many of those who were dismissed without absolution or scolded or even insulted by Padre Pio later fervently repented. Cleonice Morcaldi, a relative of Francesco, wrote:

> So many people would come here for confession and Padre Pio would send them away. But he would torment them with remorse, and he would follow them with his prayers and sufferings. Ultimately they would return, fully penitent. . . . He knew how to enter into the hearts of people. . . . But the child of Padre Pio returned fully reformed. . . . He said to me, "I know you inside and out, like you know yourself. . . ." That is why he minced no words. There was no halfway measure with him. But when it came to the poor and suffering, he had a love and a tenderness like Jesus.[11]

There was a physician whom Padre Pio ejected with one of his favorite epithets, "You pig, you!" For two years the doctor seethed and stewed. Finally he brought himself to admit that his life was like a pigsty. He returned to San

Giovanni Rotondo and was cheerfully received by Padre Pio, who welcomed his confession.

Again, there is the instance of a blind man who, on his first visit to Padre Pio, received a reception similar to that accorded the doctor. "You filthy wretch, go away!" Padre Pio bellowed. The sightless pilgrim went away in high dudgeon, excoriating the arrogant priest who had the presumption to turn a good Catholic away from the confessional. Later, when he complained to another priest about Padre Pio, the clergyman was able to draw the admission from the blind man that he was blissfully sharing home and bed with a woman to whom he was not married. Eventually, he was able to convince the blind man that this arrangement was not exactly pleasing to God and persuade him to return to Padre Pio, sincerely sorry for his sins and willing to make a change. This time Padre Pio welcomed him like a son.[12]

The fascinating story of Federico Abresch involves an apparently miraculous, at least unexplained, healing. Born in Germany in 1897, he had married an Italian woman. A nominal Lutheran before his marriage, he became a nominal Roman Catholic afterward. "I had no faith," he later admitted. He became a student of the occult and ultimately took up theosophy and became a believer in reincarnation. Out of sheer curiosity, he went to see Padre Pio in 1925.

Padre Pio did not expel Abresch from the confessional, but he did make him, as he put it, "understand immediately that in my previous confessions I had committed certain mortal sins." He then asked if his previous confessions had been in good faith: "I answered that I considered confession a good institution, socially and educationally, but that I didn't believe at all in the divinity of the sacrament. Then, deeply moved by what I had seen, I added, 'Father, now I do believe.'"

Padre Pio then explained that theosophy and reincarnation were "heresies." He asked Abresch to retire, get his thoughts together, and try to recall when he had last made a sincere confession. Pio promised to speak to him further later that day.

Abresch, "moved and shaken," did not know where to begin. He could not remember ever having made a sincere confession! When Padre Pio invited him to return for confession, however, Abresch decided to touch on the sins of his childhood. He had time to say only, "Father, I happen to be . . ." when he was interrupted. "You made a good confession when you were returning from your wedding trip," Pio said. "Leave out the rest and begin from there." Abresch, dumbfounded, was now certain that he had "come in contact with the supernatural."

> The day after we returned from the wedding trip, my wife said that she
> would like both of us to go to the sacraments, and I complied with her wish.
> I went to confession to the same priest who brought me into the Catholic

Church. He knew I was a novice, little accustomed to such things. That is why I made a good confession. But now, I ask myself: Who could have had any knowledge of these things other than Padre Pio, who has the gift of reading our most intimate thoughts and can scrutinize our conscience?

From then on, Padre Pio did not give his penitent time to think. As Federico Abresch recalled,

He concealed his knowledge of my entire past under the form of questions. He enumerated with precision and clarity all of my faults, even mentioning the number of times that I had missed Mass!

I was completely bowled over at hearing things that I had forgotten, and I was able to reconstruct that past by remembering in detail all the particulars that Padre Pio had described with such precision.[13]

In 1926, a year later, Signora Abresch began to hemorrhage, and doctors diagnosed a tumor in her womb. After two years, the tumor had grown alarmingly. Several doctors advised her to submit to surgery without delay. But Amalia Abresch was devastated by the certainty that a hysterectomy would leave her incapable of bearing children, so she went to Padre Pio. At first he advised her to have the operation, but when she told him of her desperate desire to have at least one child, he changed his mind and told her not to submit to the knife. After that, the hemorrhages ceased and, although the tumor remained, to her great delight, she conceived and, at the age of nearly forty, gave birth to a son. The boy, who was named Pio, later went on to become a priest.[14]

Eventually the Abresch family settled in San Giovanni Rotondo, where Federico opened a photography studio. For many years he was something of an official photographer for Padre Pio and his brethren, and most of the extant likenesses of the celebrated priest were taken by this man, who was led to Christ through his ministry.

What impressed visitors to Our Lady of Grace most deeply, however, was not cures, bilocations, or supernatural intuitions in the confessional (after all, not all who sought out the padre experienced these things); it was Padre Pio's Mass. I have never interviewed anyone who attended one of Padre Pio's Masses who was not deeply impressed.

"You truly saw that God was there," recalls Andre Mandato, who worshiped at many Masses at which Pio was the celebrant. It was not that he was a showman who celebrated in a way that was more dramatic or emotional than that of other priests. Members of the congregation felt, rather, that they were actually in the presence of God.

John McCaffery, a Scottish businessman based in Milan, over the years made numerous trips to see Padre Pio. He attempted to describe the stupendous phenomenon of the padre's Mass in this way:

For more than an hour one is held spellbound by the deep intensity with which it is said; not a physical intensity, for his movements are slow and deliberate, his voice full and low-pitched, but an intensity of the spirit wherein we now glimpse a Padre Pio obviously inhabiting a world other than the material world around him; at times clearly suffering, at times as though looking on things unseen by us, at times in apparent mental converse, through all and above all his evident tremendous consciousness of the significance of his words and actions; and there, clearly revealed, the bleeding perforations in his hands. In a way, when you have seen his Mass, you have seen everything, or at least you fully understand and accept everything.[15]

Andre Mandato recalls, "At the beginning of Mass, his face was really pale, just as if he were carrying our suffering, our pain, and our sin." Then, after the Consecration, his countenance underwent a radical and amazing change. His face seemed to be transfigured with radiant light. From the very first time he beheld Padre Pio's Mass, Mandato says, "I realized that the Spirit of God was there." During the course of the service, Mandato often heard Padre Pio address invisible beings. "Go away! Go away!" he sometimes heard him say, as if an evil spirit were there, trying to interfere.[16]

Although these two accounts of Padre Pio's Mass date from fifteen to twenty years subsequent to the period we are now covering, the congregations of the 1920s experienced the same thing. Even though his Mass at times lasted twice as long as that of the other priests, the faithful were literally fighting each other to get into the little church to participate in it.

Padre Pio's appeal was not entirely on the spiritual plane. During the 1920s he did all he could to improve the material condition of those around him. According to Padre Alessio, "When Padre Pio first came here, this district was as poor as India." The riot of 1920 had, of course, much to do with the misery of many of the working people. As we have seen, Pio and Francesco Morcaldi worked out a program calculated to improve the plight of the people, of which projects the one dearest to Padre Pio's heart was the hospital.

The nearest hospital to San Giovanni was in Foggia, but that was twenty-five miles away, and even by automobile (of which there were few in San Giovanni in those days), that was a full hour's drive. Padre Pio often heard about accident victims, women in labor, people suffering from heart attacks, appendicitis, and other maladies who died before they ever got to Foggia. Even when the sick and injured arrived alive, help was often slow in coming. After learning of an accident victim who was left bleeding in a hallway for days. Pio was determined to establish a hospital in San Giovanni Rotondo.

From the time of the "Massacre of San Giovanni Rotondo," Padre Pio, with the approval of his superiors, had begun to solicit funds. With the help and support of Morcaldi and three physicians, a small hospital, chiefly for emergency cases, was opened in January 1925. Called St. Francis Hospital, it had twenty beds and an operating theater of sorts. As Padre Pio insisted, medical care was free for the indigent. Dr. Angelo Maria Merla was there every day, and Dr. Bucci, from Foggia, performed surgical operations there twice a week. It was a far cry from what Padre Pio envisioned, but it was a start.

Padre Pio's other pet project was the construction of a friary in Pietrelcina. This came into being through the help of a most extraordinary lady, whose name has appeared from time to time in these pages: Mary Adelia Pyle.

Adelia McAlpin Pyle was born in Morristown, New Jersey, on April 17, 1888, one of several children of James Tolman and Frances (McAlpin) Pyle. Her family owned Herald Square in New York. Her father, who died at fifty-three in 1911, was known as the Soap King. He invented soap flakes and patented a product known as Pyle's Powder.

Little is known of Adelia's religious background. She was baptized at five months at the Church of the Covenant, which merged when she was six with another congregation to form the Brick Presbyterian Church. For six of the most formative years of her life, she sat under the celebrated Dr. Henry Van Dyke (1852-1933), preacher, educator, and author of the hymn "Joyful, Joyful, We Adore Thee" and the novel *The Other Wise Man*. Adelia must have been dissatisfied with Van Dyke in some way because when she was about ten, she loved to go secretly with her Irish governess to a nearby Roman Catholic Church. When Adelia's mother learned about this behavior, she put a stop to it, and in May 1903, at the age of fifteen, Adelia Pyle was received into membership at the Brick Church.[17]

Young Miss Pyle went to finishing school and spent some time in Europe, where she mastered five languages. While still in her twenties, she was hired as a personal secretary to the celebrated Italian educator Maria Montessori (1870-1952)). From that time on, she spent most of her time in Europe. While living in Barcelona, Spain, she had herself baptized conditionally as a Roman Catholic in the Church of Our Lady of Montserrat, much to her mother's dismay. She took the baptismal name of Mary, by which she was known for the rest of her life.

In October 1923, Miss Pyle was in search of a spiritual director when she heard of Padre Pio. Along with a Romanian Orthodox friend, she went to San Giovanni Rotondo to find him. She encountered him alone, praying in church. "Padre Pio! Padre Pio!" she cried out with great emotion, but the priest made no reply. When Miss Pyle insisted on making herself known, Pio answered testily. "What do you want? Let me pray to the Lord in peace!"[18]

When Miss Pyle proceeded to fall on her knees, Padre Pio's attitude changed. Putting his hand on her head, he said, "Daughter, don't go traveling anymore, but stay here." Again, a few days later, more insistently, he demanded, "Stay here, enter the Franciscan Third Order and build a good house for yourself and for other souls, because your permanent work will be here."[19]

Miss Pyle did as she was bidden: in 1925 she settled permanently at San Giovanni Rotondo. She took a vow of perfect and perpetual chastity, became a Franciscan tertiary, and for the rest of her life wore the brown habit and cincture and sandals. At the foot of a steep hill off to the side of the friary, she built a commodious house that resembled a little castle. Here, for more than four decades, Miss Pyle provided hospitality for many of Padre Pio's guests.

Mary Adelia Pyle is universally described as a woman of great beauty — tall, willowy, blond, blue-eyed, and had a rosy complexion. Known for great personal warmth and deep piety, "the American Lady" eventually (though not immediately) came to be celebrated by the townspeople for her simplicity, her humility, her serenity, and her stability: virtues prized in the Franciscan tradition.

One day, Padre Pio approached her and said: "There's an old organ in the church that has need of a new organist. Do you think you can play it?"

"I'm no artist, Padre, but I shall be happy to learn to play the organ so that I can serve my Lord better."[20]

And so Mary Pyle became organist at the Church of Our Lady of Grace. In time, she organized a ladies' choir called *Schola Cantorum*.

Miss Pyle had inherited a fortune from her father and was concerned to use it to help those who were suffering. Her concern for the spiritual lives of others led her to ask one day, "Can I build a friary at Pietrelcina?" She explained to Padre Pio that several residents of his hometown had been asking her to build a Capuchin friary there. Matter-of-factly, with no hint of surprise or elation, Pio answered, "Yes, do it at once, and let it be dedicated to the Holy Family."[21]

Immediately Miss Pyle placed her entire fortune at Padre Pio's disposal to construct not only a friary but also a seminary at Pietrelcina. Delegated to supervise the construction was none other than the faithful Emmanuele Brunatto, who took up residence in Pietrelcina in one of the homes owned by Pio's parents.

It will be recalled that many years before, when Padre Pio was a boy, he pointed to an open field and told Don Salvatore Pannullo that he heard singing and the ringing of bells there. Brunatto now asked Pannullo to indicate the spot. Although seventy-six years old and almost totally blind, Pati escorted Brunatto to the countryside and showed him the exact place.

The owner of the land, Alessandro Silvestri, out of love for Padre Pio, was persuaded to sell it for a modest amount. Still there remained a problem: Who would be the legal owner? Brunatto first tried to put the property in the name of the Capuchin Province of Foggia, but, apparently out of fear of the Holy Office, the provincial curia said no. Brunatto elicited a similar response from the general office of the Capuchins in Rome. The land could not be put in Mary Pyle's name because she was not an Italian citizen. Finally, Padre Pio's brother, Michele, agreed to be titular owner. As engineer and architect, Brunatto engaged a man from Rome named Todini.

On the day when the cornerstone was to be laid, all Pietrelcina gathered before the Mother Church to march, accompanied by the town band, to the spot where the new church and friary were to rise. After speeches by the mayor and other dignitaries, including Brunatto, who used the occasion for a vituperative diatribe against the Holy Office, the crowd dispersed to the nearby Church of Purgatory, which lay in ruins, to fetch stones for the rising edifice. Brunatto was amazed when he saw a sea of stones, some weighing more than a hundred pounds, being carried uphill with perfect equilibrium on the heads of women, who, with no sign of effort, brought them to the construction site and went back for more. By sundown, all the stones from the abandoned church were at the site of the new friary. That night in the sky over Pietrelcina, a huge cross of light was seen to rise from the construction site. It was observed for half an hour; then it slowly disappeared.[22]

A few days later, Luigi Cardinal Lavitrano, archbishop of Benevento, stopped by to see the construction and bless the cornerstone. Thereafter, every week at a given time, the bells of the Mother Church were rung to call the populace to go to the creek to pick up stones to carry to the new site. Brunatto was touched at seeing the villagers, including the tottering old Pannullo, only months away from his death, moving slowly up the hill with stones on their shoulders.

Soon another problem presented itself. There was no water. When Padre Pio was apprized of this, he described a certain location and told the laborers to dig there. To everyone's amazement, a large spring was found there. Thus, for at least the second time in his life, Padre Pio played the part of the water witch!

The construction of the friary, church, and seminary proceeded, though not without further difficulties, including a terrible electrical storm in which lightning killed a bricklayer. Even so, it would be twenty years before the Capuchins would finally come to Pietrelcina. That is a subject for another chapter.

A Little Light in the Thicket

In the mid 1920s, Padre Pio was cheered by the presence at San Giovanni Rotondo of his dear friend Padre Agostino Daniele. Padre Pietro, the provincial, transferred him there in 1923 to teach Latin and Greek at the Seraphic College and also to compensate Pio for the loss of Padre Benedetto. Agostino remained for two years. Writing in his diary several years later, the professor recalled, "It is needless to speak of Padre Pio's joy and mine in our living together."[1]

Both men soon discovered, however, that deep as their friendship was, there was no way to replace Padre Benedetto, especially in his capacity as spiritual director. Agostino soon realized that he was unable to plumb the depths of Pio's soul as Benedetto could.

Because of the trauma to which he had been lately subjected, Padre Pio found it difficult to talk about his spiritual state, even to Agostino. The professor obtained permission from Padre Pietro for Padre Pio to put his spiritual state into writing. Again, Pio demurred for fear that what he wrote might easily be purloined, find its way into the papers, and be the cause of his losing Agostino as well as Benedetto. "All that remains for me," Pio told the professor, "is the sole comfort of at least seeing you and of talking to you. If tomorrow someone were to learn that I am writing to you, even with the permission of the provincial, it could happen that they might prohibit even you from coming here, and what a grief that would be for both of us!"[2]

Agostino was aware, however, of Pio's ongoing inability to discern his own spiritual state, a long-standing outgrowth of his Dark Night. He often asked, "Father, pray and beg for my conversion," as if he were uncertain about his own salvation. Again, sometimes he told Agostino: "I see nothing but darkness in my soul. Will the Lord be pleased with me?" It was only through the professor's assurances, which Pio received under holy obedience, that he was calmed. "In other souls, through the grace of God," Pio told him, "I see clearly, but in my own I see nothing but darkness."[3] In addition, Padre Pio was distressed at being unable to express himself to his satisfaction. Sometimes, Padre Agostino noted, Pio would verbalize "something which he neither wants to say nor realizes he is saying,"[4] which was a terrible ordeal for Pio.

On December 13, 1923, Pio complained to Padre Pietro that he was being abandoned by everyone. "In vain I try to make acts of conformity to God's will," Pio wrote. "In vain I turn to Him. Everywhere there is silence . . . even in heaven, which has become as bronze to me."[5]

Padre Pio was soon to be deprived of the support of the kind minister provincial when, on February 23, 1924, strained beyond endurance by the ongoing crisis with the archbishop and the Holy Office, Padre Pietro dropped dead of a heart attack at the age of forty-four. He was replaced by Padre Bernardo of Alpicella, from the province of Parma. Padre Bernardo, though a just man, was constrained by Cardinal Merry del Val and the Holy Office to clap even more restrictions on Padre Pio.

On April 22, 1925, Padre Bernardo ordered that no visitors were to congregate in the sacristy, guest room, or corridor to talk with Padre Pio. The padre, furthermore, was not to stop to talk with people after hearing confessions; he was to go directly upstairs to his room. Nor was he to talk with anyone after Mass or give his hand to be kissed; he was to go directly to the choir to make his thanksgiving.

These orders were intended to put an end to the disgraceful scenes that horrified many visitors to San Giovanni, such as the fights among the local women for the privilege of kissing the holy man's hand. But the directives did curtail Pio's opportunity to be of assistance to others, which saddened him.

The directives also specified that no layman could reside at the friary, which forced Emmanuele Brunatto to leave. Brunatto went to Pietrelcina to supervise the construction of the friary complex there. But the brilliant and sensitive man was stung by his expulsion and from that moment vowed to do everything he could to "rescue" Padre Pio and discomfit Archbishop Gagliardi and the Holy Office. At the moment, however, Brunatto was occupied with the friary at Pietrelcina, where he came to know and love Padre Pio's family.

Of all his family members, Padre Pio seems to have seen the most of his brother Michele, who had returned from New York after the First World War to devote his time to farming at Pietrelcina. "He has calloused hands but a tender heart," Pio often said of him.[6] Andre and Graziella (DeNunzio) Mandato, who knew Michele well, described him to me in a 1978 interview as "a good man, a very holy man," warm, loving, and cheerful. Michele and his wife, Giuseppa, had been devastated by the death of their little son, Franceschino, who had "flown to heaven" at the age of eleven. When the child died, Padre Pio assured his brother that he would have other children. When Giuseppa bore a stillborn son shortly afterward, Pio was troubled, but insisted that his brother and sister-in-law would yet have a living child. Finally, on January 6, 1924, Giuseppa gave birth to a daughter, Pia, who lived to marry and bear eight children.

Pio's parents, now in their mid-sixties, made few trips to San Giovanni Rotondo. Early in 1925, Motherdear drove to see him, only to spend a week vainly trying to have five minutes of conversation with her son. As she packed her suitcase to return, Brunatto, who happened to be there, expressed his surprise. "Well, what am I do do?" Donna Giuseppa said. "I can't succeed in saying even a word to him. You kiss his hand for me."[7]

Padre Pio's relationship with his mother is something of a mystery. If the padre had time to see his spiritual daughters who lived in town and came to him several times a week, if he had time to talk to Morcaldi and Brunatto and Mary Pyle, it seems that he could have taken at least a few minutes to talk to his own mother, who came infrequently on a journey that took many hours. Every morning she received Holy Communion from her son's hand, but whenever she tried to approach him to say something, he would not listen or even permit her to kiss his hand. Sometime later, Motherdear stayed almost three weeks, only to return to Pietrelcina in tears. "I was there for twenty days," she told her friends, "and still I was not able to say a single word to Padre Pio. Holy Mary, why does he act that way? He doesn't even let me kiss his hand!"[8]

Pio's pat answer had always been, "The son must kiss the mother's hand and not the mother the son's," though there is no evidence that he ever kissed his mother's hand. Further, the mothers of friars commonly called them by their baptismal names, but Padre Pio never permitted his mother to call him Francesco after he entered into religious life. He always insisted that she call him Padre Pio like everyone else.

The Forgiones were soon drawn into the tempest that was raging around Padre Pio. In December 1925, Canon Giovanni Miscio, who had written letters to the Vatican denouncing Pio, now wrote an entire book "against the honor" of Padre Pio and the Forgione family. He then went to Pietrelcina, showed Michele the manuscript, and told him that he had been given an advance of 5000 lire (the equivalent of $8.29 in those days, but evidently with far more buying power) but would agree to forgo publication if Forgione would pay him the amount of the advance, which would have to be refunded.

Michele told Don Giovanni that he did not have such a sum on hand but that he was willing to sell some of his land "so that Padre Pio won't have to suffer anymore." Don Giovanni agreed. Michele, however, told Brunatto, and Brunatto hurried to Rome, where he told Cardinal Gasparri. The portly prelate exploded: "Have that canon put in jail! That will cast a little light into the thicket at San Giovanni Rotondo!"[9]

Meanwhile, so as not to have to sell land, Michele had convinced Miscio to accept 4000 lire (the equivalent of $6.63 in the exchange rate of the day) in cash and a promissory note for the rest. He paid Miscio, however, with bills whose serial numbers he had registered with the police, whom he alerted to the scheme. Within a short time, the extortionist priest was caught. When the constables burst into his home, they caught him red-handed destroying a threatening note to Michele Forgione, on which he had written, "Your days are numbered!"[10]

Padre Pio almost fainted when he learned what had happened. In vain he tried to persuade Michele not to press charges. He refused to listen to Pio, insisting, "It is my duty to defend my brother against calumny." When Pio still insisted that the matter not be taken to court, Michele informed him that the two of them would have no further contact until the case was established against Don Giovanni Miscio. Thus he left the padre fuming.

Quickly, Pio sent for Attorney Caprile, his brother's lawyer. Caprile went up to Pio's room and remained with him for an hour. Padre Raffaele D'Addario heard the two men screaming at each other at the top of their voices. When at last Caprile left Pio's room, the friar took both the lawyer's hands and pressed them between his own and pleaded, "Promise me that you won't let Don Giovanni be condemned."

Caprile told him: "Padre, you know I cannot work against my own client. Your brother is my client."

Padre Pio roared: "I have spoken! I am sending you to see that the priest is not condemned!"

"Since this is your wish," said Caprile meekly, "and since you are commanding me, I will do everything to extenuate the circumstances and to save the priest."[11]

Pio made Caprile repeat the promise. He kept it, and even though the judge in reading Miscio's manuscript found that it contained "obscene insinuations, especially repugnant in having been devised by a priest," Miscio received a suspended sentence. Until he received news of the verdict, Pio paced about, shaking his head and weeping, sighing: "A priest in jail! A *priest* in *jail*! And all because of Padre Pio!"[12]

Although Miscio did not go to prison, he lost his job as a teacher. Padre Pio, however, wrote to the state government and pleaded — successfully — for Miscio's reinstatement. After he received his teaching post back, the chastened canon went to the Forgione brothers to beg their forgiveness and thank them. Pio and Michele, themselves reconciled, embraced Don Giovanni, telling him that all was forgiven. Even in infirm old age, Miscio would totter up to the friary to visit Padre Pio, to whom he remained eternally grateful, to ask for his prayers. Near the end of his life, he told the local superiors of his desire to end his days at the friary, near his beloved Padre Pio.

Meanwhile, new fires of contention were breaking out. The same year as the Miscio affair, Padre Pio denied absolution to Maria DiMaggio, the longtime mistress of Archpriest Don Giuseppe Prencipe. So lax were the local secular clergy that it was not uncommon for those who were not homosexual to live with their women as man and wife for years. Maria DiMaggio, sixty years old, had lived with Don Giuseppe for nearly a quarter century. Padre Pio insisted that their relationship was sinful and demanded that it be terminated. While DiMaggio was willing to terminate the relationship, the archpriest was not. When, at his insistence, Maria DiMaggio continued to sleep with Prencipe, Padre Pio refused to absolve her. She went to a priest in another town, who upheld Padre Pio.

DiMaggio signed a statement in which she alleged that Don Giuseppe had originally tempted her into bed by telling her that it was not a sin because the Sacred Scriptures permit the bodily needs of a man and woman to be satisfied once a month. She contended that when, at Padre Pio's insistence, she tried to refuse the archpriest, he attempted to rape her.

When Prencipe heard of her signed deposition, he threatened to kill Maria DiMaggio unless she signed a retraction, which she did. The archbishop, who had defended Miscio to the hilt and refused to suspend any of his priestly faculties even after he was convicted, now came to Prencipe's defense, attacking Padre Pio once more for his "horrible means of hearing confessions."

During the early months of 1926, Gagliardi forwarded more anonymous letters of accusation to the new minister provincial, Padre Bernardo. Bernardo, being from outside the province of Foggia, did not know Padre Pio well enough to recognize that the accusations were false. The allegations this time were subdued enough not to be readily dismissed by someone not thoroughly acquainted with the situation. Among other things, Gagliardi, through the anonymous letters, accused Padre Pio of insisting that his spiritual children make their confessions more frequently than their usual eight-day interval, thereby implying that he was a fanatic. He further accused Pio of permitting his hand to be kissed and of lingering outside the confessional to talk with women, thereby violating the restrictions placed on him by the Holy Office.

Padre Pio was "shattered" when Padre Bernardo, in a letter, mentioned the accusations as if there were some substance to them. Responding to the charges in detail, Pio wrote the provincial, on May 18, 1926, that he had never counseled confession at any interval shorter than eight days. Only twice did he confer with women outside the confessional: once when he heard the confession of a woman who was almost totally deaf, and another time when he spoke a few words to Maria Campanile "out of pure charity and compassion, because she was ill." Regarding the hand kissing, he protested: "Anybody who has been to our church knows how many times I have shouted at them, and if they do not desist, what fault is it of mine? Do I have to strike them? Well, perhaps I would if I had good hands!"

Meanwhile, complaints against Gagliardi were being voiced more persistently, and they came not only from Padre Pio's devotees. Pope Pius XI, who still esteemed the archbishop highly, created him a count of the Roman Empire and an assistant to the pontifical throne, but there were rumblings even from within the Vatican. Bishop Valbonesi frequently referred to Gagliardi in his letters as "the vile archbishop of Manfredonia" and "that peach of a bishop." There were more complaints about sodomy in the archdiocese, about "ignorant and immoral" candidates for priestly office being preferred over men of character. There were complaints that the aging prelate no longer even took the trouble to confer the sacrament of confirmation, and that more than a thousand young people had been kept waiting for almost a decade for that sacrament. A number of priests in the archdiocese sent a petition to Pius XI, asking him to turn his attention to the "disorder, immorality," and "clerical degeneracy" that prevailed. They went on to detail charges of simony (Gagliardi was willing to offer positions to anyone willing to pay enough), the appointment and protection of men found guilty in civil courts of "infamous crimes," the keeping of false financial records and the lack of accounting for the proceeds of the sale of church ornaments, and personal immorality.

Whenever Gagliardi learned of complaints against him, he would fly into a rage. Any priest who dared to "betray" him he labeled a "viper" and stripped of his priestly faculties. He tended to blame his unpopularity on Padre Pio, and in 1926 he relieved two priests of their faculties for the crime of daring to join a delegation greeting Padre Pio on his name day.

Meanwhile, Brunatto made no attempt to ingratiate himself with the archbishop. Around this time he wrote a book, *Padre Pio of Pietrelcina*, in which he exposed the persecution of his priest-friend at the hands of the capricious and senescent archbishop. The Holy Office promptly put it on the index of forbidden books, buying up all copies, but not before Cardinal Gasparri had a chance to read it. He called Brunatto into his office and told him: "You've achieved your purpose. An apostolic visitation will take place and you will participate."[13]

A visitation is an official procedure within the Roman Catholic Church for investigating a parish, diocese, or religious community to determine whether everything is in order. An apostolic visitation of limited scope took place in March 1927. Officially, it had nothing to do with Padre Pio or Gagliardi. It was to investigate the cathedral chapter — the canons. This would include most of the local town clergy, including Miscio and Palladino. It also included the archpriest, Don Giuseppe Prencipe. The investigating team consisted of Bishop Felice Bevilacqua, Brunatto, and a secretary, Padre Alfredo Quattrino.

When the canons (priests on the staff of the cathedral who are without parish assignments and whose only obligation is to say the Office) learned that they were being investigated, they tried to go over the head of the visitation team by appealing directly to the Pope, writing a sanctimonious letter in which they portrayed themselves as innocent victims of Padre Pio, Brunatto, and their friends. They said that Pio and his colleagues had maliciously accused them of all manner of evils. At the same time, the canons insisted that the Capuchins were inventing miracle stories for the purpose of revenue. They pleaded with the Pontiff to intervene directly. Pius, however, permitted the visitation to proceed. As a result, a sordid wealth of scandal was dredged up, placing Don Giuseppe Prencipe and most of his staff in a most lurid light. Bishop Bevilacqua was horrified when the facts came to light and censured the archpriest and canons, both in his report and to their faces, for "outrages against morality."

The results of the visitation, however, were only some light slaps on the wrist. Prencipe was found guilty of immoral conduct, but "in order to avoid greater scandal," a powerful cardinal intervened to suspend the archpriest's dismissal. Palladino was suspended for a month. His intemperate harangues from the pulpit against Padre Pio had been condemned even by Prencipe. He had openly said that he did not fear God and, as for the archbishop, if Gagliardi should move against him, he would reveal the prelate's scandalous life for all to see. Several other clergy were censured, but few of them suffered very much. Of course, Brunatto, Morcaldi, and other lay supporters of Padre Pio were quite dissatisfied.

In 1928, Padre Pio was still held in great suspicion within many circles of the Church, even within his own Order. For instance, in August of that year, a Swiss Capuchin from Freibourg wrote to Padre Bernardo that he had read in a local paper that Padre Pio had been "accused, condemned, and imprisoned for crimes against morality." Meanwhile, the "notorious" Padre Pio, outwardly unflappable, continued his ministry. Those who came to see him continued to be enthusiastic, and nearly every week there were reports of some sensational cure or dramatic conversion.

One combined cure and conversion that caught the attention of the community concerned a notorious and outspoken atheist, Dr. Francesco Ricciardi, a bosom friend of Don Giuseppe Prencipe. Publicly disavowing any belief in God, Ricciardi had for years supported Gagliardi's attacks on Padre Pio. In the fall of 1928 he was diagnosed by five doctors as suffering from advanced cancer of the stomach. The physicians had pronounced him incurable and his condition hopeless.

By December, Ricciardi, who had declined precipitously, was near death. His friend Prencipe decided to approach him in hopes that the doctor might be amenable to a last-minute reconciliation with God. When the archpriest entered the room, however, the sick man threw a slipper at his head. "Go away!" he rasped. "I intend to die as I have lived!"[14]

After Prencipe left in a huff, Dr. Angelo Maria Merla, who was attending Ricciardi, ran to the friary and asked for Padre Pio. Pio wanted to leave at once but had to obtain permission from the guardian, Padre Raffaele of Sant'Elia a Pianisi. For some reason, Raffaele was at first reluctant, but he gave in to Pio's pleading and accompanied him to Dr. Ricciardi's house.

Pio entered the sick man's room alone, shutting the door behind him. No one knows what occurred between the two men, except that Ricciardi confessed his sins and received Holy Communion. When the family was readmitted to the room, they found the doctor weeping, embracing the priest. After a while, he whispered to Padre Pio: "Father, bless me one more time. There is no more hope for me, and in a little while I will be dead, and so I want to leave the world with your pardon and another blessing from you."

The family gasped at this profession of faith from a man who even a few minutes before had eschewed any belief in God. They were further amazed when Padre Pio, smiling broadly, told the doctor: "Your soul is healed, and soon your body will be healed as well! You will go to the friary and repay the visit that I have made this evening."[15]

Within three days, all signs of the cancer had disappeared and Ricciardi went to the friary to thank Padre Pio and to the church to thank God. The physician lived nearly four more years, dying at seventy-one in 1932 (of what, it is not recorded). He remained a practicing Catholic.

The healing of the atheistic Dr. Ricciardi was in stark contrast to an event that took place a few days later. On December 5, 1928, Padre Pio's mother came to San Giovanni, took a room in Mary Pyle's house, and announced that she was there to stay. It was understood that Papa Forgione would follow her early the next year, after he took care of business at Pietrelcina. After a few days, however, many friends of the family were convinced that Motherdear had come to San Giovanni not to live but to die. Nearly seventy now, the Little Princess seemed to have changed overnight from a slim, vivacious woman to an enfeebled old lady.

Even so, she attended Padre Pio's Mass every day. Mary Pyle was touched at seeing the stately old matron kiss the ground upon which her son trod after he had given her Communion. Despite her declining health, she took an active part in the conversation of the numerous guests and boarders at Miss Pyle's house. Whenever anyone ventured to criticize Gagliardi and his cohorts, Donna Giuseppa, still alert, would cut the discussion short. "Who are we to permit criticism of the ministers of God?" she would ask. "The Lord said that we ought not judge if we do not wish to be judged ourselves, and this means that we should judge neither the good nor the evil, because we can see only what people are doing, while God alone can see into men's hearts the reason why they do such things."[16]

On December 23, perhaps knowing that the end of her days was at hand, she approached Padre Raffaele, the guardian, and told him, "Take care of my son." Mary Pyle never forgot Motherdear's last trip to church. It was Christmas, bitterly cold and snowy. Despite the weather, she insisted on walking up the hill to the church and refused the offer of the use of a fur coat. "Oh, I don't want to look like a great lady, my dear," she said.[17]

After Mass, she went into the sacristy to see her son. According to Miss Pyle, Giuseppa fell to her knees at Pio's feet, "held her hands straight down like Our

Lady of the Miraculous Medal, and looked at Padre Pio as a soul must look at Jesus, and he looked at her as Jesus must look upon a soul."

Then she asked him, "Padre Pio, how can we know if before God we are not great sinners? We confess everything that we can remember or know, but perhaps God sees other things that we cannot recall."

Pio, for once devoting all his attention to Motherdear, answered her, "If we put into [our confession] all our goodwill and we have the intention to confess everything — all that we can know or remember — the mercy of God is so great that He will include and erase even what we cannot remember or know."[18]

Giuseppa then went out into the wintry air. Upon reaching her room, she collapsed and was put to bed. Doctors diagnosed double pneumonia and said that, given her age and underlying infirmity (never specified), recovery was impossible. As the days went by, praying townspeople surrounded Miss Pyle's home. Many of them expected Padre Pio to work a miracle just as he had done for the wicked Dr. Ricciardi, who was now walking about in full vigor.

If Padre Pio had been able to heal the atheistic doctor, why could he not heal his own saintly mother? When pressed about this, Pio, who always affirmed that he had no power in himself to heal and was capable only of praying to God, would only reply: "God's will be done."

Grazio and Michele hurried to the bedside of the wife and mother. Brunatto, learning the news in Rome, hastened to the Brigittine Convent to inform Graziella, or Suor Pia, that her mother was dying. With the same strange detachment that her brother had earlier displayed, Pia, who had permission to go, declined, saying, "When Mother dies, I will be here in the convent to pray for her."[19]

Padre Pio spent many hours at his mother's bedside until, at 4 A.M. on January 3, 1929, the summons came. In the words of Francesco Morcaldi, who was also there: "Her death was truly beautiful. She breathed her last serenely while they were praying. Unaided, she raised the crucifix, pressed it to her lips, [and died]."[20]

When Suor Pia was notified of her mother's death, she collapsed and, Forgione-like, immediately ran up an extreme temperature. Likewise, when the breath left Giuseppa's body, Padre Pio uttered a heartrending scream and collapsed, sobbing for hours on end, "Motherdear! My Motherdear! My beautiful Motherdear! My sweet, darling Motherdear!" His grief shocked everyone. He seemed absolutely shattered. He was unable to return to the friary or even attend the funeral. For days on end, he wept and wailed like a baby.

After several days, Padre Bernardo, the provincial, notified of Pio's extended absence from the friary, began to insist that he return, no matter what his condition was. Angelo Maria Merla and two other doctors told Bernardo that Pio was in no condition to be moved. Bernardo insisted, so Padre Pio was returned to the friary. As it was, he fainted three times before he reached his room.

Within days of his return to the friary, Padre Pio had resumed his normal duties. It was a long time, however, before he made anything approximating a full recovery. When Padre Bernardo requested him to write some meditative essays, Pio respectfully declined on the grounds that his mother's death had broken him to the extent that he was temporarily quite unable to write.

The Imprisonment

During the night of May 5, 1929, Padre Pio had a dream to which some of his colleagues attached a prophetic significance. Referring to the sixteenth-century pope Pius V, Padre Pio said: "I dreamed about St. Pius. He clearly told me that Archbishop Gagliardi will be deposed and Bishop Cuccarollo will come here in his place."[1]

The first part of the prophecy was fulfilled that October. Although it did not satisfy Morcaldi or Brunatto, the apostolic visitation of 1927 led to a second one the following year, this time to investigate the archbishop himself. Brunatto was not involved, and neither he nor the friars had any way of knowing that the investigation proved that the prelate was guilty of serious "mismanagement" of the archdiocese. As a result, the irascible old man was nudged into retirement — albeit with full honors. He spent the rest of his life with his family in the little town of Tricarico, where he had been born, enjoying the honorary title of archbishop of Lemnos. There he died, on December 12, 1941, "piously," according to a Vatican newspaper, yet never reconciled with Padre Pio. When Padre Raffaele informed Padre Pio that his old nemesis was dead, the man who had suffered so bitterly from the prelate's misguided actions simply announced that he would say Mass for him the following morning. When Padre Agostino learned the news, he wrote in his diary of the man who had once been his friend: "Speak no ill of the dead. May God receive him in glory."[2]

The second part of the prophecy of St. Pius was not fulfilled, owing, Agostino rationalized, to "the fault of men." There was indeed a prelate by the name of Sebastiano Cornelio Cuccarrollo (1870-1963), a Capuchin and bishop of Bovino who over the years had been extremely favorable to Padre Pio and, along with Bishop Valbonesi, had been so good as to inform the friars and the provincial of the various libels and slanders that Gagliardi had been disseminating in Rome. When he decided that Gagliardi needed to retire, the Pope asked Cuccarollo to take the archdiocese of Manfredonia. Cuccarollo, much to the disgust of Padre Pio, Padre Agostino, and others, declined, holding out for a more lucrative assignment, which he later obtained. "The devil has worked his wiles at Rome," a disappointed Agostino wrote when he learned of Cuccarollo's refusal. "The Lord has let men do as they please," Pio observed, "but Bishop Cuccarollo will have to answer before God because he should have obeyed the Pope and submitted to his cross!"[3]

Gagliardi was replaced by another Capuchin bishop, Andrea Cesarano, an ascetic-looking man with prominent facial bones and a patriarchal white beard. Although Padre Raffaele would characterize him as a simoniac, he seems to have been a competent bishop, a kindly man, and generally friendly toward Padre Pio. Cesarano was to govern the archdiocese of Manfredonia for the greater part of the rest of Padre Pio's life.

The tribulations of the priestly mystic were by no means at an end with the retirement of Gagliardi. Pio still had powerful enemies in Rome, chief among them, Gemelli, who continued to cast him in an unfavorable light to Pope Pius. Both Morcaldi and Brunatto were bitterly unhappy that the partial discrediting of Gagliardi had not served to remove what they felt were unreasonable restrictions on Padre Pio. Therefore they got their heads together and wrote a book called *Letters to the Church*, which contained many a juicy exposé of the private lives of prominent churchmen as well as a defense of Padre Pio. Brunatto, since his departure from the friary in 1925, had been spending most of his time shuttling between San Giovanni, Pietrelcina, and Rome. Through his contacts with Cardinal Gasparri, he was able to gain access to a great deal of privileged material. He was, of course, a persona non grata at the Vatican after it was discovered what use he was making of the materials he had uncovered.

When Padre Pio, however, learned of the forthcoming book, he seized Morcaldi by the throat. "You devil, you!" he roared. "Go, throw yourself at the foot of the Church instead of writing this garbage! Don't you set yourself up against your Mother!"[4]

For the time being, Morcaldi and Brunatto obeyed and did not distribute *Letters to the Church*. Then events caused them to reconsider. It all began when the minister general of the Capuchins, Padre Melchiorre of Benisa, at the suggestion of the Holy Office, decided to replace Padre Raffaele as guardian at San Giovanni with a man from outside the province.

On March 31, 1931, Padre Raffaele was summoned to Foggia for a private meeting wtih the provincial, Padre Bernardo, who informed him secretly that he would shortly be replaced by a new superior from the province of Milan. By the time he returned to San Giovanni Rotondo, however, the "secret" was public knowledge.

Apparently the resourceful Brunatto had his "spies" in the Vatican — influential clergy loyal to him and to Padre Pio — who immediately sent word to him and to Morcaldi whenever a decision concerning Padre Pio was in the works. At any rate, the town was soon buzzing, not only with the news that a new superior was coming from the "foreign" territory of northern Italy, but with rumors that this move was the harbinger of Padre Pio's imminent transfer. Within short order, the friary was surrounded day and night by citizens armed to the teeth, just as it had been in 1923. The townsfolk guarded the friary in shifts to make sure that Padre Pio would be taken nowhere. Barricades were thrown up in the streets so that no vehicular traffic could get to or from the friary.

In the midst of this threatening situation, on the evening of April 7, a traveler arrived at Our Lady of Grace. He was Padre Eugenio Tignola, a member of the Franciscan Observants, who was returning to Naples from a preaching assignment. He arrived in San Giovanni by bus and walked up to the friary, hoping to talk to Padre Pio about a personal problem.

Unfortunately, on the same bus from Foggia was Francesco Morcaldi, who was somehow convinced that Padre Eugenio was the sinister new guardian. Within minutes the news was all over town that the new superior had arrived and was about to spirit Padre Pio away. Soon cries were heard all over the community: "They're taking Padre Pio away! Hurry, hurry to the friary! They're taking Padre Pio away!" At about 10 P.M., an ugly mob descended upon the religious house and took up the grisly and menacing chant: "To the pillory with him! To the pillory with the stranger! Tear him to pieces! Tear him to pieces!"[5]

When Padre Raffaele refused to hand "the stranger" over, the mob uprooted a lightpole in the courtyard and used it to smash the wooden door of the friary. Raffaele met them as they poured into the enclosure, blocking the way to the stairway with his ample form. In an "authoritarian voice," he ordered everyone to leave the enclosure. "It was a dangerous thing to do," Raffaele confided to his diary, "because everyone was armed." He persuaded the mob to leave the friary when he promised that Padre Pio would speak to them.

So Raffaele went to Pio's room, ordered him to go to the choir window, which overlooked the courtyard, and calm the crowd. At the sight of his bearded face the crowd burst into wild cheers. "My blessed children," Pio began, "you have always been good. You have always conformed diligently to the grace of God. . . . Now I implore you to listen to me, as you always do, and return to your homes without harming anyone. The guest who is here with me is not the man you think he is. He is a friar who has come here for purely spiritual reasons!"

"It's not true! It's not true!" howled the crowd. They insisted that Padre Pio was being told what to say by his superiors. "What I just told you is true," Pio insisted; but when the crowd still refused to listen, Padre Pio closed the window and returned to his room. At this point, Mayor Morcaldi, who had stirred up the crowd in the first place, arrived on the scene and gained entrance to the enclosure. After conferring with Pio and Raffaele, he himself became convinced that the stranger was in fact a harmless guest. Thus he went out before the mob and pleaded with them to disperse.

When the crowd still continued to howl for the guest's blood — quite literally — Morcaldi boomed, "Do you love Padre Pio?" When cries of "Yes! Yes!" burst from the darkness, he shouted back, "Then do what he says! Do what he told you! Obey him! Go back to your homes! The guest will leave for Foggia at five this very morning!"[6]

And so, at about 2:30 A.M. on April 8, the crowd finally began to disperse. At 5 A.M., poor Padre Eugenio, nearly frightened out of his wits, set out by bus to Foggia.

Padre Raffaele had to report the damage done to the friary, and the police report of the incident soon reached Rome. As a result, the Holy Office took action. On June 11, 1931, Padre Raffaele received the following directive: "Padre Pio is to be stripped of all the faculties of his priestly ministry except the faculty to celebrate the Holy Mass, which he may continue to do provided it is done in private, within the walls of the friary, in the inner chapel, and not publicly in church."[7]

There was no way of getting out of these restrictions this time. The Holy Office, under Donato Cardinal Sbaretti (1856-1939), who had succeeded Merry del Val after the latter's sudden death the previous year, was in a mood to insist.

After Vespers, Raffaele summoned Pio to the friary parlor and, without comment, read him the decree. "God's will be done," Padre Pio said. Then he covered his eyes with his hands, lowered his head, and murmured, "The will of the authorities is the will of God."[8]

When Agostino came to see him on July 1, Pio was not as stoical. As soon as his old friend entered his room, Pio burst into tears.

"I never thought this would happen!" he sobbed.

"But it has," said Agostino. "Jesus wants it this way. Let His will be done. You must remain hanging on the cross. Men will continue to nail you to it, but in the end everything will work out for the glory of God and the good of souls."[9]

Thus began two years that Padre Pio called his "imprisonment," a trial he offered as a sacrifice to God for the needs of the unsaved. He began his day with the rest of the community. After saying the Office with his colleagues in the choir, he prepared for Mass, then went to a small oratory within the enclosure and celebrated the Eucharist in the company of one server. Because he had no congregation, no limit was set on length of his Mass, which at times lasted as long as four hours. According to Agostino though, ninety minutes was more usual. Now, at least, he was free to spend as much time as he wished in mystic communion with his God. What protracted Pio's Mass to such lengths, Agostino observed, were the Remembrance of the Living and the Remembrance of the

Dead. Pio often said that during the Mass he saw all the souls whom God was entrusting to his concern. Now, prohibited from any other contact with the faithful, he spent much time in intercession for them.

The rest of his day Padre Pio spent in study and prayer. He managed to go through volume after volume of Church history as well as pore over Scripture and the Church Fathers. The Capuchin life-style had relaxed somewhat from the days when Pio was a very young man, and the friars no longer had as many restrictions on their fellowship. Once, when Agostino asked him how he passed his time, Pio replied, "I pray and I study as much as I can, then I annoy my Brothers."

"How is it possible for you to annoy them?" Agostino asked.

"I joke the way I always joke with them, but my jokes are worse than before!"[10]

At midnight, when it was time for Matins, he would pound on his table to waken his brethren. After going to the choir to recite the Office of Matins with the rest of the community, he finally went to bed.

This was a time of great spiritual trial and testing. "I would prefer a thousand crosses," he told Agostino. "Indeed, each cross would seem sweet and light if I did not have this ordeal of never feeling certain of pleasing the Lord in what I do."[11] In November 1931, Pio spoke to the professor of "the bitter cup that is emptied, then refilled, and then comes on again, overflowing in a more terribly loathsome way." At times all celestial comforts were withdrawn. On November 15, 1931, he confided to Agostino, "Jesus is silent" — for the first time in his mature life he was having no visions.

Even so, Padre Pio never lost his supernatural illumination in spiritual counseling. Since his disciples were forbidden both to visit and to write, many of them conveyed their concerns to Padre Agostino and other friars, who relayed them to Padre Pio. More than ever, Pio seemed to be able to address the problems with supersensible wisdom.

The cessation of his visionary experience proved to be very temporary. In January 1932, Padre Pio told the professor: "Jesus frequently makes His presence felt. He speaks to my soul and grants me intellectual visions."

Some of Pio's disciples maintained that he visited them through bilocation. A nun in Florence named Suor Beniamina told Agostino, "One morning, after I had received Communion, Padre Pio appeared to me and comforted and blessed me." The professor went to Pio to determine whether this was true. "Do you often make little trips — such as, say, to Florence?" he asked.

Pio looked at Agostino and smiled but said nothing. Agostino continued to press: "A nun told me this. It is true?"

"Yes," answered Padre Pio, and that was the end of the matter.[12]

It was during the imprisonment that Padre Agostino first experienced Padre Pio's by-then-famous perfume. Ever since the time of the stigmatization, innumerable visitors had, as we have seen, reported sensing this mysterious aroma, sometimes when they kissed the friar's hand, sometimes when they were many miles away and felt that he was trying to communicate with them. Agostino remained sceptical of the reports of it until September 1931. "I don't know how many times," he wrote, "I have entered his room, spoken to him, and touched handkerchiefs that have been soaked with his blood, without ever having experienced the aroma." On this occasion he did, however. It was a scent that he could not define. "It is sweet, pleasant, delicate," he wrote. He continued to smell the fragrance for at least a week thereafter.

Meanwhile, although they could not see Padre Pio or speak or write to him, the faithful continued to pour into San Giovanni. Great busloads of visitors came to the church each day to pray for his liberation and recite the Rosary in unison in front of the friary.

In addition, Brunatto and Morcaldi were not inactive in the padre's behalf. They organized a letter-writing campaign, deluging Vatican officials with mail requesting an end to Padre Pio's segregation. Morcaldi wrote to the learned Dr. Giorgio Festa, who had examined the Padre's wounds several times and had recently prepared a scholarly work on Padre Pio and his stigmata, *The Mysteries of Science in the Light of Faith*. Because of a prohibition by the Holy Office on any publications on Padre Pio, Festa was holding back the manuscript. Now, however, with his permission, Mayor Morcaldi sent copies of the manuscript to a number of prominent churchmen. As usual, the mayor found a friend and supporter in Cardinal Gasparri. Although Pope Pius XI had recently retired him from his post as secretary of state, the eighty-year-old cardinal still wielded a great deal of influence. Having read the book, Gasparri invited Festa to talk with him. During the meeting, he said to the physician, "why not have it published?" Thus Festa went ahead and published his manuscript. Through Gasparri's influence, the Holy Office refrained from putting it on the index of forbidden books. Several great cardinals read it and were impressed.

Other obstacles remained. Just as Padre Pio's disciples thought his segregation was about to be relaxed, there came an unauthorized publication that set his case back. Early in 1932, Alberto Del Fante and Carolina Giovannini published a book called *Padre Pio of Pietrelcina: Messenger of the Lord*. In it were detailed accounts of many supernatural phenomena, such as miracles of healing, bilocation, and discernment of spirits. The problem was that the Holy Office had been warning since 1923 that the supernatural character of Padre Pio's ministry could not be confirmed, while Del Fante and Giovannini asserted in their book that it could — and that Padre Pio was, without question, "the messenger of the Lord." Not only was Pio not freed from his imprisonment, he was dealt another blow. The Seraphic College was removed from San Giovanni Rotondo.

The loss of the opportunity to minister to the teenaged boys who made up the student body left Padre Pio all the more alone. Morcaldi commented bitterly that the Holy Office considered Pio "a noxious Socrates, capable of perverting the fragile lives and souls of boys not yet tempered to monastic discipline."[13]

Others vented their wrath, not only on the Holy Office, but on some of Padre Pio's disciples. Del Fante and Giovannini were roundly reviled. Padre Agostino characterized Signorina Giovannini as a "truly fanatic, hysterical woman used by Satan to muddy the waters!"[14] His wrath also fell upon Mary Pyle, whom he accused of giving information to the authors. For a period of time, nearly everyone in San Giovanni Rotondo was of a similar opinion and turned on "L'Americana," whose complicity in the book project can by no means be established. So deeply was she held in disfavor that whenever she approached the altar rail to partake of Communion, everyone else left her to receive alone. For months no one spoke to her, and some women went so far as to recite the formulae of exorcism against her.

Worse, Morcaldi and Brunatto quarreled. Brunatto, after Festa's book had not brought a quick release of Padre Pio and after the Del Fante-Giovannini book had brought further reprisal from the Holy Office, was in favor of going ahead with the publication of *Letters to the Church*. Morcaldi, after conferring with several cardinals who promised Padre Pio's release only after all copies of the manuscript had been surrendered to them, urged his friend to comply with this request. Brunatto refused. "Go to your masters," he told Morcaldi, "and tell them that I still have material from which I can not only publish the book but even add to it!" He accused his erstwhile friend of being "a second Luther," who was "trying to dismantle the Church of Christ." Brunatto said he feared no excommunication and trusted the faithful would rise en masse once he brought the "irrefutable documents to light."[15]

The nature of these documents is not entirely known. They concerned some of the highest officials in the Church. The scandals seem to have been factual enough and lurid enough to make for considerable uneasiness within the Church when it was learned that they were on the verge of being brought to light. At any rate, Brunatto, from Paris, where he was now living, decided to go ahead in his preparation of his *Les Antichrists dans l'église du Christ* (The Antichrists within the Church of Christ).

Meanwhile, Morcaldi, through more conservative means, was effecting a breakthrough. Gasparri's replacement as papal secretary of state was Dr. Eugenio Pacelli (1876-1958), who had been apostolic nuncio to Germany. Tall, gaunt, and ascetic (He was 6'1" and weighed less than 125 pounds), with a white complexion and a hawk-like nose, no man could possibly have been as holy as he looked. He was in fact a man of great spirituality who had been a close acquaintance of the great Bavarian mystic and stigmatic, Therese Neumann. In October 1932, Morcaldi wrote to Pacelli about "the seraphic little friar," the fame of whose "heroic virtue . . . has burst the confines of the little town hidden in the mountains" where he lived. Morcaldi described how "a humanity laden with sufferings, . . . bewildered and perplexed," saw in Padre Pio a "ray of light to guide it."[16]

Pacelli, it seems, persuaded Pope Pius XI to send a personal representative to San Giovanni Rotondo to observe Padre Pio. It will be recalled that Pope Benedict XV, too, had sent personal representatives to interview and examine him. Pius XI, as we have seen, had relied solely upon the Holy Office and the advice of personal friends for an assessment of the controversial friar. Even the apostolic visitations of 1927 and 1928 had not been to investigate Padre Pio. Now, on March 14, 1933, Pope Pius finally decided to dispatch representatives to visit Padre Pio and report back to him in person. The choice fell upon a Capuchin bishop, Luca Pasetto, and Bishop Felice Bevilacqua, who had headed the visitation of 1927.

The churchmen journeyed to San Giovanni Rotondo and passed through the armed guard that had been surrounding the friary for nearly two years. The prelates asked Padre Raffaele where they might find Padre Pio. They were told that he was in the chapel, celebrating Mass. Pasetto went into the chapel to worship with him, but Padre Pio's Mass lasted so long that he got tired and came out. It was not until 10 A.M. that Pio concluded the Mass he had begun at 7 A.M.

Advised that Pasetto and Bevilacqua wanted to see him, Padre Pio went to the parlor and talked for some time with his guests. After lunch, Pasetto and Bevilacqua spent the afternoon with the stigmatic priest. They found no wild-eyed fanatic, no crazed neurotic, no embittered rebel, but a pleasant, quiet little man with a ready sense of humor. According to Raffaele, Pasetto was very much impressed with Pio's humility, his docility, and the whole of his conduct. He recognized Pio as a man of prayer and entirely godly.

The two bishops expressed their concern, both to Raffaele and to Pio, about Brunatto. Brunatto had been writing to various Vatican officials, threatening to publish his book by Easter if Padre Pio was not free by then. Bevilacqua warned Padre Pio of the terrible damage to the Church's reputation that could ensue should Brunatto's revelations become public. "The Church has a formidable weapon to neutralize scandal," Padre Pio offered. "Show that the episodes alleged in the book that might prove a source of scandal are not true."

There was silence. Bevilacqua, with shining eyes and a voice choked with tears, shook his head and said, "Unfortunately, those allegations are true."[17]

Padre Pio was very much alarmed. He wrote to Brunatto in Paris, trying to dissuade him from publishing the book. Brunatto refused to listen, contending that Pio was being forced, under obedience to his superiors, to say what he was saying. Brunatto continued to threaten the Vatican. To various cardinals and bishops, he wrote: "The price for our silence, the price of the book, is known: the liberation of the just and the removal of the guilty."[18]

Brunatto had set Easter 1933 as his deadline; but Easter came and went, and neither did he go to press nor was Padre Pio freed. Archbishop Cesarano of

Manfredonia went to the Vatican to plead the case of Padre Pio personally with Pope Pius. Still nothing happened.

Finally, on July 14, 1933, Pope Pius reversed his ban. An order came from the Holy Office that day directing that Padre Pio be allowed once more to celebrate Mass in public and that he be allowed to hear the confessions of religious within the enclosure.

Brunatto, of course, liked to take credit for the change in the friar's circumstances, but his threats were probably not the overriding factor in the decision of the Pope and the Holy Office. Padre Pio's "liberation," it seems clear, was mainly the result of the investigation of Pasetto and Bevilacqua. Padre Raffaele and others were convinced that Pope Pius changed his mind about Padre Pio when he read their report. As the Pontiff reportedly told Archbishop Cesarano, "I have not been badly disposed towards Padre Pio, but I have been badly informed about him."[19]

There is some evidence that even after he permitted Padre Pio to resume his public ministry, Pope Pius never really esteemed the stigmatized priest as a man of exceptional holiness. A Capuchin who had an audience with the Pope in 1934 was startled when Pius asked, "Suggest to me some pious person to whom I might recommend myself so as to obtain a certain grace." When the Capuchin, Padre Giuseppe of Bra, suggested Padre Pio, a look of displeasure showed on Pius's face. Cutting Padre Giuseppe short, he said, "All right! All right! I understand," blessing and dismissing him.[20] Even if Pope Pius never really appreciated Padre Pio and his ministry as others did, he ultimately came to see him as a sincere and humble priest. Thus Padre Pio was vindicated.

News of Padre Pio's liberation came on July 15, when Padre Bernardo, the provincial, came to the friary. The community was in the refectory for the evening meal. Padre Pio, who normally did not eat supper, was in the choir, praying. Padre Raffaele sent one of the friars to call Padre Pio "for an important message from the provincial." As soon as Pio was seated at his place in the dining hall, Padre Bernardo announced, "Through the will of the Holy Father, you may celebrate Holy Mass in public, starting tomorrow." As Padre Raffaele noted in his diary, there was "a clapping of hands and cheers for the Pope and for Padre Pio, who, moved and with his eyes filled with tears, left his place and went to kiss the hand of the provincial, and, with a voice trembling with emotion, asked him to convey his thanks to His Holiness."

The next day, Padre Bernardo announced to the people who happened to be in church that Padre Pio was once more permitted to celebrate Mass in public. The news spread like wildfire, and the church was packed for Padre Pio's first Mass in public in more than two years. As the beloved friar moved slowly into the church, the worshipers wept with emotion.

One person not present was Emmanuele Brunatto. He had infuriated the Capuchins by his rebuff of Padre Pio and his insistence on blackmailing the

Church. He was given to understand that he was no longer welcome in or even around the friary. Although he never saw Padre Pio again, he always maintained a keen interest in his ministry. We have not heard the last of him.

There were still many restrictions remaining for Padre Pio. For the time being, he was not allowed to hear the confessions of laypersons. The sacristy was once more off limits to all laity. (Officially, this had been the case since the mid-1920s, but enforcement of the ruling had been relaxed in the two or three years before Pio's imprisonment.) Once again, as in 1925, it was emphasized that Pio was not to stop and speak with women or permit them to kiss his hand. Pio's talks with men in the hallways were to be "few and brief," and his Mass was not to last more than a half hour (not including the distribution of Communion).

Even so, nearly everyone was overjoyed to have the beloved friar back, and Pio himself, according to Agostino, was "very much consoled" and gave thanks to God, rejoicing. As time went on, some of the restrictions were lifted. As of March 25, 1934, Padre Pio was allowed to hear the confessions of men, and as of May 12 of the same year, he was permitted to hear those of women. Thus, as he neared his forty-seventh birthday, his ministry was once again in full swing.

War and Peace

Padre Pio was forty-seven years old on May 25, 1934. He seemed to have aged perceptibly during his imprisonment. His full beard was quite gray now, although his thinning hair retained its auburn hue, and he had become somewhat paunchy.

The enlargement of Pio's waistline was by no means a result of overeating. On the contrary: as he grew older, Padre Pio tended to eat less. He had never been a heavy eater, and for at least twenty years had almost never eaten the evening meal. Now, even at noon, he ate very little. In the mid-1930s Padre Agostino observed that Pio's intake was "not sufficient for anyone who works as he does."[1] His food intake for a normal twenty-four-hour period dropped to five ounces in 1944, and to only three and a half ounces in 1945.

Likewise, the padre seemed to be able to get along with less and less sleep. During this period of his life, he slept between two and three hours during the afternoon siesta and perhaps two hours at night; and he never seemed tired. Despite his lack of food and sleep, Agostino noted that he was "always quick, always jovial, always friendly."

If he was thriving physically, however, Padre Pio continued to experience the Dark Night. Agostino wrote: "The trial continues fixed in his soul without letup. Although it does not drive him to absolute despair, it always keeps him uncertain of whether or not he is doing good or evil and whether he is pleasing or displeasing God." As Pio told the professor, "I want to please the Lord, but the uncertainty is worse than death to me."

Having longed for so many years for death as a means of attaining full union with God, Pio now began at times to dread death because of his uncertainty as to whether or not he was in God's grace. Of this dilemma he said to Agostino in

October 1934: "I'm thankful to God that He doesn't give me the time to think about this matter for long, since I have so many other things to think about. But if I did think about this terrible trial, I would surely lose my mind!"[2]

During the late 1930s his spiritual consolations were once more withdrawn, and in January 1937 he described himself to the professor as living in "pitch darkness." "I don't know how to go on anymore," Pio said. "Even the memory of your assurances . . . does not bring me comfort. It is an unspeakable torment. I do not despair, but I do not understand any of this!"[3]

What he did not understand was why God permitted this trial when he was convinced that, without it, he could accomplish more good. Padre Agostino, however, was convinced that the Lord ordered his friend's spiritual uncertainty for the purpose of keeping him humble. Certainly we will recall how Padre Pio himself, speaking of another soul, pointed out that the woman in question fell from grace through a lack of distrust in herself and too great a complacency in her own godliness. Because of this, Agostino, without a doubt, felt that it was a grace from God that Padre Pio always seemed to be unaware of any holiness on his part or of the great good that he accomplished.

It was during this period that Padre Pio composed one of his very few published works, a meditation on *The Agony of Jesus in the Garden of Gethsemane* (St. Paul, 1952). In it he propounds his characteristic doctrine of co-redemption, in which he maintains that salvation, among other things, involves sharing Christ's grief and pain for the sake of one's own salvation and that of others. He also speaks of his belief that Christ's "desolate heart has need of comfort" and that one of the duties of being a Christian is sharing Christ's bitterness and mortal anguish.

It was also during the mid-1930s that the Capuchin minister general, Padre Vigilio Dalla Zuanna of Valstagna, accorded Padre Pio, who had never been examined for his preaching license, the permission to preach, *honoris causa*. Throughout the following years, Padre Pio preached occasionally — usually several times a year. Padre Alessio remarked to me that Pio was "an ordinary preacher." The one sermon from his pen that has been published is a New Year's homily — simple, direct, and evangelical enough to pass for a sermon from his Presbyterian contemporary Billy Sunday.

Padre Pio was, in a way of speaking, entering the summertime of his ministry. With no interference from the Holy Office and with the goodwill of Padre Vigilio, he was now able to work virtually unmolested. When Padre Bernardo of Alpicella died of malaria on the last day of 1937, the man elected to replace him as provincial was none other than Padre Agostino. Bernardo had been a fair and equitable superior, but the professor was Pio's best friend. The same year Padre Vigilio's term as minister general ended, and in the ensuing election he was replaced by Father Donatus of Welle, a Belgian.

Father Donatus had heard a great deal about Padre Pio and was eager to meet him, and so, on August 7, 1938, in the company of Padre Agostino, he paid a call on Padre Pio. Donatus left a written account of his impressions. Saying that he wanted to make a close study of everything concerning the stigmatic and his environment, Donatus writes:

> I examined the stigmata and spoke frequently with Padre Pio on every kind of question: in this first encounter I wanted to inquire concerning . . . the natural humanity of the priest. Was he perhaps neurotic? hysterical? docile? violent? a dreamer? stupid? sad? fanatical? After repeated inquiries, I was able to conclude that in every sense Padre Pio was absolutely sound spiritually, and I was left with the certainty of a sincerity and a simplicity incapable . . . of saying yes when no was appropriate.

The minister general continues:

> I can and must affirm that in all the contacts I had with Padre Pio, I was deeply moved by his practice of virtue, his serenity, his humility . . . , his attitude of forgiveness that never allowed him to say a word against those who had offended him . . . , his habitual recollection . . . , his true affection towards his superiors . . . , his perfect obedience to all ecclesiastical authorities, his sane piety, and his modesty.

"Personally," he concludes his report, "I have to add that I consider Padre Pio a great saint!"[4]

Father Donatus was not the only one to hold such an opinion. When eighty-two-year-old Pope Pius XI died in February 1939, elected to replace him was Eugenio Cardinal Pacelli, who took the title Pius XII. The new Pius, whom Padre Pio came to call "sweet Christ on earth," held the Capuchin stigmatist in great esteem. From the first, the Pope encouraged the faithful to visit him. "Go ahead, it might do you some good," he often told people at audiences who, in light of the decrees of the Holy Office a decade or so earlier, asked him whether a visit to Padre Pio had papal approval. Pius XII seemed totally convinced of Padre Pio's holiness.

More and more people came to San Giovanni Rotondo each year from all parts of Italy. More and more pilgrimages to Padre Pio were organized, which did not please the padre. "I disapprove of people making pilgrimages to me," he complained to Agostino. "I wish they would discourage people from coming in groups like this. It keeps me from hearing confessions as I ought."[5] Letters were pouring into the friary in ever greater numbers. Padre Costantino Capobianco recalled in his memoirs how Padre Pio, handling a letter addressed to him, read the saluatation aloud: "To the sainted Padre Pio . . . *Sainted!* . . . Hear how *beautiful!*. . . To the *sainted* Padre Pio!"

"Now you're not getting proud, are you?" asked one of the other friars in the room.

Spreading his arms and lowering his body to imitate a boaster, Pio quipped, "Oh, yes, friend! I'm getting quite proud of it now!"[6] Thereupon he burst out laughing. For him, the idea of his being considered a saint was a big joke.

Even though he was held in such esteem by growing numbers of people, there was still no lack of difficulties. The bane of his ministry now seemed to be the hordes of fanatical women, most of them locals, who haunted the church and were facetiously called *le Pie Donne* (the Holy Women). These vixens literally fought each other for the best spots in church during the Padre's Mass and for the opportunity to make their confessions to him at the most convenient times.

One of the first problems at San Giovanni that Padre Agostino had to investigate as provincial was the claim of a certain unnamed "holy woman" of the town who swore that Padre Pio was admitting females into the friary at night. For quite a while various women continued to make similar accusations. Finally, Padre Agostino decided that it was time to investigate. A local harridan had told one of the friars that at precisely eleven o'clock that very night (long after the premises were closed to the public), a woman would be admitted to the church. Sure enough, at eleven, one of the friars saw a woman approach the friary from the courtyard, stop behind a large cross, slip behind an elm tree, then make a run for the church. The friar was convinced that she had actually entered, but a thorough search of the church and sacristy turned up nothing. Finally, it was discovered that the very woman who had predicted that a member of her gender would be admitted to the friary had been the one who had approached the church. But instead of going inside, when outside of the line of vision of the friar watching from the window, she had hidden behind some building materials alongside the wall of the friary. One of the friars, who was watching from another window, caught her emerging from behind the piles of material at a time when she thought she would not be observed. It seems that the woman, angry because she thought Padre Pio was giving too much of his time to one of her rivals, wanted to take revenge by making it appear that he was admitting a woman into the friary for immoral purposes. "You can't put anything past a jealous woman, even if she is devout!" Agostino noted in his diary.

Padre Pio was not the only reputed saint in the area. Around this time, the "Holy Woman of Rodi Garganico" was attracting quite a following. Several people asked Padre Pio what he thought of her. As he had never met the woman, all he could say was that one had to wait for the judgment of the ecclesiastical authorities. "You're just saying that out of jealousy!" complained Pio's inquirers. "You just don't want another saint around!"[7] Pio always loved to laugh about this comment.

There were many unexplained phenomena during this middle period of Padre Pio's ministry. One of the best-known instances took place on the evening of January 20, 1936. Guglielmo Sanguinetti (1894-1954), a Florentine physician about whom we shall be hearing more, and two other laymen were visiting with Padre Pio in his room when suddenly their priest-friend inexplicably dropped to his knees and asked them to pray "for a soul soon to appear before the judgment seat of God." All three guests got down on the floor and prayed with the padre. When they finished, Pio announced definitively that they had just been praying for George V, King of England.

Although news of the seventy-year-old monarch's rapidly deteriorating heart condition had been all over most of the world's newspapers for the last three days, Sanguinetti was somehow unaware of this and expressed his amazement that the padre should say such a thing, adding something to the effect that everyone knows King George is sick, but it's not been announced that he's dying.

"It is as I say," said Padre Pio.

Around midnight, Padre Pio banged on the door of Padre Aurelio. When Aurelio answered, Pio said: "Let us pray for the soul who at this moment is to appear before the judgment seat of God. It is the King of England. Let's pray together that the poor soul might be saved."

It so happened that, clutching the hand of the archbishop of Canterbury and praying the Our Father, George V died at 11:55 that night — the same time that Padre Pio had come to Padre Aurelio's room.

A similar episode took place late that year. On December 29, 1936, Padre Pio was approached by one Padre Giacinto of Sant'Elia a Pianisi, who resided at the friary of St. Anne in Foggia. Padre Giacinto came to Padre Pio on behalf of a member of his community, Padre Giuseppe Antonio of San Marco in Lamis, who was gravely ill with Bright's disease. That night, as usual, Padre Pio retired about 1 A.M. Sometime before he rose at 3 A.M., Pio opened his eyes and saw Padre Giuseppe Antonio standing in his cell. "Why, Padre Giuseppe Antonio!" he exclaimed. "What are you doing here? They told me that you were so very ill, but now I have the pleasure of seeing you well!"

"Well, all my pains are over now," said Padre Giuseppe Antonio, and vanished into thin air.[8]

The next day the community at San Giovanni Rotondo learned that Padre Giuseppe Antonio had died during the night, at approximately the time of Padre Pio's encounter with him.

There are many accounts of cures and conversions dating from the late 1930s and early 1940s. In November 1935, Padre Costantino Capobianco became ill. He went to Padre Pio and told him that he had been diagnosed as having tuberculosis of the lungs and was being ordered to report to a sanitarium in Rome the very next day. This was his second bout with the disease. "Don't worry." Pio reassured him. "This is only an excursion. The Lord intends the same results as the other time."[9] The treatment was successful. Padre Costantino was soon discharged and went on to outlive Padre Pio.

In 1939 the celebrated Italian comic playwright Luigi Antonelli (1882-1942) came to San Giovanni Rotondo. A short man with thick limbs and a dark moustache, Antonelli was known for his "sweet smile" and "the light of goodness that shone in his eyes."[10] His need was very great, as he had recently been diagnosed as suffering from cancer of the face, neck, and jaw. His doctor wanted to operate but, under direct questioning, admitted that even with surgery, Antonelli would probably be dead within six months. The playwright had been about to submit to the operation when a friend told him about Padre Pio. Thereupon he left his home in Pescara and journeyed to San Giovanni Rotondo, where he attended Mass and made his confession to Padre Pio. "I cannot repeat what he said to me," Antonelli later recounted, "because while he was speaking to me I seemed to be living in a supernatural world!"

Antonelli noticed an improvement at once, and soon his cancer was arrested. A few months later he wrote: "I don't know whether the word 'miracle' is exact from the theological point of view, but . . . we'll not split hairs upon words. . . . I am now writing . . . an article every Sunday for the *Giornale D'Italia*. I go hunting. For the past month I have been working on a comedy which will be produced at the Manzoni Theatre in Milan. I don't know what the doctors may think about it, I don't know what x-rays and histological examination may reveal . . . but today I feel that I am miraculously cured."[11]

When Antonelli refused surgery, his doctors warned him that he would be dead within three months; yet he survived for three years, working and active for most of that time. Before he finally succumbed, he told his experiences to another noted author, the Argentinian Dino Segre (1893-1975), who wrote under the pen name of Pitigrilli.

Pitigrilli was well known both in Italy and South America. By his own admission, he was a materialist, though he had been a seeker of truth for some time. When, at Foggia, Antonelli had told him about the dramatic improvement in his health and urged him to go to San Giovanni Rotondo, he did so.

Pitigrilli attended Padre Pio's Mass, sitting far back in the church. As far as he could tell, he was completely unknown and unrecognized. To his amazement, during the part of the Mass when the priest urges the congregation to pray for various intentions, Padre Pio said: "Pray, brethren. Pray fervently for someone who is here among you today, someone who is in great need of prayer. One day he will approach the Eucharistic table and will bring many with him who have been in error like himself."

Although not called by name, Pitigrilli was convinced that Padre Pio had him in mind. Feeling as if his heart were breaking, he dissolved in tears. When he approached the padre for confession, Pio said to him: "What profiteth a man to gain the whole world and lose his soul? Truly, God is good to you."

Pitigrilli underwent a deep and lasting conversion experience. Returning to Buenos Aires, he went to his publisher immediately and insisted that certain of his works that were not consistent with the Christian faith be withdrawn. For the thirty odd years that remained of his life, Pitigrilli wrote plays and books with a Christian message, laboring for the faith that he once despised.

Perhaps the most famous phenomenon of supernatural repute from this period involved Monsignor Fernando Damiani, vicar general of Salto, Uruguay. We will recall that it was to Damiani that Pope Benedict XV characterized Padre Pio as an extraordinary and holy man and that it was the same priest who had made the friar known to Mother Teresa Salvadores when she appeared to be dying of cancer in Montevideo in 1921.

According to Padre Hugo Caballero, one of the few people still alive in 1981 who remember Damiani, the monsignor was "an honest, kindly man who was in love with the liturgy and the beautiful and fascinating ceremonies of . . . that period. Not a man given to mystical experiences, he was a practical man, but very pious."

Damiani had served as a college chaplain in Salto before going to Chile early in his career to join a contemplative religious community. After a time he returned to Uruguay, where as a priest in the rural parish of Rosario, he became a social activist, founding a number of agricultural unions and workingmen's savings banks. Eventually he was named general director of all the Church's social works in Uruguay.

In 1937 Damiani visited Padre Pio in San Giovanni Rotondo. He was then sixty years old, suffering from severe coronary disease, and in great pain. He asked no cure, saying merely that he had come to San Giovanni because he wanted to die near Padre Pio.

While staying at the friary, he had a major heart attack and lay for hours at the point of death. He asked for Padre Pio, but to his dismay, the friar remained in the confessional and did not come to him until he was through hearing his penitents. "Why didn't you come earlier?' demanded the old prelate. "I could have died already!"

"I knew that you would not die," said Padre Pio matter-of-factly, "and so I continued to hear confessions." He told Damiani that he was to die in Uruguay. "When your hour does come," Pio assured the old man, "I promise to see to it that you are well assisted spiritually."

When he was able to travel, Damiani returned to Uruguay. There he continued his ministry, but his heart grew steadily worse. In September 1941, Damiani was presiding over a congress on vocations at Salto. The episcopal mansion in which Damiani lived was filled with visiting priests, monks, and prelates, including Uruguay's three bishops: Alfredo Viola, the local incumbent, Antonio Maria Barbieri (1892-1979), archbishop of Montevideo, and Miguel Paternain, bishop of the diocese of Florida in south central Uruguay. Also present was Alberto Levame, papal nuncio to Uruguay.

Damiani stayed up until 11 P.M., talking in his room with Archbishop Barbieri. A little past midnight, Barbieri, who had retired to his room, was awakened by a knock at his door. He opened it. The room and the corridor were both dark, but he thought he could make out the form of a man in a Capuchin habit. "Go to assist Msgr. Damiani," said the friar. "He's dying." The knocking at the archbishop's door was overheard by a priest by the name of Padre Francisco Navarro, who was awake and praying in the chapel on the same floor.

In the meantime, Barbieri ran to Damiani's room. The door was unlocked, and when he got no response to his rapping, he went inside and found Damiani in the throes of another heart attack, speechless, and apparently dying.

Across the bed where he writhed, breathless and contorted with pain, Damiani had a little writing table. On it were scattered pills for his angina pectoris as well as a note written in a faltering hand. It seemed to be the sketch or outline of a telegram: "Padre Pio — San Giovanni Rotondo — the unrelenting spasms in my heart are destroying me — Damiani." Damiani had apparently collapsed before being able to send the telegram.

Unclosing his eyes and seeing Barbieri there, Damiani mustered the strength to ask the archbishop to administer the sacrament of the sick (the "last rites"). Running to fetch the necessary materials, Barbieri awakened everybody in the mansion and told Navarro to go to Damiani's room at once to hear his confession. After this was done, the dean of the cathedral, who had reached Damiani before Barbieri was able to return, anointed the old man. A few minutes later, medical assistance arrived, but the efforts of the doctors were to no avail, and around 12:30 in the morning, on September 12, 1941, Fernando Damiani, vicar general of Salto, died, surrounded in his final hour by four bishops, and six other priests! As Padre Pio had promised, he died well assisted.[12]

The presence of the mysterious monk who knocked on Barbieri's door and advised him that Damiani was dying cannot be explained by natural means. Padre Navarro, who was out of bed and fully awake, heard it as clearly as Barbieri did. There were no Capuchins at the residence other than Barbieri himself, and everyone else who was staying there denied having alerted the archbishop to Damiani's heart attack. All of them maintained that they had been informed of the crisis by Barbieri. All those who were present at Damiani's deathbed were convinced that it had been Padre Pio who appeared through bilocation to rouse the guests in the house.

William Carrigan, who was to be closely associated with Pio a few years later, recalled, in an interview he gave me in January 1979, that Padre Pio once told him: "These people think I have miracles. I have no miracles." Whenever anyone did come to thank him for an extraordinary grace, he would say, "If you think you have received a grace, go to our Lord and thank Him, not me."

The fact remains that thousands of people came to San Giovanni each year in search of miracles. Partly because of this, Padre Pio founded his *Casa Sollievo della Sofferenza* (Home to Relieve Suffering), his great hospital to minister to the needs of both soul and body.

An earthquake in San Giovanni Rotondo in 1938 not only severely damaged the friary, forcing Padre Pio and several other friars to sleep in a trailer for several weeks, it also rendered inoperable the thirteen-year-old St. Francis Hospital. Pio was not interested in having it renovated, however. It was too small and inadequate, and he had grander plans in mind.

Instrumental in the construction of the *Casa* were three physicians. One of them was Guglielmo ("Willy") Sanguinetti from Florence, whom we first met in Padre Pio's room the night King George died. Sanguinetti was a stocky man, about five-feet-six. Although only in his mid-forties, he was grey and prematurely bald. Described as a marvelous man by all who knew him, he was genial, warm, and vibrant. He and his wife, Emilia ("Mi"), had first come to San Giovanni Rotondo sometime between 1933 and 1935. Willy had not been very much interested in Padre Pio. Having lost his religion in college, he professed to believe that the cosmos was nothing more than a jumble of sensations. It was Mi who prevailed upon him to go. After he met Padre Pio, Sanguinetti's life was radically changed: he became a fervent Christian.

"You, Doctor, are the man who will come here and build my hospital," Padre Pio had said to him early in their acquaintance, possibly on their first meeting. Sanguinetti protested that he was neither achitect nor engineer — simply a medical doctor. Undaunted, Pio insisted that Willy was his man. Sanguinetti continued to protest, explaining that he was not sufficiently wealthy to give up his practice, leave the Florentine suburb where he resided, and come to San Giovanni to live on faith. "God will provide," assured the padre.

A short time after he returned to Florence, Sanguinetti was amazed when he won a large sum of money in a lottery. With it he was able to purchase a large farm to provide a substantial rental income. He still had enough left over to buy a house in San Giovanni Rotondo. There he set up a practice ministering to the health needs of the growing number of pilgrims, many of whom were deathly sick.

The second doctor was a veterinarian from Perugia by the name of Mario Sanvico. Like Sanguinetti, he was about forty, and, also like him, he is described as a man of great personal goodness. He too had been approached by the padre, who informed him, "You will collaborate with me in the construction of a hospital." Sanvico too left his practice to settle in San Giovanni Rotondo.

The third doctor was a pharmacist from Zara, Yugoslavia, named Carlo Kiswarday. He had come to San Giovanni with his wife some years before on a visit, only to be startled when Padre Pio insisted, "I want you to make your home here." Like his two colleagues, Kiswarday left his home to come to San Giovanni.

On the night of January 9, 1940, Padre Pio called the three physicians, all now in residence at San Giovanni, to his room and announced his plans in full. Producing a nearly worthless fifty-lire piece, he announced, "I want to make the first donation for the Home to Relieve Suffering."

This little coin had a poignant history. After the earthquake had damaged the

St. Francis Hospital, an old woman had approached Pio, urging him to rebuild. "I want to make a contribution," she said. "It isn't much, but it's all I have."

Padre Pio, knowing that the woman was destitute, refused the coin. "No, Madame, I won't take it," he said. "You can't afford it, and I don't expect it of you."

Still the old woman persisted, cheerfully expressing her willingness to sacrifice. "Oh, I could do without buying matches, and I could go to my neighbors for a light for my fire."

"Mercy, no! I can't accept this," said the padre.

"Well, Padre, I guess it is too small," replied the widow.

At this point Padre Pio broke down. "Give it to me. Give it to me at once! This is the handsomest donation I could ever hope to receive."[13]

For years Padre Pio kept the coin pinned on the inside of his habit, next to his heart, producing it periodically to gaze at it and weep. He said that it embodied for him the spirit of sacrifice that characterized the Sangiovannese as they worked with him to build the Home to Relieve Suffering.

When Dr. Sanvico asked him why he wanted to give the hospital such a peculiar name, Pio told him that he did not care for the word *hospital* or *clinic* or *institution*. For him, especially after his own experiences during the First World War, *hospital* meant a place of horror and suffering. What he envisioned, however, was a place to *relieve* suffering, where science as well as religion combined to work for the welfare of the soul as well as the body. The aim of *La Casa Sollievo della Sofferenza* was, as Padre Pio put it in a letter to Pope Pius, "To introduce to the care of the sick a concept more profoundly humane and more supernatural, that places the sick in ideal conditions both from a material and spiritual point of view, to the end that the patient might be led to recognize those working for his cure as God's helpers, engaged in preparing the way for the intervention of grace."[14]

Though all three doctors were enthusiastic about the project, they advised Padre Pio that the time was not propitious for such a monumental endeavor, with the European war on the verge of engulfing the entire world. When his heart was set on something, however, Padre Pio was never a man to take no for an answer.

Accordingly, the doctors announced the plans and began to solicit contributions. Almost immediately, people began to respond. Within four days, seven people had made contributions, including Pio's nephew Ettore Masone and three of his closest disciples, Elena Bandini, Pietro Cugino (whom we will meet in a later chapter), and Cleonice Morcaldi. Their contributions amounted only to the equivalent of $1.60. As days went on, most of the contributions were equally meager. Coming from poor working people, the contributions often represented a great sacrifice, but they were not nearly enough for the costly work at hand. The first — and for several years, the only — large donation came from none other than Emmanuele Brunatto, now a successful Paris businessman. Although out of favor with the Capuchins, Brunatto never ceased to revere his beloved master, and now he sent a donation of 3.5 million francs — the equivalent of $79,500!

The hour was not propitious, however, and the work progressed very slowly, chiefly because of the Second World War, which engulfed Italy a few months after Padre Pio's meeting with the three doctors. The project, in fact, ground to a near standstill during the years of blood and terror that were to follow.

Padre Pio had been very much alarmed by the rise of Hitler and his "religion of blood," and after Mussolini allied himself with him in the Rome-Berlin Axis of October 1936, Pio had become very much depressed. "Don't you remember how, along about 1920 or 1921," he reminded Agostino at the time, "I predicted that the League of Nations wouldn't last? I told you, 'These nations are going to tear each other to pieces!' Well, you see, it's happening!"[15]

As German troops rampaged through Europe, many Italians expected a speedy end to the war — and one in Italy's favor. Padre Pio had no such illusions. Much to the annoyance of some of his patriotic confreres, he predicted: "We are still at the beginning. The war will last a long time. We will see it spread from country to country like a rampaging flood, spreading devastation, carnage, and death. May the Lord save us!"[16]

Just as he predicted, the war gradually began to turn against the Axis. In June 1943, Agostino asked about its outcome, and Pio made some "ugly predictions." "People are hardened," he said. "They do not turn to God, and the Lord is not moved to compassion."[17]

Around that time, a delegation came from Mussolini, asking for advice. Padre Pio's feelings toward *Il Duce* had become quite negative. Feeling that Mussolini had done a good job at first, Pio came to take a dim view of the increasing pressure the dictator exerted to force Italians to join the Fascist Party. As Pio later explained to American visitors: "It reached the point that one couldn't get sugar, flour, or oil without a Fascist card. It was blackmail. Even the children's books were full of Fascist propaganda."[18] Therefore, when the messengers from Mussolini approached him, Padre Pio snapped, "So *now* you come to me, after you have destroyed Italy! You can tell Mussolini that nothing can save Italy now! Nothing! Tell him, 'You have destroyed her!'"[19]

When many of his fellow countrymen expressed dismay at the prospect of Italy losing the war, Pio begged to differ. William Carrigan, in a 1979 conversation with me, quoted Padre Pio as saying: "To win the war would not mean that we won it but that Germany would win it. Then we would fall under Nazi slavery, which is the most diabolical slavery that one can imagine!"

The bombs began to fall on Italy. In the summer of 1943, Foggia was bombed, the friary of St. Anna was badly damaged, and Padre Agostino temporarily had to move the headquarters of the province to San Giovanni Rotondo.

During September, the friars heard the false report that the Pope was being held a prisoner in the Vatican by the Nazis, who were occupying Rome. Pio was so distraught that he immediately ran a high fever and had to go to bed, murmuring dire prophecies. "Germany will be destroyed," he said, "because she is cursed by God."

Naturally, people began to ask him whether their town or dwelling would be spared the bombs that were plummeting down on most of the major cities. Sometimes he seemed to know. When a man from Genoa asked if his city would be bombed. Pio began to weep. "Genoa will be bombed," he groaned. "Ah, oh, how they will bomb that poor city! So many homes, buildings, and churches will crumble!" The inquirer began to quake with terror. "Be calm," Pio told him. "Your house will not be touched." And so it happened. In June 1944, the Allies bombed Genoa to a heap of rubble, but within a huge area of burnt-out ruins, the only house standing was that of the man to whom Padre Pio had prophesied.[20]

Asked whether San Giovanni Rotondo would be bombed, the padre replied that it would not. "The Lord, through His infinite goodness, will spare this blessed place and all the Gargano."[21] This too came to pass. There are many stories concerning Allied pilots who attempted to bomb San Giovanni but were stopped by the apparition of a "monk" standing in the air with his arms outstretched. There are fliers who swore that they had sighted a figure in the sky, sometimes of normal size, sometimes gigantic, usually in the form of a monk or priest (almost always identified as Padre Pio). The sightings were too frequent and the reports came from too many sources to be totally discounted. Almost all of them seemed to coincide with the malfunctioning of equipment on the planes, rendering them incapable of discharging their bombs. There are, however, no signed depositions available to be consulted.

There were other unusual stories, many of them having to do with miraculous deliverances. Several people from Foggia, where thousands were killed in the air raids, said that a bomb, falling into a room where they were huddled, landed near a photograph of Padre Pio. They claimed that when it exploded, it "burst like a soap bubble." Others reported that while bombs were raining down upon the city, they cried, "Padre Pio, you have to save us !" While they were speaking, a bomb fell into their midst but did not explode. When Padre Pio heard these stories, he would often say, "Stop! You're giving me a swelled head!"

The war years brought loss to Padre Pio's family as well as to his country. In January 1944, Pio's sister-in-law Giuseppa, wife of his brother, Michele, died in Pietrelcina at the age of sixty. Her sole surviving child, Pia, there at the bedside, testified that both her dying mother and the family physician, Andrea Cardone, saw Padre Pio appear in bilocation at the foot of the bed, while she herself, seeing nothing, smelled his "characteristic perfume." The next month, Pio's sister Pellegrina died in Chieti. What reaction he had to her death is unknown.

Pellegrina had long been the black sheep of the Forgione family, and it appears that there had long been little or no communication between her and the rest of the family. Whose fault this was will probably never be known. No matter how strained or limited the relationship, Padre Pio must have felt some grief, which along with that for his beloved sister-in-law and his anguish over the war, led him to remark to Padre Agostino in March 1944: "I am beginning to reflect upon that great passage to eternity, but I don't think I'm ready yet. I tremble and pray."[22]

The World for a Parish

Depressing as the war was to Padre Pio (and to everyone else), it was the means of opening the third phase of his ministry — his ministry to the world. To this point his fame had chiefly been confined to Italy. Now, largely a result of the arrival of American soldiers, he would be sought out from the four corners of the globe.

During the earlier part of the war, the area around Foggia had been infested with Nazis, who had built an air base in that agricultural and railroad center. In 1943, British and American troops dislodged them and stationed their own personnel in their place. The Germans had shown almost no interest in Padre Pio. Exactly two of their soldiers had taken the pains to call upon Padre Pio. In contrast, the Allied troops, especially the Americans, showed great enthusiasm for the Prophet of the Gargano. By Christmas Eve of 1943, Padre Agostino was recording in his diary: "Every Sunday, American soldiers come to hear Padre Pio's Mass. All of them are amazed and contrite, even the Protestants."[1]

This influx of American military personnel to San Giovanni Rotondo was to a large extent a result of the efforts of Mary Pyle and the director of the Adriatic section of the American Red Cross, William Carrigan.[2]

Carrigan, a graduate of the Catholic University of America in Washington, D.C., with a major in psychology, had worked as an assistant in the psychology department there until he was appointed to his position with the Red Cross at the outbreak of the war. He traveled with the Fifteenth Army Air Force and shared with me his vivid recollections of his arrival in Foggia and his encounter with Padre Pio.

The troops, along with Carrigan, reached Naples late in 1943 in the midst of a terrible thunderstorm. The city was a ghost town. The retreating Germans had ruined the water supply, with the result that there were queues blocks long in front of every spring or fountain in and about the city. People waited all night to obtain water. There was no power and little food. Many of the churches, seized by the Germans for the quartering of troops, had been left stripped bare and defaced.

The next day, Carrigan headed to Foggia in a convoy. "The very life had been bombed out of Foggia," Carrigan recalled. More than eleven thousand people had been killed in the bombings of the previous months, and most of the survivors had fled. The few who remained rummaged amid the rubble for scraps to eat.

Shortly after arriving in Foggia, Carrigan began to hear reports from the soldiers about a man up in the mountains who had the wounds of Christ. It happened that some American soldiers, while searching for eggs, had found themselves at San Giovanni Rotondo, where they had met fellow countryperson Mary Pyle, who offered them hospitality and regaled them with stories about Padre Pio. When the soldiers returned to their base and told their buddies about "the man in the mountains," a number of them wanted to visit the holy man. Because the Army had no available transportation for "a pleasure trip," several of the soldiers approached Carrigan.

A devout Catholic, Carrigan agreed to furnish transportation. On a cold winter's day with eight inches of snow on the ground, he and twenty American soldiers made their way to San Giovanni Rotondo. Padre Pio was well into his Mass when they entered the little church. There was no heat, and even though the Americans wore heavy overcoats, they were chilled to the bone. But, as Carrigan recounted to me: "It wasn't long before I experienced a physical warmth. Quickly I realized that he was very unique."

There was indeed something quite unusual going on. During the Consecration, Padre Pio seemed to undergo a transformation. He seemed to take on physical sufferings. "Though I knew nothing about the bodily stigmata," Carrigan said, "I noticed that he leaned on the altar, first on one elbow and then on the other, as if he were trying to relieve a pain in his feet. Moreover, at the words of the Consecration, it seemed as if he were having great difficulty in speaking the *Hoc est enim corpus meum* (This is my body)." Carrigan recalled:

> He shouted the words. He hesitated and bit them off as if he were in physical pain. Then when he reached for the chalice, he jerked his hand back rather violently, as if the pain were so great he could not grasp it. He hesitated as if he needed to restore his strength. . . . I was close enough to observe his facial expression. There was much twitching of the muscles. I saw tears rolling down his cheeks. Occasionally he would jerk his head to one side or the other, as if he were suffering special pains in the head and neck. The Consecration took two or three times as long as it took the average priest, yet . . . I seemed to understand. I felt an unusual participation in the sacrifice of this holy man.

Carrigan noted that after the bread and wine had been consecrated,

> it appeared as if the suffering had subsided. Padre Pio appeared exhausted
> and leaned over the altar for several minutes, as if he were in deep commun-
> ion with the Lord. Then something else happened to me. I felt that truly this
> man at this moment in time was in very close communion with our Lord,
> and, not knowing anything about him, he seemed to be so credible that I
> found myself hastily bringing to this altar and placing in the hands of Padre
> Pio my family, my friends, and those I knew were in special need, as well as
> the soldiers I was committed to serve. After some minutes, Padre Pio seemed
> to have his strength restored, and proceeded to distribute Communion to
> the faithful.

After the Mass, Padre Pio received visitors in the sacristy. Because of the war,
the church was nearly empty and the Americans had easy access to Pio. Carrigan noted a man "of average stature [Pio was actually, as we know, only 5'5"
tall], slightly on the heavy side, and slow of pace." There was nothing in his conversation or facial expression to indicate that he was suffering. On the contrary,
he was vital, lively, and cheerful.

Carrigan knelt to receive the padre's blessing, but the friar held him up by the
elbows as he started to kneel.

"*Americano?*" he asked.

"*Si! Si, Padre!*" replied Carrigan.

Through an interpreter, Pio told Carrigan that he and his group were the first
American military personnel he had met during the war. He made it clear that
he was delighted to see the *Americani*. After that, Pio let Carrigan kiss his un-
gloved and wounded hand. "My lips felt the rough scales of the blood crystals
that formed around the wounds," Carrigan recalled. "I also experienced the
aroma that is so frequently discussed. I was at first of the impression that it was
due to medication, but I couldn't identify it. It was very pleasant, but I thought
nothing of it at the time." Padre Pio spoke to each of the soldiers and allowed all
the men to kiss his wounded hands.

Carrigan felt as if his life would never be the same. Summing up his impressions of Padre Pio, he recalled:

> He was so thoroughly imbued with the love of Christ and so thoroughly con-
> vinced of the movement of Christ in the world that he exuded an unusual
> credibility to all who came under his influence. . . . He confirmed the faith
> of those who were already strong, and, for those who were uncertain and
> had questions, he brought a certain understanding. . . . Since I met Padre
> Pio at that Mass so many years ago, I can truthfully say that I have had no
> doubts or fears of contradiction regarding Christ's being who He said He is:
> the Savior of the world.

Carrigan decided right then that he wanted to make it possible for soldiers who needed spiritual guidance to go to Padre Pio. Pio was enthusiastic and at once contacted Archbishop Cesarano to arrange for a Midnight Mass on Christmas Eve for the Americans (midnight Christmas Masses are not customary in southern Italy).

In the meantime, Carrigan approached the chaplain of the Fifteenth Army Air Force, Father John Saint-John, a Jesuit. Although he had never heard of Padre Pio before, Saint-John was amenable to Carrigan's suggestions, and a few days later, he, Carrigan, and another large group of soldiers went to San Giovanni Rotondo.

Padre Pio was ready for his guests. Beaming, he gave each soldier and airman a rosary or medal. When the fliers knelt before him, he laid his hands on the wings on their uniforms and blessed them. Whenever some of the soldiers managed to speak a little Italian, Pio "lit up with joy."

Thus Carrigan and Father Saint-John began to organize pilgrimages of American soldiers to Padre Pio. These grew in frequency and numbers throughout 1944 and 1945. The men were warmly welcomed by the friars and, especially, by Miss Pyle, who fed as many as she could in her home, quickly endearing herself as a mother-figure to the servicemen.

Padre Pio himself seemed to know but one English word — "Okay!" Fortunately, there was no lack of interpreters. Besides Miss Pyle, there was a Hungarian refugee priest who spoke beautiful English. Less fluent was Padre Agostino, who, with his squat frame and massive white beard, reminded some of the men of Santa Claus. "Zi' Orazio," Pio's father, had been living in Mary Pyle's home since 1937 and was delighted at the arrival of the *Americani* because it gave him a chance to revive his almost forgotten English. His son Michele, who spent much of his time at San Giovanni Rotondo since his wife's death, also spoke some English. Carrigan remembers him as a thin man and "very spiritual."

Despite the language barrier, Carrigan knew personally of hundreds of men who received "reconfirmation of their faith" through their encounters with Padre Pio. He knew nearly as many who underwent outright conversions.

Carrigan vividly recalled a soldier who had become a discipline problem. He had become lackadaisical about his work and was frequently reluctant to carry out commands. The soldier agreed to talk with Padre Pio. As the man was Italian-American, no interpreter was needed. After fifteen minutes of conversation, the soldier's attitude changed radically. "Everything will work out well for him," the padre assured Carrigan.

That afternoon, the soldier, walking through the ravaged streets of Foggia, came upon some children who were kicking a ball made out of string and cloth. He learned that more than eight thousand children were roaming the streets. There were no schools to attend, and many of the boys spent their time robbing soldiers or inviting them, for a fee, to their sisters' beds. Quickly, the soldier persuaded his unit to organize a recreational program for the children. As he had previously worked for a recreational center in Chicago, he was able to send there for a supply of baseballs, basketballs, and other equipment.

Carrigan recalls another soldier he took to see Padre Pio. This man, too, was a serious discipline problem. Immediately after they returned from the interview, the soldier's commanding officer said to Carrigan: "What did you tell that lad? He's now a model soldier!" Carrigan replied that it was a quarter of an hour with Padre Pio that did the trick. Again, a third man, after merely seeing Padre Pio vesting for Mass, confessed: "In that moment it seemed as if my whole mind was turned around. I felt a complete turnaround in my thinking." He left the sacristy renewed in his determination to live a Christian life.

Padre Pio encouraged the American servicemen who spoke to him to contribute to the poor, and he expressed a desire for particular units to adopt needy families. He also told them about the hospital that he was building. Never asking for contributions, he simply told them: "This is a work of God. When you return to the States, tell people about it." In this way, after the war, a steady stream of contributions began to flow in from America.

For a period of about two years, William Carrigan saw a great deal of Padre Pio. On several occasions he was permitted to eat at the refectory and even stay overnight at the friary. Carrigan was impressed by the atmosphere of the friary. Pious old Padre Agostino, Carrigan said, though "kind and gentle," maintained strict discipline. No smoking was permitted. The friars were not even permitted to accept cigarettes and cigars from the GI's. "The monastery was a model of brotherly love." According to Carrigan, "Spirituality oozed from the place."

There was no obvious rivalry or jealousy. Although Agostino was guardian, it was Pio who seemed to be the unofficial leader, the "magnet" of the community.

Despite Padre Pio's great spiritual presence, most of the Americans found Padre Pio "the sort that you could have gone fishing with," Carrigan later recalled. There was nothing mysterious about him. Nor did Carrigan see any evidence of mystical charisms.

Even though he spoke almost no English, Padre Pio seemed to understand the Americans when they spoke. Carrigan and his companions communicated with Padre Pio by means of sign language, Church Latin, and the few scraps of Italian and English that the speakers had in common.

The Red Cross director was impressed by the padre's asceticism. "I need very little of the world's goods," Pio said to him. "A cover for my body, enough food to survive, and a little rest, and that's enough." Carrigan saw for himself that the padre's physical needs were indeed minimal. At the midday meal — the only one he took with his brethren — he "never ate all that was put before him. What he ate was nothing compared to the other friars, many of whom were great eaters." In the evening, Pio would sip a little wine or fruit juice. He especially loved pineapple juice, and after Carrigan and other American officials and soldiers returned to the States, they saw to it that he had a regular supply for the rest of his life. Carrigan, whose room was across the hall from Pio, noted that he never seemed to sleep any longer than four hours a night.

One night Padre Pio invited his American guest to pray with him in the choir. He escorted him to his stall and bade him kneel beside him. "He locked his arm in mine," Carrigan recalls. "I felt a unique relationship to him."

Padre Pio was not a man one could easily refuse. In 1945 Amalia Abresch, whom we met in an earlier chapter, once again fell deathly ill. Pio sent for Carrigan. "She is going to die unless she gets to the hospital at Ancona," he told Carrigan. The Red Cross official began to make excuses. There was still fighting around the city. Many of the roads had been destroyed.

The padre was adamant: "Get an army ambulance and take her there."

"Padre, you *know* I can't do that! You know as well as I do that the U.S. Army does not permit its vehicles to be requisitioned for civilian use."

Pio was firm. "You *must* take her up to Ancona, or else she will die."

"I don't think I can help you," protested Carrigan.

The next morning, Carrigan went to the military hospital and explained the problem to the colonel in charge. To his amazement, the colonel insisted that Carrigan use the ambulance. Within a short time, Carrigan was in the ambulance, heading for San Giovanni Rotondo. He fetched Signora Abresch, who, though deathly ill, smiled all the way to Ancona. Three or four weeks later Padre Pio again sent for Carrigan. "It's time to get the ambulance again to fetch Signora Abresch," he said. "She's well now."

Carrigan reported the story of a remarkable conversion: In 1945, a Jewish journalist from Rome wanted to write a story about Padre Pio but had no interest in Christianity. Getting out of his car, he asked for Padre Pio. It happened that the person he addressed was the man he sought. Padre Pio bowed to the Jew and said, "At your service, sir." Amazingly, the Jew fell to his knees, took the padre's hands and kissed them. "Will you receive me into the Church?" he asked. It was an instant conversion and just as much a surprise to the newsman as it was to everybody else!

Before Carrigan left for the States, he wrote a story about Padre Pio for the Catholic News Service, telling about the Sunday pilgrimages of soldiers and the great numbers of them whose lives had been changed. Within months, practically all the Roman Catholic periodicals had used the story. This publicity was an apparent cause of a rapid and dramatic increase of mail from the United States.

Another was Mary Pyle, who, because of illness in her family, returned to New York briefly after the war. She used this opportunity to speak of Padre Pio and his ministry, and was thus instrumental in drawing the attention of many Americans to the man who was already celebrated throughout Italy.

By December 1945 the volume of mail from all parts of the world had grown to more than a hundred letters a day. By March 1947 more than two hundred a day were arriving. Four priests were unable to handle the correspondence adequately. Working full time, they were still unable to reduce the backlog of ten to fifteen days by sending out a form letter saying that the padre was praying for the correspondent, who should remember to pray and to trust in God at all times.

Although nearly overwhelmed by confessions and prayer requests, Padre Pio still found time to be concerned about his family, the state of Italy, the opening of the friary and seminary at Pietrelcina, and the construction of the *Casa*.

On a happy note, in May 1945, Padre Pio officiated at the wedding of his only niece, Pia Forgione, to a teacher named Mario Pennelli. The couple settled in San Giovanni Rotondo and eventually raised a family of eight children. Pia's father, Michele, soon came to live with them year-round.

That same year, Pio's only nephew, Ettore Masone, fell ill. Masone, who had suffered from epilepsy since childhood, had come to live at San Giovanni Rotondo in 1940 after the death of his father. At the end of the war, however, he returned to Pietrelcina to open a movie house. When he asked his uncle's advice, the padre told him simply to be careful about the kind of movies he showed. "You don't want to contribute to the propagation of evil," he warned.[3]

Shortly after he opened the theater, however, Masone had a severe epileptic crisis. Pneumonia set in, then pleurisy. Mary Pyle, who had gone to Pietrelcina to look after him, phoned Padre Pio when doctors advised an operation. All Pio could tell her was, "Well, if it's necessary, they must operate."

Even after the surgery, Masone failed to gain and was sent home in a state worse than that in which he had come to the hospital. Not yet thirty, he was resigned to death and told his friends to pray, not for his recovery, but for the salvation of his soul. Soon he fell into what seemed to be a deep sleep. "I found myself at the gates of heaven," Masone wrote, "where my sister Giuseppina, who had been dead for many years, was standing. Then I also saw Padre Pio. Both of them were unwilling for me to enter into heaven."[4]

Meanwhile, Masone's doctors and friends were convinced that he was in a coma and dying. Hearing him repeat, over and over, "Zio Pio! Zio Pio!" they remembered that his mother, moments before her death, had also reported seeing Padre Pio. Certain that death was imminent, Masone's relatives phoned a nearby friary to make funeral arrangements for the next day.

No sooner had they done this than Masone came to his senses and told them to stop their lugubrious preparations. "I'm not dying anymore!" he said. When the priests came the next day to conduct his funeral, they found, not a corpse, but a man well on the way to recovery.

The following year brought sadness to Pio's heart. Papa Forgione had become a fixture at San Giovanni Rotondo. So humble was this old man that he never introduced himself as Padre Pio's father. Although bent and wizened, Zio Orazio remained vigorous until the spring of 1946, when, at the age of eighty-five, he suffered a bad fall, from which he never fully recovered. By early October, it was apparent that Grazio was slipping from this world. Padre Pio spent most of the last four days of Papa's life with him. The old gentleman would eat only when his son spoon-fed him. Then, at 9:30 on the evening of October 7, Grazio's soul was freed. Padre Pio broke down completely, as he had done when his mother died, and was unable to leave Miss Pyle's house. While funeral services were being conducted, he lay sobbing on the bed where his father had died. When he was able to return to the friary, it was a week before he was able to do any more than say Mass and then go to bed.

Padre Pio was not a political man, but he voted regularly and frequently expressed strong opinions about events and personalities. As we have seen, he did not think highly of Mussolini — at least at the end — but he thought the world of Franklin D. Roosevelt. When William Carrigan spoke disparagingly of the President during the war, Pio countered by saying: "Don't talk that way. Roosevelt is a great man! If it weren't for him, we wouldn't be coming out of this thing!"

The Fascist peril past, the padre grew concerned about the growing strength of the Communists. Men gathered once or twice a week under the red banner in nearly all the towns. Padre Pio viewed this with great alarm.

To combat the red peril, Pio neither gave speeches nor organized meetings. He simply prayed and exercised his right to vote. On June 2, 1946, he voted for the Constituent Assembly and in the simultaneous national referendum to decide the fate of King Umberto II and the Italian monarchy. The Padre was mobbed at the polls as people swarmed about him to kiss his hand. When he returned from voting, swelling crowds hailed him with cheers and applause. When the Christian Democrats won an absolute majority over the Communists in the Assembly, many of the Marxists began to blame the unassuming little friar for their defeat. "By his very presence he took votes away from us!" several of their spokesmen groused.

The referendum abolished the monarchy. Padre Pio never talked much about the monarchy, but some of those close to him believe that he opposed it because of the royal family's heavy involvement in Freemasonry, another ideology that he found totally unacceptable.

There was an even wilder scene at the elections that took place in the spring of 1948. This time, convinced that the fate not only of Italy but of the whole world was at stake and that everything would be lost in the event of a Communist victory, Padre Pio took it upon himself to write to Premier Alcide De-Gasperi, expressing his support for the Christian Democrats. With the elections a few weeks away, Padre Agostino noted in his diary that Pio was "lining up victory on the side of law and order" by "jawboning" every official or private citizen with whom he had any influence.

Many of the Communists did not take kindly to such priestly involvement in the political arena. A few days before the elections, a Communist from the nearby town of San Marco in Lamis was electioneering from the back of a truck. As he passed within earshot of the friary, he bellowed, "Down with Padre Pio!" Moving away from the friary, he continued his politicking, doubling back into the town. Five minutes after he had reached the center of town, he was seized with terrible pains and had to give up his haranguing and return home. He was taken to a hospital, and physicians, opening him up, found that he had only a few days to live.[5] Padre Pio's followers attributed the orator's collapse and terminal illness to divine retribution. They made a similar interpretation of an accident that took place on election day.

On April 18, Padre Pio arrived at the polls by automobile. As he was about to enter the balloting place, a woman ran into the street, shrieking obscenities at him. After she wearied of heaping imprecations on the little friar's head, she stepped toward the polling place, slipped and fell, broke her leg, and had to be taken to the hospital without having the opportunity to vote.[6]

The Christian Democrats were victorious in the elections, and Padre Pio, who rejoiced immensely, was hailed by many people as instrumental in keeping Italy from going Communist at this crucial time. As in the elections of 1946, many Communists took Padre Pio's trip to the polls as a personal affront and did not hesitate to blame him for their defeat.

Padre Pio was as much concerned with the friary and seminary at Pietrelcina as he was with the national elections. Twenty years after work had begun, the building complex was finished but unoccupied. Completed just before the outbreak of hostilities, it had been requisitioned by the government for the billeting of troops. Padre Agostino was naive enough to rejoice, assuming that the government would ensure that the premises would be returned in optimum condition. Quite the opposite: the building was occupied, in turn, by Italians, Germans, New Zealanders, and Poles, who smashed all the furniture and covered the wall with obscenities in an assortment of languages.

In addition, many Church officials, especially Archbishop Agostino Mancinelli of Benevento, were opposed to the location of a Capuchin friary at Pietrelcina. Padre Pio was so disgusted with Mancinelli's refusal to state any reason for his opposition that, in July 1946, when a priest from the archdiocese of Benevento conveyed the prelate's greetings, Pio retorted, "Tell him that . . . souls are being lost and the enemies of God are wreaking havoc, all because the Archbishop sleeps and does not want the friars at Pietrelcina." Declaring that "the responsibility is all his," Pio added: "Benevento was bombed and lost the cathedral and episcopal residence as a punishment for the Archbishop. My heart bleeds to say this, but it's true. . . . Worse, not even after this punishment from God is the Archbishop willing to understand his responsibility. He is truly hard of heart!"[7]

The "enemies of God" were neither Marxists nor Fascists nor Nazis — rather, they were members of a Pentecostal sect! For some years a preacher named Cavaluzzo had been operating at Pietrelcina, holding evangelical meetings, distributing books, tracts, Bibles, money, and even baptizing people in the river! His group had even gone so far as to ask the mayor if they could purchase the vacant friary to use as their church, and the mayor, good Catholic that he was, in terror and alarm had turned to Padre Pio for help.

Though Padre Pio had great respect for Jews, for him Pentecostals were, for some reason, "enemies of God," and "the foes of our Holy Religion."[8] Perhaps the group in Pietrelcina was an extremist sect with bizarre and unwholesome practices. We don't know. Determined that something had to be done at once to provide a Capuchin presence in Pietrelcina, Pio, in December 1946, dispatched the faithful Marquess Giuseppe Orlando. "God has chosen you to do this work," he told the man who in many ways had replaced Brunatto as his troubleshooter. "Go to Rome and succeed."

The marquess set out at once for the Eternal City, really at a loss as to what to do. Uncannily, things worked out. He made the right contacts, and at the right time. He learned Mancinelli's real reason for opposing the Capuchins. The archbishop told Orlando frankly: "The Capuchins cannot come to Pietrelcina because it would raise the question of their interests against those of the parish clergy. . . . Everyone would give their . . . offerings to the Capuchins because they are Padre Pio's monks, and no longer to the secular clergy, and I have to defend the secular clergy because they are my dependents."[9] The prelate conceded that if a means were found to compensate the clergy who stood to lose the most by the Capuchin presence, he might be disposed to change his mind.

Furthermore, Orlando learned that the Francsican Observants of Paduli were lobbying the Vatican against the establishment of a Capuchin friary at Pietrelcina. Why? Because Pietrelcina was too close to Paduli and the Capuchins would infringe upon the rights of the Observants to solicit alms and money in that region. As the Observant provincial angrily told Orlando, "Only we can solicit in that area!" The priestly marquess shook his head and thought to himself, "Monks against monks!"[10]

At Rome, Orlando found a champion in Luigi Cardinal Lavitrano, who promised to work on Mancinelli. He sent an aide to Benevento to persuade the archbishop. Within a few days, Mancinelli acquiesced, the Sacred Congregation for Religious agreed, and all obstacles to opening the friary were removed.

In January 1947, Orlando returned from Rome. Padre Pio was in bed when he heard the sound of applause coming from the corridor. Getting up, he found Orlando and several colleagues beaming from ear to ear. When he learned that Orlando had succeeded, he embraced him, kissed him, and blessed him, weeping with joy. "See, Peppino," Pio said. "God chose you to accomplish this work!" The marquess was curious about "all those fortuitous meetings." "Were they a matter of coincidence?" he asked.

"Yes," replied Padre Pio, "but there is Somebody up there who arranged those coincidences!"[11]

When the friary was opened in July, Mancinelli led the parade and celebrated the solemn Pontifical High Mass. Padre Pio had been invited but sent Mary Pyle (who, as we will recall, paid for the construction out of pocket) and Padre Raffaele as his representatives. Though Padre Pio never saw the friary at Pietrelcina in person, Mercurio Scocca believed that he had done so by bilocation. Some years later, when a statue of St. Mary was dedicated, Scocca came to Pio, regretting his absence.

"Now that shows just how much you know," said Pio to his lifelong friend. "I was there! How many steps lead to the building? There are nine, aren't there?" Scocca, after checking to make sure that the edifice did have nine steps, became convinced that Pio had indeed been there.[12]

At the same time that he was negotiating for the opening of the friary at Pietrelcina, Padre Pio was working feverishly to make the *Casa Sollievo della Sofferenza* a reality. During the war, money had been coming in for this project in bits and trickles. Padre Pio had launched an appeal throughout Italy. Donations were numerous, but most of them were small, often amounting only to a few cents. By late 1946, Dr. Sanguinetti informed Padre Pio that they had not raised sufficient funds to begin construction. Pio seemed unperturbed. Around that time, a world-famous opera singer (probably Beniamino Gigli, who was a devotee of Padre Pio) came to San Giovanni Rotondo. Announcing that he had gotten a new contract, he quoted the amount he was making in excess of the previous one. He then declared that he was donating the extra money to the hospital. Sanguinetti determined that the donation, even to the decimal point, was the precise sum needed to begin construction. Thus, in May 1947, the work began, supervised by Sanguinetti and the architect Don Angelo Lupi (d. 1969).

Sanguinetti became a self-taught construction expert. He drove trucks, supervised laborers, located technical experts, and selected materials. As his friend John McCaffery recalls, "In the matter of ensuring that there would be no exploitation in quality of goods or in costs, he was like a tiger."[13]

After a few months, however, money ran out and construction stopped. It appeared that the great work was in deep trouble, but relief was not long in coming. During the summer of 1948, the eminent British economist, conservationist, and humanitarian Barbara Ward (1913-1981) came to Italy to write a report on the postwar reconstruction of the country for her magazine, the *Economist*. She was particularly interested in the work of the United Nations Relief and Rehabilitation Administration (UNRRA). Miss Ward was in fact engaged to the deputy director of UNRRA in charge of operations in the field, Commander Robert Jackson. As Miss Ward, afterward baroness of Lodsworth, recounted in a letter to me shortly before her death:

> When I reached Rome, I stayed with Italian friends, the Patrizis. Marchese
> Bernardo Patrizi, learning that I was to go on to Taranto, urged me to break

my journey at Foggia and allow him to take me up to San Giovanni Rotondo to encounter the saintly Padre Pio, who, with his stigmata, his endless hours in the confessional, and his reputation for healing the sick, was already the drawing power for immense pilgrimages from Italy and . . . other lands.

Miss Ward and the Patrizis set out together, passing through the baking heat of Foggia into the cooler air of the Gargano hills. Arriving at San Giovanni Rotondo, they spent the night with Willy and Mi Sanguinetti, whom the baroness remembers as "a charming, highly intelligent, and utterly devoted pair."

The next day Miss Ward attended Padre Pio's Mass and was deeply impressed. Afterward she and the Marquess Patrizi had a long talk with Dr. Sanguinetti. The physician explained how, in the years since he had come to San Giovanni, the responsibility of caring for sick and dying pilgrims had largely fallen upon his shoulders. "He confessed that the problem of caring for the deeply sick was nearly defeating him, despite the neighborly cooperation of the whole village," the baroness recalls.

Then he explained to Ward the plans for the *Casa.* "Subscriptions are constantly coming in and I have no doubt that they will continue to do so." Sanguinetti said. "But they just aren't enough! Signor Lupi, the architect, and I have dedicated ourselves to the preparation of plans and estimates. We are confronted, however, with the stark fact that we haven't enough money to carry through a hospital project of this size."

He explained that hospitals and medical centers were desperately scarce in southern Italy, and the Foggia district was no exception. "A well-conceived and well-run hospital would serve the health of the whole region," he said, "and, by its elevation among the hills of the Gargano, it would be more suitably sited than out in the burning summer plains."

"It was this assurance of a wider usefulness," recalls the baroness, "that prompted me to wonder whether the hospital — for which, after all, local funds had already been collected — might not be the recipient of aid from UNRRA, since the restoration of health services was part of its official mandate." Miss Ward thereupon wrote her fiancé, asking that the hospital be considered part of the rehabilitation of the Foggia region. As a result, UNRRA made a grant of $325,000 for the construction of the *Casa.*

Work proceeded rapidly. Lupi, though several hours short of his degree, was quickly acclaimed as an architectural genius. Father Dominic Meyer (1892-1966), who came from America in 1947 to be Padre Pio's English correspondence secretary, described Lupi as "architect, constructor, superintendent, and a lot of other things for the new hospital. Through his genius, all manner of necessary equipment and supplies are being made here. This saves a lot of money and gives the poor people here work." In a letter to a relative, he speaks with enthusiasm of Lupi and the new facility:

The tile for the flooring, for wainscoting, window sashes, bathroom equipment, etc., are made of imitation marble. The material he gets from the . . . mountain behind the hospital. . . .

The lime for the plaster he likewise extracts from the stone, having built a special lime kiln. Then, from the scaffolding and other wood left over from the building frame, he makes some of the finest furniture, tables, chairs, etc. Iron beds are also made, as well as wrought iron furnishings. The chapel is a gem. Floors and pillars are in mosaic.[14]

As work progressed, there remained an embarrassing problem. In awarding the UNRRA grant, Robert Jackson had requested that the hospital be named for Fiorello H. LaGuardia (1882-1947), the recently deceased director general of UNRRA. Padre Pio did not like the idea. He did not want his Home to Relieve Suffering called a hospital. And, having never met LaGuardia, he was not keen on having the *Casa* bear his name. Soon, Padre Pio and "the Society" (board of directors) of the hospital found an ingenious solution. When the *Casa* was finally opened several years later, on the side of the building they erected a little plaque expressing gratitude to the United Nations and stating that the building was named for Fiorello LaGuardia. However, at the top of the building, in neon letters, they placed the sign LA CASA SOLLIEVO DELLA SOFFERENZA.[15]

A Day with Padre Pio

Padre Pio's day began each morning about 3:00, when his alarm clock sounded and he rose to prepare for Mass. Although he never celebrated the Eucharist earlier than 5 A.M. and the community never rose before that hour, Pio loved to spend several hours in prayer and meditation before approaching the altar. His very first prayers each morning were for the Pope. By the side of his bed in Room No. 5, he kept three little pictures, which were illuminated by a lamp: St. Michael the Archangel on one side, the Virgin Mary in the middle, and the Pope on the right. He had his window shade adjusted so that the first light of day — still several hours off — would shine on the Holy Father's portrait.

Padre Pio was not the only person in San Giovanni Rotondo awake in the wee hours of the morning. A great line of men and women began to form fairly early in the evening, and when the church doors opened at 4:30, there invariably ensued a furious scramble, as many hundreds of people competed for seats in a church that comfortably seated no more than two hundred.

Most of the commotion was caused by the large, noisy coterie of local women who called themselves "the Pious Ladies." These women were not the intimate disciples, such as Mary Pyle, the Campanile sisters, the Garganis, or the Morcaldis. Rather, they were what in the United States might be called groupies, women who hysterically mobbed Padre Pio almost in the same way that their more secular sisters would a few years later mob Elvis Presley and the Beatles.

Few of these pious ladies waited all night for a good seat in church. The long line of people who waited patiently without the benefit of a rest room in the cold night air was composed mostly of out-of-towners. A few minutes before the church doors opened, the Pious Ladies would suddenly appear, forming what

John McCaffery likened to a "flank position" near the head of "the enemy column."[1] The instant the doors were opened, they would charge the "enemy ranks" and battle their way to the front of the church, armed with hat pins and pocketbooks, jabbing, kicking, and even biting. In the early 1950s, the wife of the Chilean ambassador had her nose nearly bitten off by one of the Pious Ladies. I have interviewed several Americans who spoke of being "attacked by hostile natives," as if they were in some primeval jungle.

As the local harridans surged into the church, often literally trampling their victims, Padre Agostino, who remained guardian until 1952, would frequently post himself in the choir overlooking the church below and roar reproaches at them. "You uneducated ignoramuses!" he would thunder. "Don't you know that you are in the house of the Lord?"[2] To no avail. The Pious Ladies crowded into the seats toward the front of the church, and the rest of the throng had to pack in behind them.

A hush came over the crowd as Padre Pio appeared and slowly made his way to the altar. For him the Mass was indeed something special. He defined it as "a sacred fix with the Passion of Jesus," in which "all Calvary" was, not reenacted, but re-presented, or extended to the present.[3] The Mass was not a "bloody sacrifice," and if anyone called it that, Pio would call him a heretic. Rather it was a participation in Jesus' sacrifice, apart from any merit or worthiness on the celebrant's part or that of anyone worshiping with him.

In his Mass, in a sense, Padre Pio relived Christ's passion. At various points he said that he experienced in a mystical way the crowning with thorns, the scourging, the crucifixion, and even the death of the Lord. In fact, he told a colleague, "All that Jesus has suffered in His Passion, inadequately I also suffer, as far as is possible for a human being. And all this against my unworthiness, and thanks only to His goodness."[4]

Within the Mass, however, Padre Pio admitted to an intense mystical involvement with the unseen world. He apparently saw, as in a vision, the entire Passion, and actually felt, physically, the wounds of Jesus. When he read the Epistle and Gospel of the day's Mass, he identified so closely with their content that he frequently would shed copious tears. During the offering of the bread and wine, Padre Pio often remained motionless for moments on end, as if "nailed by a mysterious force," gazing with moistened eyes upon the crucifix. At these moments, he said, his soul was "separated from all that is profane." At the Commemorations of the Living and the Dead, he maintained that he saw all his spiritual children at the altar, "as if in a mirror."[5]

During the Consecration, Padre Pio seemed to suffer most intensely. He seemed to feel the horrible weight of sin — his own sins and those of all mankind — and the enormity of God's immense and unmerited love. As he communed, he professed to feel physically the "kiss of Jesus," all over his being. He spoke of Communion as "all one mercy, all one embrace. . . ."[6]

Thus the Mass ended with many of the worshipers — even the Pious Ladies — awestruck and in tears. Barbara Ward Jackson, in her memorandum to me, dated February 16, 1980, spoke of her experience of the four-hour Mass she attended in 1947. Despite the length of the Mass, she recalled

> the profound hush of expectancy, hope, and anguish that fell on that vast congregation. . . . I cannot remember, in all those hours, any sound above the whimper of sick children and the whispered words of comfort of their mothers. Whoever they were — the healthy, the young, the curious, the penitents, the hopelessly crippled, and, above all, sick children and their parents longing for a miracle — the hushed and awed silence covered everyone. It was almost as though, without signs or cures, one were living through a minor miracle. Never have I heard a silence so full of prayer and anguish and hope.

The silence ended with the Mass. As Padre Pio made his way into the sacristy, many of the Pious Ladies, finding once more their voices, shriekingly surged toward him. Some of them, standing on pews, held out babies or religious articles to be blessed. Others grabbed at his cincture or his vestments. William Carrigan told me that on one occasion a woman grabbed Pio's arm and would not release it. "All right, take it! You can have it!" the padre told her. "Just let me go!"

Other times the good padre was not so good humored. Carrigan recalls another instance when a frantic woman literally flung herself into Padre Pio's path and lay clutching the hem of his alb, screaming and moaning, beseeching the padre for some favor or other. Backing away, the padre roared, "You get up from there!" Seemingly furious, he ordered her to leave instantly. When he reached the sacristy, he confessed to Carrigan that he was not really angry, "You've got to be sharp with these people," he explained. "It's the only thing they understand!"

Likewise, reporters and photographers were unwelcome. "Throw them out! Call the police!" he was known to shout if they pressed in on him. He seldom posed for a picture, and, when he did, it was for his friend Federico Abresch. Nearly all of the numerous likenesses of Padre Pio were totally candid, totally unsolicited, and totally undesired on his part. During his stint as guardian, Padre Agostino had a standing policy of noncooperation with reporters. A man had only to identify himself as a newsman for Agostino to lay a hand on his shoulder and politely but firmly tell him that it was his custom never to speak to reporters or permit his friars to do so. Then he would show him the door.

The faithful and devout were always welcome in the sacristy, the area where he and the other priests put on and removed their vestments. As we have seen, at times the authorities in Rome put the sacristy off limits to laypersons. When worshipers were permitted there, however, Padre Pio was never averse to greeting them, exchanging a few pleasantries, and blessing those who desired to be blessed. After removing his vestments, Padre Pio would proceed to the choir on the balcony above the little church, there to make his prayers of thanksgiving. After that he was ready to hear confessions.

Padre Pio, of course, could hear only a certain number of confessions in a day. After the Second World War, with large numbers of visitors from many nations, the wait was terribly long. If one wanted to make one's confession to Padre Pio, he joined a long line of penitents in the morning. Apparently, throughout the night, two lines formed, one for the Mass, the other for the confessional. If the padre did not get to the penitent that given day, the individual would have to return the next morning and get in line again.

There was no way of keeping one's place in line from day to day. A woman who had been, let us say, fourth in line at the time Padre Pio heard his last confession the day before would have to go to the rear of the line when she arrived the next morning. Even if she managed to be one of the first four to arrive, she risked the chance of being bumped out of line, sometimes at the last minute, by some Pious Lady who claimed that the spot was hers. If the hapless visitor did not give in, she was liable to be kicked, punched, or even dragged out of line by her hair!

Some Pious Ladies were more civil. They would offer to keep places in line for visitors who did not care to wait all night. Of course, they charged a substantial fee!

Things reached an ugly pass one day in 1950. A woman from Sicily had been waiting a week, standing all night, constantly being dislodged by the Ladies. At length, she was first in line. It was then that several women punched and shoved their way ahead of her. Desperate, the Sicilian woman drew a knife and threatened her attackers. The Pious Ladies immediately began screaming that the Sicilian was about to kill them. Padre Pio, irate, left the confessional and demanded to know what was going on. The Pious Ladies told him their side of the story, and Pio, having no idea whatsoever about what was going on, turned on the poor Sicilian, told her he would not hear her confession, and ordered her to return home.

When the woman reported the incident to the provincial, who was at that time none other than Padre Paolino DiTommaso of Casacalenda, he pressed Father Clement Neubauer of Milwaukee, the minister general, for permission to issue tickets for confession. At first, Clement told him that this smacked more of the theater than of the Church, but Paolino eventually got his way. Thereafter, all those wishing to make their confessions to Padre Pio had to register in person at the church. Tickets were given to local people; tickets of a second color to people from out of town. Two lines were formed, one for locals and one for visitors. To guard against the black market, each ticket had to be signed in person in front of a priest by the person to whom it was issued. The priest also had to sign it and date it. This system, in force for the remainder of Padre Pio's life, drastically cut down on the violence and the circus atmosphere that became almost a way of life after the Second World War.

Foreigners were carefully screened so as to permit only those fluent in Italian to approach Padre Pio. Many believed that the padre had the "gift of languages," that an American or Russian, for instance, could miraculously understand and be understood by him. There had been, indeed, some remarkable occurrences. We will recall how, during the years preceding the First World War, Padre Pio had no trouble understanding Padre Agostino's letters in French and Greek, even though he was uninstructed in either language. In the 1940s, another inexplicable happening of this type was recorded. A Swiss priest came to make his confession to the padre. Since the visitor spoke no Italian and Padre Pio spoke no German, they conversed in Latin. Before he left, the Swiss priest asked the padre to pray for a certain lady. To the visitor's amazement, Pio replied, "*Ich werde sie an die göttliche Barmherzigkeit empfehlen*" (I will commend her to divine mercy).[7]

Normally, however, Padre Pio spoke only Italian and, of course, his native Neapolitan dialect. A penitent ignorant of these languages was sure to cause embarrassment for himself and annoyance on the part of the padre. Occasionally, as we have seen, Padre Pio would hear a confession in Latin, but usually he preferred not to and would often tell those intent on doing so to seek a more learned confessor.

Padre Pio spent all morning after Mass as well as several hours in the afternoon hearing confessions. Mornings he usually heard the confessions of women; afternoons, those of men.

For some, there was nothing unusual about making one's confession to Padre Pio. "I went to him for confession many times, and there was nothing unusual," William Carrigan told me. "It was just as normal as apple pie." Great numbers of those who had the opportunity to make their confession to the padre, however, have testified that there was indeed something unusual, if only the wisdom, the compassion, the insight, and the clarity with which he heard and counseled them. For most of the people, most of the time, Padre Pio was unable to reveal the future or bring to light hidden sins the penitent himself had forgotten. The padre was able, however, to understand and advise as few other priests or counselors could.

There are reports too numerous to be ignored about Padre Pio's demonstrating supernatural insight in the confessional. We have already read the accounts of Andre Mandato and Federico Abresch. Graziella Mandato, wife of Andre, told me in August 1978 that the same sort of thing happened when she first confessed to Padre Pio in the 1940s. "I was too scared to talk," she said, "but Padre Pio told me everything that I did wrong."

Clarice Bruno, an American-born Franciscan tertiary who first called upon Padre Pio in the 1940s, has left a detailed account of her first session in the confessional with Padre Pio. The entire interview took less than two minutes. The moment she entered the confessional, Padre Pio announced, "I will do the talking." With that, he began "reciting my sins to me, pausing between each one so that I could confirm it by saying, 'Si, Padre.'" At one point he said, "You have been impatient and lost your temper . . . but you immediately repented."

Immediately Miss Bruno remembered how, the previous day, she had lost her temper with a waiter in a local restaurant. "I hope I repented," she told the padre.

"I *said* that you repented right away," Pio responded.

"He was not asking — he was telling me," Miss Bruno recalled.

Then, "suddenly, in the middle of the confession, contrary to custom, and before I had, therefore, the occasion to formulate my question, he gave me the advice that I, in that moment, particularly needed." Thereupon, he absolved her and closed the little door between them. The confession was over, and Miss Bruno left the church feeling "lighter" and "at peace with God."[8]

Although Graziella Mandato recalls that Padre Pio was always "very sweet" to her when she made her confessions, he was, as we have already seen, noted for his curtness towards those who came out of curiosity or were unwilling to make a sincere confession. "He wasn't an easy confessor," Padre Tarcisio Zullo of Cervinara, a colleague, recalled. "Your veins trembled and your pulse beat faster when you knelt before him. With his searching eyes, he would seek out the most secret wounds in your soul. You could hide nothing from him, even if you were very clever."[9]

Miss Bruno wrote of a lady who entered the padre's confessional for the first time, only to have him ask "Don't you hear someone crying?" When she responded in the negative, he repeated the same question a second and a third time. Finally he said, "That was the child you murdered years ago!" The woman left the confessional convulsed with sobs. She had undergone an abortion years before but had told no one about it and had even blotted it from her own mind.[10]

Padre Tarcisio recalls climbing the stairs one day beside Padre Pio when a man ran up and asked him to hear his confession. Padre Pio gave the man a severe look. "Don't you see how black you are? Go," he said, "and put things in order, change your way of life, and I will hear your confession."

When Padre Tarcisio scolded him for his harshness, Padre Pio answered, "If you only knew how many arrows pierced my heart before displeasing that brother of mine! But, if I don't do this, they will not be converted to God!"[11]

Padre Pio could be especially severe with women who, he felt, came to him inappropriately attired. Any woman whose skirt failed to reach to the mid-calf or whose sleeves did not cover three quarters of the length of her arm was ordered out of the confessional. Thérèse Lanna of New York, in a conversation we had in 1980, vividly recalled the experience of two acquaintances who presented themselves to Padre Pio in dresses with see-through sleeves and plunging necklines. "Out! Out! Out!" he shouted. Taking quite literally St. Paul's injunction in 1 Corinthians, chapter 11, long after most churchmen had forgotten about it, Padre Pio refused to speak to any woman who had the temerity to enter the church with her head uncovered. Nor would he have anything to do with a woman with the stench of tobacco on her breath. Although he was not averse to talking a pinch of snuff to clear his sinuses on occasion, he was death on cigarettes, especially for women. To a kindergarten teacher from Rome named Nerina Noe, he once snarled, "Women who smoke are disgusting!"[12] Signorina Noe never again felt a desire for cigarettes after that memorable encounter! Clarice Bruno also testified to a healing of her addiction to nicotine through Padre Pio.

Although he was a strict man, Padre Pio was also compassionate. He never counseled asceticism. In fact, he often advised against extreme penances. Father Joseph Pius recalls how grieved Padre Pio was when he learned that a woman, trying to imitate him by offering herself, without any spiritual counseling, as a Victim of Divine Love, lost her mind and had to be institutionalized. Another time, a lady came to him saying: "Dear Father, I want to help. Give me some suffering."

"Ah, but my dear, you already have such trouble, and you want to help me in suffering?" Pio replied. "Think about your present troubles and don't court additional ones!"[13]

Another time, an overzealous woman, as a penance, picked some noxious weeds from the meadow and ate them despite warnings that she was liable to contract typhus from doing so. When Padre Pio learned of this, he told her: "I won't permit any more of this madness! There are many ways to do penance, such as offering to the Lord whatever trouble comes to us day by day. It is up to the Lord to give us our cross. If still He has not sent you one, it is because He is not sure that you could bear it."[14] It was only a few, rare individuals that Pio counseled to offer themselves as victim-souls.

Except for lavatory and coffee breaks, the padre would ·stay in the confessional all morning. At noon he would go to dinner in the friary refectory. "We usually had to grab him from the confessional to go to dinner," Padre Raffaele D'Addario recalled in an interview in 1971. He would drink a glass or two of wine or fruit juice and take a few bites of food. By 1950 he seldom ate more than a half ounce of food in a twenty-four-hour period.[15] He liked cheeses, pasta, fish, and fried sausage, but never swallowed more than a few mouthfuls before professing, "I'm stuffed."

Even so, approaching his early sixties, Padre Pio continued to grow stouter. In the late 1940s he fell violently ill with one of his vomiting attacks and was unable to eat for eight days. Dr. Sanguinetti, on weighing him, was astounded that the priest had actually gained weight during this period. Incredulous, he asked the padre why he remained so stout even though he ate so little.

"Assimilation. Everything depends on assimilation," was the reply.

"But there's nothing to assimilate if you don't eat."

"Well, every morning I take Communion."

"No," said the doctor, "no, you're not convincing me. You must be hiding some food somewhere so as to trick me."

"I haven't eaten anything, just as you have seen," replied Pio. "But we must think of the parable in the Bible about the sower. The grain fell on good ground and produced a hundredfold. You see that my soil is good and I have produced much!"

"Very well," said Sanguinetti. "These are spiritual things. What does the spirit have to do with the body?"

Pio went on to say that he was nourished solely by the Eucharist. "Don't you recall that saint who lived solely on the Host, who took as nourishment each morning only the Host and ate nothing until the following morning?" he asked. "Well, it is the Lord who does this, and not I. It is the Lord who is working in me!"[16]

After lunch, Padre Pio went into the garden for about a half hour for recreation, one of two periods in the day free for unrestricted socializing. Often laymen came to join Pio and his brethren as they stood about and chatted. It was during these times that Padre Pio loved to tell funny stories. Although he could be earthy, he was never coarse. When anyone insisted on telling a dirty story, he would either ask them to leave or excuse himself. Nearly all the stories he told had some religious moral; many of them concerned saints or Bible figures. For instance, he told a story about a tailor who died and went to heaven.

"Now this tailor, who used to curse and swear," said Pio, "was a crude, drunken lout, and when he died, he found himself a beggar before St. Peter. St. Peter took the Book of Life and read it and decided to throw the tailor out. When he learned what St. Peter was about to do, the tailor screamed and hollered until St. Joseph, who happened to be nearby, came running and asked St. Peter what the matter was.

"When the tailor saw St. Joseph, he threw himself on his knees and besought him, saying, 'Dear St. Joseph, you remember that I always prayed to you. I was a pig, yes, even a hog, it's true, but every day I thought about you because you were always one of my favorite saints, because you were a working man.'"

St. Joseph was moved, and seeing the tailor tearing out his hair, he told St. Peter to let him enter the pearly gates. St. Peter, however, refused. Thereupon St. Joseph went to the Madonna and said: "Listen, Mary, I don't count for anything around here anymore in this heaven. I ask a favor of St. Peter, and he won't let a fellow in. My recommendations count for very little. Let's leave."

The Madonna answered, "You're right! I'm sure that Peter was misbehaving, and besides, I'm your wife, and the wife must follow the husband. Therefore, I'm coming with you. But let's not leave Our Lord here, because He's our Son. Let's go and take Our Lord with us."

Then the Holy Spirit saw the Madonna, Jesus, and St. Joseph leaving, and decided to go along with them, flying overhead. Pio continued, "God the Father also followed them as well as the other saints. Then St. Peter opened the gate of heaven and let the tailor in."[17]

Sometimes Padre Pio would reminisce about his army life and his commanding officers, and sometimes even imitate the unsteady gait of the drunkard. " 'Why, O Lord,' said the inebriate, seeing a centipede walking on the wall, 'did you give this critter a hundred legs and me, who can't stand up straight, only two?' "[18]

He used to tell about two men from the backwoods who had just heard about the invention of the train and decided to take a ride.

"Where do you want to go?" asked the ticket seller.

"What business is it of yours?" said the bumpkins.

Once on board, the hayseeds become terrified when the train roared into a tunnel.

"Where are we going?" asked the one.

"I think we're going into hell!" whimpered the other.

"Don't worry," said the first, confidently. "We have round-trip tickets!"[19]

Whenever anyone talked about making him a saint, Padre Pio used to say, "Before they make me a saint, they'll have to put Lucifer on the main altar of St. Peter's!"[20] Other times, referring to the fact that southern Italians are called macaroni eaters, he used to say: "If they make me a saint, anyone who comes to me seeking a favor will have to bring me first of all a crate of macaroni. For each crate of macaroni, I'll grant a favor!"[21] Jesting about his own profession, he used to say, "Three things are useless: washing a donkey's head, adding water to the ocean, and preaching to nuns, monks, and priests!"[22]

One day a fashionably dressed lady with a troubled countenance approached him. "Padre, today I turn sixty!" she whined. "Say something nice to me."

With a roguish smile, the padre whispered in her ear, "Death is near!"[23]

Another time Pio received a message from a woman asking his advice as to whether she should undergo shock treatments. "Tell her," he said, "if she isn't a fool already, she surely will become one if she has the shock treatments!"[24]

The august Padre was not averse to playing pranks, either. One day he was hosting some relatives from Pietrelcina. He arranged for them to dine in the guest room of the friary. While the adults were at table, engrossed in their food and conversation, Padre Pio noticed that the six-year-old boy looked bored. Leaving unobserved through the main doorway, he went around to a little service window and, from without, peered through and got the attention of the child. Holding his fingers to his lips as a signal for him to keep quiet, Pio beckoned the boy to climb through the little window. Taking the child into his arms, Pio carried him upstairs to his room, where he gave him two chocolate bars. After a few minutes, he brought the boy back downstairs and slipped him through the window again, instructing him to take his place once more at table. The adults, busy talking and eating, had not noticed his absence.

Padre Pio, still standing at the service window, began to bang on the wall, shouting, "What's the matter, is everybody asleep?" When the diners finally looked up, Pio announced, "I've been standing here for one hour calling you and you haven't heard. Were you all, perchance, in ecstasy?"

"But, Padre Pio, that's just what they say about you!" announced a bewildered guest.

"Then what's the matter? I've been standing here for an hour and you haven't heard," the padre continued with a straight face.

The guests were sure that Padre Pio was joking. "Well, if you don't believe me," said Pio, "ask the boy. Ettoruccio, what did we do?"

"Uncle Pio is a nice man. He took me and carried me to his cell," the boy replied.

The adults all laughed, thinking that the child was just agreeing with anything Padre Pio said — that is, until he produced the chocolates. The family left the friary believing that what Padre Pio had told them was true![25]

Recreation at an end, Padre Pio usually took a short siesta. His practice of sleeping an hour or two, ordered by his physicians in the 1930s, was apparently short-lived. After the Second World War, he occasionally went to bed for a catnap. Usually he went to the veranda to pray the Rosary. This was a very important devotion to him, without which he considered the Christian life incomplete. Whenever he had a spare moment, in the hallway, on the stairs, even going to and from the confessional, he could be seen fingering his beads. In fact, he once told one of his superiors that he said more than thirty Rosaries each day. He called the Rosary his weapon against the devil, and often, in old age, when he could not find his rosary, he would ask one of his brethren, "Where is my weapon?" He insisted that his spiritual children make the Rosary part of their daily devotions.

At some point during the early afternoon, Pio joined the community for the afternoon Office, after which he lingered on his knees in the choir, in deep meditation, sometimes as long as two hours. Padre Agostino spoke of this period as a "true spiritual and physical repose."

By the late 1940s, Padre Agostino, among others, began to feel that Padre Pio had attained "spiritual union," the highest degree of mysticism. During the summer of 1945, Agostino observed that Pio's "interior life is always lifted up in God, whose presence he feels almost with his senses." By the end of that year, Agostino saw fit to observe that Pio's long-standing spiritual trial was becoming less excruciating. A few days before Pio's sixtieth birthday, the professor wrote in his diary about the "life of continual union with the Lord" in which Pio's spirit "is not distracted from the thought of God even when he is speaking to others. Even outwardly, to a perceptive observer, he seems always to be dominated by a never-ending meditation on heavenly things."[26] Agostino felt that this "intimate union with God" had much to do with Pio's immense energy and his need for only minimal sleep and nourishment. "He never seems to grow weary, as if he were made of iron," Padre Agostino commented when Padre Pio was sixty-six years old.

After he finished his meditation, Padre Pio would sometimes work on his correspondence with his secretaries. Forbidden to answer letters himself, he sometimes directed his secretaries how to answer requests. Most of the letters, as we have seen, were simply answered with a form letter promising the padre's prayers.

It may seem that by this point Padre Pio had done a day's work, but we have only come to mid-afternoon. Around this time, Padre Pio would resume hearing confessions. Later, around 4:30, it was time for Vespers and Benediction, during which the Eucharist is held aloft in a monstrance for the faithful to adore. For many years, Padre Pio officiated daily at this rite. The *Schola Cantorum*, accompanied by Mary Pyle on the harmonium, sang fervently, and many worshipers were moved to tears at the sight of Christ's very body, hidden under the species of bread, held in the wounded hands of Padre Pio.

After Benediction, Padre Pio again would go into the garden — for ten or fifteen minutes. Father Joseph Pius recalls his love of "Brother Sun and Sister Moon," the trees, the flowers, the rocks, the wind and, above all, the animals. Like St. Francis, Padre Pio seemed to have an uncanny ability to communicate with them. Father Joseph Pius told me, in 1978, of an incident when the padre was sitting in a grove of pine trees, trying to talk to some of his spiritual sons, only to have almost all conversation drowned out by the chattering of the birds. According to the Brooklyn-born priest, Pio looked up at his feathery "sisters" and bade them, "Be quiet!" "There was silence until he finished his conversation."

At the supper hour, Pio would usually join his brethren for a glass or two of fruit juice and a cookie or cracker.

At sundown the townspeople gathered to await his blessing beneath the window of the choir overlooking the town. This long-standing custom had, as we have seen, attracted sharp criticism from the Holy Office years before. As early as 1919, when he was a little boy, Pio's nephew, Ettore Masone, recalled "extraordinarily large crowds" that would pack the courtyard in front of the friary, crying, "Padre Pio! Padre Pio!" until he appeared at the window. They would stand there, cheering, waving handkerchiefs, blowing kisses, and serenading the padre with hymns while he looked down upon them, smiled, and blessed them. Though that was Padre Pio's last appearance of the day, as far as the public was concerned, his work was by no means over.

The evening was spent in various pursuits. Sometimes it was spent with Sanguinetti, Lupi, Kiswarday, and Sanvico, conferring on the progress of the *Casa*. Occasionally he would deliver a lecture in town to members of the Franciscan Third Order. The Sangiovannese, as we have seen, were so fanatical that he could not so much as begin to think about accepting invitations to speak outside the city limits. At one of these spiritual talks, in a private home, Padre Pio once more exhibited his Franciscan affinity with God's creatures. According to a story told me by Father Joseph Pius Martin, there was a canary chirruping in a cage while Pio was trying to lecture. Pio turned to the bird and said, "Now I have to praise God." To everyone's astonishment, the canary went to the bottom of the cage and remained silent until the lecture was concluded.

During the evenings, Pio would hold spiritual conferences with other priests and counsel them on personal problems. He did not like to hear the confessions of other Capuchins, however. He told them that each of them had his own spiritual director and that he felt that his primary responsibility was to the lay persons who came to seek him. Often in the evenings, Padre Pio would join his secretaries for more work on the correspondence.

Late in the evening, Pio joined the community in Compline, the night Office. After that, the rest of the community retired for the night, but Pio stayed up to study Scripture and pray. Before retiring to his room, however, he always stopped at Padre Agostino's room to talk with his beloved professor. When it was time to go, he would remove his skullcap, join his hands, bow, and ask for Agostino's blessing. After Agostino had blessed him, Pio would kiss his hand, embrace him, and go to his room.

During most of his time at Our Lady of Grace, Padre Pio resided in Room No. 5, an eight-by-ten bedroom and study typical of the friary. The room was not really very austere. It had an excellent view of what must have been a breathtaking expanse of countryside — before it was fouled by electrical wires and the ugly cement apartments that began to spring up like toadstools in later years. In the room was a desk, a nightstand, a washbasin, a chamber pot, and an armchair. On one wall there hung a grisly, bloody crucifix, such as is popular in the south of Italy. On another were pictures of Pio's parents, Mary Pyle, St. Michael, Mary, and the Pope. For years the padre insisted on sleeping on a hard, rough pallet, characteristic of the austerity of the Order when he was younger. When Dr. Sanguinetti came to San Giovanni Rotondo, however, over Pio's protests, he provided the ascetical friar with a comfortable modern bed. The superiors had to order Pio to sleep in it.

Padre Pio sat in his room, reading the Bible (often with tears in his eyes) and praying until 12:45, when it was time for Matins. Then he would thump on his table loud enough to awaken the twenty or so friars in residence, wash, and go to the choir. It was only at 1:30 that he lay down for a maximum of two hours' sleep, his twenty-two-hour day at an end.

Padre Pio was often asked how he managed to do so many things in the course of a day. "You must do three or four things at once!" someone said.

"They say that Napoleon could do four things at once," the padre replied. "I'm not Napoleon, but three I can pull off!"[27]

The Charismatic

Reports of miracles attributed to Padre Pio proliferated after the Second World War. With increasing frequency, Italian newspapers carried headlines such as these: PRODIGIOUS CURE ATTRIBUTED TO PADRE PIO — PARALYTIC WALKS THROUGH INTERCESSION OF PADRE PIO — MIRACULOUS CURE OF A WOMAN SICK WITH CANCER — AFTER SIX YEARS OF TORTURE, LITTLE OLD LADY IS HEALED — CURE OF A NUN AT BOLOGNA AFTER THIRTY YEARS OF SUFFERING.

These stories of healings, bilocations, prophecies, and other supernatural phenomena tended to create the image of Padre Pio as a man who knew everything and could do everything.

This conception of Padre Pio as a "fairy godfather" has troubled many of his well-meaning supporters. William Carrigan, for instance, said emphatically, "In all my experience with Padre Pio, I never, *never* observed anything miraculous." Carrigan, though he has boxes full of testimonies of healings and other miracles, maintained during our 1980 interview that they are useless. He said he would never make them public "because the stories are just too far-out to be true."

Carrigan points out that most of the people who surrounded Padre Pio, with the exception of Dr. Sanguinetti, were not particularly objective. Even Mary Pyle, who loved to relate the amazing occurrences in Padre Pio's ministry, for all her New York background and high-class education, seemed to Carrigan "a little hazy on facts." He is inclined to dismiss many of the incidents she recounted as simply "folklore."

The problem with many of the accounts is the lack of documentation. Since most of those who surrounded Padre Pio never had the slightest doubt that miracles regularly occurred, they seemed to think it unnecessary to go to any pains to provide extensive documentation for them. As a result, many of the accounts that have come down to us lack names, dates, and other specifics.

Yet, not everyone who recorded the remarkable events of Padre Pio's ministry was a superstitious, credulous peasant. Carrigan felt that Padre Agostino tended to be uncritical in accepting miracle stories, yet his diary reveals that he always insisted on adequate documentation when, as guardian of the friary, people came to him claiming to have received supernatural favors.

Perhaps the most reliable source of information concerning these extraordinary occurrences is Father Dominic Meyer. Born Henry Lewis Meyer in Belleville, Illinois, on July 22, 1892, he entered religion at twenty-three as a novice in the Friary of St. Bonaventure in Detroit. He was ordained at thirty in Marathon, Wisconsin, and later earned a doctorate in sacred theology at the Gregorian University at Rome. For many years he was professor of dogmatic theology. Father John Schug, who studied under him, remembers Father Dominic as a very austere-looking man, tall (5'10") and gaunt, with dark, sunken eyes, sunken cheeks, bushy beetle brows, a long, dirty-grey beard, and, rather incongruously, a pot belly.

"A primitivist, completely unconcerned about his physical appearance," is the way Father Schug discribed him. "He was characterized by a complete lack of self-consciousness." A man of few words but of profound thought, Father Meyer was extremely reserved and seldom showed signs of emotion. Meyer became convinced of the factual nature of many of the reported supernatural occurrences in Padre Pio's life. "There's no need for any exaggeration," he remarked of Padre Pio. "The truth is stranger than fiction." Some of the best-documented miracles are those described by Dr. Meyer during his tenure as English secretary to Padre Pio from 1948 to 1961.

This chapter will recount some of the "miracles" from the late 1940s and early 1950s, and then discuss Padre Pio's gifts, or charisms. Most of the miracles from these years are healings.

On June 10, 1945, there came to San Giovanni Rotondo a Signora Massari, a native of San Marco la Catola and a resident of the town of Volturara Appula. For twenty years she had been totally deaf. Padre Agostino noted in his diary that she "asked the grace of the Lord [for a cure] through the intercession of Padre Pio." While attending one of the Masses, she suddenly began to hear the priest chanting. As she left the church, she heard the bell ringing, and then she heard people talking.

Padre Agostino, hearing of her cure, insisted on seeing the lady. Finding that she did, in fact, hear perfectly, he proceeded to interview her traveling companions, who insisted that until that very day she had been stone deaf. Agostino requested extensive medical documentation, but if he ever received it, it is not to be found today. Was it all a hoax? Was the woman's problem hysterical in nature? Was she really healed of a physical condition beyond the competence of any physician to treat? No one can say with absolute certitude.

Again, in November 1947, Padre Agostino noted in his diary that he had received a medical certificate documenting the almost instantaneous cure of a uterine disease, a condition for which surgical intervention would have been necessary. Apparently, the diary entry refers to the cure that took place spontaneously through Padre Pio's prayers. Presumably the medical certificate, stowed away somewhere in the friary archives, tells the name of the patient and the specific medical condition that was relieved.

Better-documented is the cure of Maria Rosa De Angelis in the spring of 1948. A medical certificate signed by Dr. Antonio Buda of Laureano, of the region of Calabria, in the south of Italy, stated that medical examinations on March 25, 1947, revealed that the patient was suffering from "an aneurysm of the ascending aorta." When he examined the woman again on July 24, 1948, he found "a noticeable improvement . . . with a marked reduction of the aneurysmic swelling. The reason for the verified improvement," the physician added, "cannot be attributed to the usual medical treatments."[1]

In early 1949 a woman from Milan named Carla Minola was ill with "acute ascending myelitis," which is an inflammation of the spinal cord, sometimes fatal, so-called because the ensuing paralysis starts with the lower extremities and ascends to the arms and chest and throat. Minola was in "great agony" when suddenly she professed a cure through Padre Pio's prayers. Her doctor, Professor Grossoni, while admitting the "instantaneous cure" and expressing "amazement" to his colleagues, attributed the recovery to "special radiotherapy." Padre Agostino, however, considered the doctor absurdly sceptical and was convinced enough of the miraculous nature of the cure to chronicle it in his diary.

Perhaps the best known of the cures attributed to Padre Pio was the "miracle of Ribera," named for the town near Palermo, Sicily, where a little girl named Gemma DiGiorgio was born in 1939 — apparently with a severe congenital defect.

Signorina DiGiorgio maintains that as a child she was totally blind. She told Father John Schug in an interview in July 1971: "I had no pupils in my eyes. I had no sight at all. When I was three months old, my mother took me to a very famous oculist [Professor Contino] in Palermo. He told her that, without pupils, I would never be able to see."[2]

In the spring of 1946, a nun in Gemma's hometown wrote to Padre Pio about the child. Instead of the usual form letter, she received a note urging that Gemma be brought to Padre Pio in person. At the first opportunity, Gemma's grandmother took the child to San Giovanni Rotondo, where the Padre heard the girl's First Confession, administered her First Communion, and made the Sign of the Cross on her eyes.

As of 1971, it was certain that Signorina DiGiorgio did indeed have normal vision, though her eyes were abnormal-looking. Father John Schug, agreeing that she had no pupils, noted: "She looks like a blind person. Her eyes are sallow and lusterless. But there is no doubt that she can see. I saw her reach for a phone book, check a number, and dial the number without groping. . . . Questioned by a Sicilian Capuchin . . . , she described the progress in construction of a building fifteen yards away and mentioned the colors of the various sections of the building."[3]

Yet there remains a question as to what exactly was (and is) the matter with Gemma's eyes. When he learned of the alleged cure, Padre Agostino spent two full years trying to obtain documentation. Finally, in February 1948, he received an affidavit from Dr. Contino, who had examined Gemma when she was three and who had seen her since her reputed cure. Saying nothing about a lack of pupils, Contino maintained that "she was not born blind, but her ability to see was uncertain."[4] He stated that he examined the child again in December 1947 and found that there was now no question that the child could see, for she could count his fingers at a distance of about sixteen feet. Dr. Sanguinetti, who was trained in ophthalmology, studied Dr. Contino's affidavit and told Agostino that he did not think the cure exceeded natural powers. Father Joseph Pius, who wrote to me in August of 1979, offered this opinion: "Gemma has pupils. As a matter of fact, the entire eye is one very large pupil."

The facts that can be definitely established are these: (1) Gemma DiGiorgio was born with a severe congenital defect of the eyes; (2) before the prayers of Padre Pio were enlisted, her vision was either quite defective or altogether non-existent; (3) thereafter, although the physical defect remained unchanged, Gemma was able to see normally.

As usual, Padre Pio was reluctant to speak about the cure. When a great furor developed over it, he coldly asked a man who was going into raptures about "the miracle of the blind girl," "Did you witness it?" The man was speechless. "I said, 'Did you witness it?' " When the man still could not find his tongue, Padre Pio repeated his question for a third time. The man went away without uttering another word.

Father Dominic described the case of Lucia Bellodi, which involved not only a physical cure but a bilocation as well. It took place June 12, 1952, on the feast of Corpus Christi. In addition to Father Dominic's account, we have a deposition from Bellodi herself, written on June 4, 1955.

Bellodi was twenty-one. Since she was fourteen, she had been suffering from a severe case of diabetes insipidus, which resulted from an attack of encephalitis. Not to be confused with diabetes mellitus, or sugar diabetes, this is a chronic metabolic disorder frequently associated with damage to the pituitary gland and characterized by a failure of the body to maintain its water content through the limiting of the formation of urine. Those afflicted with diabetes insipidus excrete enormous quantities of urine — often nearly ten gallons a day. To compensate for the loss of fluid, they are constrained to drink a similar quantity of liquids.

Donna Lucia, a farm girl from near Modena, had been totally incapacitated ever since the disease manifested itself. "The doctors who treated me during this period made use of every modern treatment," she wrote, "but I grew worse rather than better. My disease . . . was resistant to every therapy." She was first treated at a hospital in Mirandola, than at a sanatorium at Gaiata, then at a hospital at Sondrio, and then at one in Modena. Finally, at twenty, she was declared incurable and placed in a nursing home.

Her condition was indeed deplorable. She was drinking up to twelve gallons of water a day. When she went to sleep, nurses had to insert in her mouth a rubber hose attached to a jar holding six gallons of water, since she had to drink even while she slept. It she did not, she would hemorrhage from her mouth and her tongue would swell to the point that she could not close her mouth. Inasmuch as she was constantly urinating, her bed linen had to be changed several times a day. Almost every two weeks she underwent epileptoid crises accompanied by high fevers, violent headaches, delirium, and loss of consciousness.

As the nursing home was run by the Church, Lucia heard the nuns talking about Padre Pio and gradually developed a great devotion to him: "I often prayed to him but never asked the grace of a cure. Rather I asked him to give me resignation to my affliction or else free me through death."

On the feast of Corpus Christi in 1952, Bellodi had one of her crises. That morning, during a period of consciousness, she expressed a desire to go to Mass. After making her confession, she collapsed and had to be put to bed. She remained semiconscious until two in the afternoon, drinking more than ever. "Around 2 P.M.," she writes, "at the very height of the crisis, when the staff . . . believed that I was about to die, since I was all cold, I fell asleep. Yet, before I did, I smelled all around me a fragrant perfume of violets and inquired as to its source. I had slept about half an hour when the nurse and the nun who was assisting me shook me awake. They wanted me wide awake so that I would not have a hemorrhage."

They noted that she had not been drinking water, and they were concerned because her teeth were clenched so tightly that they were unable to insert the tube.

Just before she woke, Lucia heard these words, spoken by an invisible presence: "Get up, Lucia, because you are cured. This evening or tomorrow, come here to see me at San Giovanni Rotondo." At this point, Lucia says: "I awoke and sat up in bed, declaring that I was cured and wanted to get up. They thought at first that I was raving, but when I told them what I heard, they told me that I should go into the chapel to thank the Lord."

She climbed the stairs "with a firm and sprightly step." "I felt wonderful," she declared, ". . . as if I hadn't suffered at all for seven years."

The doctors examined her immediately and at once declared that hers was a case of "divine intervention." They did not release her to go to San Giovanni that evening or the next morning as she had been bidden in her dream. It was July 12 before she was permitted to go to Padre Pio. When she did, he greeted her warmly, told her that he had been waiting for her and that he had recognized her before the Lord.

Father Dominic, who met Lucia Bellodi, was himself of the opinion that she had been miraculously cured. Bellodi, pronounced completely healthy by her doctors, returned home to a strenuous life as a farm laborer. In 1961, at the age of thirty, she married. Several years later, she disproved her doctors' predictions that her long sickness had rendered her incapable of becoming a mother. [5]

Father Dominic Meyer is the source of the account of another remarkable providence that occurred the same summer. According to Dr. Meyer, Maria Palma Carboni, a native of the town of Confiento, was a servant in the home of a wealthy Tuscan family. In April 1952 she was seized with what was first taken to be "a nervous crisis." Taken to a local hospital, she grew worse. Doctors were baffled by her condition. Some diagnosed "mental hysteria," others a lesion of the brain.

Shortly after she was returned to her family home on a nearby farm, relatives became convinced that she was possessed by demons. "Her condition," Dr. Meyer wrote, "was such as to terrify everyone, not only by its violence, but by its strangeness. During the day she was normal. But as soon as night came, she became violent, beat herself, and began 'to speak with the devil.' she knew beforehand just how long the conversation would last, and she told the bystanders it would last 35 or 47 minutes, etc."

Carboni claimed that she could see the devil. Others in the room felt a sinister presence. Windows rattled, and there was a loud rapping on the door. People came from all around to see Maria Carboni shrieking, gibbering, and writhing in unspeakable agony.

The local priest, one Don Deglesposito, was at first sceptical and thought that Carboni was suffering from mental illness. As the days went by, he was forced to change his mind. "For three nights," he wrote to Fr. Meyer, "the girl had such severe attacks that four persons could hardly keep her in bed. Her eyes were closed. She screamed that the devil wanted to enter by the window. At the same time (there were ten people in the room), we heard the windows rattle, doors slam, and felt the small house tremble."

He went on to describe how the unfortunate woman "recited poems she never heard before, from classical authors." Deglesposito sprinkled the sick woman and the room with holy water, but all to no avail. Deglesposito then decided to take Maria to San Giovanni Rotondo. He hired a taxi and set out with the sick woman, another priest, and two of her relatives. En route they had "dozens of accidents," including two collisions with a truck. On the way Maria had not less than thirty-three violent attacks.

On June 20, 1952, Carboni, Deglesposito, and company finally arrived at San

Giovanni. Carboni was placed on a bench in the church and lay there, seemingly unconscious, until Padre Pio approached her and blessed her. "Poor little thing!" he said. "Who knows what she has suffered! Let's hope that she will get better." Then he left.

From that moment, Maria Palma Carboni was perfectly normal. She returned home, and the friars at San Giovanni kept in touch with her for some time. One of Carboni's relatives, an inveterate Communist, was so impressed by her cure that he became a Christian.[6]

Perhaps the best-documented cure associated with Padre Pio — the one that can be classed most unambiguously as a miracle — took place in February 1949. A learned physician with whom I discussed many of Padre Pio's alleged healings told me that if the facts have been correctly reported, there is no question about the cure of Giovanni Savino being contrary to every known law of nature. Every disease — cancer, diabetes, or any other — he explained, is subject, even though very rarely, to spontaneous remission. There have been cases in which diseases considered terminal and incurable by every physician in attendance have suddenly and inexplicably disappeared. For a missing part of the body to be restored, however, is quite another matter. There is no way that such a thing can occur by natural means. Yet this is precisely what seems to have happened to a laborer named Giovanni Savino. There is excellent documenation for the occurrence.

Savino was still alive on July 17, 1971, when Father John Schug interviewed him. For days Father Schug had tried to arrange a meeting, but until that time Savino, a modest, retiring man, had been unwilling. When he finally agreed to tell his story, he did so reluctantly.

Savino, a construction worker, was a Franciscan tertiary and a fervent spiritual son of Padre Pio. Every morning, before going to work, he would go to the Padre's Mass and afterward solicit his blessing. On the morning of February 12, 1949, Padre Pio did an unusual thing. Placing his hands on Savino's head in blessing, he embraced him and said, "Courage! I'll pray to the Lord that it may not cause your death." This alarmed Savino, who could not pry out of Padre Pio what it was that was endangering his life. Padre Pio did the same thing on the next three mornings. On that third morning, February 15, Savino confided nervously to Padre Raffaele, "Something is going to go wrong today." Nevertheless, resigning himself to whatever had to be, he went to work on an addition to the friary.

Around 2 P.M., Savino and another worker placed a charge of dynamite under a huge boulder. Savino set the charge and lit the fuse. It did not go off. After a few minutes, he decided to have a look. As he approached, the charge detonated, blowing the boulder to bits and hurling rock fragments against Savino's face. The laborer was blown off his feet, his face burned and torn by the blast.

Padre Raffaele and Dr. Sanguinetti were at Savino's side within moments, and Father Dominic Meyer also came to see if he could help before the injured man was taken to a hospital in Foggia. All three men noted that among Savino's numerous other injuries, his right eye was gone entirely. They agreed that "the socket was empty." Doctors in Foggia confirmed the fact that the right eye had been completely annihilated and the left one so badly damaged that there was little likelihood of his ever seeing out of it again.

"For three days I was in shock," Savino recalled. "My whole head and face were bandaged. . . . They thought they could save [the left eye] by an operation. They said that there was nothing they could do for my right eye. It was completely gone."

On February 18, Savino heard the surgeon enter the room. He told him that Padre Pio had just wordlessly paid him a visit. He was certain of this because as he was speaking to Pio in his mind, he became aware of his characteristic aroma.

On the morning of February 25, Savino woke at 12:30 or 1:00. "I could hear the breathing of the two or three men sleeping next to me," he said. "I felt someone give me a light slap on the right side of my face, the right side where the eye was completely gone. I asked, 'Who touched me?' There was nobody. Again I smelled the aroma of Padre Pio. It was beautiful."

Later that morning an ophthalmologist came to examine Savino's left eye. For the first time since the accident, his face was unbandaged. To their amazement, the doctors found that his shattered face was fully healed and covered with new skin. Savino, however, was most delighted at the fact that he could see. "I can see you!" he said excitedly to the eye specialist.

"Turn . . . so that you can see me with your left eye," said the ophthalmologist, preparing a chart.

"No, I see you with my right eye. I don't see anything out of my left eye."

"Are you crazy?" demanded the doctor. "I am telling you that your right eye isn't there anymore. I'm treating only your left eye."

When Savino insisted, the doctor, who had been paying attention only to the left eye, saw to his utter astonishment that Savino had a right as well as a left eye. The specialist, till then an atheist, was converted on the spot. "Now I believe too," he exclaimed, "because of what my own hands have touched!"[7]

For the rest of his life, Savino was blind in his left eye, the one that had been damaged but not lost in the explosion. He maintained good vision, however, in the right eye, which had apparently materialized after its predecessor had been emulsified!

Father Dominic Meyer asked Savino, shortly after his recovery, how he knew that it was Padre Pio who had slapped him. Savino replied, "I know his touch." Father Dominic wrote: "This explanation was too simple for a hardened sinner like me. . . . This would have been a case of bilocation . . . because Padre Pio had never left San Giovanni Rotondo, and a miracle."[8]

The question is sometimes raised as to whether Savino's eye was completely blown from his head. Father Joseph Pius Martin, who had been asked which miracle attributed to Padre Pio was the most striking, researched that question extensively in 1981. "It had to be that pertaining to John Savino," he says. Although Savino has been dead since 1974, his widow, various members of his family, and a number of people who had examined Savino after his accident are still alive. After conducting numerous interviews, Father Joseph Pius is satisfied that Savino's right eye had been totally macerated. "When he arrived at the hospital at Foggia," Martin says, "doctors found in the socket a small amount of bloody flesh. The eye had been shattered into a bloody jelly." He was also able to affirm that every doctor connected with the case was positive that there was no way, according to even the most liberal interpretation of the laws of nature, that an eye so completely destroyed could regenerate itself.

How is one to interpret the various supernatural occurrences with which Padre Pio's ministry abounded? It is well to discuss in detail some of the most important supernatural or supersensible aspects of the padre's ministry: his perfume, his healings, his gifts of knowledge and bilocation.

These things all fall into the category of charisms. Such supernatural gifts were clearly attributed in the Bible to several individuals, most notably, apart from Christ, to Moses, Elijah, and Elisha, in the Old Testament; and to the Apostles Peter, John, and Paul, in the New. While nowhere is it stated that such charisms are to be considered normative for the faithful, it is clearly affirmed in the Gospel according to St. Mark, chapter 16, that these signs will accompany those who believe. Jesus said that his followers will have the ability to cast out demons in his name, speak in new tongues, handle serpents, drink deadly poison without harm, and heal the sick.

St. Paul (in 1 Corinthians, chapter 11) describes these specific spiritual gifts: the utterance of wisdom, the utterance of knowledge, faith, healing, miraculous powers, prophecy, the ability to distinguish between spirits, various kinds of tongues and their interpretation. He makes it clear that there are varieties of gifts and that the Spirit distributes them as he wills.

St. James (chapter 5), speaking specifically about spiritual healing, advises the elders of a given congregation to pray over the sick and anoint them with oil in the name of the Lord. Although this is set forth as a ministry accessible to all Christians, he adds that the prayer of a person who is holy has great power.

Thus, it appears from Scripture that the Apostles worked many miracles and were endowed with various charisms and that these phenomena would be found within the Church at large. The closer a person is to God, however, the greater power he could expect to have.

Padre Pio was a charismatic in the New Testament sense, namely, in that he was the recipient of a number of supernatural gifts similar to those described in the Bible. Those close to him were convinced that his prayers were especially potent because of his intimacy with God.

Padre Pio was genuinely concerned, however, that because of his gifts, people would tend to treat him as if he were a kind of witch doctor who could manipulate the will of God. Reacting with alarm to the throngs who all but mobbed him, Pio often denounced their devotion to him as paganism and fanaticism. Time and time again when people came to ask him for graces, Pio reminded them that, though he could and would pray for them, "The grace is the Lord's to give."

He knew well that being a charismatic is no guarantee of being a saint. Pharaoh's magicians were able to imitate many of the miracles that God worked through Moses and Aaron. Many mystical phenomena have, with fairly good foundation, been attributed to Buddhist, Hindu, and Moslem holy men, and even to animist witch doctors. It has always been understood that witches and warlocks, in league with the devil, can produce many "signs and wonders." The Holy Office was worried that Padre Pio might be a man with great supernatural gifts who would lead men away from traditional Christian teachings. Certainly there were contemporary examples of this type of individual in Rasputin in Russia and Edgar Cayce in America. Anyone who entertained such a worry, however, had only to spend a short time with Padre Pio to be aware that his teachings were strictly in harmony with the Bible as well as the Roman Catholic Church.

One sign of Padre Pio's genuine Christian holiness was his modesty. He did not like to be praised for his goodness. "You are all so mistaken," he would say. "It is you who are good, not I. . . . God made all things. His creation includes the stars and the humblest domestic utensils. I belong to the second category." Speaking of his charisms, he said: "I realize to the full the greatness of the gifts that God has bestowed upon me. But that terrifies me because I know only too well what miserable use I have made of them. If He had given them to the lowest scoundrel in the world, he would have employed them better. I dread the thought of death and having to answer for it."[9] Again, to his nephew Ettore Masone, Pio said: "I am fearful because of all the Lord has given me, since the more we are given, the more we are responsible before Him. I am fearful because of all the goodness and mercy that He has shown me."[10]

There is good evidence that Padre Pio had most of the gifts of the Spirit described by St. Paul in 1 Corinthians. In addition, he displayed a gift not mentioned by St. Paul but described elsewhere in Scripture, notably in Acts 8:26-40, in the account of St. Philip and the Ethiopian eunuch — the gift of bilocation. Another gift universally ascribed to Padre Pio, which is nowhere mentioned in Scripture, was the mysterious fragrance or perfume that seemed to emanate from his person.

The "odor of sanctity" is not unique to Padre Pio. It has been associated with several other mystics, notably St. Teresa of Avila. A similar aroma has been ascribed to a stigmatic named Brother Gino Burresi, who lives today near Rome.

There can be no question that a strange and delightful fragrance was often perceived in association with Padre Pio. Without exception, those I interviewed who spent any time at all with Padre Pio experienced the aroma at some time or other. Padre Alberto D'Apolito, one of Padre Pio's colleagues for many years, wrote in 1978: "The reality is that hundreds of thousands of individuals, even unbelievers, have testified and continue to testify that they have suddenly and inexplicably perceived the perfume of Padre Pio at San Giovanni — in the church, in the corridor, in the courtyard, in the inns — as well as hundreds of miles away, especially in moments of danger."[11]

We have seen how medical men, such as Festa and Romanelli, were aware of the aroma and tried in vain to find a scientific explanation. A certain Dr. Amanzio Duodo of Veglio Mosso Picco testified that on February 15, 1950, he was talking with friends, one of whom was describing a visit to San Giovanni, when "suddenly and unexpectedly an intense perfume of violets enveloped us all. It lasted about a half hour, although the doors and windows were open. Later on, a pungent and strong odor of perfume assailed us." Dr. Eduardo Bianco, who was present that evening, wrote that he too smelled the odor of violets. "On various other occasions," he added, "I have repeatedly perceived odors of roses, violets, and carnations, whose source was positively not artificial. I wish also to declare that these observations of mine elude all scientific explanation, although I have done my best to rationalize them."[12]

Frequently, this fragrance was perceived when Padre Pio was not present physically. William Carrigan, normally quite sceptical of miracle stories, perceived the aroma while writing at his desk at Foggia. "I had no trouble in identifying the aroma as that of Padre Pio," he told me. "It wasn't something you could confuse with any other odor."

Even after Padre Pio's death, the aroma has continued to manifest itself. Robert H. Hopcke of North Plainfield, New Jersey, is a Lutheran seminarian who has never met Padre Pio. Hopcke was in Philadelphia in mid-September 1978, visiting his friend Vincent Mandato prior to leaving for a year's study in Florence. Mandato was devoted to Padre Pio. On Sunday morning, the two young men went to Mass at a Catholic church near the University of Pennsylvania campus. In a letter to me dated June 30, 1980, Hopcke recounts:

> At Mass, just before the homily, I remember smelling very distinctly the odor of roses. . . . I didn't think much of it, and it seemed to go away only to come back again, just as sweet and just as strong, during the Creed. At that time, I recall looking around to see who the woman was nearby who had doused herself with so much scent, but there was no woman near us. I tried to locate a flower arrangement in the church that could be giving off such a perfume, but again, there was no arrangement nearby, and no roses in the church at all. I thought perhaps it could be the scented candles, but the strength of odor was such that the faraway candles would have had to fill the

church with their scent, and surely I would have smelled such a powerful fragrance immediately upon entering the church and not halfway through the Mass. The odor seemed to fade again, and came back for the third and final time during the consecration of the Host. It faded again. I thought the experience a little odd but promptly put it out of my mind.

That is, until my friend Vince asked me after Mass . . . , "Did you smell something strange in church today?"

I said that I had and he told me . . . to ask his father when I returned home to North Plainfield what the fragrance could have been. We spent the rest of the day together and that night, at the train station, said goodbye to one another for an entire year. . . . Intrigued by the whole affair, I hurried over to the Mandato's house as soon as I arrived home.

The senior Mandato had been very close to Padre Pio in his native Italy when he was young. Hopcke said nothing more to him than, "You know, today, while Vince and I were in church this morning, we both smelled something very strange in the air."

He finished the description for me. "It was very sweet and very strong, like the scent of roses, a garden of roses in decline, and it came and went a number of times, three or four times. . . ."

"Why, yes!" I answered, surprised at the accuracy. "And it came right before the homily, during the Creed, and during the consecration of the Host."

Mrs. Mandato jumped off her chair and kissed me. "*Hai ricevuto una grazia* — you have received a grace. The spirit of Padre Pio was with you and Vincent today in church. His spirit is often accompanied by just that scent of roses. Surely Vincent was invoking his protection for you for the coming year in Italy and the scent of roses was his assurance that he will be with you."

Hopcke concludes:

Not having known Padre Pio personally, as have the Mandatos, and having, I like to think, a very rational, logical mind, I neither totally believe nor disbelieve the stories of Padre Pio. The sheer volume of them tends to make me believe that something indeed miraculous took place in the presence of this obviously holy, devout Capuchin. However, the farfetched character of many of these tales reactivates the sceptic within me. Nevertheless, I cannot deny what I smelled that day in church. . . . And I cannot deny that before I even spoke of what I had smelled, Mr. Mandato had described it perfectly. . . .

According to most people who perceived the scent, it was manifested to convey a message from Padre Pio. Padre Alberto said that the waves of perfume were a sign of Pio's spiritual presence. There is little on record to indicate what Padre Pio thought about the fragrance. McCaffery wrote that the Padre commented about it just once to him, remarking merely that the aroma was "just sweets for the children."[13] Incredibly, no one else seems to have thought to ask him, point-blank, about the phenomenon!

Of more obvious benefit to others was Padre Pio's gift of healing. One friar who worked closely with Padre Pio estimated that approximately one thousand healings of major illnesses or injuries have been associated with his fifty-year ministry.

In his approach to disease, however, Padre Pio differed somewhat from many of his contemporaries who had "healing ministries." Unlike many of those of the Pentecostal persuasion, Padre Pio never taught that one had a right to claim a healing. Very seldom did he even lay hands on the sick, much less say, "Be healed!" Most of the healings took place apart from the padre's physical presence.

In his approach to those who besought from him a grace for healing, Padre Pio was undramatic, making every effort to draw attention away from himself. If approached in person, Padre Pio, if he made any response at all, usually said simply, "I will bless you," and very quickly and perfunctorily made the Sign of the Cross over the person's head. Often he would say, "Let's pray to God."

"I knew from experience," Padre Alessio told me in September 1978, "that when Padre Pio said to the sick person, 'I'll pray for you,' or 'Let's pray to God,' they seemed always to be healed. On the other hand, if he said, 'Let's resign ourselves to the will of God,' or said nothing at all, the grace of healing was not to be."

People unable to approach the padre in person were often granted a cure by contact with some object that had been touched by him. When Mother Teresa Salvadores was ill in 1921, for instance, friends applied one of Padre Pio's gloves to her body. This is not a superstitious or blasphemous practice. In the Bible it is written, "And God did extraordinary miracles through the hands of Paul, so that handkerchiefs or aprons were carried from his body to the sick, and diseases left them and evil spirits came out of them" (Acts 19:11-12). Most often, however, cures took place after Padre Pio simply exhorted the pilgrim or correspondent to pray to God. The healings were sometimes instantaneous, sometimes rapid, sometimes gradual. When anyone came to thank him for a miraculous cure, the padre vehemently refused any credit. "Don't thank me, thank God," he would say.

As is evident by his involvement in a hospital project, Padre Pio was not at all averse to the ministrations of medical doctors. Throughout his long life, he submitted to them, undergoing surgery at least three times. "It's our duty to do all we can to be healed," he told his nephew Ettore Masone. "God wants us to help ourselves in seeking healing, and we have the duty to submit . . . to medicines and other treatment."[14] That is, even though it may be God's will, one is to seek relief from the illness or infirmity first by the usual means.

Father Joseph Pius once had a boil "in a very upsetting location." He went to Padre Pio, begging him, "Make it go away!" The padre said nothing, and the hapless friar ended up having to submit to a most painful surgical operation. After Joseph Pius was discharged, Padre Pio, without making any specific reference to him, said in his presence to a group of friends and colleagues when the subject turned to divine healing: "Now, for instance, if you have a boil, you've got to follow the doctor's advice and medicate and clean it, and perhaps even submit to surgery. Miracles occur only when human intervention cannot achieve the purpose."

At times, however, he seemed to know when medical treatment would be useless or counterproductive, and he was known to advise against operations that doctors had recommended. The friars often referred to him as "the doctor," and many of his circle would not undergo any serious medical treatment without first consulting him. During the early 1950s, when Padre Costantino Capobianco had a sinus problem, he had x-rays taken, and three doctors separately recommended surgery. Before submitting to the knife, Padre Costantino consulted Padre Pio.

"What are these things?" asked Pio when he saw the x-rays. When Costantino told him what they were, Pio said authoritatively, "And they're all wrong."

Padre Costantino subsequently consulted a fourth specialist, who determined that the x-rays had been misinterpreted and that there was no need for an operation. Costantino's affliction abated without surgical intervention.[15]

Some years later, the same Padre Costantino was advised to undergo surgery for an intestinal problem. "I understand well," he told his doctors, "but first I want to hear what Padre Pio has to say. It isn't a question of the worth of your hand. . . . I wish to consult Padre Pio because he has another telephone and another radar."

The surgeon, in front of his colleagues and assistants, replied, "Go, Padre. Go to Padre Pio because when I am faced with a difficult case, I go to him too!"

Padre Pio recommended the operation, Padre Costantino underwent it, and it was successful.[16]

Father Joseph Pius tells the story of an eminent plastic surgeon by the name of Piero Mellilo, who suffered a cerebral hemorrhage. Doctors found that the cause of the problem was a severe aneurysm of one of the blood vessels in his brain and advised a very delicate and dangerous operation. They warned him that without the surgery, death was certain. Further, his condition was so precarious that the slightest physical movement was liable to precipitate a second and fatal stroke.

Uncertain as to whether to go through with the brain surgery, Mellilo made a phone call to the Friary of Our Lady of Grace, hoping to speak with Padre Pio. Normally Padre Pio would not be called to the phone, but since it rang just as he was walking past, Pio answered it. When Mellilo told him about the situation, Padre Pio snapped: "No, don't have the operation! Tell those confounded doctors to go operate on themselves! You get out of there!"

When Mellilo's doctors learned that he had decided to forego the surgery, they warned him that if he left the hospital, he would surely have a massive hemorrhage and drop dead on the floor before he ever reached the street. As the plastic surgeon dressed and headed toward the exit, doctors and nurses followed, expecting him to collapse any moment. He reached home feeling fine and more than two decades later was still practicing.

Conversely, Padre Pio seemed to know when collapse or death was near, even for an apparently healthy person. For instance, in May 1962, Padre Teofilo of Pozzo della Chiana, the former minister provincial, visited San Giovanni Rotondo in the midst of a grueling preaching tour. Padre Pio warned him against taxing his strength. Padre Teofilo, a dynamic man, assured Pio that he was in excellent health and had no problem in keeping such a schedule.

"Oh, what are you doing!" exclaimed Padre Pio. "Don't you know that your life is hanging by a thread of parsley?"

Padre Teofilo laughed it off. Four months later he was dead of stomach cancer.[17]

Around the same time another priest, Padre Dionisio, spoke of his plans to go to Venice for further studies. "Studies! Studies!" said Padre Pio. "Think of death!" Bewildered and offended, Padre Dionisio went away, while Padre Pio shrugged his shoulders and remarked to a colleague, "There's nothing I can do." Twenty days later, Padre Dionisio dropped dead.[18]

Very often, when Padre Pio could not obtain the grace of a physical healing, he was granted permission by God to take upon himself the patient's physical sufferings. Padre Alessio remembers several instances in which people, in the last stages of cancer, asked Padre Pio to pray for their healing. Pio told them or sent word that it was not God's will that they be delivered from their sickness but that he would take their sufferings upon himself. In almost all of these circumstances, Padre Alessio recalled during our interview in 1978, the sick person never suffered any more pain, even though the illness persisted and ultimately proved fatal.

Perhaps Padre Pio differed the most from those of Pentecostal bent in that he did not believe that relief of suffering was always God's will. Francis MacNutt, a Roman Catholic prominent in the popular charismatic movement, has written, in *Healing* (Notre Dame, 1974), that "the ordinary will of God is that man should be whole" (p. 102). Although he certainly emphasized the love and compassion of God, Padre Pio would probably never have made such a statement.

He certainly would not have agreed with the contention of his American Methodist contemporary Oral Roberts, who says that God desires that all Christians have health, material prosperity, and spiritual consolations *at all times*.[19] Surely he would reject Roberts's contention that good works necessarily result in physical and material blessings.[20]

Padre Pio, of course, founded a hospital "for the relief of suffering" and often prayed for and obtained material — even financial — blessings. Unlike many Pentecostal and neo-Pentecostal "charismatics," he did not feel that physical health and prosperity were necessarily normative, much less that their absence signified a deficiency in one's commitment to God. Stressing the value of redemptive suffering, Pio often told those whose prayers he knew could never be granted, "Let's resign ourselves to the will of God." He urged the sufferer to offer his pain and anguish to God to be joined to that of Jesus for the redemption of souls. Accordingly, he sometimes looked with favor when certain people declined a gift of healing that was available so that they might offer their suffering as a sacrifice to God. This is well illustrated in the case of two blind men.

One of these was Pietro Cugino, known about San Giovanni as "Blind Pete." Cugino, who was born about 1913, lost his eyesight when he was a child. One day he called on Padre Pio. The padre greeted him with these words: "You're lucky, Pietruccio [Pete], that you don't see the filth and the slime of this world! You have less occasion to offend the Lord." To this statement, which many would find harsh and unfeeling, he added, "Tell me the truth. Have you ever desired to get back your sight?"

Pietruccio responded that he had never thought about it before. Pio persisted: "Would you like to have your eyesight restored? Again Pietruccio answered in a noncommittal way.

"What do you mean, you don't know?" Pio demanded. "Do you or don't you want your sight?"

"Padre, I have to think about it."

"If you desire," said Pio, "we will pray to the Madonna, who is so good . . ."

"Padre," Pietruccio said, "I was born with sight. At age twelve, the Lord took it away. If the Lord took my sight, He had His reasons. Now, why should I pray against the will of God? Why should I ask again for what He first gave me and then took away?"

"Do you or don't you want your sight?" asked Padre Pio.

"Padre," Pietruccio at last responded, "the Lord knows what He is doing. I always want to do the will of God. If the Lord should restore my sight and this should be the occasion of sin, I renounce it." When Padre Pio heard this, he embraced Blind Pete and blessed him.[21]

Another instance concerned a man from northern Italy, Salvatore Sciogliuzzi, who in middle age, probably in the late 1940s, lost his sight. He had been a government employee but could no longer work after becoming blind. With several children and a wife to support, he was in dire financial circumstances. The disability pension he had applied for had not yet been approved. Depressed not only about his disability but about his finances too, he went to Padre Pio. "Trust in God," Pio told him, "and in a little while everything will work out."

Sciogliuzzi left San Giovanni — still blind but in good spirits. Soon he obtained his pension and was situated more comfortably. Each year he would go back to San Giovanni Rotondo to visit Padre Pio, and he never embarked on any major undertaking without asking his counsel.

One day, however, Sciogliuzzi's youngest son asked him, "Why don't you ask Padre Pio to give your sight back?"

"Why don't *you* ask him?" replied the father.

And so the son went to talk to Padre Pio. "May I ask you for something?" said the boy.

"What do you want, Son?" asked the priest.

"The grace for my father's sight."

"Why do you ask me?" answered Pio. "Ask your father."

The boy returned in confusion to his father, who inquired, "Did you ask Padre Pio?"

"Yes," said the boy, "but I don't understand. He said to ask you."

The father kissed the boy and told him: "Padre Pio told me when I first came to him that any time I want to ask for the grace, the grace is there. But, when I thought of how much Jesus suffered for us, I said to Jesus, 'I give up my sight for Thy glory!' "

Sciogliuzzi was a good friend of Andre Mandato. One day both of them were at San Giovanni Rotondo when Sciogliuzzi made his way into Mandato's hotel room, quite agitated and confused. When his friend asked him the reason, Sciogliuzzi asked him what Padre Pio looked like. "Is he a . . . heavy man with a grey beard?" Told that he was, he became even more agitated.

That day Sciogliuzzi and a number of others had been waiting at the foot of the stairs that led from the friars' living quarters to the hallway. He heard slow, heavy steps. Lifting his head, he *saw clearly* "this monk with a grey beard. A stout, heavy man. He smiled at me," Sciogliuzzi said, "and then I became blind again."[22]

One wonders whether either Cugino or Sciogliuzzi really could have obtained the grace of sight had they requested it outright. Perhaps Padre Pio was able to interpret God's purpose in their affliction so effectively that each willingly embraced his handicap when he became convinced that it was necessary in God's plan of redemption.

There are some who believe that, through rare occult powers, Padre Pio had knowledge of what is known as the akashic chronicle. According to some teachers of occult science, every thought and action that takes place in the physical world is recorded in the *akasha*, or "astral light," which fills all space. They also believe that certain people with extrasensory powers can read the record of the past through or in this celestial medium.

It cannot be denied that Padre Pio often knew many things that he could not possibly have learned through normal means. Most remarkable was the knowledge he sometimes manifested in the confessional. Without ever having met the penitent, he at times would astound the person by giving the date of his or her last confession and detailing specific acts that could have been known only to the person kneeling before him. During both world wars, many women came to him to inquire whether their husbands or sons missing in action were alive or dead. Whenever Pio answered them definitively, the man in question would invariably turn up alive if Pio said he would.

The normally skeptical Carrigan has said that the closest thing to a supernatural manifestation he ever observed in Padre Pio occurred when the Red Cross official was informed that he was going to be transferred to Leghorn. He had been told that an official newly arrived from the States was to replace him. Shortly thereafter, Carrigan, with Padre Pio in the friary garden, told his priest-friend that he expected to be transferred soon to Leghorn.

"Why?"

Carrigan told him that he honestly did not know. Padre Pio then fell silent. He gazed across the valley illuminated by the setting sun. Then he made a cryptic statement: "He will go, and you will stay."

Although Carrigan has been deeply hesitant to attribute this statement to supernatural wisdom, it happened as Padre Pio said.

Carrigan recalled another incident. There was a lady whose son had been serving in the Italian Army. The war was over, and the boy had neither come home nor been heard from. She expressed her concern to Padre Pio, who promised, "I will pray." One day, some time later, he told her: "I can't find him on the other side. He must be alive."

Later the lady got a letter from her son. He was confined in the prisoner-of-war camp in North Africa and eventually returned home.

Many, if not most, of the letters that reached the friary asked questions that required supernatural knowledge. Dutifully, Pio's secretaries read many of these letters to him. Father Meyer wrote: "Often when I lay questions before him from letters which I must answer, he says, 'Tell them to be resigned and to trust to the mercy of God,' or, 'There is no answer to that question.' Many continue to ask whether or not their boy or husband, missing in action, is still alive. . . . Sometimes he answers definitely, 'He is dead.' But more often he merely gives an evasive answer to show that God did not reveal this to him."[23]

Padre Costantino recalls a certain professor Filippo de Capua, whose wife was expecting their first child. Specialists both in Foggia and Naples told him that either the mother or the child was liable to be lost at the time of delivery. The horrified husband went to Padre Pio, who assured him, "Neither the mother nor the child will die." Understandably, de Capua was still very much troubled. Padre Pio then remarked sternly, "It is not yet written in the decrees of God, but if anything happens, it will be because of your lack of faith!"[24]

Sometimes Padre Pio answered people's questions before they asked them. Father Dominic wrote in July 1949: "During the war a man came here to go to confession to Padre Pio. Some persons, very dear to him, had been killed in a bombardment, and he didn't know whether they were prepared to meet a sudden death. He hesitated to ask Padre Pio for a direct revelation. But Padre Pio, reading his heart, said to him, 'They are all saved!' "[25]

Father Joseph Pius was present when a woman inquired about the soul of her husband, who had taken his life. Joseph Pius, who was then studying for the priesthood, recalls that Padre Pio appeared to be gazing into the other world, somehow focusing on it. "There's very little hope," he said at first. Then his face darkened further and he turned to her and announced. "There's no hope."

There were definitely many times when Padre Pio was not supernaturally enlightened. For instance, his nephew Ettore Masone was put out of college because he had epilepsy and the administration did not want to take responsibility for him. When Padre Pio heard that the boy was no longer in school, he assumed — incorrectly — that he was a dropout.

"Get away from me, you bum!" he shouted at the astounded boy. "You have a lot of gall just to come into my presence!"

"Why are you talking to me this way, Uncle?"

"Because you dropped out of college! Go away!"

"Uncle, read this letter."

Pio took the letter, read the true reason for Ettore's dismissal, laid his head on his desk, and began to sob.[26]

From Pio's letters to Agostino and Benedetto between 1910 and 1922, it is clear that the source of his supersensible wisdom in those years was not some psychic power. When he was asked a question the answer to which was beyond his normal physical and mental powers to give, he did not consult some astral record; he asked Jesus. Sometimes Jesus gave him the answer; sometimes he did not. For example, after the death of a close friend, Pio prayed aloud: "Jesus, You know how much I love You. Do not be offended if I say that this time You were cruel to me. You took my friend . . . without first telling me, just as You have done so many times with other people."[27]

Perhaps Padre Pio's supernatural knowledge could best be described as prophecy (he was widely known as the Prophet of the Gargano and the Prophet of the People). In the popular imagination, a prophet is one who can tell the future. Padre Pio, although at times he could foretell the future, did not fit this category. He did, however, fit the category of prophet as understood in Scripture. The Hebrew term for prophet is *navi*, "one who is called." A prophet, in the biblical sense, is God's mouthpiece, a man or woman called to convey the

Lord's will. This, basically, was the role played by Padre Pio. Both in answer to various questions from inquirers and, more important, in spiritual counsel in the confessional, Padre Pio, when given supernatural illumination, made known the will of God.

Even stranger than Padre Pio's gift of prophecy was his gift of bilocation, in which he was mysteriously propelled, as he put it, "through an extension of [his] personality," into different parts of the world and even into the spiritual realm.

Padre Carmelo of Sessano, who served as guardian of Our Lady of Grace in the 1950s and whom William Carrigan characterized as "one of the smartest monks I've ever met," told John McCaffery that Padre Pio, in bilocation, was "appearing all over the place." Describing an incident that took place around 1953, he told about a concert that took place in the hall adjoining the monastery.

> Padre Pio had been asked if he would like to join the group of friars who would be there.... He assented willingly and ... followed the various items with obvious interest and appreciation. At the interval, however, whilst the others chatted, he placed his arms on the back of the chair in front of him and rested his head on them, remaining silent and motionless. His companions, thinking he was fatigued, left him undisturbed, and thus he stayed for about five minutes. Then, as the interval was ending, he sat back again and resumed contact with the others. No one thought any more about it.

The next day, however, Padre Carmelo went to visit a sick man and was amazed when he expressed his appreciation for permitting Padre Pio to call on him the previous evening. Carmelo, of course, knew very well that Padre Pio was at the concert all evening and had gone straight to the friary when it was over. When he told the man and his family this, he was told: "Yes, yes, Father! Of course he did! He came here last night. Didn't you know?" When Carmelo asked the exact time, their answer corresponded to the time when Padre Pio seemed to be resting in fatigued abstraction.[28]

Padre Alessio recalls similar instances. On one occasion he entered the padre's room and found him shivering. The weather was warm, but he appeared to be freezing. He also seemed to be in a trance. Alessio piled blanket after blanket upon the quaking form without obtaining him any noticeable relief. He later learned that the mystic had been hearing the confession of a man dying high in the snowy mountains.

Reports of bilocation came from all over the world, from Hawaii to St. Peter's, where Padre Pio allegedly put in an appearance at the canonization of St. Thérèse of Lisieux in 1925. Many of these stories are doubtless the product of hearsay or fertile imaginations. Many, no doubt, resulted from people seeing what they wanted to see. Any unexpected encounter with an unknown bearded man dressed in monkish attire would be, for many of the pious, an instance of Padre Pio in bilocation. Still, there are some well-documented cases, such as that of the Marchioness dei Boschi.

With regard to these occurrences, it is well to note that from 1918 onward, Padre Pio never left San Giovanni Rotondo, so that these mysterious occurrences cannot be explained through the assumption that Padre Pio was actually there in person. There would have been no way for him to be away from the friary without being missed.

In some of the better-documented accounts of bilocation, the padre was seen as if in a vision. There are accounts of his touching and being touched, but many seem to be of the nature of the appearance by the bedside of Maria Campanile's sister in 1918, in which he was seen "spiritually" by one woman and not at all by another.

Many of those familiar with occult science have interpreted Padre Pio's bilocations as "astral projections." Whatever one labels what he himself described as a "prolongation" or "extension" of the personality, Padre Pio seemed to have had little control over it. As Padre Alessio told me in 1978, Pio never liked to talk about the matter, but when questioned, he usually said, "I only know that it is God who sends me. I do not know whether I am there with my soul or body, or both of them."

With regard to Padre Pio's various charisms, one wonders why more people did not ask him directly for detailed explanations. Perhaps those who went to him minded to do so were moved as was a Protestant who recounted his experiences to William Carrigan: "I had a whole bunch of questions for him. When I came into his presence, I couldn't think of one. He just overwhelmed me."

Although Padre Pio was a charismatic in the sense that he was graced by charisms similar to those ascribed to the Apostles, there were some distinct differences between his ministry and the ministries of some modern-day neo-Pentecostal charismatics. Unlike most modern "charismatics," Padre Pio did not emphasize "baptism in the Holy Spirit" or tongues; further, he put a much greater stress on redemptive suffering.

Most modern charismatics regard the "baptism in the Spirit" as immensely important. They speak of a tangible religious experience, a "sensible consolation," as many would describe it, in which by being "filled" with the Holy Spirit, one is empowered to live a more dynamic Christian life. An excellent description of this experience comes from the pen of Corrie ten Boom (1892-1983), the Dutch Presbyterian author and lecturer, a contemporary of Padre Pio whose teachings and theology were in many ways very similar to his. In the mid-1950s, when Miss ten Boom was ill, a minister visiting her laid hands on her and prayed. She wrote:

> I felt a great stream of power flowing through me. Such great joy! The mourning left and I wanted to sing with David: "Thou hast turned for me

my mourning into dancing: thou hast put off my sackcloth and girded me with gladness" (Psalm 30:11). I felt the presence of the Lord Jesus all around me and felt love flowing through me in an ocean of grace. My joy became so intense that I finally prayed, "No more, Lord, no more!" My heart felt it was about to burst, so great was the joy. I knew that it was that wonderful experience promised by Jesus — the Baptism in the Holy Spirit.[29]

She concluded that this "was the beginning of a new spiritual blessing that each day brings me into a closer walk with the Lord Jesus."

If Padre Pio ever had such an experience, it was at his confirmation, when he was twelve. Years later he described to Agostino how he "wept with consolation in [his] heart" whenever he thought of his confirmation because

I remember what the Most Holy Spirit caused me to feel that day . . . a day unique and unforgettable in all my life! What sweet raptures the Comforter made me feel that day! At the thought of that day, I feel aflame from head to toe with a brilliant flame that burns, consumes, but gives no pain.[30]

In this experience, Pio had a glimpse of God's "fullness and perfection."

Some charismatics today teach that such experiences should be normative for all Christians. Padre Pio never taught that they should be normative, much less expected, or even sought. In his case, the experience was entirely unbidden. All charisms and consolations, he felt, are bestowed through the inscrutable wisdom of God rather than through any actions on the part of creatures to bring them about.

There is some evidence, too, that Padre Pio spoke in tongues. We will recall the testimony of Klugkist, who heard Padre Pio speak in a language unintelligible to others. Here again, Pio never taught that such a gift should by any stretch of the imagination be considered normative, nor is there any record of his ever having encouraged anyone to seek it. If he ever spoke in tongues, except on these isolated occasions, he did so in private.

Perhaps the greatest difference between Padre Pio and many of the charismatics of the late twentieth century was his emphasis on redemptive suffering. "Something *good* is going to happen to *you*" is the motto of Oral Roberts. Padre Pio would surely have found this promise misleading, for he admitted the possibility that something very bad — at least from an earthly point of view — might happen to one, and that life, though not without its pleasures, is full of suffering. He taught that a servant is not above his Master and that, as Christ suffered, His followers can likewise expect to suffer. He taught that Christians, unless they have a special calling as Victims of Divine Love, should not court suffering. Nevertheless, they should expect it and, when it comes, offer it to God. His was not a "rose garden" theology. He believed very strongly in the words of St. Paul that say that we are "heirs with Christ, provided that we suffer with him so that we may also be glorified with him."

'A Magnificent Work of Charity'

In his sixth decade, Padre Pio still appeared vigorous. Padre Agostino noted in his diary that his old friend seemed to be "in robust good health." A reporter for *The New York Times* described him as "hale and hearty-looking, with a clear skin, a bushy beard and head of hair, a tendency to corpulence, a pleasant smile, . . . twinkling brown eyes." His gentle voice, the reporter wrote, was "disconcertingly interrupted by what can only be described as pleasant grunts."[1]

Professor Giuseppe Sala, M.D., who became Padre Pio's physician in the mid-1950's, recalled in 1981 that the friar enjoyed "reasonably good health" and never complained about physical infirmities. Five feet five inches tall in his prime, Pio then weighed about 170 pounds. His blood pressure was excellent for a man of his years, and his other vital signs were normal. Nor was he anemic, despite the stigmata. Sala is not certain about Padre Pio's exact caloric intake, except to say that "No normal man could eat as sparingly as he did and still live!"

Nevertheless, age was creeping up on the celebrated priest. He continued to be subject to respiratory problems and to the sudden fevers that had visited him all his life. In his late fifties, Pio had a couple of agonizing attacks of kidney stone but had been able to void the stone without recourse to surgery. His eyesight, which had given him trouble from time to time throughout his life, showed the usual changes common in a man of his age. Spectacles were prescribed, but the firm-minded friar could not be persuaded to wear them. Padre Pio was more concerned about his hearing. At one point he confided to Agostino that he feared he was growing deaf. "I'd rather be carried to the confessional in a chair than to be unable to hear confessions at all."[2] As it turned out, he never lost his hearing, but arthritis increasingly impaired his mobility until, in the last six months of his life, he was forced to use a wheelchair.

At the moment, however, Padre Pio was working as hard as ever. He was *discreto* (counselor) of the religious community. This meant that he had to vote on all actions that the community undertook. He had also to check and sign the friary registers. This office, which he continued to hold until his death, was the only one he ever held within the community.

His spiritual life continued in its usual intensity. Padre Agostino commented during the Christmas season of 1953: "The Padre's life is always the same, notwithstanding the continuous crush of his sacred ministry. His interior life is always rapt in the contemplation of God and union with Him. His mystical union with God is habitual and definitely real. His outward deportment is a source of admiration and joy to anyone who approaches him or speaks with him."[3]

Visitors continued to come in ever greater numbers from all parts of the world. He showed no partiality to any race or nationality, though Father John Schug was told by a friar at San Giovanni Rotondo that Pio was a bit "frightened" of American Negroes! His visitors included numerous celebrities. After the victories of the Christian Democrats at the polls after the Second World War, Padre Pio was continually consulted by political leaders, including Aldo Moro, Antonio Segni, Mariano Rumor, and Giovanni Leone, all of whom headed the Italian government at one time or another. Figures from the world of art and music came to see him too.

Meanwhile, people from all over the world were coming to settle at San Giovanni Rotondo to be near the Man of God. One lady, a former practitioner of Oriental religions, settled near the friary. "There is no place on earth in which you get so much light for the interior life as at San Giovanni Rotondo," she declared.[4] Many agreed with her wholeheartedly.

All the while, the construction of the *Casa* was proceeding steadily. By the fall of 1950 the main building was well on its way to completion, and on October 21, Padre Pio was able to tour the structure. "I do not know what to admire more," he wrote, "the structure for its perfect harmony, or the kindness of Dr. Sanguinetti. Praise to God and sincere thanks to our benefactors and to all who have contributed to the realization of this work of Christian charity."[5]

In addition to supervising the construction of the building, Sanguinetti was also beautifying the environment. Visitors to San Giovanni had always commented on the barrenness of the terrain. A passionate ecologist, Sanguinetti singlehandedly covered the desolate, red, rocky hills with groves of evergreen trees. He planted one seedling after another over a period of several years. Because the mountainside was mostly rock, he often had to use dynamite to blast out holes large enough to accommodate the carloads of soil that he had to haul up the slopes by mule, since the incline was so steep that no truck could negotiate it. By the mid-1950s, the area had been transformed, and cypress trees encircled the friary.

Along with his work on the *Casa*, Padre Pio was busy organizing prayer groups. These cells of Christians who met together weekly or monthly to pray together were a rarity in Italy in those days, and Padre Pio created something of a stir by calling for their formation. Actually, he was inspired by Pope Pius XII, who for years had been urging "men, women, and young people" to come together in prayer meetings.

Padre Pio first began establishing prayer groups in 1947, announcing, "It is time to unite both intentions and actions: to offer Our Lord collective prayers imploring His mercy for a humanity that appears to have forgotten Him."[6] He had, of course, been holding prayer meetings with his spiritual children for more than thirty years, but now he wanted his followers to go into the world to disciple others. By 1950, prayer groups had been established in twenty-three Italian cities. As the years went by, more and more Padre Pio Prayer Groups began to spring up all over the world. Christians met together to pray for their own intentions, for Padre Pio's ministry, for world peace, for the Pope, for the Church, and especially for the *Casa*. Without prayer, he said, the work was a plant with neither water nor air. Pio insisted from the start that each group be under the supervision of a Roman Catholic priest. This was to guard against any insinuation that he was desirous of starting a new church. In light of future events, this was indeed a prudent move.

At any rate, the movement that the padre envisioned as "a tremendous chorus" linking "heaven to earth and men to God" grew rapidly. By the time Padre Pio died, his "prayer army" numbered more than seven hundred groups in fourteen countries.

Meanwhile, work on the *Casa* was nearing conclusion, but many of Padre Pio's friends were becoming concerned about the administration. After 1946 the hospital had belonged to the Anonymous Society, a sort of board of directors, headed by Sanguinetti, Sanvico, and Kiswarday. Padre Paolino, once more a member of the community at San Giovanni, was worried about this arrangement. As things now stood, the members of the Society could bequeath their shares of the hospital to their heirs. "The original directors are honest men," he told Pio, "but what will happen when they die?" The Marquess Giuseppe Orlando likewise expressed his concern. "Tomorrow the heirs of the founders might be Protestants, Communists, Jews, or atheists," he said. "And then what?"[7]

Paolino, the marquess, and others expressed their feelings to the curia (board of directors) of the Capuchin Order. For a time various ideas were bandied about, such as putting the *Casa* directly under the Order or placing the hospital under the proprietorship of the church of *Santa Maria delle Grazie*. Finally, in 1954, it was agreed that the proprietorship of the *Casa* would be awarded to a special branch of the Franciscan Third Order, of which Pio was made director.

The wisdom of this action soon became apparent to everyone when, on September 9, 1954, Sanguinetti suffered a massive heart attack and died almost instantly. He was sixty. Seven months later Sanvico succumbed to cancer at the age of fifty-five.

Padre Pio was particularly shattered by the passing of Sanguinetti. For several days he was unable to do anything other than celebrate Mass, and for months one had only to mention Sanguinetti's name for Pio to burst into tears. "But Padre," his friends affirmed in an attempt to comfort him, "he has gone to his reward!"

"He has indeed," admitted Pio, "but, you know, not only the mind, but the human heart claims its share."[8] Apparently God had not warned him of Sanguinetti's imminent death, as he often did in the case of many of Pio's loved ones. "You took him without first telling me . . . ," Pio complained to his Lord. "If You had told me that You were going to take him, I wouldn't have given him to You. I would have snatched him out of Your hands!"[9]

"We all have to die," said another well-meaning friend.

"We all have to die, it is true," replied Padre Pio, "but the Lord should have spared him to me for just a little longer, because the opening of the *Casa Sollievo della Sofferenza* is near at hand, and I don't know what I'm going to do! I just don't know what I'm going to do!"[10]

Even without Sanguinetti, preparations went ahead for the opening of the *Casa*. Within months of the doctor's passing, Padre Agostino began to complain that he and Padre Pio had to suffer because of the faulty administration of some of the newer directors. Padre Raffaele, the vicar, characterized some of these men as "petty, ambitious, and none too bright."

Nevertheless, on May 5, 1956, the great day arrived: the *Casa* opened. The massive crowds that packed into San Giovanni beheld a platform full of dignitaries from both Church and State. Representing the Italian government were the minister of state, Signor Braschi, and the president of the Senate, Signor Menzagora. Padre Benigno of Sant'Ilario Milanese, the minister general of the Capuchin Order, was there, as was Giacomo Cardinal Lercaro, archbishop of Bologna.

The *Casa* opened its doors by playing host to an international seminar of the European Society of Cardiology, and several world-famed physicians shared the platform with the padre. The president of the society, Dr. Gustav Nylin of Sweden, declared that the hospital was "a magnificent work of charity." An American physician, Dr. E. H. Wagersteen, commented: "It saddens me to think that in the world there is only one Padre Pio. It is a pity that there are not more." The celebrated friar blushed at the compliment and laughed, "God forbid!"[11]

Padre Pio thanked his benefactors from all over the world for their cooperation. "This is the product which Providence, assisted by all of you, has created!" he said. "I present it to you! Admire it, and then let us all bless the Lord Our God!" He charged the doctors to "bring God to the sick! It will be more valuable than any other treatment. . . . You have the mission of curing the sick, but if at the patient's bedside you do not bring the warmth of loving care, I fear that medicines will not be of much use!"[12]

Although not physically present, Pope Pius XII lauded the *Casa* as "the fruit of a lofty instinct of an ideal." Within a year he would honor Padre Pio's request to be appointed lifetime administrator of the *Casa*. In doing so, he relieved the friar of his vow of poverty so that he could handle and supervise the donations.

The Pope was not the only one deeply impressed by the hospital. A reporter from *The New York Times* described the *Casa* as "one of the most beautiful as well as one of the most modern and fully-equipped hospitals in the world. It even has a helicopter landing place on the roof for emergency patients. . . . Its different shades of lovely green marble, its fine tile-work, its bright, pleasant rooms . . . , its ultra-modern operating rooms, laboratories, and kitchens, its little chapel with its precious stained-glass windows, its staff of top-flight surgeons and specialists — every detail — make it as beautiful and up-to-date a place to take away suffering as one can hope to find."[13]

Padre Pio's spiritual daughter Clarice Bruno was also impressed by the "airy, cheerful rooms," which had oxygen outlets and radio earphones beside each bed, something unusual for the time and place. Like the reporter from *The Times*, she was delighted by the absence of "hospital white" and the fact that "everything is in color." While the *Casa* was under construction, Dr. Kiswarday had complained to Padre Pio that too much was being spent on luxuries. Unimpressed by the argument, the padre replied that nothing was too good or too beautiful for the sick and suffering.

The five-story hospital, dwarfing the friary and church a stone's throw away, boasted four operating theaters, a radiology and pharmaceutical department, a blood bank, and a medical library. About half of the six hundred beds planned for the facility were available. There was a center for nurses and one for interns, and a movie theater! The entire building was air-conditioned.

In accordance with Padre Pio's concern that the *Casa* be a place to serve the poor, he made certain that hospital fees were reasonable. As late as 1971, the typical daily rate was the equivalent of $14.75! Most patients had insurance, but those without it were covered by a fund maintained by contributions from all over the world.

Padre Pio continued to emphasize that the *Casa* was not only for the relief of sick bodies but for the benefit of the whole person. "The suffering patient," he declared, "must have in himself the love of God by a wise acceptance of his pains and a serene meditation on his destiny before God. Here the love of God must be strengthened in the spirit of every patient through his love of Jesus crucified. Here patients, physicians, and priests shall be reservoirs of a love which will communicate itself to others in proportion to the extent it is found in them."[14]

Padre Pio made it a point to visit the hospital frequently, going from bed to bed, praying with the patients and speaking words of cheer. As he made his way slowly down the corridors, patients and staff alike would line the way, begging his blessing. On special holy days, he celebrated Mass in the chapel.

On the first anniversary of the inauguration of the *Casa*, Pio announced plans for a medical and religious center, a "hospital city," which would include an international center where doctors and medical students would not only further their professional studies but also "their formation as Christians." In addition, he announced plans for a religious retreat house on the mountain as well as a home for retired priests. Moreover, he called for the construction of a Way of the Cross on the hillside. Still this was not all. The padre announced plans for the establishment of Christian day-care centers as well as centers for handicapped and retarded children, not only in the immediate vicinity, but throughout southern Italy. He also called for the establishment of a Christian mental health institute. "These are not simply my works," he insisted, "but they are God's works, just as He shows me."[15]

Padre Pio lived to see the beginning of the construction of the Way of the Cross, with the stations executed in bronze by the celebrated sculptor Francesco Messina, whom the padre personally invited to execute the work. Eventually, a retreat house was opened at San Giovanni Rotondo. Centers for spastic and retarded children were inaugurated there and in the cities of Manfredonia and Termoli. To this day, not all of the Padre's plans have been fulfilled.

With the opening of the *Casa*, Padre Pio was now an international figure. He was offered a weekly radio program in which he could speak to all the sick of Italy. He could have become another Oral Roberts or Kathryn Kuhlman, but he elected to stay clear of the electronic church. "I always pray for the sick," he said. "Rather than talk to them [on radio or television], I prefer to speak a prayer to God on their behalf."[16]

Padre Pio was plunged into "terrible anguish" when Pius XII, the "beautiful little Pope," died on October 9, 1958, but he was comforted when, according to Padre Agostino, he was accorded a vision of Pius in his heavenly home. Padre Pio also rejoiced greatly in the election of Pius's successor, the aged patriarch of Venice, Angelo Roncalli, who became Pope John XXIII. The very first apostolic blessing the new Pontiff betowed was upon Padre Pio. As months went by, however, it became apparent that Pope John was not as supportive of Padre Pio as his predecessor had been.

In the meantime, a large new church, seating two thousand, was being constructed adjacent to the old one. With the opening of the *Casa*, the inadequacy of the old church became all too apparent. The confusion, the fights, and the stampedes that had been a part of the scene at San Giovanni for years were becoming intolerable. Beneath the new church, construction of a crypt was begun as a final resting place for Padre Pio's remains when his time should come.

That hour seemed all too near when the church was first opened. For the first time in forty years, Padre Pio was completely prostrated by illness. In late April, physicians diagnosed bronchial pneumonia. Early in May, they called his illness pleurisy and ordered absolute bed rest. After May 5, he was confined to his room, unable to celebrate Mass or hear confessions.

Three times during May, Pio's physicians drew more than a quart of bloody fluid from his pleural cavities without bringing relief. Padre Carmelo of Sessano, the guardian, summoned well-known specialists. After making various tests, they arrived at a grim diagnosis: "pleural neoplasm with bloody exudations." They recommended a terrible regimen of chemotherapy.

With solemn faces, three doctors entered Pio's room and told him that he had cancer and had no more than a few months to live. To their shock, the sick man burst out laughing and told them they did not know what they were talking about.

Dr. Giuseppe Sala, Pio's physician at the time, agreed with his patient and took violent exception to the diagnosis of cancer. Saying that Pio was suffering from nothing more than a "pleural inflammation superimposed on a chronic bronchial catarrh," he forbade the chemotherapy and ordered treatment for pleurisy and nothing more.

Pio grew no better. Every day, by means of a loudspeaker installed in his room, he listened to the services in church. After the service, through a microphone, he gave a brief address to the worshipers. That was all he could do. On the second of July he decided to drag himself to the *Casa* to celebrate Mass for the patients there. When Mass was finished, Pio was in such great agony that he had to remain at the hospital. After two days he was carried back to the friary on a stretcher.

When it became known in Vatican circles that Padre Pio was gravely ill, the papal secretary of state, for some reason, decided to play doctor and insist that Pio return to the *Casa* for treatment. This distressed the padre, who said that he wanted to die at the friary. He conceded that if the order to return to the *Casa* came from Rome, he would obey it. Dr. Sala and Padre Raffaele managed to intercede with Rome and obtain permission for Padre Pio to remain at the friary.

On August 5, a statue known as the Pilgrim Madonna was brought by helicopter from Fatima, Portugal, where it normally reposed, representing the celebrated apparition of the Virgin Mary to three local children in 1917. The statue was brought to San Giovanni Rotondo by helicopter, and for several says the faithful gathered in prayer and devotion before the image.

The likeness was brought into the Church of Our Lady of Grace, where Padre Pio, sick as he was, was determined to venerate the Lady it represented. Pale and weak, he was carried into the sanctuary and managed to kneel before the image and drape a golden rosary around it. Then, breathless and in pain, he was carried back to bed.

When the statue was being conveyed away by the helicopter, Pio murmured,

"Dear Mother, ever since you came to Italy [he is referring to the fact that the statue was on tour], I have been immobilized by sickness. Now that you're leaving, aren't you going to say even a word to me?"

In the twinkling of an eye, the padre felt "a mysterious force" surge through his body. Immediately he shouted, "I'm healed!" and leaped from his bed. [17]

Pio felt completely cured. Within two weeks he had resumed all his duties. He did not hestitate to declare that he had been miraculously delivered through the intercession of the Virgin Mary. When someone disputed this, he told him, "I know that I was still sick and felt so very, very bad. I prayed to the Madonna, and the Madonna healed me. If they don't want to believe it, then let them put the Madonna on trial. It was she who healed me." [18]

Although he had been returned to reasonable bodily health for a man of seventy-two, all was not smooth sailing for Padre Pio. The next few months would unleash a storm of controversy very nearly as intense as that which broke over his head in the 1920s.

'Just in Time for My Golden Jubilee'

On July 29, 1960, there arrived at San Giovanni Rotondo a stranger, Monsignor Carlo Maccari. A representative of Pope John XXIII, he came to conduct an apostolic visitation to investigate Padre Pio and his ministry, especially as it related to the *Casa Sollievo della Sofferenza*. The day before, Padre Pio, learning of the planned inquiry, lamented: "They will make my life impossible! They will put me in an unfavorable light and they will force me to surrender to various obediences!"[1] And so it happened. The international acclaim and adulation that had been heaped upon the aging priest since the opening of the *Casa* now burst like a bubble, and by the end of the year, Padre Pio was being treated by much of the media like some discredited charlatan.

The Maccari investigation had its origin in a number of events. One of the most serious had to do with charges of mismanagement within the *Casa*. Padre Raffaele, the old vicar of the friary, wrote in a memorandum he composed for the "sake of history," that after the deaths of Sanguinetti and Sanvico, the "relationship of mutual trust" that had previously existed between the friary and the *Casa* had dissipated. Carlo Kiswarday, the last of the original directors, died that summer. Shortly before his passing, he complained to Raffaele and others that things weren't going well and that he was aware of certain irregularities.

Both the friars and the hospital administators began to distrust each other, especially with regard to the handling of offerings. Some of the Capuchins complained that money sent to the *Casa* but intended for the church and friary was not handed over by the administrators. Likewise, the hospital administrators complained that funds intended for the *Casa* but mailed in care of Padre Pio were not forwarded to their proper destination.

Although no one seriously suspected him personally of skullduggery, Padre Pio, since Pope Pius had freed him from his vow of poverty, had been sarcastically dubbed "the World's Richest Monk" by some newspapers. Many contended that huge sacks full to the brim with money came addressed to him each day. There were charges that some of Padre Pio's followers were misappropriating funds, diverting financial contributions from their intended purpose. The mail at the friary, or at least some of it, was now being handled by laypersons, nearly all of them local people, who were not above gossiping about the contents of letters involving personal problems. Accordingly, Padre Emilio of Matrice, who succeeded Padre Carmelo of Sessano as guardian in 1959, directed that henceforth all mail addressed to Padre Pio or the friary was to be handled only by members of the religious community. Some of the Pious Ladies, who had apparently relied upon their cronies in the mail room for juicy tidbits of gossip, accused the guardian of instituting his new policy for the purpose of isolating Padre Pio. Others declared that Padre Emilio had banned laymen from the mail room so that the greedy friars could appropriate with impunity money intended for the *Casa*.

Forty years of warnings and reproofs by two generations of superiors along with periodic provisions and restrictions by the Holy Office and Capuchin generalate had been quite unable to prevent the stampedes that occurred when the doors opened for Padre Pio's Mass. Padre Agostino, who was back at Our Lady of Grace after a third stint as minister provincial, became increasingly concerned about the disorder, which was actually becoming greater. As always, he shouted at the Pious Ladies as they scrambled for the best seats. As the crowds grew greater and more aggressive and he grew older and sicker (he was eighty in January 1960 and in agony from gout and arthritis), he grew more irritable and his language became rather intemperate. Finally, the doctor had to order the old man to bed at the hours when religious services were held in the church. Agostino never knew that these periods of rest were ordered to keep him from contributing to the confusion in the church.

Visitors were appalled to see not only hundreds of women fighting for the best places but chains and locks on the pews closest to the altar. Some of the Pious Ladies had in recent years taken to installing chains around their pews so that they might stroll leisurely to their places. As they had done for four decades, the crew of Pious Ladies still followed the padre about, snipping off pieces of his vestments when they could. All about the friary, worshipers saw the hucksters pulling off their time-tested trick of selling bandages dipped in animal blood as having come from Padre Pio's wounds.

Some of the Pious Ladies, jealous of the attentions that Padre Pio paid some of his disciples, made the preposterous charge that the seventy-three-year-old priest was having sexual relations with them. The accusations of fornication reached their height after Padre Pio's illness of 1959. It was contended that one of the grande dames spent an undue amount of time alone in Padre Pio's hospital room during the two days that he was a patient in the *Casa*. Padre Giustino of

Lecce, a member of the community, wrote in a memorandum that at the time of Pio's hospitalization, "In the cellars of San Giovanni Rotondo people were sniggling that . . . Padre Pio had slept with C. . . ."[2]

To scotch these sordid rumors, Padre Emilio decided to hide tape recorders in the places where Padre Pio usually conversed with visitors, hoping thereby to prove that all of his conversation was holy. This was not the first attempt to bug Padre Pio. Several years before, Padre Carmelo of Sessano, during his tenure as guardian, had hidden a microphone-recorder under his habit to switch on when gems of wisdom fell like drops of dew from the lips of the venerable padre. "Just imagine," Carmelo exclaimed, "if we had tapes of St. Francis and St. Anthony today! What a wonderful story it would be for us all! Well, let's give future generations the benefit of this great saint we have here!"[3]

Padre Carmelo found, however, that he could not switch the machine on subtly enough to avoid Padre Pio's notice. As Carmelo bluntly admitted later: "When I switch on, he switches off! Each time I set the machine in motion, he immediately goes mute!"[4]

This time the bugging was done more expertly, and the matter was more serious. The whole project seems to have been monumentally asinine. Padre Giustino bugged the guest room and several other places where Padre Pio was wont to converse with visitors, as well as the area where he usually heard the confessions of men. He did *not* plant microphones and recorders in the women's confessional or the bedroom, which would seem to be the most important places to bug if one hoped to refute — or confirm — a charge of sexual immorality.

Padre Giustino is said to have made thirty-six tapes during a three-month period, many of them of confessions. When Padre Pio eventually discovered the microphone wires, he was aghast and immediately sent for his old friend, the aged Francesco Morcaldi, the former mayor. Morcaldi, horrified and indignant, apparently leaked the story to the press. Next, Pio notified the archbishop of Manfredonia, Andrea Cesarano. The bishop hurried to the friary to deal with the "impious sacrilege." When he arrived, Padre Pio threw his arms around him and sobbed, "My own brethren are doing this to me!"[5]

Padre Pio was not the only member of the community who was indignant. When they learned of the bugging, a good many of his colleagues, especially the older ones, were up in arms about such a flagrant violation of the confidentiality of the confessional. "We are terrified by these events," Padre Paolino wrote to a friend in France, "and we cannot understand what would have led the padre's confreres to act in such a way. We cannot, however, deny the facts. . . ."[6]

Soon the story was all over the newspapers, causing many to question further what was going on at the friary. Rumor had it that the tapes were being sent to the Vatican for the amusement of Church big shots.

There was yet another near crisis during the mid-1950s. The Capuchin Order had made several disastrous investments through a financier named Giovambattista Giuffre, who called himself "God's Banker." He promised a ninety-percent interest on investments. Giuffre invited Padre Pio to invest hospital funds in his banks. Pio, however, with no need of supernatural intuition, responded: "Ninety-percent interest! There's something fishy here!" and declared that he was not interested. Although no funds from Our Lady of Grace or the *Casa* were invested in "God's Bank," incredibly, a considerable number of gullible Capuchin leaders invested money with Giuffre. When, inevitably, his banks failed, the Order found itself in debt up to the capuche. Rumor had it that the minister general of the Capuchins, Father Clement Neubauer (1891-1969), was trying to pressure Padre Pio into lending him hospital monies so that he could pay the Order's debts. It was bruited about that Father Clement and other high officials in the Order were infuriated by Padre Pio's refusal to lend them funds and were searching for ways to get the hospital out of his hands. Some newspapers began to charge Father Clement with denouncing Padre Pio to Pope John as "a poor administrator . . . immoral . . . disobedient . . . rebellious . . . and an instigator of heresy." Here they were mistaken. Father Clement, nicknamed Padre Vedremo ("Father We'll See"), was a phlegmatic, undemonstrative man. Yet he confided to friends that he "completely believed in Padre Pio."[7]

Yet, although Padre Pio enjoyed the support of the minister general, as well as such other highly-placed Church officials as Cardinal Lercaro, Giuseppe Cardinal Siri, archbishop of Genoa, and Giovanni Battista Cardinal Montini, archbishop of Milan, he had enemies too. For some reason, there were Church officials who looked askance at the padre's prayer groups and denounced him as a "fanatic" and a "charismatic."

One of Padre Pio's more measured and moderate critics was Albino Luciani (1912-1978), bishop of Vittorio Veneto, afterward patriarch of Venice and, finally, Pope John Paul I. In his diocesan bulletin of February 4, 1960, he wrote that Padre Pio's ministry was like "an indigestible dainty." He was concerned that the padre appealed to people with an "exaggerated craving for the supernatural and the unusual." He went on to say, "The faithful have need for solid bread (the Mass, the catechism, the sacraments), which nourishes them, not chocolates, pastries, and sweetmeats that burden and beguile."[8] Luciani was particularly troubled by the pilgrimages to Padre Pio, especially those organized by mail.

Less temperate in his criticism was Girolamo Bortignan, bishop of Padua. Though he was himself a Capuchin, he seems to have been unalterably opposed to Padre Pio. He strongly denounced the prayer groups, refused to permit them in his diocese, and suspended priests who attempted to organize them. The reason he gave was that the prayer groups tended to be the occasion for "exaggerated manifestations" (tongue-speaking? healing?). In May 1960 he complained to Pope John that Padre Pio was a "charismatic" and was fostering a schism.[9]

Thus, while Padre Pio continued to exercise his ministry in much the same way that he had for the last forty years, storms of controversy were raging about him. There were calls from different quarters for an investigation of the various charges and countercharges: the alleged financial irregularities, the charges of immorality, the charges of heresy. According to Padre Raffaele, the formal request for an apostolic visitation was made by Father Clement, who wanted an inquiry into the fiscal affairs of the *Casa* and the friary. Pope John dispatched Maccari to investigate not only the financial affairs of the *Casa* but also the "life and virtue of Padre Pio."

The most complete and perhaps the most evenhanded account of the Maccari investigation comes from a memorandum written by Padre Raffaele. Despite his attempt to be fair, his disgust and contempt for Maccari, or "Macaroni," are undisguised. Nearly everyone who dealt with the visitator felt that he was unduly biased against Padre Pio. As Raffaele put it, Maccari "practically ignored the report he received from the Order, but was well informed by those who saw the work of the Capuchin Fathers in a bad light, and thus he came to San Giovanni Rotondo well imbued with ideas against the one and in favor of the other."[10]

Maccari began his visitation at the end of July, with Don Giovanni Barberini as his secretary. Although Padre Pio was somewhat uneasy, not all of his friends initially considered the visitation a bad thing. Padre Agostino, for one, appalled by the continuing pandemonium in church, as well as by his suspicions of financial mismanagement on the part of the present *Casa* administration, welcomed the visitation. Convinced of a "diabolical conspiracy" at the *Casa*, even toward the end of the investigation he confided to his diary, "Let's hope that Satan will come away with broken horns and thus the adorable omnipotence of God will be glorified!" On the other hand, Padre Raffaele and others were very soon quite dissatisfied with Maccari's "totally prejudiced" approach.

Maccari lodged at the *Casa*. The first day he went to the friary, assembled the community, was introduced to Padre Pio, and read the decree naming him the apostolic visitator and representative of Pope John XXIII. He announced that he would be interviewing all the friars at Our Lady of Grace, but, according to Raffaele: "He called a pair of religious, and no more. The others waited in vain."

Early in his visitation, Maccari alarmed Padre Pio's supporters by conferring with the archpriest of San Giovanni Rotondo, Don Michele DeNittis, who had succeeded Don Giuseppe Prencipe upon his death in December 1956. There was still some hostility on the part of the local clergy, especially on the part of DeNittis. Raffaele noted that the day after Maccari met with the archpriest, the visitator summoned all the surviving members of the faction who had tried to undermine Pio in the 1920s. A local priest favorable to the padre overheard DeNittis telling Don Domenico Palladino, "Well, Dumi, the hour of revenge has come!"

A layperson who was a fervent follower of Padre Pio hurried to Padre Raffaele. "Padre," he told the old vicar, "after Maccari talked with DeNittis, all the dubious characters from the old days went up to see the visitor. What are we going to do?"

"Nothing," replied Raffaele. "No one must be hindered from going to the visitor, so as not to make matters worse."[11]

After Maccari interviewed those who had an axe to grind either against Padre Pio or the Capuchins, he got around to interviewing the spiritual daughters — the real disciples, not the groupies. Afterward they came to the vicar and other longtime supporters of Padre Pio, horrified because Maccari had asked them explicit questions about Pio's sex life.

A few days later, Maccari called Padre Raffaele and began to question him, too, about Padre Pio's sex life. Raffaele could not brook such nonsense and cut the visitor short: "All I can say is that if all priests, both secular and religious, prelates included, had the baptismal purity and innocence of Padre Pio, the Church would be truly holy in all her members! I have nothing more to say!"[12]

Maccari then addressed the charges of fanaticism and complained about the shysters who peddled crudely painted likenesses of the padre along with their usual faked relics, all within the shadow of the friary. "This is superstition, not faith!" he contended.[13] Raffaele reminded the visitor that this kind of person haunted religious sanctuaries all over the world — "even at Rome, which, under the very eye of the Vatican, teems with Jewish shysters." He added that at San Giovanni there were also "souls who have renounced the world and who live a true Christian life with convincing faith!" Maccari was also appalled that Padre Giustino and another friar had taken to visiting a fortune-teller. Raffaele's excuse, that his brethren were suffering from overwork, went over like a lead balloon.

Maccari's attitude remained unchanged. "From the way he talked," Padre Raffaele wrote, "he seemed to want to let me understand that he thought that everything connected with Padre Pio was a sham and a show."[14]

Meanwhile, Maccari's secretary, Don Giovanni Barberini, was "acting more like a police detective than a priest." Raffaele recounts that the secretary went into the restaurants, saloons, and shops, trying far into the night to wheedle information and opinions about Padre Pio out of the people there. Padre Pio was especially repelled by Barberini and tried to avoid him whenever possible. When he did encounter Barberini, according to Padre Raffaele, Pio's "face changed and reflected a sense of nausea."

Barberini came to the friary and announced that he had been assigned the task of examining all correspondence. He began opening all letters, even confidential ones, checking the offerings to see if the Capuchins were really passing on to the *Casa* those so designated. He even followed the mailman as he handed over his sack of letters to the receptionist, and shadowed the receptionist as he distributed the mail. "He thought he would find millions of lire and uncover who knows what scandal!" Raffaele wrote. "Poor deluded man!" Raffaele helped Barberini go through the mail for two mornings, then announced that he would no longer be a party to such tomfoolery. "We are religious, not thieves!" he sniffed.

At length, Maccari decided to interview Padre Pio. A time was set and Pio appeared at the designated spot only to have Barberini sweep in to tell him that Maccari was too busy and could not come. Pio, though greatly irked because he had to forego hearing confessions to present himself for the interview, let the incident pass and "withdrew to his room in holy peace."

Later on that day, Maccari summoned Padre Pio again, and the two men were closeted for some time. When Pio emerged from the conference, Raffaele noted that he seemed "serious and serene." Though reticent in reporting what had been said, Pio implied that Maccari had accused him of showing favoritism toward his spiritual daughters in preference to other local women. Maccari had also apparently accused him of not handing over the money originally donated for the *Casa* to the Pope so that the Pontiff could have built a hospital in Rome or some other large urban center and not in such a miserable hole in the wall as San Giovanni. One thing Maccari had said had hurt Pio especially deeply: "A month after you are dead, your hospital will have to close its doors!"

When Maccari left San Giovanni Rotondo on October 1 — after a two-month stay — he promised to return again soon, but he never did. Provisions and restrictions were not long in coming however.

First of all, Padre Emilio of Matrice, who had earned the opprobrium even of Maccari by his stupid bugging of Padre Pio's confessional, was relieved of his office as guardian and transferred. Padre Giustino was sent away. So was Padre Raffaele. Maccari concluded that the old vicar, a part of the community since 1924, had been there too long. Replacing Emilio as guardian was a Sicilian friar, Padre Rosario of Aliminusa, who had previously been assigned to Palermo. A gaunt, Lincolnesque man, he was characterized by Padre Raffaele as "upright, calm, prudent, reflective, and full of love and good sense." Padre Alessio, who had joined the community in 1959, recalled in an interview twenty years later that Rosario had "a great love for Padre Pio."

On January 31, 1961, Alfredo Cardinal Ottaviani (1890-1979), prefect of the Holy Office, sent a long memorandum to Padre Rosario, making several stipulations. He stated that Maccari's visitation had uncovered "not a few violations of the religious Rule." Therefore, in order to "stop the repetitions of acts that have the character of a cult directed towards the person of the padre," Ottaviani laid down a number of rules reminiscent of those handed down by Cardinal Merry del Val years before.

It was forbidden for priests or bishops to serve at Padre Pio's Mass. The time of his Mass was to be varied from day to day. Women were not to converse with Padre Pio as he entered or left the confessional, and they were barred completely from the church during the hours when he was hearing confessions — unless they had a ticket to the confessional. Men were barred from the sacristy during the times when the padre was vesting there, and they were forbidden to join him during recreation time in the garden. Railings were to be erected around the women's confessionals in the church so that penitents waiting in line would be forced to keep their distance and unable to eavesdrop. And, last, it was absolutely forbidden for the padre to converse with women alone, anywhere.

These provisions raised a great outcry. When he tried to carry out Ottaviani's directions, Padre Rosario was denounced as "the Jailer" and the "Rosary of the Devil." Morcaldi felt that these restrictions heralded a return to the "atmosphere of noisy vengeance" of the Gagliardi years. Meanwhile, many newspapers took the side of Padre Pio's detractors and printed disparaging stories about him and interviews with such vituperative detractors as Don Domenico Palladino, who vented forty years of detestation for the stigmatized Capuchin.

Padre Pio's genuine spiritual daughters made the matter worse. These women wielded a great influence over the padre, especially as he grew older. He tended to accept as fact whatever they said. After the Maccari investigation, some of them tried to convince the padre to leave the friary and take up residence at the *Casa*. To the horror of Padre Rosario, the old man seemed ready to do it.

Rosario refused to allow him to go, but some of the ladies convinced Pio that they had an order from the Vatican, overruling the local superior. It came to Padre Rosario's attention one night that Padre Pio was about to slip away to the *Casa*. Since Rosario had no knowledge of any order from the Vatican assigning him to the *Casa*, he cringed at the possibility of being put in the unenviable position of being forced to discipline an old man almost universally acclaimed as a saint. For several nights, he was forced to lock Padre Pio in his cell. Predictably, this action, when it became known to the public, as it inevitably did, brought howls of indignation from the padre's followers and a storm of scorn upon the head of Padre Rosario.

Padre Pio, as submissive to authority as ever, never complained or held any bitterness against Rosario. As he had done with Padre Agostino and succeeding superiors, Pio knelt down in front of Padre Rosario each night to ask his blessing. At last the guardian told him that it was inappropriate to let a man of Pio's age and stature kneel down before him and kiss his hand. With great reluctance, Pio agreed that each night the two would "embrace and kiss each other."

Padre Bernardino of Siena has written: "Prohibitions rained down on him, and Padre Pio went on with life as usual. He was calm and obedient to the slightest hint. . . . [He] did not judge his superiors' actions. He bowed his head and obeyed."[15] Padre Rosario testified that when he communicated the orders of the Holy Office to Padre Pio, "He received the orders in a spirit of humility and obedience, without raising any objection."[16] Pio did once remark to a friend, Dr. Giovanni Gigliozzi, "I'm a prisoner," when he saw the huge iron bars being erected around the confessionals.

It did hurt him greatly that all of this confusion was occurring around the time of the fiftieth anniversary of his priestly ordination. "Just in time for my Golden Jubilee," he remarked to John McCaffery.

"Well, Padre, you *did* ask to suffer, didn't you?" responded his friend.

Then, embracing McCaffery, Pio said, "Now you understand what it is all about."[17]

Padre Pio was cheered, however, by the many tributes and congratulations that poured in on the occasion of his anniversary. Perhaps he was touched the most by the letter from the archbishop of Milan, Cardinal Montini, who greeted the "most venerable Father," offering his "congratulations for the immense graces that have been bestowed upon you and which have been dispensed by you." Two years earlier, Padre Pio had told a man named Alberto Galleti: "Tell the Archbishop that he will one day be Pope, and to be prepared. Mind you, tell him this!" When Montini received the message, he laughed and said, "Oh, these saints can get some strange ideas!"[18]

Padre Pio's difficulties were not at an end. He had already signed a will leaving the *Casa* to the Vatican at his death. On November 17, 1961, however, Father Clement came personally to Padre Pio, along with the new minister provincial, Padre Torquato of Lecore, and other Capuchin officials, informing him that Pope John had revoked the decree of his predecessor dispensing Pio from his vow of poverty. They asked him to sign the *Casa* over, there and then, to the custody of the Vatican Bank, which he did without any argument.

When the *Casa* passed from Padre Pio to the Vatican, many of his followers were further enraged. One of the most incensed was Emmanuele Brunatto. He charged that since he had contributed nearly $80,000 to the committee for the construction of the *Casa* in 1941, and since the money was donated exclusively to Padre Pio, it was "illegal" and "immoral" to try to shift the hospital out of the Padre's hands.

Brunatto, nearly seventy but still given to extreme actions, was determined to submit Padre Pio's case to the United Nations! He wrote another one of his briefs, contending that Padre Pio was subject to illegal acts which were infringements of the "fundamental liberties" described by the Universal Declaration of Human Rights of 1948 and the European Convention of Human Rights of 1950. He maintained that since experience had demonstrated that it was impossible for the padre to obtain justice from judiciary and administrative officials in Italy, both lay and ecclesiastical, it was appropriate that the case of Padre Pio be taken up by the United Nations. Brunatto circulated his memorandum among the delegates to the United Nations and even toyed with the idea of sending copies to all fifty American governors!

When Padre Pio learned what Brunatto was doing, he ordered him to cease and desist. "Rest assured," Pio wrote, "everything will return as it was before." In closing, he consoled Brunatto. "It will not remain for us to eat of the fruits of our actions because these belong to the Lord. Bear up, and you will see that every disillusionment will not crush you."[19] Brunatto did not defy Padre Pio as he had done in 1933. He acquiesced to the padre's requests, and nothing more was heard of taking Padre Pio's cause to the UN.

A change in Padre Pio's situation took place on June 3, 1963, when Pope John XXIII died. He was replaced by none other than Cardinal Montini, who took the name Paul VI. Within months, most of the restrictions imposed after the Maccari visitation were relaxed, as Pope Paul authorized Cardinal Ottaviani to announce that Padre Pio was to be permitted to "carry out his ministry in full liberty."

'I Can't Bear
My Cross Anymore!'

By the middle 1960s, Padre Pio was growing feeble. His arthritis was making it increasingly difficult for him to get about, his asthma and bronchitis were worse than ever, and other infirmities of advancing years were multiplying. Mary Pyle wrote a friend that Padre Pio was having great difficulty in breathing but continued to say Mass and hear approximately fifty confessions nearly every day. "He has to be supported when he walks or says Mass," she remarked, "but his strength is holding up this poor old world."

He must have felt increasingly alone. With the passing years, more and more of his old friends and acquaintances disappeared into the invisible world. On May 14, 1963, his dearest and oldest friend, "the Professor," Padre Agostino, was called to heaven, having attained the age of eighty-three. Pio was with him when he died. Bedridden and in great pain for months, Agostino's death was no surprise. Still, his passing crushed Padre Pio, who for months could not pass his old friend's room without bursting into tears.

In October of the next year, another longtime friend, the ancient Padre Paolino, died at the *Casa* after a long illness. Then, the following February, word came that Emmanuele Brunatto had died in Rome, very suddenly, of a heart attack, at the age of seventy-two. The old priest did not show the slightesᵗ sign of surprise. It seemed he already knew.

His brother Michele, who was living with his daughter near the friary, was likewise nearing his earthly end. Mary Pyle, too, was failing and had already sustained several strokes.

There were younger (or comparatively younger) members of the community who were devoted to Pio — men such as the padres Onorato, Aurelio, Eusebio, Pellegrino, Mariano, and Alessio, and "Brother Billy" from Brooklyn (later Father Joseph Pius). There were increasing numbers of younger disciples, but their presence could not, of course, erase the loss of those who had gone before.

As he grew older, Padre Pio seemed to soften his theology. "I believe that not a great number of souls go to hell," he remarked. "God loves us so much. He formed us in His image. God the Son Incarnate died to redeem us. He loves us beyond understanding. And it is my belief that even when we have passed from the consciousness of the world, when we appear to be dead, God, before He judges us, will give us a chance to see and understand what sin really is. And if we understand it properly, how could we fail to repent?"[1] When President John F. Kennedy was assassinated in November 1963, Padre Pio broke down and wept. When Padre Aurelio, equally distressed at the loss of a personage highly esteemed in Italy, asked him to pray for the dead man's salvation, Padre Pio replied: "It's not necessary. He's already in Paradise."[2] He also remarked that he believed that Mussolini was in heaven.

As Padre Pio grew weaker in body, hell seemed to renew its physical attacks on him. From the mid-1960s there are numerous accounts of diabolical molestations. Evenings the padre was in the habit now of sitting in his armchair, praying the Rosary. His eyes had grown too dim to permit him to read much anymore. Some of the younger friars, especially Padre Alessio, were assigned to watch over him and assist him if necessary. On several occasions, more than one of the friars witnessed the old man being hurled from his chair onto the floor by some invisible force. Padre Alessio slept in the room adjoining Pio's and would be called several times a night by the old priest, who begged him to stay with him. He was terribly afraid that demonic forces would hurl him from the bed. Padre Alessio himself never actually saw Padre Pio thrown about, but the old man's terror was all too evident. Padre Mariano once saw Padre Pio's countenance fixed as if in great terror. "What do you see?" he asked.

"I see a head," said Pio, and Mariano questioned him no more.[3]

The friars were aware that they were not dealing with the irrational fears of a weak and confused old man who tended to fall from his bed and chair. More than once there was evidence of a physical beating.

A member of the community recalled to Father John Schug that he and Padre Onorato had gone downstairs for a cup of coffee: "We had left Padre Pio with a buzzer attached to the arm of his chair. All he needed was a hand motion to call for help. Everything was fine. Within the space of five minutes, Padre Onorato returned and heard Padre Pio pleading out loud, 'Help me! Help me!' He rushed into the room and found Padre Pio sprawled on the floor, beaten and bruised."[4]

On July 5, 1964, a possessed woman from near Bergamo in northern Italy was brought to the friary for exorcism. Padre Pio, too old and weak to undertake it himself, supervised one of the younger priests in performing the exorcism. During the rite, the woman roared in an unnatural voice, "Pio, we will see you tonight."

That night, Padre Pio was alone in his room. At ten o'clock some of his colleagues heard a terrific crash. Running to his room, they found the padre on the floor in a pool of blood. His face was swollen and discolored, and he was bleeding profusely from his nose and from a deep cut on his forehead. There were no signs of forced entry, nothing was broken, and everything was in its usual place except for a pillow that, instead of being in Pio's armchair, was neatly tucked beneath the old man's bleeding head.

The guardian, Padre Carmelo of San Giovanni in Galdo, asked who had put the pillow under his head. Weakly, Pio replied, "The Madonna."

The next day the exorcism commenced anew. "Last night I was up to see the old man upstairs," the possessed woman roared. "I hate him so much because he is a fountain of faith. I would have done more, except the Lady in White stopped me."

The young friar did not succeed in exorcising the demon. Padre Pio told the friars that hers was a case of a victim soul who had to suffer a little longer before she could be freed.

Padre Pio's injuries were real. His gash required stitches. For five days he could not celebrate Mass in public. As Father Joseph Pius recalls: "His face was cut above the right eyebrow. His eyes were black, all black under the eyes. His shoulders were terribly bruised. I saw it."

Two years later, a visitor to the friary came up to Padre Pio and said, "The last time I was here was when that little devil hurt you."

"*Little* devil!" exclaimed the venerable man. "They weren't little at all. They had the hooves of Lucifer to beat me with!"[5]

The world situation deeply saddened Pio at this stage of his life. He was appalled by the rampant materialism and immorality that he saw about him. One of the things that disgusted him most was modern television programming. By the mid-1960s, Capuchins were permitted to watch TV, which did not please Padre Pio, who felt that the programs did not lead to the virtues desirable in Christian living. He also feared that excessive television viewing was a factor in the destruction of family life: instead of talking to each other, family members tended to spend evenings staring gape-mouthed, like zombies, at the set. He strongly advised anyone who asked his opinion not to buy a television set. Although he had once cautiously approved of his nephew's running a movie theater and had authorized a cinema in the *Casa*, Padre Pio grew increasingly negative about motion pictures. When the subject was broached, he was known to say, "The devil is in it!" On at least one occasion he told a penitent that the reason his car had broken down the night before was that he was en route to the movies!

Padre Pio was exceedingly pessimistic about the world situation and the future. He seemed to see the future, and it filled him with horror. When Pio was questioned as to what the coming years would bring, Father Joseph Pius reports,

he often said, "Can't you see that the world is catching on fire?" There are
many accounts of grim and grisly prophecies from the padre's lips, but most of
them are unsubstantiated. As Padre Pio frequently said, "If I said all the things
people said I say, I'd have to be talking all the time." Father Joseph Pius does
recall some prophecies about coming world events but has said that it is best
that they not be disclosed lest they prove too unsettling.

What perhaps troubled the padre most were the changes within his own
beloved Roman Catholic Church. The 1960s were a time of change, as the Second Vatican Council convened between 1962-1965. Indeed, in 1964 Mary Pyle
wrote her friend Coletta Kehoe, "So many Bishops from the ecumenical council
come up to see Padre Pio that sometimes it seems that the Council is at San
Giovanni Rotondo."

Padre Pio accepted humbly the changes that came as a result of the Council.
Like many elderly priests, he requested and received a dispensation to continue
to celebrate the Tridentine Latin Mass. He did occasionally attend a Mass in the
vernacular but made no comment whatsoever about it.

What saddened him immeasurably was the attitude of dissent and unbelief
that seemed to be rife within the Church. He was almost embittered by the protests and criticism leveled at the Pope and at the Church in general by various
radical priests and laymen. Wondering at their behavior, Pio's comment was,
"Thank God I am old and near death!"[6]

A Capuchin official named Padre Clemente of Santa Maria observed that
what caused Padre Pio great sadness in the last years of his life was the abandonment of ancient traditions by many Capuchins and, above all, the great decrease
in vocations to the Order. Indeed, in the wake of Vatican II, there was some talk
(never really taken seriously) of discarding the traditional Capuchin habit. One
day, to play an odd sort of joke, one of his colleagues came to Pio during recreation with a tape measure in his hand. "I have to take measurements," the
younger man explained.

"Whose?"

"Yours."

"Mine? Do you want to make me another habit?"

"No. I have to take measurements for trousers. One never knows. Don't you
know that the Special General Chapter is in session? Maybe they will order us to
wear civilian dress. So we'd better be ready."

The humor was lost on the old man, who started to weep. "Have you lost your
senses?" he cried. "I have lived and I will die with this blessed habit on. Do you
understand?"[7]

The crowning blow took place early in 1965. Padre Pio's sister Graziella, as we
know, had been a member of the Brigittine Order for nearly fifty years, living
in the motherhouse at Rome. Many considered her a saint in her own right and,
en route either to or from visits to Padre Pio, would call on her. Several people I

interviewed, who asked not to be identified, were not so enthusiastic. "Her religious life," said one, "was ordinary, without any special sign of divine intimacy." Another simply said, "I was never impressed."

Perhaps an indication of Padre Pio's opinion of her, at least in later years, is illustrated by the following incident. A man who had just visited Suor Pia in Rome remarked to Padre Pio, "What a beautiful person your sister is!"

"Go away from here!" Padre Pio said tartly. "Don't come to me talking this rubbish!"

"Padre, it's true. She's so good and holy."

Rather bluntly, the old man replied: "Look. I am the best one in my family. Only one surpassed me, but she [Felicita] is no more."[8]

At any rate, Suor Pia must have been a strong-willed woman. In the wake of Vatican II, her convent was subject to sweeping changes. Suor Pia vigorously objected to the liberalization of her way of life and, at the age of seventy, left the convent and took an apartment in Rome with another dissenting nun. Shortly thereafter she appeared at San Giovanni Rotondo and asked to speak with her brother.

Padre Alessio accompanied Padre Pio to the guest room, where he saw Suor Pia, tall, gaunt, and haggard, looking older than her years, dressed conservatively but in civilian clothes. Seeing her thus, Pio burst into tears and snapped, "Just look at what you have become!" Pia tried to explain the reasons for her departure from the convent, but Pio refused to accept her arguments. He did concede that she had valid grievances and that the changes of which she complained were certainly bad. Nothing, however, could excuse her breach of the precept of obedience. Speaking of the new, liberal superiors, Pio told her: "They are wrong and you are right, but still you must obey. You must return." Suor Pia refused. Padre Pio then told Alessio to take him back to his room and turned away from his sister, weeping uncontrollably.

At once he began to pray to heaven that Suor Pia would return to the Brigittines. It was hard enough for him to accept the fact that young nuns and monks were walking out of their convents and monasteries, but now his own seventy-year-old sister had joined their ranks! For him a traditionalist rebel was as bad as a radical one.

He fervently prayed that Pia might return to the Brigittines, but heaven was as brass. "God does not answer my prayers anymore!" he sobbed. "Hithertofore Our Lady has never denied me a grace. Now she doesn't listen to me either!" The padre's tearful petitions were rejected, as Suor Pia never returned to her Order. She did join the Congregation of the Sorrowful Mother, but this action did not satisfy her brother, who considered her still to be in a state of disobedience. The two never spoke again, although Pia, only seven months from her own death, did attend her famous brother's funeral. She died in Rome, April 30, 1969. Though never dispensed from her vows, she maintained that she remained faithful to them. To this day she remains an acute embarrassment to her family. More than a decade after her death, Pia Forgione-Pennelli is said to react with violent outbursts followed by stony silence at the mere mention of the name of her aunt and namesake. The full story will probably never be known.

Padre Alessio felt that the defection of his sister was the crowning sorrow of Padre Pio's life, and the fact that the urgent request he made to the Lord was denied constituted his "last trial." In this ordeal, it seems that the words of Christ on the cross "My God, my God, why hast Thou forsaken me?" were more than ever fulfilled in him. While God still granted many more of Pio's requests, and while this certainly was not the first denial, there was something about God's refusing Pio this grace that devastated him. The Dark Night, which had somewhat abated during his middle years, now returned with a vengeance, and more than ever he felt his soul plunged into deepest darkness; more than ever before, he felt forsaken by God. "I cannot bear my cross anymore," he said repeatedly. "He hardly ever talked after that," Padre Alessio recalls. "He might as well have been called the Silent Friar."

'Give Me the Obedience to Die!'

Padre Pio's health declined precipitously after Suor Pia's defection. He began to complain of "unbearable insomnia," a bit odd in a man who for sixty years had never permitted himself more than four hours of sleep. Now his rest was troubled. He mumbled, moaned, and prayed in his sleep. One of his younger colleagues, Padre Eusebio, observed that his slumber was punctuated with sighs and invocations, such as: "My Jesus, my mother Mary, I offer up to you the groaning of my poor soul!"

Well-meaning doctors prescribed Valium and barbiturates, and the frail old man became dependent on them. Dr. Sala resorted to "white lies" to keep the padre from taking too many pills. When the ailing priest asked him for more medicine, Sala would tell him that he was leaving town for a few days and that Pio would have to make do with his present supply for the time being. The padre, ungraced by supernatural illumination in this instance, believed him. News of the padre's use of tranquilizers and sleeping pills spread to many of the disciples and to the townspeople, who became incensed and bitterly excoriated his doctors and colleagues. Some even claimed that the padre's superiors were ordering him to take the pills so as to destroy his mind and his ministry. When Padre Pio fell seriously ill in the spring of 1965, several newspapers published reports, based on "informed sources," contending that the holy man was actually suffering from "severe barbiturate intoxication." At any rate, Pio recovered and threw away all his medicines, deciding that it was better to suffer from depression and insomnia than to be drugged.

Although many of his disciples, continuing to believe in the prediction of the Pietrelcinese astrologer of so many years ago, confidently expected him to live to be ninety-nine, Padre Pio knew that his days were drawing to a close. By 1966 it was plain that he had a serious heart condition. In the ensuing months he had several crises of arrhythmia, with a precipitous drop in blood pressure. More and more he was subject to crushing pains in his chest. Moreover, his respiratory problems were worsening. He had increasingly severe attacks of asthma and bronchitis and at times could scarcely speak. His voice, once a melodious baritone, was now reduced to an old man's croaking whisper. For some years he had, as we have seen, been suffering from arthritis; now he also had osteoporosis, a painful deterioration of the bones, and could barely walk. He grew so feeble that he could no longer even turn himself in bed. He had to be assisted in dressing, bathing, and even, much to his great humiliation, in the most intimate necessities of life. "I am reduced to a state of helplessness," he lamented. "May the Lord call me now because I am no longer permitted to be of any use to my brethren."

During his last three years, he gradually withdrew from life. He never laughed or joked. He no longer came down to the refectory for dinner or joined his colleagues for recreation. He could no longer read. When not going about his sacred ministry, he simply sat by himself, praying the Rosary in silence. Father Joseph Pius, who was with him a great deal during his last three years, felt that the old man was gradually withdrawing from everything he loved in anticipation of death.

Although he still felt unworthy and unsure of his salvation, Padre Pio was glad at the approach of death. He frequently told his superior, Padre Carmelo: "Give me the obedience to die."

Despite his growing debility, he continued his ministry. As he had refused to take a vacation (a privilege accorded to Capuchins) for half a century, he refused to do so now. He no longer officiated at Benediction, but he continued to say Mass every morning to a packed church. Padre Alessio would help him dress and get to the church. Then the younger man would lie down and try to get a little sleep. Pio had gotten so bad that he was calling for Alessio nearly every five minutes during the night, and the younger priest got almost no rest. Though Padre Alessio would set his alarm clock for the time when the Mass would be ended, he always slept through its ring. Without fail, over a period of weeks in this routine, Alessio would be jolted awake by a loud knocking at the door. Answering it, he would find no one there. He would rush from his room and reach the church just as the padre was finishing his Mass. This continued until one day Padre Pio warned him, "Young man, please don't make my angel have to wake you every morning." After that, Padre Alessio never had any trouble waking up on his own.[1]

Padre Pio continued to hear about fifty confessions each day, and the Lord, who saw fit to deny his prayers concerning his sister, continued from time to time to grant him the gift of supernatural illumination. The venerable priest likewise continued to listen to the many requests that came to him in the mail, and each evening around eight, he would greet the growing crowds from nearly every country on earth who came to wave to him and serenade him with hymns. He even continued, as he had done all his life, to excercise his right to vote, participating in municipal elections within months of the end of his life.

Although his physical powers were waning, many of Padre Pio's colleagues felt that his spiritual life had intensified. One day Padre Costantino entered his room and was struck by what he saw. "His countenance was shining with a rosy flame of light such as I had never seen before and shall, I think, never see again. It was for but an instant, but I shall never forget it."[2] This phenomenon was observed in Moses when he came down from Sinai with the two tables of the Law in his hands. It is written that "the skin of his face shone because he had been talking with God" (Exodus 34:29).

Frequently during the night, Padre Alessio heard Padre Pio, sitting in his favorite armchair, talking to unseen guests, apparently in bilocation. Padre Pellegrino, who at times also watched the old man at night, said to him one day, "Padre, you can't deny that now and then you go off to Paris, or London, or Berlin, or somewhere else, and at the same time remain comfortably in San Giovanni Rotondo by bilocation. . . ."

"Yes," Pio answered, "whether it's true or not that I am found in various places by bilocation, trilocation, or whatever, you must ask God and not me. All I can tell you is that I always try to remain attached to the thread of His will. For this reason, I am always where I am."[3]

There continued to be reports of healings. Two of them, both of which occurred in the last year of the padre's life, are worth mentioning.

On Christmas Eve 1967, twenty-year-old Agnese Stump arrived at San Giovanni Rotondo with her father and brother. She had been having terrible pain in one of her legs, and doctors were advising an operation. She asked Padre Pio whether she should submit to the knife. "Go ahead and have the operation," he told her. "Don't be afraid. I'll assist you with my prayers. But remember, nothing will be done without my hand."

The doctors took a biopsy and determined that she was suffering from osteosarcoma — a very deadly form of bone cancer. Several doctors wanted to amputate the limb; others said it was too late. Donna Agnese, despite the pleas of her parents, refused the amputation.

Within a short time, she was in a terrible way. "The bone was all eaten up and looked like a black sponge," she said. "I couldn't stand on my left leg. The bone couldn't support me. It was full of pus." The doctors, certain that the cancer had entered her bloodstream, awaited the fatal outcome. All they could do was to immobilize the leg in a cast so that it would not shatter, and wait.

They waited and prayed. Donna Agnese did not die. The pains went away. Her leg, however, remained in a cast. After some months, the cast was removed and the leg was found to be completely normal. There was no trace of the disease in her body, and the large expanse of bone that had been destroyed had entirely grown back.[4]

As of 1979, Donna Agnese Stump was "in perfect health" and living in the city of Pavia. When Father John Schug visited her, she showed him before-and-after x-rays of her leg. Though not a physician, Father Schug was able to see a radical difference between the two sets of x-rays.

Early in 1968, Giuseppe Scatigna of Palermo, Sicily, developed a swelling in his groin. His doctors, neglecting to perform a biopsy, assured him that it was only an "impacted gland." Gradually the lump grew bigger and more painful. When laboratory tests were finally made, they revealed that he was suffering from metastatic melanoma — a virulent form of cancer.

The Scatignas went to see Padre Pio, who agreed to pray for him. The sick man begged for just five more years of life so that he could see his adopted daughter grow up.

The doctors in Sicily had given up on him when Scatigna sought admission at the *Casa*. Even there, the doctors considered his case hopeless but decided to admit him "out of charity." After further tests, they informed him that he had two days to live: the cancer had diffused throughout his body. Scatigna was in such pain that he could scarcely move. His skin was yellow. He could eat nothing.

His wife went to the friary and begged for a piece of Padre Pio's clothing with which to touch her husband. The guardian consented. She touched the sick man with the cloth, and immediately he felt better. A few days later more x-rays were made. To everyone's amazement, there was no trace of cancer in Scatigna's body. Within days he went home.[5]

Giuseppe Scatigna enjoyed a number of years of good health before he died a "beautiful and happy death" in the spring of 1978, at age fifty-five. The cause of death was another form of cancer, apparently unrelated to his illness of a decade before. Before he died, he commented: "I wanted five years so that our daughter could grow up. Padre Pio obtained nine, so I am grateful."

There was to be no cure for Padre Pio, however. By the spring of 1968 he coughed constantly. His lungs were torn by asthma and bronchitis. Overnight he seemed to shrivel, and his once stocky form was reduced to skin and bone. He experienced crushing pains in his chest and a sense of suffocation. "I can't go on any longer!" he murmured. "Lord, what more can I do on this earth? Come and take me!"[6] Now confined almost constantly to a wheelchair, he celebrated Mass seated.

He grew very depressed. When Padre Raffaele came to see him, Pio remarked: "I can't do anything anymore. I am helpless in every way." Raffaele recalled: "I remember a day when, after hearing confessions, he began to cry like a baby. He was mortified that he could not even rise from bed by himself, and he was very much humiliated in front of those priests assigned to stay at his side day and night."[7]

On April 26, 1968, the padre was told that his eighty-year-old disciple Mary Pyle had been taken to the *Casa* after suffering another stroke. Would he like to go to see her? He shook his head and said, "No, I'm going to pray to the Lord that He might take her home to heaven with the angels." Later, told that she was gone, he said, "Now, at long last, she will be able to listen to the celestial harmonies without having to play the organ!"[8] They buried her in the marble mausoleum in the same town cemetery that contained the mortal remains of Padre Agostino and Padre Pio's parents, and which, only the previous May, had received those of his brother, Michele.

By the spring of 1968, Pio's stigmata had become less evident. According to some witnesses, the marks were no longer visible on the feet, although the pain persisted. On the hands there were now only scabs, with just a touch of redness. His colleagues viewed this as a sign of approaching death. As Padre Onorato put it, "The ministry was finished, so the signs were finished."[9]

By July, the Man of God, now eighty-one, was practically bedfast and frequently in great pain. Often unable to celebrate Mass, he spent entire days in his room, praying. Often he exclaimed: "Pray for me. I am afraid of finding myself before Christ. I have not properly responded to His love and to His infinite graces."[10] Workmen were still engaged in the construction of his burial cyrpt beneath the new church. "When the tomb is finished, then I will die," he often said. To various spiritual children who wrote expressing a desire to visit, he sent word that they had better do so now or they were likely to be too late. His niece Pia Forgione-Pennelli discussed some plans for the next year.

"But I won't be here next year."

"Then where will you be, dear Uncle?"

"Dead."

In early September the friars were alarmed because Padre Pio stopped eating altogether. Sometimes he could be coaxed to put a slice of fruit in his mouth, but he would vomit almost immediately. Continually he begged his brethren to pray for him.

Padre Pio took pen in hand just one more time, on September 12, 1968. He was distressed at the worldwide criticism that was being leveled against Pope Paul VI in the wake of his "birth control encyclical," *Humanae Vitae*. The dying man wrote the Pontiff:

> I know that your heart is suffering much these days in the interest of the Church, for the peace of the world, for the innumerable necessities of the people of the world, but, above all, for the lack of obedience of some, even Catholics, to the high teachings that you, assisted by the Holy Spirit and in the name of God, are giving us. I offer you my prayers and daily sufferings as a small but sincere contribution on the part of the least of your sons in order that God may give you comfort with His grace to follow the straight and painful way in the defense of eternal truth, which never changes with the passing of the years. Also, in the name of my spiritual children and the

Prayer Groups, I thank you for your clear and decisive words that you pronounced, especially in the last encyclical, *Humanae Vitae*, and I reaffirm my
faith, my unconditional obedience to your illuminated directions.

May God grant victory to the truth, peace to His Church, tranquillity to the
world, health and prosperity to Your Holiness, so that once these fleeting
clouds are dissipated, the Kingdom of God may triumph in all hearts, guided by your apostolic work as Supreme Pastor of all Christianity.[11]

September 20, 1968, was the fiftieth anniversary of the stigmatization. Bent
over almost double with pain, Padre Pio celebrated Mass that morning. Later in
the day he attended the public recitation of the Rosary as well as the Benediction. That evening one of his brethren wished him another fifty years. "What
harm have I ever done to you?" demanded the old man.[12]

San Giovanni Rotondo was packed with crowds of people, not only with those
who wanted to celebrate the fiftieth anniversary of the stigmatization, but also
with those who had come for the First International Convention of Prayer
Groups, which was to begin in two days. That night there was a great candlelit
parade in which nearly everyone in town participated. A great sea of light
moved slowly up the road to the friary. Gathering in the courtyard of the friary,
the crowd took up the chant "Long live Padre Pio! Long live Padre Pio!" and
shot off fireworks in his honor.

The people were disappointed that Padre Pio did not appear at the window.
The beloved old priest, worn out by sickness, lay fast alseep. When morning
came he had not the slightest idea that a celebration had taken place in his hon-
or.

The next day, September 21, he was too weak to say Mass or hear confessions.
That morning he had another attack of breathlessness and palpitations of the
heart. As the terrible pain once more gripped his chest, he clutched Padre
Carmelo's hand, looked at him, and whispered, "This is the end! This is the
end!" Yet by afternoon he was sufficiently improved to attend Vespers and
Benediction; and in the evening he was wheeled to the window to bless the
huge throng.

The prayer group convention officially began September 22. It seemed as if
nearly all of the padre's disciples were present. The *Casa* was decked with lights
and festive banners. The hotels and inns, filled to capacity, had been booked for
months. "What a celebration!" said the padre when informed of the activity.
"I'm so confused I think I'd like to run and hide!"[13]

Pio wanted to say his usual Mass without chant that morning at five, but
Padre Carmelo persuaded him to celebrate a sung Mass for the festive occasion.
The crowd broke into a cheer as he appeared, helped by three friars — a tiny,
bent, haggard, and tottering figure, his face and nearly bald skull parchment-
white, his rheumy eyes seemingly fixed on another world. A hush fell on the

throng as, falteringly, he began the Mass. For the first time in anyone's memory, he did not attempt to hide his hands at any point in the service. To the amazement of everyone there, there was no trace of any wound.

Haltingly, he proceeded with the Mass. The congregation had to strain to hear his feeble, quavering voice. At the conclusion, while being helped from the chair at the altar into his wheelchair, his wasted limbs gave way entirely. He would have toppled to the ground had not the friars in attendance caught him. As he was wheeled away, he held out his arms to the congregation, calling weakly, "My children! My children!"

That morning, for the first time in days, he decided to hear confessions. Since no one expected him to be up to a turn in the confessional, very few came. He spoke briefly to several women who had gathered in the sacristy. Cleonice Morcaldi remembered that "he could hardly sit erect in his chair. He had a cadaverous look."

Padre Pio spoke to his nephew Ettore Masone, who was there with his five-year-old son, Pio. Masone wanted to ask his uncle if, the night of the festivities, he had been in ecstasy rather than sleeping. Why was it that he had not heard all the noise?

"You want to know too much," the old man said. "Kiss my hand and go about your business."

Masone was alarmed at the padre's appearance. "Leave me alone. I'm weary, very weary," said Pio. He turned to the little grandnephew. "You carry my name," he said. "I want you to live up to it, understand?"[14]

That morning the crypt was blessed. At 10:30, held erect by two friars, he blessed the throngs from his window. That afternoon he was told that the first stone had been laid in place for the Way of the Cross he had desired for so long. At 4:30 he attended Benediction, after which he again blessed the throngs from the window. His face was marked by great suffering. He waved his handkerchief lightly but without the usual enthusiasm. His eyes were glassy, and he stared ahead as if into another world.

Padre Pio retired to his bed, murmuring: "I belong more to the other world than to this one. Pray to Our Lord that I might die!"[15] In deep pain, Pio could not sleep. Padre Raffaele, in town for the celebration, looked in on him. Returning to his colleagues, he said, "I don't like the way he looks." He summoned a physician, Professor Bruno Pavoni. After the doctor briefly examined the sick man, Raffaele demanded why he had given Pio nothing for pain. "He doesn't want it," said Pavoni.

Raffaele was now certain that Padre Pio would never see another dawn. He returned to the room, bent over, and kissed his old friend on the forehead. Pio embraced him and returned his kiss. "Thanks for everything," he whispered. "May the Lord reward you for your love."[16]

That evening Pio kept calling Padre Pellegrino, who had been his nurse-companion since Padre Alessio had gone to Ireland to study. Between nine and midnight, he must have called five or six times. Each time he simply asked what time it was. He seemed melancholy and agitated.

Just after twelve on the morning of September 23, Padre Pio called Padre Pellegrino once more, took his hand and, with moistened eyes, begged him, "Stay with me, my son." Again he asked the time, and this time added the question, "My son, have you said Mass yet?"

When Pellegrino replied that it was still too early, the old man answered, "This morning you will say Mass for me."

He asked to make his confession. Then he said to Padre Pellegrino, "My son, if the Lord calls me tonight, ask all my brothers to forgive me for all the trouble that I have caused them, and ask all our fellow priests and my spiritual children to say a prayer for my soul."

Padre Pellegrino then requested a last blessing for all the fellow priests, spiritual children, and for all the sick. "Of course, I bless them all," said the padre. "Ask the guardian to give them all this last blessing from me."[17]

After renewing his vows of poverty, chastity, and obedience, Padre Pio expressed a desire to get out of bed. It was now 1:30 A.M. Padre Pellegrino helped him out of bed, but Pio walked unaided into the veranda with surprising sprightliness. Turning on the light, he sat down. Five minutes later, however, he wanted to go back to his room. Suddenly he was so weak that Pellegrino had to fetch the wheelchair.

Back in his room, he collapsed into his armchair. Fixing his eyes as if into the other world, he whispered, "I see two mothers."[18]

Pellegrino, seeing that Pio's breathing had become labored and his face and lips were turning blue, announced that he was going to fetch Dr. Sala. "Don't call anybody," Pio begged. But the younger priest went anyway, leaving Pio with Padre Raffaele, who was shortly joined by the guardian and three other friars.

When Padre Pellegrino returned a few minutes later with Dr. Sala and Dr. Gusso, Pio was sinking rapidly. Sala took his pulse. It was weak. His extremities were cold. Pio, still conscious, kept repeating, very slowly, "Jesus . . . Mary . . . Jesus . . . Mary . . ."[19]

Padre Carmelo administered the Sacrament of the Sick (the "last rites").

Sala was giving Padre Pio oxygen and injections to stimulate his failing heart, but the old man was beyond all that now. The little group gathered around the armchair to recite the prayers for the dying as the padre's head sank to the left and his eyes closed.

"Padre! Padre!" cried Sala, his eyes filling with tears.

As if summoned from the other world, Padre Pio opened his eyes, looked at Sala, and then closed them again, forever. His breathing ceased. Sala and two other doctors, who had just arrived, began to administer artificial respiration and pounded on the patient's chest. The heart started again, and there followed the sound of several more breaths. Then silence. It was 2:30. The face was, according to Sala, "pale, distended, and bloodless," the lips "slightly parted, like a little bird's." Dr. Giuseppe Gusso observed "the clinical signs of death, the most peaceful and sweet I have ever seen."[20]

Epilogue:
An Imitator of Christ

More than a hundred thousand people gathered at San Giovanni Rotondo on September 26, 1968, to pay their last respects to the man they had come to know as the twentieth-century St. Francis, to gaze upon his embalmed body, and to follow the solemn cortege through the streets of the city and back again to the church.

As a sign of respect, citizens draped their best tablecloths and Persian carpets from windows and rooftops, and displayed enormous pictures of Padre Pio. The minister general of the Order, Father Clementinus of Vlissingen, who led the procession, was joined by representatives of other religious Orders as well as by secular clergy and governmental officials. After an outdoor funeral Mass, the mortal remains of the Prophet of the Gargano were placed in the crypt beneath the church.

After Padre Pio died, many newspapers predicted that San Giovanni Rotondo would dry up and die like an uprooted plant, yet visitors have arrived in even greater numbers since the padre's death. Thousands continue to come from all parts of the earth to visit the sites associated with his remarkable ministry.

Visiting San Giovanni Rotondo ten years after the padre's passing, I questioned one of the friars about reports of miracles during Padre Pio's lifetime. "It would be more significant," he answered, "to talk about miracles that have taken place since his death." A second friar told me that he knew of approximately a thousand healings that have been attributed to the heavenly intercession of Padre Pio — as many as had been attributed to him during his long life.

Father Joseph Pius told me that the friary's archives contain documents of the case of an actor in Ceylon (now Sri Lanka). X-rays taken in October 1968 — a month after Padre Pio's death — revealed a large hole in the man's heart. En route to London for surgery, the actor broke his journey at Rome, where he invoked the intercession of Padre Pio. No sooner had he done this than he felt his heart pounding so violently that he feared he was having a coronary. After a few minutes, though, he felt fine and resumed his trip to London. He was astounded to learn that x-rays taken after his arrival indicated no need for surgery. The hole in the heart, clearly visible in the x-rays taken shortly before, was gone!

Father Joseph Pius also knows of a woman from Palermo, Sicily, who was in Padua in June 1976 for surgery on a perforated ulcer. Back home, one of the Padre Pio prayer groups interceded for her. Shortly before she was to have a large portion of her stomach removed, the woman "saw" Padre Pio, in broad daylight, beside her bed. He placed his hands on her abdomen. Instantly she felt a change, and doctors were soon able to confirm that all evidence of the ulcer had vanished. She left the hospital, needing neither surgery nor medication.

Padre Alessio, a few years ago, told of a woman in Poland who lay dying in the last stages of cancer. A friend "prayed to Padre Pio," touched the sick woman with a relic, and immediately she rose from her bed cured.

Every day the friars at San Giovanni Rotondo receive letters such as this:

> You may recall that my son John was struck down by an unknown disease when he was only 6 mos. old. He is now 4¼ yrs. old and has proved Doctors wrong by living so long. . . . Understandably, he is not yet able to walk around by hisself as of yet, but we feel that it will not be too long before he does. We all owe this to Pio Padre intercession as we have been praying to him every day since the son was took sick.

Or this:

> I must write and tell you that, through the intercession of Padre Pio, my son went to Confession again after an absence of about 9 yrs. I had been hoping and praying for a long time, then one day I promised I would visit Padre Pio's tomb and send a letter to have it published in the magazine "The Voice of Padre Pio," if my son returned to the Faith, and within a few weeks, through God's grace, he went to confession and returned to the Faith.

Or this:

> Our grandson, born May 15, 1978, hours after he was born stopped breathing. The nurses & dr. started him breathing again. Later a second & third time he stopped breathing again. When I found out about it a third time, I immediately started praying to Padre Pio & asked him to go to our grandson's bedside and help him. The baby was baptized by the hospital chaplain. All kinds of tests were made & they found nothing wrong. He is now home & growing & healthy, thanks to Padre Pio and our dear Lord.

These letters testify to Padre Pio's continuing, even growing, reputation as much as they seem to exhibit evidence of his intercession from heaven. Indeed, some might question the miraculous nature of the events described as well as the theological propriety of "praying to Padre Pio." Certainly some of the padre's spiritual children carry their zeal to extremes. One of them said to me, "You get better results by praying to Padre Pio than you can by praying to St. Anthony, St. Francis, the Madonna, or even God!"

Padre Pio's spiritual children look eagerly toward the day when their beloved friar is officially declared a saint by the Roman Catholic Church. The preliminaries for the cause for his canonization began in 1969. In November 1980 the cause received apostolic approval.

From a secular point of view, Padre Pio was an eminent humanitarian who established a first-rate hospital in a remote area previously notorious for the woeful inadequacy of its health care. He set up institutions for the physically handicapped and the mentally afflicted. Without trying to be, Padre Pio was an important political force, who helped keep Italy from going Communist in the years immediately following World War II and even afterward. He was, moreover, a powerful influence in favor of traditional morality and against artificial birth control, abortion, and the "sexual revolution." Such accomplishments, though not appreciated by everyone, establish Padre Pio as a historical figure of major importance.

More than that, Padre Pio Forgione of Pietrelcina was one of the giants of the Christian faith, as it is traditionally understood, both as a "charismatic" and as a man of great personal holiness.

Many say that Padre Pio was a saint. "Look how many gifts he had," they say, "and how many miracles he did." This, they reason, is proof of his holiness. Charismatic gifts, however, are not necessarily proofs of holiness; and many extremely holy people, St. Thérèse of Lisieux for example, were essentially without such gifts as healing, visions, and supersensible knowledge.

Others who were by no means Christian or holy in the traditional sense of these words — people like Grigori Rasputin, Edgar Cayce, Rudolf Steiner, and Helena Blavatsky — abounded in gifts that apparently went beyond the powers of nature.

Padre Pio's holiness can be established by the manner in which he used his extraordinary gifts, not simply by the fact that he had them. He could have used his charisms for his own personal advancement and prestige. He could have grown arrogant and mercenary. He resisted these temptations. According to universal testimony, he remained humble, simple, and unassuming, using his gifts not for his own glorification but for the benefit of mankind.

Some may still question the reality of Padre Pio's charisms. The skeptic will claim that the so-called miracles can, if studied carefully enough, be explained by natural means. If one believes strongly in Christ, *everything* is a miracle: the sunrise, the changing of the seasons, the growth and development of flowers, the structure and composition of the human body — indeed, all creation! On the other hand, if one rejects scriptural belief, very often nothing, no matter how extraordinary, is recognized as miraculous.

Perhaps Padre Lorenzo had a point in making no effort at meticulous documentation of all reports of miracles. What was important to him — and to Padre Pio — was the greatest miracle of all, faith in God, on which everything else depends. And not even the most hardened skeptic can deny that Padre Pio brought about the miracle of faith in the lives and hearts of thousands of men, women, and children throughout the years.

As I am not a Roman Catholic, I have perhaps a concept of sainthood different from that of most of Padre Pio's spiritual children. Yet even the most cursory reading of Scripture will reveal that the sanctity to which all Christians are called is a total, absolute, and unconditional dedication of the self to God in Christ Jesus. Padre Pio lived this commitment in a striking and intense way. Whatever one may think of his charisms, the propriety of his offering himself as a Victim of Divine Love, his ministry, or his theology, there can be no doubt that Padre Pio gave himself over entirely to his Lord. The most fervent atheist will be forced to admit, even if he believes that the padre dedicated his life to a delusion, that his commitment was total. His entire life was given over to God and to the service of man. The only thing Padre Pio cared about in this world was saving souls. To him, everybody was "a soul" and the object of his intense concern, a concern so powerful that he was willing to immolate himself for that soul's welfare.

Padre Pio was a man who, like all men, was influenced by his family, by his environment, by his education. He was a man who, like all men except One, made mistakes and had human faults and failings. He was, unlike most men and women, an individual who had totally surrendered himself to his Savior, Christ; a man who strove from childhood to his last breath to be an imitator of Christ. No suffering — physical, spiritual, or emotional — was so great as to stay him in this mission. When his total dedication to the Christian faith is considered on the basis of Scripture as well as of Christian tradition, no one can seriously deny that Padre Pio is one of God's saints.

Notes

AdR	Alessandro da Ripabottoni, *Pio of Pietrelcina: Infancy and Adolescence* (San Giovanni Rotondo, 1969).
Agostino	Gerardo DiFlumeri, ed., *Padre Agostino da San Marco in Lamis: Diario* (San Giovanni Rotondo, 1975).
Beata	Lino da Prata and Alessandro da Ripabottoni, *Beata te, Pietrelcina* (San Giovanni Rotondo, 1976).
Bernardino	Bernardino of Siena, "Padre Pio: The Church — The Blessed Mother," *Acts of the First Congress on Padre Pio's Spirituality* (San Giovanni Rotondo, 1978).
Capobianco	Costantino Capobianco, *Detti e anedotti di Padre Pio* (San Giovanni Rotondo, 1973).
Carty	Charles Mortimer Carty, *Padre Pio: The Stigmatist* (Rockford, Illinois, 1963).
Ch & Ci	Francobaldi Chiocci and Luciano Cirri, *Padre Pio: Storia d'una vittima* (Rome, 1968) — volume number added if other than volume I.
Cireneo	Alessandro da Ripabottoni, *Padre Pio da Pietrelcina: Il cireneo di tutti* (San Giovanni Rotondo, 1978).
Cruchon	Georges Cruchon, "The Stigmata of Padre Pio," *Acts of the First Congress on Padre Pio's Spirituality* (San Giovanni Rotondo, 1978).
D'Apolito	Alberto D'Apolito, *Padre Pio da Pietrelcina: Ricordi, esperianze, testimonianze* (San Giovanni Rotondo, 1978).
Leone	Gherardo Leone, *Padre Pio: Infanzia e prima giovinezza (1887-1910)* (San Giovanni Rotondo, 1973).
L'Umanita	Alessandro da Ripabottoni and Grazio and Carmela Micheli, *L'Umanita di Padre Pio nella sua vita e nei suoi scritti* (San Giovanni Rotondo, 1975).
McCaffery	John McCaffery, *Tales of Padre Pio: The Friar of San Giovanni Rotondo* (Kansas City, 1978).

Masone   Ettore Masone, "Mio zio Padre Pio," a continuing article in the periodical *La Casa Sollievo della Sofferenza* (San Giovanni Rotondo).

Massa   Bonaventura Massa, *Maria Pyle: Passo beneficando tutti* (San Giovanni Rotondo, 1975).

Matthews   Herbert L. Matthews, "Padre Pio: A Lesson in Simplicity," *New York Times Magazine*, July 29, 1956.

Meyer   "Letters of Father Dominic Meyer," *The Voice of Padre Pio*.

Napolitano   Francesco Napolitano, *Padre Pio of Pietrelcina: Brief Biography* (San Giovanni Rotondo, 1978).

Pagnossin   Giuseppe Pagnossin, *Il Calvario di Padre Pio* (Padua, 1978) — volume number added if other than volume I.

Paolino   Padre Paolino da Casacalenda, *Le mei memorie intorno a Padre Pio*, G. DiFlumeri, ed. (San Giovanni Rotondo, 1978).

Pio I   Pio da Pietrelcina, *Epistolario I: Corrispondenza con i direttori spirituali (1910-1922)* (San Giovanni Rotondo, 1973).

Pio II   Pio da Pietrelcina, *Epistolario III: Corrispondenza con le figlie spirituali (1915-1923)* (San Giovanni Rotondo, 1977).

Schug   John A. Schug, *Padre Pio: He Bore the Stigmata* (Huntington, Indiana, 1976).

Underhill   Evelyn Underhill, *Mysticism: A Study in the Nature and Development of Man's Spiritual Consciousness* (New York, 1961).

Voice   *The Voice of Padre Pio,* English edition, publication of the National Centre for Padre Pio, Inc., 11 N. Whitehall Road, Norristown, Pennsylvania 19401.

Venafro   Gerardo DiFlumeri, *La permanenza di Padre Pio a Venafro* (San Giovanni, 1977).

Vivifier   Tarcisio of Cervinara, "Padre Pio as Confessor: Extraordinary and Unique Vivifier of Dead Souls," *Acts of the First Congress on Padre Pio's Spirituality* (San Giovanni Rotondo, 1978).

Itemized notes follow:

Introduction: 'The Second Saint Francis'

1. "Padre Pio, R.I.P.," *National Review*, Oct. 22, 1968, pp. 1050-1051.
2. *Voice*, vol. III, No. 1, 1973, p. 16.
3. *Voice*, vol. I, No. 3, 1971, p. 3.
4. *Voice*, vol. V, No. 3, 1975, pp. 12-13.
5. Rudolf Bultmann, *Kerygma and Myth* (New York, 1961), p. 5.

Chapter 1
The God-Is-Everything People

1. Rev. John A. Schug, unpublished manuscript.
2. Rev. John A. Schug, unpublished manuscript.
3. Leone, p. 14.
4. Pagnossin, p. 349.
5. *Beata*, p. 105.
6. *Beata*, p. 229.
7. *Beata*, p. 206.
8. Leone, p. 35.
9. "Our Blessed Lady and Padre Pio," *Voice*, vol. VII, No. 2, 1977, p. 5.
10. Leone, p. 31.
11. *Beata*, p. 143.
12. "Our Blessed Lady and Padre Pio," p. 5.
13. Leone, pp. 41-42.

Chapter 2
'Il Bello Francesco'

1. AdR, p. 3.
2. Leone, p. 26.
3. AdR, p. 100.
4. Cruchon, p. 128.
5. Cruchon, p. 128.
6. *Voice*, vol. IV, No. 3, 1974, p. 13.
7. Leone, p. 76.
8. Leone, p. 28.
9. Leone, p. 28.
10. Leone, pp. 73-74.
11. *Beata*, p. 128.
12. Agostino, p. 25.
13. *Beata*, p. 113.
14. *Beata*, p. 239.
15. *Beata*, p. 207.
16. *Beata*, p. 109.
17. Leone, p. 89.
18. *Beata*, p. 186.
19. *Beata*, p. 185.
20. *Beata*, p. 186.
21. AdR, p. 37.
22. Leone, p. 83.
23. AdR, pp. 39-40.
24. *Beata*, p. 135.
25. *Beata*, p. 136.
26. *Beata*, p. 73.
27. *Beata* pp. 134-135.
28. Pio I, pp. 1281-1282.
29. Pio I, p. 1283.
30. Pio I, p. 1284.

Chapter 3
An Example to All

1. *St. Francis of Assisi: Writings and Early Biographies*, Marion A. Habig, ed. (Chicago, 1973), p. 57.
2. Geoffrey Chaucer, *The Canterbury Tales*, Nevill Coghill, trans. (Hammondsworth, Middlesex, 1963), pp. 25-26.
3. Leone, p. 14.
4. Underhill, p. 302.
5. Underhill, p. 313.
6. Underhill, pp. 313-314.
7. Pio I, p. 807.
8. Bernardino, p. 155.
9. Leone, pp. 120-123.
10. *Beata*, p. 224.
11. *Cireneo*, p. 25.
12. *L'Umanita*, pp. 158-159.
13. Agostino, p. 80.
14. *Cireneo*, p. 32.
15. Pellegrino Funicelli, "The Bible and Padre Pio," *Voice*, vol. II, No. 4, 1972, p. 16.
16. St. Teresa of Avila, *The Way of Perfection* (Garden City, N.Y., 1964), p. 213.
17. John of the Cross, *Counsels of Light and Love* (New York, 1977), p. 30.
18. *Counsels of Light and Love*, pp. 42,43.
19. *Counsels of Light and Love*, p. 33.
20. Agostino, p. 186.
21. Gerard Greene, *All on Fire: A Story of St. Gemma Galgani* (Notre Dame, 1953), pp. 68-69.
22. Francis McGaw, *Praying Hyde* (Minneapolis, 1970), p. 37.
23. Agostino, pp. 40-41.

Chapter 4
Heavenly Secrets

1. Underhill, p. 287.
2. Underhill, p. 282.
3. Pio I, pp. 373-375.
4. Pio I, pp. 373-375.
5. Pio I, pp. 373-375.
6. Pio I, p. 56.
7. Pio I, p. 259.
8. D'Apolito, pp. 251-252.
9. D'Apolito, pp. 253-262.
10. *Venafro*, p. 80.
11. *Cireneo*, p. 29.
12. *Cireneo*, p. 29.

Chapter 5
'A Holy Priest, a Perfect Victim'

1. Pio I, p. 179.
2. Pio I, p. 180.
3. Pio I, p. 185.
4. Pio I, p. 188.
5. Pio I, p. 182.
6. Pio I, p. 192.

7. Gerardo DiFlumeri, *The Mystery of the Cross in Padre Pio of Pietrelcina* (San Giovanni Rotondo, 1977), p. 22.
8. Pio I, p. 219.
9. Pio I, p. 219.
10. Pio I, p. 224.
11. Agostino, p. 131.
12. Pio I, p. 224.
13. Pio I, p. 199.
14. Pio I, p. 200-201.
15. Pio I, p. 204.
16. Pio I, p. 210.
17. Pio I, p. 217.
18. Pio I, p. 198.
19. Pio I, p. 229.
20. Pio I, p. 231.
21. Pio I, p. 206.
22. Pio I, pp. 207-208.
23. Pio I, p. 304.
24. Pio I, p. 1277.
25. *Beata*, p. 209.
26. Pio I, p. 234.
27. Pagnossin II, p. 358.

Chapter 6
Strange Events at Venafro

1. *Venafro*, pp. 67-68.
2. Pio I, p. 234.
3. Pio I, pp. 237-238.
4. Pio I, pp. 239-240.
5. Pio I, pp. 240-241.
6. Agostino, pp. 268-269.
7. Agostino, p. 66.
8. *Venafro*, p. 84.
9. John of the Cross, *Counsels of Light and Love* (New York, 1977), p. 41.
10. Agostino, p. 269.
11. Agostino, pp. 35-36.
12. Agostino, p. 37.
13. Agostino, pp. 37-40.
14. Agostino, pp. 40-44.
15. Agostino, p. 47 (passage translated by Liliana Gagliardi).
16. Agostino, p. 47 (passage translated by Liliana Gagliardi).
17. Agostino, p. 48 (passage translated by Liliana Gagliardi).
18. Agostino, p. 48.
19. Agostino, p. 49.
20. Agostino, pp. 66-67.
21. Agostino, pp. 56-57.
22. Pio I, pp. 442-443.
23. *Venafro*, p. 77.
24. *Venafro*, pp. 76-77.
25. Underhill, p. 59.
26. *Venafro*, pp. 70-71.
27. *Venafro*, p. 72.
28. Agostino, p. 255.

Chapter 7
The Double Exile

1. *Beata*, p. 205.
2. Pio I, p. 276.
3. Pio I, p. 363.
4. Pio I, p. 256.
5. *Beata*, p. 94.
6. *Beata*, pp. 193-194.
7. *Beata*, pp. 195-196.
8. Pio I, pp. 442 and 443.
9. *Beata*, p. 203.
10. *Beata*, p. 203.
11. *Beata*, p. 194.
12. *Beata*, p. 194n.
13. Pio I, p. 302.
14. Pio I, p. 315.
15. *Beata*, pp. 205-206.
16. Pio I, p. 330.
17. Pio I, pp. 338-339.

Chapter 8
The Dark Night of the Soul

1. Pio I, p. 420.
2. Pio I, pp. 420-421.
3. Pio I, p. 461.
4. Pio I, p. 304.
5. Pio I, p. 308.
6. Pio I, p. 424.
7. Pio I, p. 462.
8. This manuscript was to be found, in 1971, in the New York Public Library, Lincoln Center branch.
9. Underhill, p. 198.
10. Underhill, p. 381.
11. Pagnossin, vol. I, p. 9.
12. Underhill, p. 383.
13. Underhill, p. 399 (citing John of the Cross's *Dark Night of the Soul*).
14. Teresa of Avila, *The Life of Teresa of Jesus: The Autobiography of St. Teresa of Avila* (Garden City, N.Y., 1960), p. 192.
15. Underhill, p. 401.
16. Underhill, p. 417.
17. Underhill, p. 417 (quoting from Jacob Boehme's *Threefold Life of Man*).
18. Pio III, pp. 1006-1008.
19. Pio I, pp. 264-265.
20. Pio I, p. 273.
21. Pio I, p. 382.
22. Pio I, p. 297.
23. Pio I, pp. 327-328.
24. Pio I, p. 300.
25. Pio I, p. 682.
26. Pio I, p. 476.
27. Pio I, pp. 640-641.
28. Pio I, p. 466.
29. Pio III, pp. 164-165.

30. Pio III, p. 194.
31. Pio III, p. 196.
32. Pio III, pp. 614,619.
33. Pio III, pp. 311-312.
34. Pio III, pp. 341-342.
35. Pio III, pp. 677-678.
36. Vivifier, p. 253.

Chapter 9
Between Barracks and Friary

1. Pio I, p. 473.
2. Pio I, p. 779.
3. Pio I, pp. 375-376. Pio's explanation of this case closely parallels an explanation offered in The Life of Teresa of Jesus: The Autobiography of St. Teresa of Avila (Garden City, N.Y., 1960), p. 192.
4. Pio I, p. 439.
5. Pio I, p. 479.
6. Pio I, p. 496.
7. Pio I, p. 500.
8. Pio I, p. 519.
9. Pio I, p. 468.
10. Pio I, p. 495.
11. Pio I, p. 579.
12. Pio I, p. 582.
13. Pio I, pp. 587-588.
14. Pio I, pp. 587-588.
15. Pio I, p. 704.
16. Pio I, p. 709.
17. Pio I, pp. 727-728.
18. Agostino, p. 258.
19. Pio I, p. 730.
20. Agostino, p. 261.
21. Timothy Ware, The Orthodox Church (Hammondsworth, Middlesex, 1964), p. 48.
22. Agostino, pp. 260-261.
23. Pio I, p. 767.
24. Agostino, p. 261.
25. Pio I, p. 773.
26. Agostino, pp. 261-262.
27. Paolino, pp. 57-59.
28. Paolino, pp. 62-68.
29. Pio I, p. 792.
30. Pio I, p. 821.
31. Paolino, p. 236.
32. Pagnossin, p. 9.
33. Pio III, p. 266.
34. Pio III, p. 978.

Chapter 10
The Spiritual Director

1. Pio III, p. 185.
2. Pio III, p. 238.
3. Pio III, pp. 48-49.
4. Pagnossin, p. 40.
5. Pagnossin, p. 41.
6. Pio III, p. 59.
7. Pio III, pp. 250-251.
8. Pio III, p. 251.
9. Pagnossin, p. 41.
10. Pagnossin, p. 41.
11. Pio III, pp. 666-667.
12. Pio III, p. 48.
13. Pio III, p. 55.
14. Giovanni Gigliozzi, The Spouse's Jewels (Subiaco, 1958), p. 106.
15. Pagnossin, p. 42.

Chapter 11
The Stigmata

1. Pio I, p. 803.
2. Pio I, pp. 837-838.
3. Pio I, pp. 1027-1028.
4. Pio I, p. 1030.
5. Pio I, p. 1063.
6. It is interesting to compare Padre Pio's forthcoming description with a passage from St. Teresa's Autobiography: "It pleased the Lord that I should sometimes see the following vision. I would see beside me, on my left hand, an angel in bodily form — a type of vision which I am not in the habit of seeing, except very rarely. Though I often see representations of angels, my visions of them are of the type that I first mentioned [intellectual]. . . . He was not tall, but short, and very beautiful, his face so aflame that he appeared to be one of the highest types of angel who seem all afire. . . . In his hands I saw a long golden spear and at the end of the tip I seemed to see a point of fire. With this he seemed to pierce my heart several times so that it penetrated to my entrails. When he drew it out, I thought he was drawing them out with it and he left me completely afire with a great love for God. The pain was so sharp that it made me utter several groans, and so excessive was the sweetness caused me by this intense pain that one can never wish to lose it, nor will one's soul be content with anything less than God." The Life of Teresa of Jesus: The Autobiography of St. Teresa of Avila (Garden City, N.Y., 1960), pp. 274-275.
7. Pio I, pp. 1065-1066.
8. Pio I, pp. 1068-1069.
9. Paolino, pp. 103-104.
10. Paolino, pp. 114.
11. Pio I, p. 1091.
12. Pagnossin, p. 24.
13. Pagnossin II, p. 357.
14. Pio I, p. 1095.
15. Masone, September 1973, p. 20.
16. Beata, pp. 230-231.
17. Paolino, p. 117.

Chapter 12
Holiness or Hysteria?

1. René Biot, *The Enigma of the Stigmata* (New York, 1962), pp. 19-22.
2. Biot, p. 30.
3. Joan Carrol Cruz, *The Incorruptibles* (Rockford, Illinois, 1977), p. 103.
4. Cruchon, p. 124.
5. Cruchon, pp. 124-128, passim.
6. Cruchon, pp. 132-133.
7. Cruchon, pp. 128-132, passim.
8. Cruchon, pp. 129-138, passim.
9. Schug, pp. 82-83.
10. Carty, p. 30.
11. Cruchon, p. 129.
12. Cruchon, pp. 129-131.
13. Padre Alessio Parente, interview, San Giovanni Rotondo, September 5, 1978.

Chapter 13
The Rumor of Sanctity

1. Pio I, p. 1129.
2. Pio I, pp. 1146-1147.
3. Paolino, pp. 160-161.
4. Paolino, pp. 342-343.
5. Paolino, pp. 143-144.
6. "Letters from a Russian Prince," *Voice*, vol. VIII. No. 1, 1978, pp. 11-12.
7. Pagnossin, p. 3.
8. Pagnossin, pp. 4-7.
9. Pagnossin, pp. 24-25.
10. Pagnossin, p. 206.
11. Pagnossin, pp. 205-206.
12. Pagnossin, p. 201.
13. Pagnossin, pp. 139-174, passim.
14. Pagnossin, p. 147.

Chapter 14
The Friar and the Archbishop

1. McCaffery, p. 64.
2. Pio I, p. 1181.
3. Pio I, pp. 1247-1248.
4. Pagnossin, pp. 128-129.
5. Francobaldo Chiocci, *I nemici di Padre Pio* (Rome, 1968), p. 43. Passages used in this chapter were translated by Robert H. Hopcke.
6. Chiocci, p. 44.
7. Chiocci, p. 44.
8. Chiocci, p. 46.
9. Pagnossin, pp. 517-518.

Chapter 15
The Raging Tempest

1. Carlo Falconi, *Popes in the Twentieth Century, from Pius X to John XXIII* (Boston, 1967), p. 217.

2. C.C. Martindale, "Padre Pio of Pietrelcina," *The Month*, New Series, vol. 7, No. 6, June 1952.
3. Pagnossin, p. 153.
4. Pagnossin, p. 168.
5. Pagnossin, p. 165.
6. Mary F. Ingoldsby, "Padre Benedetto Nardella: The Man Who 'Formed' Padre Pio," *Voice*, vol. VII, No. 4, 1977, p. 13.
7. Pagnossin, pp. 175-176.
8. Pagnossin, p. 182.
9. Pagnossin, p. 182.
10. Pagnossin, p. 189.
11. Capobianco, p. 61.
12. Pagnossin, p. 208.
13. Pagnossin, p. 260.
14. Pagnossin, pp. 232-233.
15. Pagnossin, p. 252.
16. Pagnossin, p. 260.
17. Pagnossin, p. 225.
18. Silvestro Mischitelli, "Between the Blessed Sacrament and a Gun," *Voice*, vol. I, No. 3, 1971, p. 13.
19. Mischitelli, pp. 13-14.
20. Pagnossin, pp. 238-239.

Chapter 16
'The Light of the Gargano'

1. *L'Umanita*, p. 430.
2. Padre Pio to Alberto Costa, bishop of Malfi and Rapolla, Dec. 10, 1922. Letter furnished by Giuseppe Pagnossin.
3. *Voice*, vol. IX, No. 1, 1979, p. 12.
4. Napolitano, pp. 140-141.
5. Carty, pp. 161-162.
6. Napolitano, pp. 141-142.
7. Schug, p. 51.
8. Schug, pp. 51-52.
9. Schug, pp. 132-133.
10. D'Apolito, pp. 243-246.
11. D'Apolito, pp. 127-130.
12. McCaffery, pp. 133-134.
13. Massa, p. 39.
14. Massa, p. 14.
15. Massa, p. 41.
16. Massa, p. 16.

Chapter 17
'A Little Light in the Thicket'

1. Agostino, p. 62.
2. Agostino, pp. 65-66.
3. Agostino, pp. 62-65.
4. Agostino, p. 65.
5. Pagnossin, p. 175.
6. *Beata*, pp. 224-225.
7. Pagnossin, p. 537.
8. *Beata* pp. 224-225.
9. Pagnossin, p. 272.
10. Pagnossin, p. 276.

11. Pagnossin, p. 286.
12. Pagnossin, p. 283.
13. Pagnossin, p. 292.
14. Pagnossin, p. 402.
15. Pagnossin, p. 401.
16. Unpublished manuscript in the possession of Rev. John A. Schug.
17. Pagnossin, p. 537.
18. Unpublished manuscript, Rev. John A. Schug.
19. Unpublished manuscript, Rev. John A. Schug.
20. Unpublished manuscript, Rev. John A. Schug.

Chapter 18
The Imprisonment

1. Pagnossin, p. 543.
2. Agostino, p. 267.
3. Pagnossin, p. 543n.
4. Pagnossin, p. 564.
5. Pagnossin, pp. 580-582.
6. Pagnossin, p. 583.
7. Pagnossin, p. 573.
8. Pagnossin, p. 605.
9. Agostino, p. 79.
10. Agostino, p. 79.
11. Agostino, pp. 93-94.
12. Agostino, p. 82.
13. Pagnossin, p. 376.
14. Agostino, p. 84.
15. Pagnossin, p. 643.
16. Agostino, p. 84.
17. Pagnossin, p. 682.
18. Pagnossin, p. 667.
19. Schug, pp. 105-106.
20. Pagnossin, p. 689.

Chapter 19
War and Peace

1. Agostino, p. 102.
2. Agostino, p. 96.
3. Agostino, pp. 113-114.
4. Pagnossin II, p. 24.
5. Agostino, p. 124.
6. Capobianco, p. 66.
7. Agostino, p. 159.
8. Agostino, p. 115.
9. Agostino, pp. 100-101.
10. *Giornale d'Italia* (Pescara), Nov. 22, 1942.
11. Carty, pp. 113-114.
12. Agostino, pp. 198-199.
13. McCaffery, p. 21.
14. Ch & Ci, p. 255.
15. Agostino, p. 115.
16. D'Apolito, p. 75.
17. Agostino, p. 162.
18. William Carrigan, interview, Nov. 29, 1979.
19. Dorothy M. Gaudiose, *Prophet of the People: A Biography of Padre Pio* (New York, 1974), p. 137.
20. Schug, pp. 155-156.
21. D'Apolito, p. 75.
22. Agostino, p. 164.

Chapter 20
The World for a Parish

1. Agostino, p. 163.
2. The entire body of material concerning Padre Pio and the American soldiers and airmen comes from interviews with William Carrigan (Nov. 29, 1979; Jan. 21, 1980; and Aug. 18, 1980) and Joseph Peterson of Hillsdale, New York (Aug. 21, 1980).
3. Masone, December 1973, p. 20.
4. Masone, December 1973, p. 21.
5. Agostino, p. 187. (In an account by Karl Wagner, a Viennese writer, the man drops dead on the spot when the curse he hurls against Padre Pio recoils upon him.)
6. Agostino, p. 187.
7. Pagnossin, p. 95.
8. Pagnossin, p. 91.
9. Pagnossin, p. 92.
10. Pagnossin, p. 93.
11. Pagnossin, p. 94.
12. *Beata*, p. 208.
13. McCaffery, p. 20.
14. Meyer, vol. V, No. 2, 1975, p. 17.
15. Matthews, p. 11.

Chapter 21
A Day with Padre Pio

1. McCaffery, p. 77.
2. Paolino, p. 203.
3. Tarcisio of Cervinara, *Padre Pio's Mass* (San Giovanni Rotondo, 1975), p. 20.
4. *Padre Pio's Mass*, p. 20.
5. *Padre Pio's Mass*, pp. 30-31.
6. *Padre Pio's Mass*, p. 36.
7. Paolino, p. 167.
8. Clarice Bruno, *Roads to Padre Pio* (Rome, 1969), pp. 79-80.
9. *Vivifier*, p. 257.
10. Bruno, p. 187.
11. *Vivifier*, p. 260.
12. Bruno, p. 183.
13. Masone, November 1973, p. 20.
14. Masone, January 1974, p. 21.
15. Meyer, vol. V, No. 3, 1975, p. 10.
16. Masone, February 1974, p. 20.
17. *L'Umanita*, pp. 168-169.
18. *L'Umanita*, p. 162.
19. Schug, p. 117.
20. Pellegrino Funicelli, "Beatification Process," *Voice*, vol. VIII, No. 1, 1978, p. 9.
21. "Beatification Process," p. 8.
22. Napolitano, p. 198.
23. Schug, p. 118.
24. Napolitano, p. 209.
25. Masone, September 1973, p. 20.
26. Agostino, p. 182.
27. Capobianco, p. 47.

Chapter 22
The Charismatic

1. Agostino, p. 193.
2. Schug, p. 176.
3. Schug, p. 180.
4. Agostino, p. 186.
5. Ch & Ci, pp. 670-672.
6. Meyer, vol. V, No. 3, 1975, pp. 15-16.
7. Schug, pp. 172-175.
8. Meyer, vol. V, No. 1, 1975, pp. 3-4.
9. McCaffery, pp. 66-67.
10. Masone, November 1973, p. 21.
11. D'Apolito, pp. 89-90.
12. Schug, p. 211.
13. McCaffery, p. 9.
14. Masone, January 1974, p. 20.
15. Capobianco, pp. 68-70.
16. Capobianco, pp. 71-74.
17. Capobianco, pp. 32-34.
18. Schug, p. 134.
19. Oral Roberts, *A Daily Guide to Miracles and Successful Living by Seed-Faith* (Tulsa, 1975), p. 35.
20. *A Daily Guide*, pp. 68ff.
21. D'Apolito, p. 187.
22. Andre Mandato, inverviews, Aug. 1 and Nov. 19, 1978.
23. Meyer, vol. V, No. 2, 1975, p. 15.
24. Capobianco, pp. 75-76.
25. Meyer, vol. V, No. 2, 1975, p. 15.
26. Masone, October 1973, p. 21.
27. D'Apolito, p. 98.
28. McCaffery, p. 26.
29. Corrie ten Boom, *Tramp for the Lord* (Old Tappan, N.J.), p. 62.
30. Pio I, p. 471.

Chapter 23
'A Magnificent Work of Charity'

1. Matthews, p. 38.
2. Agostino, pp. 221-222.
3. Agostino, p. 219.
4. *Voice*, vol. VIII, No. 4, 1978, p. 15.
5. Augustine McGregor, "The Miracle of Faith," *Voice*, vol. VIII, No. 3, 1978, p. 14.
6. Napolitano, pp. 150 and 153.
7. Paolino, p. 211n.
8. McCaffery, p. 66.
9. D'Apolito, p. 98.
10. D'Apolito, p. 98.
11. Schug, p. 223.
12. Schug, p. 222.
13. Matthews, p. 11.
14. McGregor, p. 15.
15. Schug, pp. 225-226.
16. McGregor, p. 15.
17. Agostino, p. 240.
18. Pagnossin II, p. 294.

Chapter 24
'Just in Time for My Golden Jubilee'

1. Pagnossin II, p. 260.
2. Ch & Ci, vol. III, p. 460.
3. McCaffery, p. 114.
4. McCaffery, p. 115.
5. Luis-Jesus Luna Guerrero, *El Padre Pio: Tragedia de Fe* (Madrid, 1975), p. 111.
6. Pagnossin II, p. 144.
7. Letter, Rev. John A. Schug to Rev. C. Bernard Ruffin, April 28, 1980: *I discussed these charges against Father Clement with Father Adrian Holzmeister, a classmate and lifelong friend of Father Clement. Also, Father Adrian was Father Clement's appointee as first Provincial of the newly formed New York-New England Province at the time the Giuffre affair was boiling in Italy. Clearly, the two Capuchins maintained their closeness during these years. Father Adrian told me that they discussed Padre Pio and that Father Clement "completely believed in Padre Pio," and that the accusations against Father Clement were not true.*
8. Pagnossin II, p. 89.
9. Pagnossin II, p. 93.
10. Pagnossin II, p. 98.
11. Pagnossin II, p. 99.
12. Pagnossin II, p. 99.
13. *Time* magazine, April 24, 1964, p. 81.
14. Pagnossin II, p. 99.
15. Bernadino, p. 158.
16. Fernando da Riese Pio X, *Padre Pio da Pietrelcina: Crocifisso senza croce* (Rome, 1975), p. 384.
17. McCaffery, pp. 110-111.
18. Pagnossin II, p. 26.
19. Pagnossin II, p. 209.

Chapter 25
'I Can't Bear My Cross Anymore'

1. McCaffery, p. 67.
2. Padre Aurelio of Sant'Elia a Pianisi, interview, July 19, 1971.
3. Schug, p. 55.
4. Schug, p. 55.
5. Schug, p. 55 (also corroborated by Father Joseph Pius Martin in interview, September 6, 1978).
6. Bernardino, p. 149.
7. Bernardino, p. 149.
8. Masone, January 1974, p. 21.

Chapter 26
'Give Me the Obedience to Die'

1. Padre Alessio Parente, lecture, Holy Comforter Lutheran Church, Washington, D.C., Jan. 4, 1979.

2. Capobianco, p. 77.
3. Pellegrino Funicelli, "Padre Pio's Trips by Air,"
   Voice, vol. VII, No. 3, 1977, p. 17.
4. Transcript of interview wtih Agnese Stump in
   possession of Rev. John A. Schug.
5. Schug, pp. 181-185.
6. D'Apolito, p. 308.
7. Pagnossin II, p. 359.
8. Massa, p. 39.
9. Schug, p. 241.
10. D'Apolito, p. 308.
11. *Voice*, vol. III, No. 2, 1973, p. 12.
12. Schug, p. 232.
13. Napolitano, p. 232.
14. Masone, March 1974, p. 21.
15. Napolitano, p. 237.
16. Padre Raffaele D'Addario of Sant'Elia a Pianisi,
    interview, July 19, 1971.
17. Schug, pp. 237-238.
18. "The Last Days of Padre Pio," *Voice*, vol. I, No.
    1, 1971, p. 11.
19. Schug, p. 239.
20. Schug, p. 241.

Index